Off we go ~ at last!! LOL, T xmas 2000 xxx

Prague

John King
Richard Nebeský

LONELY PLANET PUBLICATIONS
Melbourne • Oakland • London • Paris

MAP 1 GREATER PRAGUE

PLACES TO STAY & EAT

1 Pension BoB
2 Tour Hotel
3 Autokemp Džbán &
  TJ Aritma Hostel
5 TJ Hvězda Praha Hostel
6 Hotel Praha
9 Camp Sokol Troja
10 Camp-Pension Herzog
11 Camp Fremunt
12 Autocamp Trojská
13 Camp Dana Troja
15 Hotel Stírka
17 Botel Neptun
20 Pension Praga
21 Interhotel Olympik II
22 Interhotel Olympik Praha
23 Hotel Čechie
24 Autokemp Žižkov
  (Pražačka Camping)
26 Hotel Rhea
27 Hotel Don Giovanni
30 Slavia Hotel

33 Domov Mládeže
36 Hotel Markéta
37 Kolej Kajetánka Hostel
39 Hotel Pyramida
40 Motorlet Císařka
42 Hotel Golf &
  Caravancamp Motol
43 Hotel Kavalír
46 Hotel Tourist
48 Intercamp & Ubytovna
  Kotva Braník
49 Pension Bohemians
50 Botel Racek
52 Hostel Podolí
53 Hotel Panorama
55 Hotel Beta
58 Hotel ILF
59 Sky Club Brumlovka
60 Hotel Kačerov
61 Restaurace Eureka
62 Hotel Globus
63 AV Pension Praha

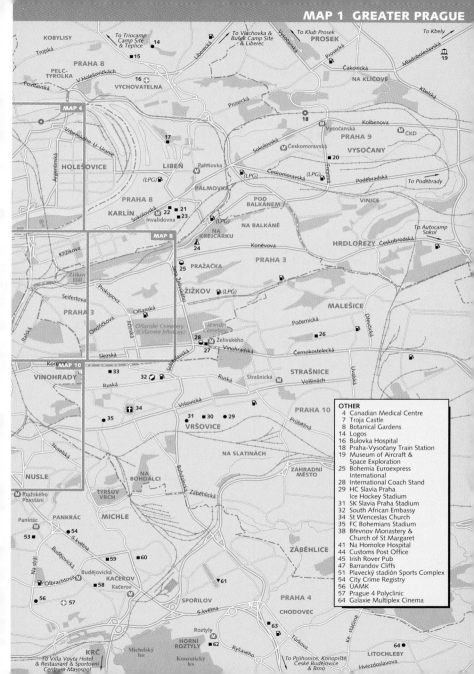

MAP 1 GREATER PRAGUE

OTHER
4 Canadian Medical Centre
7 Troja Castle
8 Botanical Gardens
14 Logos
16 Bulovka Hospital
18 Praha-Vysočany Train Station
19 Museum of Aircraft & Space Exploration
25 Bohemia Euroexpress International
28 International Coach Stand
29 HC Slavia Praha Ice Hockey Stadium
31 SK Slavia Praha Stadium
32 South African Embassy
34 St Wenceslas Church
35 FC Bohemians Stadium
38 Břevnov Monastery & Church of St Margaret
41 Na Homolce Hospital
44 Customs Post Office
45 Irish Rover Pub
47 Barrandov Cliffs
51 Plavecký stadión Sports Complex
55 City Crime Registry
56 ÚAMK
57 Prague 4 Polyclinic
64 Galaxie Multiplex Cinema

Prague
3rd edition – March 1999
First published – June 1994

Published by
Lonely Planet Publications Pty Ltd A.C.N. 005 607 983
192 Burwood Rd, Hawthorn, Victoria 3122, Australia

Lonely Planet Offices
Australia PO Box 617, Hawthorn, Victoria 3122
USA 150 Linden St, Oakland, CA 94607
UK 10a Spring Place, London NW5 3BH
France 1 rue du Dahomey, 75011 Paris

Photographs
All of the images in this guide are available for licensing from
Lonely Planet Images.
email: lpi@lonelyplanet.com.au

Front cover photograph
Detail of the elegant 15th century Astronomical Clock on Prague's Old
Town Hall (Joe Cornish, Tony Stone Images)

ISBN 0 86442 624 0

Contents

2 Contents

PLACES TO STAY   135

PLACES TO EAT   150

ENTERTAINMENT   166

SHOPPING   174

EXCURSIONS   177

LANGUAGE   194

GLOSSARY   199

INDEX   212

MAP SECTION   217

The Authors

John King
John grew up in the USA, destined for the academic life, but in a rash moment in 1984 he headed off for a look at China, took up travel writing, and never looked back. After a decade in Hong Kong, John, his wife Julia Wilkinson (also a travel writer) and their two children are now based in south-west England. John is also co-author of Lonely Planet's *Czech & Slovak Republics, Portugal, Karakoram Highway, Pakistan, Central Asia* and *Russia, Ukraine & Belarus* guidebooks.

Richard Nebeský
Born one snowy evening in the grungy Prague suburb of Žižkov, Richard got a taste for travelling early in life, when his parents dragged him away from the 'pretentious socialist paradise' of Czechoslovakia after its invasion by Warsaw-Pact troops. A stint on campus was followed by a working tour of the ski resorts of the northern hemisphere and an overland odyssey across south Asia. Since joining Lonely Planet in 1987, he has co-authored Lonely Planet's *Central Europe* and *Eastern Europe* phrasebooks and the *Czech & Slovak Republics* guidebook. Othe titles he has helped to update include *Central Europe, Eastern Europe, France, Australia, Indonesia, Russia, Ukraine & Belarus, South-East Asia* and *Thailand*.

From the Authors
John King I owe great thanks to my co-author, Richard, for hard work on this edition, including much that only he, as a native Praguer, could have done. I'm grateful to Cathy Lanigan and Michelle Lewis for support, good humour and much patience as the manuscript materialised; and to Tim Ryder and Dale Buckton, who converted it into a real book. Sacha Pearson of Lonely Planet's Oakland office provided quick and cheerful research help.

In Prague, Václav Novotný, director of the Prague Information Service, and his staff dug hard for background information. Zee Plumley and Helena Parmová walked me through the permits maze. Lukas Codr untangled the telephone system and helped with Internet matters. Thanks also to Alexander Cesar of Baker & McKenzie.

Peter Mills of Rail Europe went beyond the call of duty with extensive research. For their usual generous help I am again grateful to Paul Gowen, Touring Information & Research Manager at the RAC, and Sue Hall of the Cyclists' Touring Club.

Finally and most importantly, I thank my wife, Julia, and my children, Kit and Lia, who saw much less of me than they should have during this project; and Neliza Rumbaua, who took up much of the slack.

Richard Nebeský I'd like to warmly thank Luděk and Zdena Bartoš, and Lenka and Jarda Průcha, for information and help, and for making my stay in Prague a pleasant one; my parents for invaluable advice and support; and Petr Mařík and Zdena Li for insight into artistic Prague. Thanks also to Hana Urychová of PIS, Martin Měkota, Míša Bartošová, Blanka and Olin Valovy, and Míta and Tonda Kulišovy. Also *děkuji* to John, my co-author, and to the Lonely Planet staff who worked on this guide.

This Book

John King and Richard Nebeský researched and wrote the first edition of *Prague*. Richard updated the second edition, and this edition was updated by John and Richard.

From the Publisher

This third edition of *Prague* was edited in Lonely Planet's London office by Tim Ryder, with help from Katrina Browning. The proofing was done by Dorinda Talbot. Michelle Lewis designed the book and Dale Buckton handled the bulk of the mapping, with assistance from Michelle, Sara Yorke, Tony Battle and Tom Fawcett. Dale also designed the cover. David Rathborne did the indexing, with help from Dorinda, and last-minute layout corrections were handled by Paul Bloomfield. Nicky Castle drew the illustrations, Gadi Farfour designed the colour pages, and the photographs were supplied by Lonely Planet Images.

Thanks to Leonie Mugavin for her help with the Health section, to Quentin Frayne for his speedy magic with the Language chapter, to Dan Levin and Chris Lee Ack for sorting out the Czech fonts, and to Simon Calder for providing up-to-the-minute Getting There & Away information.

Thanks

Many thanks to the following travellers who used the last edition and wrote to us with helpful hints, useful advice and interesting anecdotes:

Douglas & Clarice, Simon Adelman, Nicola Antonucci, Barry Appleby, Rosalind Ardee, Leanne Biuvet, Tommy Busk, AW Cole, Richard Colebourn, Philip Connor, Dr Peter J Cox, Jazz Dhiman, Kari Dolezal, Joanna Easthill, Niclas Ekstrom, Jan Fidrmuc, Richard Foxell, Clare French, Bryan Glendon, Richard Graham, Sandro Gramaglia, Kristna Halfmann, Vanessa Hammond, John Hanrahan, Caroline Hanssen, Robin Hart-Jones, Richard Hauch, Eric Hauser, Sarah Howard, Lloyd Kahn, Michael J Kierans, Gottfried Knott, Karen Kramer, Steve Lack, Anders Larsson, Ben Laurie, Sami & Minna Laurikainen, FW Luther, Federick M, Oka Maeda, Adam Mattsson, Michela Monti, Kevin Nicholls, Koari Noguchi, Jill Norton, Catherine Pembrey, Garrett Prestage, George Ratcliffe, John Raven, I & N Richardson, Michele Ricks, Inge Roose, Timo Schrama, Willy Duarte van Selm, Penelope Shortland, John Smilgin, Maria Snarski, John Swerby, Petr Vacha, FM Vletter, Mark Wallem, Colin Watkins, Robert Watson, B Westerberg, Sean D Williams, Herreman Yvan.

Foreword

ABOUT LONELY PLANET GUIDEBOOKS

The story begins with a classic travel adventure: Tony and Maureen Wheeler's 1972 journey across Europe and Asia to Australia. Useful information about the overland trail did not exist at that time, so Tony and Maureen published the first Lonely Planet guidebook to meet a growing need.

From a kitchen table, then from a tiny office in Melbourne (Australia), Lonely Planet has become the largest independent travel publisher in the world, an international company with offices in Melbourne, Oakland (USA), London (UK) and Paris (France).

Today Lonely Planet guidebooks cover the globe. There is an ever-growing list of books and there's information in a variety of forms and media. Some things haven't changed. The main aim is still to help make it possible for adventurous travellers to get out there – to explore and better understand the world.

At Lonely Planet we believe travellers can make a positive contribution to the countries they visit – if they respect their host communities and spend their money wisely. Since 1986 a percentage of the income from each book has been donated to aid projects and human rights campaigns.

Updates Lonely Planet thoroughly updates each guidebook as often as possible. This usually means there are around two years between editions, although for more unusual or more stable destinations the gap can be longer. Check the imprint page (following the colour map at the beginning of the book) for publication dates.

Between editions up-to-date information is available in two free newsletters – the paper *Planet Talk* and email *Comet* (to subscribe, contact any Lonely Planet office) – and on our Web site at www.lonelyplanet.com. The *Upgrades* section of the Web site covers a number of important and volatile destinations and is regularly updated by Lonely Planet authors. *Scoop* covers news and current affairs relevant to travellers. And, lastly, the *Thorn Tree* bulletin board and *Postcards* section of the site carry unverified, but fascinating, reports from travellers.

Correspondence The process of creating new editions begins with the letters, postcards and emails received from travellers. This correspondence often includes suggestions, criticisms and comments about the current editions. Interesting excerpts are immediately passed on via newsletters and the Web site, and everything goes to our authors to be verified when they're researching on the road. We're keen to get more feedback from organisations or individuals who represent communities visited by travellers.

Lonely Planet gathers information for everyone who's curious about the planet – and especially for those who explore it first-hand. Through guidebooks, phrasebooks, activity guides, maps, literature, newsletters, image library, TV series and Web site we act as an information exchange for a worldwide community of travellers.

Research Authors aim to gather sufficient practical information to enable travellers to make informed choices and to make the mechanics of a journey run smoothly. They also research historical and cultural background to help enrich the travel experience and allow travellers to understand and respond appropriately to cultural and environmental issues.

Authors don't stay in every hotel because that would mean spending a couple of months in each medium-sized city and, no, they don't eat at every restaurant because that would mean stretching belts beyond capacity. They do visit hotels and restaurants to check standards and prices, but feedback based on readers' direct experiences can be very helpful.

Many of our authors work undercover, others aren't so secretive. None of them accept freebies in exchange for positive write-ups. And none of our guidebooks contain any advertising.

Production Authors submit their raw manuscripts and maps to offices in Australia, USA, UK or France. Editors and cartographers – all experienced travellers themselves – then begin the process of assembling the pieces. When the book finally hits the shops some things are already out of date, we start getting feedback from readers, and the process begins again …

WARNING & REQUEST

Things change – prices go up, schedules change, good places go bad and bad places go bankrupt – nothing stays the same. So, if you find things better or worse, recently opened or long since closed, please tell us and help make the next edition even more accurate and useful. We genuinely value all the feedback we receive. Julie Young coordinates a well-travelled team that reads and acknowledges every letter, postcard and email and ensures that every morsel of information finds its way to the appropriate authors, editors and cartographers for verification.

Everyone who writes to us will find their name in the next edition of the appropriate guidebook. They will also receive the latest issue of *Planet Talk*, our quarterly printed newsletter, or *Comet*, our monthly email newsletter. Subscriptions to both newsletters are free. The very best contributions will be rewarded with a free guidebook.

Excerpts from your correspondence may appear in new editions of Lonely Planet guidebooks, the Lonely Planet Web site, *Planet Talk* or *Comet*, so please let us know if you *don't* want your letter published or your name acknowledged.

Send all correspondence to the Lonely Planet office closest to you:

Australia: PO Box 617, Hawthorn, Victoria 3122
UK: 10A Spring Place, London NW5 3BH
USA: 150 Linden St, Oakland CA 94607
France: 1 rue du Dahomey, Paris 75011

Or email us at: talk2us@lonelyplanet.com.au

For news, views and updates see our Web site: www.lonelyplanet.com

HOW TO USE A LONELY PLANET GUIDEBOOK

The best way to use a Lonely Planet guidebook is any way you choose. At Lonely Planet we believe the most memorable travel experiences are often those that are unexpected, and the finest discoveries are those you make yourself. Guidebooks are not intended to be used as if they provide a detailed set of infallible instructions!

Contents All Lonely Planet guidebooks follow the same format. The Facts about the Country chapter or section gives background information ranging from history to weather. Facts for the Visitor gives practical information on issues like visas and health. Getting There & Away gives a brief starting point for researching travel to and from the destination. Getting Around gives an overview of the transport options when you arrive.

The peculiar demands of each destination determine how subsequent chapters are broken up, but some things remain constant. We always start with background, then proceed to sights, places to stay, places to eat, entertainment, getting there and away, and getting around information – in that order.

Heading Hierarchy Lonely Planet headings are used in a strict hierarchical structure that can be visualised as a set of Russian dolls. Each heading (and its following text) is encompassed by any preceding heading that is higher on the hierarchical ladder.

Entry Points We do not assume guidebooks will be read from beginning to end, but that people will dip into them. The traditional entry points are the list of contents and the index. In addition, however, there is a complete list of maps and an index map illustrating map coverage.

There's also a colour map that shows highlights. These highlights are dealt with in greater detail in the Facts for the Visitor chapter, along with planning questions and suggested itineraries. Each chapter covering a geographical region begins with a locator map and another list of highlights. Once you find something of interest in a list of highlights, turn to the index.

Maps Maps play a crucial role in Lonely Planet guidebooks and include a huge amount of information. A legend is printed on the back page. We seek to have complete consistency between maps and text, and to have every important place in the text captured on a map. Map key numbers usually start in the top left corner.

Although inclusion in a guidebook usually implies a recommendation we cannot list every good place. Exclusion does not necessarily imply criticism. In fact there are a number of reasons why we might exclude a place – sometimes it is simply inappropriate to encourage an influx of travellers.

Introduction

Kidnapped for 40 years by communism, Prague (Praha), historic heart of Bohemia and one of Europe's most beautiful cities, is 'home' again. The romantic image of the city that Czechs lovingly call Golden Prague refuses to go away, in spite of the unfortunate, if civil, 'Velvet Divorce' of 1993 that split the country into Czech and Slovak republics, and the excesses that have accompanied Prague's rise in the tourism charts.

The romantic vision extends even to politics. As Eastern Europe's communist regimes fell like dominoes in 1989, the 'Velvet Revolution' in Czechoslovakia stood out for its swiftness and dignity. The Czechs had already captured our imaginations with the aborted 'Prague Spring' of 1968 and, we felt, they'd make a good job of liberation. They confirmed it by choosing a playwright and moral philosopher as their new president.

Reliable figures on the number of visitors to the city are hard to come by. City hall estimates at least 2.6 million in 1996, 85% of them from abroad. Another source says 108 million people visited the Czech Republic in 1997, of which most probably spent time in Prague. Numbers are levelling out after a post-1989 surge, in part because there aren't enough rooms. In summer the hotels of this former eastern-bloc backwater are packed to bursting, and its narrow lanes are choked with Dutch tour groups, German weekenders and Italian school children. The city has discovered shifty waiters, crooked cabbies, pickpockets and other flotsam that collects in the wake of tourism. Prices keep rising, and the owners of newly privatised buildings scramble to repair them before they fall down. In the evenings, downtown streets are full of restless Czech teenagers, and graffiti now mars many handsome façades.

And yet Prague remains for most of us a fairy tale come true – the 'city of 100 spires', its compact medieval centre a web of cobbled lanes, ancient courtyards, dark passages and churches beyond number, an architectural smorgasbord of Romanesque, Gothic, baroque and Art Nouveau – all watched over by an 1100-year-old castle with liveried guards. Veteran travellers (and some locals) lament not having it to themselves any more, and of course it must have been easier before 1989 – no crowds, no billboards, nobody shooting car commercials in the backstreets.

But there's a different kind of fizz now. Prague is incredibly youthful: thousands of twenty-something westerners have settled here as artists, consultants and entrepreneurs, and journalists continue to effuse about a 'new Left Bank'. Known already for its classical music and literary life, and in this century for ground-breaking visual arts and cinema, the city has also become a magnet for top-flight jazz and rock.

Meanwhile, from the open door of a backstreet pub comes the clatter and chatter of Czechs enjoying the best beer in the world, and from the open window of a recreation centre come the strains of an out-of-tune amateur string quartet. In some ways Prague carries on as it always has, and Czechs welcome visitors with grace and 'Prague-matism', not only for their money but as new neighbours.

Facts about Prague

HISTORY

Prague's history has echoed not only through the Czech lands but across Europe. Among Prague flashpoints with major international consequences have been the rise and subsequent bloody splintering of the Hussite movement in the 15th century; the 17th century anti-Habsburg uprising that set off the Thirty Years' War; and the communist putsch of 1948.

Prehistory

The oldest evidence of human habitation in the Prague valley dates from 600,000 BC, but more numerous clues were left by mammoth-hunters during the last ice age, about 25,000 years ago. Permanent farming communities were established around 4000 BC in the north-western parts of Prague, and the area was inhabited continuously by various Germanic and Celtic tribes before the arrival of the Slavs. It was from a Celtic tribe called Boii that Bohemia got its name, a name still used today for the western part of the Czech Republic.

The Coming of the Slavs

In the 6th century, two Slav tribes settled on opposite sides of a particularly appealing stretch of the Vltava River. The Czechs built a wooden fortress where Hradčany stands today, and the Zličani built theirs upstream at what is now Vyšehrad. They had barely dug in when nomadic Avars thundered in, to rule until the Frankish trader Samo united the Slav tribes and drove the Avars out. Samo held on for 35 years before the Slavs reverted to squabbling.

In the 9th century Prague was part of the short-lived Great Moravian Empire, under whose second ruler, Rastislav (ruled 846-870), emissaries were invited from Constantinople and Christianity took root in the region. The Moravians were ultimately undone by internal conflicts, especially with the Czechs, who finally broke away from the empire.

Přemysl Dynasty

Prague Castle was built in the 870s by Prince Bořivoj as the main seat of the Přemysl dynasty, with Vyšehrad sometimes serving as an alternative in the 10th and 11th centuries (see the Vyšehrad section in the Things to See & Do chapter for notes on the mythical founding of this dynasty).

Christianity became the state religion under the rule of Wenceslas (Václav), Duke of Bohemia (ruled approximately 925-935), 'Good King Wenceslas' of the old Christmas carol (though in fact he never was a king) and now patron saint of the Czech Republic.

In 950, the German king Otto I conquered Bohemia and incorporated it into the Holy Roman Empire. By 993 Přemysl princes had forged a genuine Slav alliance, and ruled Bohemia on the Germans' behalf until 1212, when the pope granted Otakar I the right to rule as a king. Otakar bestowed royal privileges on the Old Town, and Malá Strana was established in 1257 by Otakar II.

Přemysl lands stretched at one point from modern-day Silesia to the Mediterranean Sea. However, their Austrian and Slovenian domains were lost when Otakar II died and his army was thrashed at the 1278 Battle of Moravské Pole (fought near modern-day Dürnkrut in Austria) by the Austrian Habsburgs.

Prague's Golden Age

The murder of Wenceslas III in 1306 left no male heir to the Přemysl throne. Two Habsburg monarchs briefly ruled Bohemia until the Holy Roman Emperor, John of Luxembourg (Jan Lucemburský to the Czechs), also became King of Bohemia by marrying Václav III's daughter Elyška in 1310. Under the rule of John's son,

Charles (Karel) IV (ruled 1346-78), as king and Holy Roman Emperor, Prague grew into one of the continent's largest and most prosperous cities, acquiring its fine Gothic face, and landmarks including Charles University, Charles Bridge and St Vitus Cathedral.

The Hussite Revolution

The late 14th and early 15th centuries witnessed the Church-reform movement led by Jan Hus (see the boxed text below). Hus' eventual conviction for heresy and his death at the stake in 1415 sparked a nationalist rebellion in Bohemia led by the Hussite preacher Jan Želivský. In 1419 several Catholic councillors were flung from the windows of Prague's New Town Hall by Želivský's followers, thus introducing the word 'defenestration' (literally, the act of throwing someone out of a window) to the political lexicon.

Jan Hus

Jan Hus was the Czech lands' foremost, and one of Europe's earliest, Christian reformers, anticipating Martin Luther and the Lutheran Reformation by a century.

He was born into a poor family in southern Bohemia in 1372. At the age of 18 he enrolled at Charles University, and two years after graduating he started work as a teacher there. Five years later he was made dean of the philosophy faculty, at a time when the university was caught up in a struggle against German influence.

Like many of his Czech colleagues, Hus was inspired by the English philosopher and radical reformist theologian John Wycliffe. The latter's ideas on reform of the Roman Catholic clergy meshed nicely with growing Czech resentment at the wealth and corruptness of the higher clergy, who together owned about half of all Bohemia, and their heavy taxation of the peasantry.

Prague reformers had in 1391 founded the Bethlehem Chapel (see under Staré Město & Josefov in the Things to See & Do chapter), where sermons were given in Czech rather than Latin. Hus preached here for about 10 years, while continuing his duties at the university.

Because German masters at the university enjoyed three votes to the Czech masters' one, anti-reform attitudes officially prevailed there. In 1403 the masters declared many parts of Wycliffe's writings to be heresy. During the Great Schism (1378-1417), when Roman Catholics had two popes, the masters opposed the 1409 Council of Pisa that was called to sort things out. This so infuriated Wenceslas IV that he abrogated the university constitution and gave the Czech masters three votes to the Germans' one, leading to a mass exodus of Germans from Prague.

In the chaos surrounding the Great Schism, one pope was persuaded to prohibit preaching in private chapels such as Bethlehem Chapel. Hus refused to obey, and was excommunicated, though he continued to preach at the chapel and teach at the university. But a disagreement with Wenceslas IV over the sale of indulgences cost him the king's support, and the Council of Constance, called to put a final end to the Schism, convicted Hus of heresy, and he was burned at the stake in 1415.

After the death of Holy Roman Emperor and King of Bohemia Wenceslas IV in 1419, Prague was ruled by various Hussite committees. In the 1420s a split developed in their ranks between radical Taborites, who advocated total war on Catholics, and moderate Utraquists, who consisted mainly of nobles and were more concerned with transforming the Church.

In 1420, combined Hussite forces led by the military commander Jan Žižka successfully defended Prague against the first anti-Hussite crusade, launched by Sigismund, the Holy Roman Emperor. In 1434 the Utraquists agreed to accept Sigismund's rule in return for religious tolerance; the Taborites kept fighting, only to be defeated in the same year at the Battle of Lipany.

Following Sigismund's death, George of Poděbrady (Jiří z Poděbrad) ruled as Bohemia's one and only Hussite king, from 1452 to 1471, with the backing of Utraquist forces. He was centuries ahead of his time in suggesting a European council to solve international problems by diplomacy rather than war, but he couldn't convince the major European rulers or the pope. After George's death, two weak kings from the Polish Jagiellonian dynasty ruled Bohemia, though real power lay with the Utraquist nobles, the so-called Bohemian Estates.

Habsburg Rule

In 1526 the Austrian, Catholic Habsburgs were again asked by the Czech nobility to rule Bohemia. In the second half of the century the city enjoyed great prosperity under Emperor Rudolf II, and was made the seat of the Habsburg Empire. Rudolf established great art collections, and renowned artists and scholars were invited to his court. A huge fire in 1541 laid waste many sections of Malá Strana and Hradčany.

A blow to Czech fortunes for the next 300 years was an ill-fated uprising of the Bohemian Estates in 1618, which began when two Habsburg councillors and their secretary were flung from an upper window in Prague Castle. This sparked off the Thirty Years' War, devastating much of

Europe, Bohemia in particular; a quarter of the Bohemian population perished.

The following year the Bohemian Estates elected Frederick of the Palatinate as their ruler. But because of ineffective leadership, low morale among their heavily mercenary army, and limited international support, the crucial Battle of Bílá Hora (White Mountain) on 8 November 1620 was lost by the Protestants almost before the first shots were fired. The 'Winter King' (so-called because he ruled Bohemia for just one winter) fled and the 27 nobles who had instigated the revolt were executed in Old Town Square.

The defeat slammed the door on Czech independence for almost three centuries. Czechs lost their privileges, rights and property, and very nearly their national identity through forced Catholicisation and Germanisation. During the Thirty Years' War, Saxons occupied Prague from 1631 to 1632, and Swedes seized Hradčany and Malá Strana in 1648. The Old Town, though unconquered, suffered months of bombardment. Prague's population declined from 60,000 in 1620 to 24,600 in 1648. The Habsburgs moved their throne back to Vienna, reducing Prague to a provincial town, although it did get a major baroque face-lift over the next century, particularly after a great fire in 1689.

In the 18th century the city was again on the move, economically and architecturally. The four towns of Prague (Staré Město, Nové Město, Malá Strana and Hradčany) were joined into a single, strong unit by imperial decree in 1784.

The Czech National Revival

In the 19th century, Prague became the centre of the so-called Czech National Revival (České národní obrození), which found its initial expression not in politics – political activity was forbidden by the Habsburgs – but in Czech-language journalism, literature and drama. Important figures included linguists Josef Jungmann and Josef Dobrovský, and František Palacký, author of *Dějiny národu českého* (History of the

Czech Nation). A distinctive architecture also took form; Prague landmarks of this period include the National Theatre, the National Museum and the New Town Hall.

While many of the countries in post-Napoleonic Europe were swept by similar nationalist sentiments, social and economic factors gave the Czech revival particular strength: educational reforms by Empress Maria Theresa (ruled 1740-80) had given even the poorest Czechs access to schooling; a vocal middle class was emerging with the Industrial Revolution; and Austrian economic reforms, plus changes in industrial production, were forcing Czech labourers into the bigger towns, cancelling out the influence of large German minorities there.

Prague also joined in the 1848 democratic revolutions that swept Europe, and the city was the first in the Austrian Empire to rise in favour of reform. Like most of the others, however, Prague's uprising was soon crushed. But in 1861, Czechs defeated Germans in Prague council elections and edged them out of power forever, though the shrinking German minority still wielded substantial influence well into the 1880s.

WWI & Independence

Czechs had no interest in fighting for their Austrian masters in WWI, and neighbouring Slovaks felt the same about their Hungarian rulers. Many defected to renegade legions fighting the Germans and Austrians.

Meanwhile, Tomáš Garrigue Masaryk, Edvard Beneš and the Slovak Milan Štefánik began to argue the case – especially in the USA with President Wilson – for the Czechs' and Slovaks' long-cherished dream of independence. President Wilson's interest was in keeping with his own goal of closer ties with Europe under the aegis of the League of Nations (the unsuccessful precursor to the United Nations). The most workable solution appeared to be a single federal state of two equal republics, and this was spelled out in agreements signed in Cleveland in 1915 and then in Pittsburgh in 1918.

As WWI drew to a close, Czechoslovakia declared its independence, with Allied support, on 28 October 1918. Prague became the capital, and the popular Masaryk, a writer and political philosopher, became the republic's first president.

On 1 January 1922, Greater Prague was established by the absorption of several surrounding towns and villages, growing to a city of 677,000. Like the rest of the country, Prague experienced an industrial boom until the Great Depression of the 1930s. By 1938 the population had grown to one million.

WWII

Unfortunately the new country was not left to live in peace. Most of Bohemia's and Moravia's three million German speakers wished to join Greater Germany, and in October 1938 the Nazis occupied the Sudetenland (the border regions with Germany and Austria), with the acquiescence of Britain and France in the infamous Munich Agreement. On 15 March 1939, Germany occupied all of Bohemia and Moravia, declaring the region a 'protectorate', while Slovakia proclaimed independence as a Nazi puppet state.

Prague suffered little physical damage during the war, although the Germans destroyed the Czech underground – and hundreds of innocent Czech villagers – in retaliation for the assassination in Prague of SS General and Reichsprotektor Reinhard Heydrich (see the boxed text).

Prague's community of some 120,000 Jews was all but wiped out by the Nazis, with almost three-quarters of them – and some 90% of all the Jews in Bohemia and Moravia – dying of starvation or exterminated in camps from 1941. For more on the Jews of Prague, see the boxed text under Staré Město & Josefov in the Things to See & Do chapter.

On 5 May 1945 the population of Prague rose against the German forces as the Red Army approached from the east. US troops had reached Plzeň, but held back in deference to their Soviet allies. The only help for Prague's lightly armed citizens came from

FACTS ABOUT PRAGUE

The Assassination of Heydrich

In response to strikes and sabotage by the increasingly well organised Czech underground, in 1941 the German government replaced its Reichsprotektor in Bohemia and Moravia with the SS General and anti-subversion specialist Reinhard Heydrich, who cracked down on resistance activities with a vengeance.

In a clandestine operation, Britain trained a number of Czechoslovak paratroopers for an attempt to assassinate Heydrich. Astonishingly, it succeeded. Two paratroopers, Jan Kubiš and Jozef Gabčík, managed on 27 May 1942 to wound Heydrich as he rode in his official car in the city's Libeň district, and he later died of his wounds. The assassins and five co-conspirators fled but were betrayed in their hiding place in the Church of SS Cyril & Methodius, and in the ensuing siege all were killed or committed suicide.

The Nazis reacted with a frenzied wave of terror, including the annihilation a month later of two entire Czech villages, Lidice and Ležáky (see the Excursions chapter for more on the grim fate of Lidice), and the more or less complete shattering of the underground movement.

Russian soldiers of the so-called Vlasov units, former POWs who had defected to the German side and now defected in turn to the Czech cause (they subsequently retreated to western Bohemia and surrendered to the Americans). Many people died before the Germans began pulling out on 8 May, having been granted free passage out of the city by the Czech resistance movement.

Most of Prague was thus liberated by its own residents before Soviet forces arrived the following day. Liberation Day is now celebrated on 8 May; under communism it was 9 May.

Expulsion of Sudeten Germans

In 1945 Czechoslovakia was re-established as an independent state. One of the government's first acts was the expulsion of Sudeten Germans from the borderlands. By 1947 nearly 2.5 million Sudetenlanders had been stripped of their Czechoslovak citizenship and their land, and forcibly expelled to Germany (mainly Bavaria) and Austria. Thousands died during forced marches.

Despite a 1997 declaration of mutual apology for wartime misdeeds by the Czech Republic and Germany, the issue still brings emotions to the boil. Most Sudeten survivors feel their Czech citizenship and property were taken illegally. Many Czechs, on the other hand, remain convinced that Sudetenlanders forfeited their rights when they sought help from Nazi Germany, and that a formal apology by President Václav Havel in January 1990 was unwarranted.

Communism

In the 1946 elections, the communists became the republic's dominant party with 36% of the popular vote, and formed a coalition government with other socialist parties.

Tension grew between democrats and communists, and in February 1948 the communists staged a coup d'état with the backing of the Soviet Union. A new constitution established the Party's dominance, and government was organised along Soviet lines. Thousands of non-communists fled the country.

The 1950s were an era of harsh repression and decline as communist economic policies nearly bankrupted the country. Many people were imprisoned. Hundreds were executed and thousands died in labour camps, often for little more than a belief in democracy. In a series of Stalin-style purges organised by the Communist Party, many people, including top members of the party itself, were executed.

The 'Prague Spring' & Charter 77

In the late 1960s Czechoslovakia enjoyed a gradual liberalisation under Alexander Dubček, the reformist general secretary of the Czechoslovak Communist Party. These reforms reflected a popular desire for full democracy and an end to censorship – 'socialism with a human face', as the party called it in its April 1968 'Action Programme'.

But Soviet leaders grew alarmed at the prospect of a democratic society within the Soviet bloc, and its certain domino effect in Poland and Hungary. The brief 'Prague Spring' was crushed by a Soviet-led Warsaw Pact invasion on the night of 20-21 August 1968. Prague was the major objective; Soviet special forces with help from the Czechoslovak secret service, the StB, secured Ruzyně airport for Soviet transport planes.

At the end of the first day, 58 people had died. Passive resistance followed; street signs and numbers were removed from buildings throughout the country to disorient the invaders.

In 1969, Dubček was replaced by the orthodox Gustav Husák and exiled to the Slovak forestry department. Around 14,000 Party functionaries and 280,000 members who refused to renounce their belief in 'socialism with a human face' were expelled from the Party and lost their jobs. Many other educated professionals became street cleaners and manual labourers.

In January 1977, a group of 243 writers, artists and other intellectuals signed a public demand for basic human rights, Charta 77 (Charter 77), which became a focus for opponents of the regime. Prominent among them was the poet and playwright Václav Havel (see the boxed text on the next page).

The 'Velvet Revolution'

The communist regime remained in control until the breaching of the Berlin Wall in November 1989. On 17 November, Prague's communist youth movement organised an officially sanctioned demonstration in memory of nine students executed by the Nazis in 1939. But the peaceful crowd of 50,000 was cornered in Národní street, where hundreds were beaten by police and about 100 were arrested.

Czechs were electrified by this wanton official violence, and the following days saw non-stop demonstrations by students, artists and finally most of the populace, peaking in a rally on Letná plain by some 750,000 people. Leading dissidents, with Havel at the forefront, formed an anti-communist coalition, which negotiated the government's resignation on 3 December. A 'Government of National Understanding' was formed, with the communists as a minority group. Havel was elected president of the republic by the federal assembly on 29 December.

The days following the 17 November demonstration have become known as the 'Velvet Revolution' (Sametová revoluce) because of its almost totally nonviolent character.

The 'Velvet Divorce'

Free elections to the federal assembly in 1990 were won by Civic Forum (OH) and its Slovak counterpart, People Against Violence (VPN). But Civic Forum soon split, over economic policy, into the right-of-centre Civic Democratic Party (ODS), led by Václav Klaus, and the left-of-centre Civic Forum led by Jiří Dienstbier. Klaus forced through tough economic policies, the success of which gave the ODS a slim victory in 1992 elections.

Václav Havel

Havel was born in October 1936, the son of a wealthy Prague restaurateur. His family's property was confiscated after the communist *putsch* of 1948, and as the child of bourgeois parents, he was denied easy access to education. He nevertheless finished high school and studied for a time at university before landing a job at the age of 23 as a stagehand at the Theatre on the Balustrade. Nine years later he was its resident playwright.

His enthusiasm over the liberal reforms of the 'Prague Spring', and his signature on the Charter 77 declaration, made him an enemy of the Husák government. His works – typically focusing on the absurdities and dehumanisation of totalitarian bureaucracy – were banned, his passport was seized and altogether he spent some four years in jail for his activities on behalf of human rights in Czechoslovakia.

The massive demonstrations of November 1989 thrust Havel into the limelight as a leading organiser of the non-communist Civic Forum movement, which pressed for democratic reforms and ultimately negotiated a new government of national reconciliation. Havel himself was elected president of the country the following month, and the first president of the new Czech Republic in 1993.

In 1998 he was re-elected, but this time with the slimmest of margins, and his health has been failing. Nevertheless the dignified former playwright is now clearly the Czechs' favourite elder statesman.

Meanwhile, separatists headed by Vladimír Mečiar won 1992 elections in Slovakia, depriving the ODS of a parliamentary majority. The very different economic positions of Mečiar and Klaus made compromise almost impossible, with Mečiar favouring gradual transformation and independence for Slovakia. The two leaders decided that splitting the country was the best solution, and on 1 January 1993, Czechoslovakia ceased to exist for the second time this century.

Prague became the capital of the new Czech Republic, and Havel was elected as its first president.

After the Divorce

The first Czech-only elections, in 1996, ended inconclusively. Klaus' ODS gained a relative majority but even with coalition partners, the Civic Democratic Alliance (ODA) and the Christian & Democratic Union (KDU-ČSL), it failed to score a parliamentary majority and was forced to negotiate with the second-strongest party, the Social Democrats (ČSSD). The ODS and its minority government were unable to govern effectively, and seemed to have lost the will for change. Allegations of corruption began to multiply, foreign investment slacked off and the Czech economy began to slump.

In December 1997 Klaus was forced to resign over a party-finance scandal, though in addition the fragile partnership with the KDU-ČSL was nearing collapse. President

Havel succeeded in patching together an interim government, headed by former central bank boss Josef Tošovský. In January 1998 Havel himself barely managed to get re-elected president, by a margin of just one vote.

The 1998 elections were again unsatisfying. The ČSSD won only 74 of 200 parliamentary seats, with the ODS a close second. In July, Havel asked the ČSSD leader, Miloš Zeman, to form a new government, though he only managed to do so with the help of the ODS, who in return insisted on several ministerial posts, the watering down of some of the ČSSD's left-of-centre positions, and the appointment of Václav Klaus as parliamentary speaker.

Affordable housing remains in short supply in Prague, the health system is under strain, and pollution and crime rates are up. Nevertheless, Prague's booming tourism and a solid industrial base have left its citizens in better economic shape than the rest of the country. Unemployment here is minimal, shops are full, and many buildings have had or are getting face-lifts.

In the international arena, the Czech Republic has joined the big league: it is on course to join NATO in 1999 and in the running for acceptance as a member of the EU by 2003.

CLIMATE

The Czech Republic has a transitional climate between maritime and continental, characterised by hot, showery summers, cold, snowy winters and generally changeable conditions. A typical day in Prague during June to August sees the mercury range from about 12 to 22°C. Temperatures from December to February push below freezing. Wide variations are common, sometimes surpassing 35°C in summer and -20°C in winter.

The closest thing to a 'dry season' is from January to March, when total precipitation (mostly as snow at that time) is less than a third of that during the wettest months, from June to August. And yet January averages as many 'wet' days (about

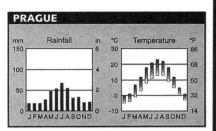

two out of five) as do the summer months. Summer's long, sunny hot spells tend to be broken by sudden, heavy thunderstorms. May and September have the most pleasant weather.

ECOLOGY & ENVIRONMENT

During most of the year, Prague's air is fairly breathable. But in mid-winter the air can get foul with vehicle emissions, particularly during inversions (a meteorological phenomenon in which air temperature increases with altitude, causing ultra-stable conditions). If you're just here for a few days, there's little to worry about, though Prague residents suffer from high rates of respiratory ailments.

Radio and TV stations provide bulletins about pollution levels, and the Prague Information Service (see Tourist Offices in the Facts for the Visitor chapter) should be able to tell you of any risk.

Central Prague's traffic is more and more gridlocked as the number of new cars soars. Plans for a ring road around the city have so far been stalemated by opposition from every council through which it would pass.

The Vltava River is marginally polluted upstream (south) of Prague but seriously polluted downstream. See Health in the Facts for the Visitor chapter about drinking the tap water.

Czechs have been recycling waste for a long time; you'll find large bins for glass, plastics and paper all over town. Most bottles are recyclable, and the price of most bottled drinks includes a deposit of 3 to 10 Kč, refundable at supermarkets and food shops (some beer bottles only have a 0.40 Kč deposit).

GOVERNMENT & POLITICS

Prague is the capital of the Czech Republic and the seat of government, parliament and the president. The city itself is governed separately from other regions of the country by the Local Government of the Capital City of Prague, headed by a council and a mayor. The acting body of this government is the municipal office together with the council. Prague is divided into 10 districts and 57 suburbs, governed by district and local governments.

Since 1989, Prague citizens have voted heavily (typically about 60%) for right-of-centre parties. Václav Klaus (whose constituency includes Prague) and his Civic Democratic Party (ODS) collected over 42% of the city's popular vote in the 1998 elections, while the two other right-leaning parties together polled another 20%. Prague was in fact the only town in the country where the ODS polled at the top.

But country-wide, the ODS is now in opposition to the left-of-centre Social Democrats (ČSSD), led by Miloš Zeman, the current prime minister. Klaus, the force behind many of the country's post-1989 reforms and now speaker of the parliament, is still regarded by many as a Thatcherite, though his policies tended to be a practical mix of market reforms and socialism.

The Communist Party still has a solid, doctrinaire core of elderly followers. In the 1998 elections they gathered 11% of the vote, slightly up from 1996.

ECONOMY

Since the Industrial Revolution, Bohemia and Moravia have specialised in light industry, and in Central Europe their combined industrial output was once second only to Germany's. Under communist rule, industry and agriculture were nationalised, and heavy industry (mainly

Scandals Galore

Since 1989 scandals have convulsed every major Czech party, though none led to anybody's downfall until a flap over party finance in the ruling Civic Democratic Party (ODS) brought down the government and cost Václav Klaus his job as prime minister (though he held on to the party leadership).

The ODS and its former coalition partners, the Civic Democratic Alliance (ODA) and the Christian & Democratic Union (KDU-ČSL), as well as the ruling Social Democrats (ČSSD), have been accused by one another and by the media of failing to declare campaign donations, of falsifying donors' names and of offering and accepting bribes.

In 1998 the ODS tried to do the right thing by publishing a list of its major donors and hiring a top western accounting firm to audit its books, but the plan backfired when numerous undeclared donations and expenditures were uncovered, and several listed donors denied ever giving money to the party.

The ČSSD has its own so-called Bamberg scandal, in which its leader, Miloš Zeman, is alleged to have negotiated (in the German town of Bamberg) large donations to the party without the knowledge of party elders. The affair is under investigation by the BIS (the Czech secret service).

Zeman himself has become something of a laughing stock for his 'discovery' in 1996 and 1998 of 'secret documents', later shown to be bogus, that accused major figures, including the president, former minister of the interior Jan Ruml, and the BIS itself, of illegal activities.

steel) was introduced along Soviet lines. Other important industries include vehicles, machinery, armaments, cement, plastics, cotton, ceramics and beer.

Agricultural products include sugar beets, wheat, potatoes, corn, barley, rye, hops, lumber, cattle, pigs, poultry, horses and carp. The country lacks natural energy sources apart from large deposits of low-quality brown coal in North Bohemia and North Moravia. Its natural gas comes mainly from Russia, and via a new pipeline through Germany from Norway.

About 9% of Prague's population is employed in manufacturing, making it the largest industrial centre in the republic. Major industries are textiles, machinery and food; Karlín and Smíchov are the two major industrial suburbs. Most of the population is employed in service industries, including tourism-related ones.

At the time of writing, the Czech economy, for years considered one of the healthiest in the former eastern bloc, was struggling. Inflation was 10.8% in 1997, the gross domestic product (GDP) growth rate had fallen to 1%, unemployment stood at 4.8% (but just 1.2% in Prague), and the country was experiencing its first budget deficit (1% of GDP) since 1993. Other problems were a drop in foreign investment, growing public and government debt (170 billion Kč) and a lack of effective regulation of the business sector. In 1997 the koruna was devalued by 12%.

The average monthly wage in 1998 was about 10,900 Kč (US$340), enough for a reasonably comfortable life – although for Prague residents living in the central tourist zones, costs have gone through the roof.

Privatisation

In 1990 the government embarked on an ambitious privatisation programme. The 'small-privatisation' phase included restitution – the return of property to pre-1948 owners or their descendants – and the sale of smaller enterprises through auctions or straight to foreign buyers. All of Prague's hotels and restaurants are now privately owned, though the government still owns, and subsidises, most theatres and museums.

A 'large-privatisation' phase has concentrated on large enterprises, and small ones that had not yet found buyers. Sales were conducted mainly through a coupon system, in which every citizen had a chance to become a shareholder, or by auction. An important element was the April 1993 re-opening of the Prague stock exchange.

A protracted third phase is now focusing on a handful of large, over-staffed and low-productivity companies, including most major banks. It is taking longer than planned, in part because since 1996 the ODS has lacked the majority needed to push privatisation and other reforms through parliament, and in part because many of the already privatised companies had been bought by the banks themselves.

POPULATION & PEOPLE

Czechs are West Slavs, as are Poles, Slovaks and Lusatians (Sorbs). Roughly one out of 13 Czech citizens lives in Prague, whose 1997 population was estimated to be 1,214,000, equivalent to about 2450 people per sq km.

In addition to Slovak and Romany (Gypsy) minorities, there are significant numbers of expatriate foreigners – especially Ukrainians, Americans and Germans – living and working in Prague. Based on work-permit statistics and educated guesses about the ratio of legal to illegal workers, it's thought there are between 20,000 and 60,000 of them.

ARTS
Music

Before Christianity, folk songs and dances were the main forms of music in the Czech lands. The Church tried to replace these with Christian songs, and introduced Gregorian plainsong. Hussite reformers promoted hymns in Czech and drew on popular folk melodies, providing fertile ground for the future development of Czech music. Remnants of old Czech tunes can still be found in Protestant German hymns.

The Counter-Reformation put a lid on Czech musical culture. Above the village level, it survived only among a handful of musicians composing and playing at the courts of other European rulers. The most notable of these expatriates was Jan Dismas Zelenka, who worked in Dresden during the 18th century.

The musical spirit returned in the mid-19th century with the rise of several great composers during the early stages of the National Revival. Bedřich Smetana (1824-84), the first great Czech composer, incorporated folk melodies into his classical compositions. His best-known works are *Prodaná nevěsta* (The Bartered Bride), *Dalibor a Libuše* (Dalibor & Libuše) and *Má Vlast* (My Country).

Antonín Dvořák (1841-1904) spent four years in the USA where he lectured on music and composed the symphony *From the New World*. Among his other well known works are the two *Slovanské tance* (Slavonic Dances; 1878 and 1881), the operas *Rusalka* and *Čert a Káča* (The Devil & Kate) and his religious masterpiece *Stabat Mater*. Another prominent composer of this generation was Zdeněk Fibich (1850-1900).

Moravian-born Leoš Janáček (1854-1928), who also incorporated folk elements into his heavier music, is one of the leading Czech composers of the 20th century. Never as popular as Smetana or Dvořák in his native country, his better-known compositions include the opera *Jenůfa*, the *Glagolská mše* (Glagolithic Mass) and *Taras Bulba*, while one of his finest pieces is *Stories of Liška Bystrouška*.

Other well known composers are Josef Suk (1874-1935) and Bohuslav Martinů (1890-1959).

Jazz Jazz has a grip on Czech cultural life that is unmatched almost anywhere else in Europe. It was already being played by amateurs and professionals in the mid-1930s, mostly for dancing. Czech musicians remained at the forefront of the European jazz scene until the communist takeover in 1948. In the late 1950s, Prague Radio had a permanent jazz orchestra led by Karel Krautgartner.

Restrictions were gradually lifted in the 1960s. One of the top bands in this period was the SH Quartet, which played for three years at Reduta, the first Czech professional jazz club, in Prague. Another leading band was the Junior Trio, with Jan Hamr and the brothers Miroslav and Allan Vitouš, who all left for the USA after 1968. Jan Hamr (keyboards) became prominent in 1970s American jazz-rock as Jan Hammer, while Miroslav Vitouš (bass) rose to fame in several American jazz-rock bands.

Rock & Pop Rock was often banned by communist authorities because of its 'corrupting influence', although certain local bands, and innocuous western groups such as Abba, were allowed. Karel Gott and Helena Vondráčková were the two most popular Czech pop stars before 1989.

The pioneers of Czech rock (*Big Beat* in Czech), Sputnici, were the best known of several 1960s bands recycling American hits. Malostranská beseda in Malá Strana was a popular venue. But serious rock remained an underground movement for small audiences in obscure pubs and country houses. Raids and arrests were common. Fans included political dissidents such as Václav Havel. Plastic People of the Universe achieved international fame by being imprisoned after a 1970s show trial intended to discourage underground music.

Since 1989, rock and post-rock bands have proliferated. Though Prague's club scene is lively, many of the city's finest venues (especially those in city-owned properties) have shut down as a result of court actions over noise.

Popular bands on the home front include pop-oriented Buty; hard-rock bands Lucie and the less refined Alice; and even a country & western rock band, Žlutý Pes (Yellow Dog). More alternative are several veteran outfits, including the grunge band Support Lesbiens, and Visací Zámek (Padlock). Lucie Bílá, diva of 1990s Czech pop, started out sounding like a toned-down Nina Hagen, but has lately turned to rock musicals and Czech versions of American and British hits. Newer talent includes Patti Smith-like Načeva, and avant-garde violinist and vocalist Iva Bittová, who has made first-rate classical and modern recordings.

Literature

The earliest literary works were hymns and religious texts in Old Church Slavonic, replaced by Latin in the late 11th century. The 14th and 15th centuries saw the appearance of reformist theological texts, mostly in Czech, by Jan Hus and others.

With the imposition of the German language after the Thirty Years' War, Czech literature entered a dark age, re-emerging only in the early 19th century in the Czech-language works of the linguists Josef Dobrovský and Josef Jungmann. In the mid-19th century, František Palacký published a five volume history of Bohemia and Moravia.

Karel Hynek Mácha, possibly the greatest of all Czech poets, was the leading representative of romanticism in the early 19th century; his most famous lyrical work is *Máj* (May). Mid-19th century romanticism produced outstanding pieces about life in the country – especially *Grandmother* by Božena Němcová (the first major woman Czech writer), and Karel Erben's *Flowers*.

The radical political journalist Karel Havlíček Borovský criticised the Habsburg elite and wrote excellent satirical poems. Two poets of the time who took much inspiration from Czech history were Jan Neruda (who also wrote *Povídky malostranské* or Prague Tales, a collection of stories about daily life in Malá Strana) and Svatopluk Čech.

At the end of the 19th century, Alois Jirásek wrote *Staré pověsti české* (Old Czech Legends), a compendium of stories from the arrival of the Czechs in Bohemia to the Middle Ages, as well as nationalistic historical novels, his best being *Temno* (Darkness). A major political philosopher and writer of his time was Tomáš Garrigue Masaryk, later to become the Czechoslovak Republic's first president.

One of the best-known Czech writers of all is Franz Kafka. Along with a circle of other German-speaking Jewish writers in Prague, he played a major role in the literary scene at the beginning of this century (see the boxed text 'Kafka's Prague' in the Staré Město & Josefov section of the Things to See & Do chapter). His two complex and claustrophobic masterpieces are *The Trial* and *The Castle*. Others in the same circle were critic Max Brod and journalist Egon Erwin Kisch.

Among their Czech-speaking contemporaries was Jaroslav Hašek, now best known for *Dobrý voják Švejk* (The Good Soldier Švejk), which is full of good, low-brow WWI humour about the trials of Czechoslovakia's literary mascot, written in instalments from Prague's pubs.

The post-WWI Czech author Karel Čapek is famous for a science-fiction drama, *RUR* (Rossum's Universal Robots), from which the word 'robot' entered the English language. Well known poets of the interwar years are Jaroslav Seifert (awarded the Nobel Prize for Literature in 1984) and Vítěslav Nezval.

The early communist period produced little of literary value, though the 1960s saw a resurgence of writing as controls were relaxed. Writers such as Václav Havel, Josef Škvorecký, Milan Kundera and Ivo Klíma produced their first works in the years preceding the 1968 Soviet-led invasion. Klíma's best-known novel is *The Ship Named Hope*.

After the invasion some, including Havel, stayed and wrote for the underground *samizdat* press or had manuscripts smuggled to the west. Others left, producing their best work in exile. Kundera's best novel is probably *The Joke*; two other well known works are *The Unbearable Lightness of Being*.and *The Book of Laughter and Forgetting* Two good reads by Škvorecký are *Cowards* and *The Bride of Texas*. Other important figures of this time are philosopher Jan Patočka and poet Jiří Kolář.

Until his accidental death in 1997, the Czech Republic's leading contemporary novelist was Bohumil Hrabal. One of his most notable novels, *The Little Town That Stood Still*, portrays with good humour the interactions of a small, close-knit community. Another popular Hrabal work is *Closely Watched Trains*.

Painting

The luminously realistic, 14th century paintings of Magister Theodoricus (Master Theodoric), whose work hangs in the Chapel of the Holy Cross at Karlštejn Castle and in the Chapel of St Wenceslas in St Vitus Cathedral, influenced art throughout central Europe.

Another gem of Czech Gothic art is a late 14th century altar panel by an artist known only as the Master of the Třeboň Altar; what remains of it is in the Convent of St George in Prague Castle.

The baroque era saw a surge of Catholic religious art, dominated in Bohemia by Petr Brandl.

The Czech National Revival in the late 18th and early 19th centuries witnessed the appearance of a Czech style of realism, in particular by Mikuláš Aleš and the father and son Antonín and Josef Mánes. Alfons Mucha is well known for his late 19th century Art-Nouveau posters. Czech landscape art developed in the works of Anton Kosárek, followed by a wave of impressionism and symbolism at the hands of Antonín Slavíček, Max Švabinský and others. The earliest notable woman painter, Zdenka Braunerová, concentrated on painting and sketching Prague and the Czech countryside.

In the early 20th century, Prague developed as a centre of avant-garde art, centred on a group of artists called Osma (The Eight). Prague was also a centre for Cubist painters, including Josef Čapek. The functionalist movement flourished between WWI and WWII in a group called Devětsil, led by the adaptable Karel Teige. Surrealists followed, including Zdeněk Rykr and Josef Šíma.

Forty years of communism brought little art of interest, at least through official channels. Underground painters of the time included Mikuláš Medek, whose abstract, surrealist art was exhibited in out-of-the-way galleries, and Jiří Kolář, an outstanding graphic artist and poet. Some of the never-exhibited artists of the postwar years have surfaced since 1989.

Sculpture

Medieval sculpture, like medieval painting, served religious ends. In the 12th and 13th centuries, sculpture evolved from ornamentation into realism. The 14th century saw further realist tendencies, represented by the portraits of royal and noble figures in St Vitus Cathedral. Soon a more decorative style took over, best exemplified by the anonymous *Krumlov Virgin* in the Convent of St George at Prague Castle.

Gothic realism in the latter 15th century brought more lively forms, including the work of the so-called Žebrák Master of Sorrows, in the Convent of St George at Prague Castle.

In the baroque era, religious sculpture sprouted in public places, including 'Marian columns' erected in gratitude to the Virgin for protection against the plague. Two outstanding baroque sculptors were Matthias Braun and Ferdinand Maximilian Brokoff. An important late 18th century figure was Ignác František Platzer, whose decorative statues can be seen throughout Prague.

Bohemian sculpture declined until a mid-19th century revival , a principal figure of that time being Václav Levý. Josef Václav Myslbek dominated sculpture in the latter 19th century with his romantic Slavonic style. His students, including Stanislav Sucharda, produced brilliant symbolist pieces. Other sculptors were the impressionists Ladislav Šaloun and Josef Mařatka.

One of the best-known Cubist sculptors was Otto Gutfreund. In the 1920s he switched to realism, influencing the next wave of sculptors such as Jan Lauda, Karel Pokorný and Karel Dvořák. Surrealism followed, one of its best-known figures being Ladislav Zívr.

Cinema

The pioneer of Czech cinema was the architect Jan Kříženecký, who made three comedies in American slapstick style that were shown at the 1898 Exhibition of Architecture and Engineering.

The domestic film industry took off in the early years of this century, and Czechs were leading innovators. The first film ever to show full frontal nudity was Gustaf Machatý's *Extase* (Ecstasy, 1932), a hit (and a scandal) at the 1934 Venice Festival. Revealing all was one Hedvige Kiesler, who went on to Hollywood as Hedy Lamarr. Hugo Haas directed a fine adaptation of Karel Čapek's anti-Nazi science-fiction novel *Bílá nemoc* (White Death) in 1937. Fear of persecution drove him to Hollywood, where he made and starred in many films.

The Nazis limited the movie industry to nationalistic comedies, while under communism the focus was on low-quality propaganda films. A 'new wave' of Czech cinema rose between 1963 and the Soviet-led invasion in 1968. Its young directors escaped censorship because they were among the first graduates of the communist-supervised Academy of Film. It was from this time that Czech films began to win international awards.

Among the earliest outstanding works was *Černý Petr* (Black Peter, known in the USA as *Peter & Paula*, 1963) by Miloš Forman, who fled after 1968 and became a successful Hollywood director with films such as *One Flew over the Cuckoo's Nest* and *Amadeus*. Other prominent directors were Jiří Menzel, Věra Chytilová and Ivan Passer.

Some post-1968 films critical of the regime were banned or their production stopped. Probably the best film of the following two decades was Menzel's internationally screened 1985 comedy *Má vesnička středisková* (My Sweet Little Village), a subtle look at the workings and failings of socialism in a village co-operative.

Directors of the post-communist era are struggling to compete with Hollywood films, as well as the good Czech films of the 1960s. So far the only one who has succeeded is Zdeněk Svěrák, whose 1994 hit *Akumulátor* was the most expensive Czech film produced to date. In 1996 it was surpassed at the box office by the internationally acclaimed *Kolja*, about a Russian boy raised by a Czech bachelor (played by the director's father). A year later *Kolja* won the best foreign film awards at the Cannes Film Festival and the US Academy Awards.

The Czech film studios at Barrandov in south-west Prague are also known for their world-class animated and puppet films, many of which were made from the 1950s to the 1980s. The best of the puppet films, *A Midsummer Night's Dream*, was produced by the talented Jiří Trnka.

Theatre

Czech-language theatre did not develop fully until the 16th century. Themes were mostly Biblical and the intent was to moralise. At Prague's Charles University, Latin drama was used for teaching. The best plays were written by Jan Ámos Komenský (John Comenius) in the years before the Thirty Years' War, after which plays in Czech were banned. German drama and Italian opera were popular during the 17th and 18th centuries, when many theatres were built.

In 1785, Czech drama reappeared at the Nostitz (now Estates) Theatre, and Prague became the centre of Czech-language theatre. Major 19th century playwrights were Josef Kajetán Tyl and Ján Kolár. Drama, historical plays and fairy tales flourished as part of the Czech National Revival. In 1862 the first independent Czech theatre opened: Prague's Temporary Theatre (Prozatimní divadlo).

Drama in the early years of the Czechoslovak Republic was led by the brothers Karel and Josef Čapek, and also

František Langer. Actor and playwright EF Burian later became known for his experimental dramas.

Under communism, classical theatre performances were of a high quality, but the modern scene was stifled. Exceptions included the pantomime of the Black Theatre (Černé divadlo) and the ultra-modern Magic Lantern (Laterna Magika), founded by Alfréd Radok.

Many fine plays, including those by Václav Havel, went unperformed locally as a result of their anti-government tone, but appeared in the west. In the mid-1960s, free expression was explored in Prague's Theatre on the Balustrade (Divadlo Na zábradlí), with works by Havel, Ladislav Fialka and Milan Uhde, and performances by the comedy duo of Jiří Suchý and Jiří Šlitr.

Marionette & Puppet Theatre Marionette performances have been popular in Prague since the 16th century. A major figure of this art form was Matěj Kopecký (1775-1847).

Marionette theatres opened in Prague and Plzeň in the early 20th century. Josef Skupa's legendary Spejbl & Hurvínek (the Czech Punch & Judy) attracted large crowds, and still do.

Even during communism, puppet and marionette theatre was officially approved and popular, and Czech performances were ranked among the best in the world, especially in the films of Jiří Trnka.

Architecture

The earliest Slavonic buildings in Bohemia were wooden and have not survived. The earliest nonperishable structures were stone-built **Romanesque** rotunda-churches, though most have since been incorporated into larger churches. Prague's finest Romanesque structure is the Basilica of St George in Prague Castle; another example is the Rotunda of St Martin at Vyšehrad.

The 13th century brought the **Gothic** style in buildings and entire town centres, with arcaded houses built around a central square. Czech Gothic architecture flourished during the rule of Charles IV, especially in the hands of the German architect Peter Parler, best known for the eastern part of St Vitus Cathedral. Other fine Gothic structures are Týn Church, the Powder Tower, the Convent of St Agnes, and Charles Bridge and its towers.

Renaissance architecture appeared in the early 16th century, with Italian designers invited to Prague by Habsburg rulers. The emphasis was more on chateaux and merchant houses than on churches. The mixture of Italian and local styles gave rise to the unique 'Czech Renaissance' style, featuring heavy ornamental stucco decorations and paintings of historical or mythical scenes. A fine example is the Summer (or Belvedere) Palace at Hradčany; on a smaller scale is Dům U minuty, part of the Old Town Hall.

Re-Catholicisation and reconstruction after the Thirty Years' War introduced the **baroque** style in Habsburg palaces, residences and new churches. This was the grandest period in Bohemian architecture, responsible for the baroque 'face' of Prague today. In the early 18th century a Czech baroque style emerged. Its best-known practitioners were the Bavarian father and son Kristof and Kilian Ignatz Dientzenhofer, the Italian Giovanni Santini and the Bohemian František Kaňka. The best example among dozens is the Dientzenhofers' St Nicholas Church in Malá Strana.

The 19th century saw various **revival** movements – neoclassical, neo-Gothic, neo-Renaissance – which in the middle of the century coincided with the Czech National Revival. One of the finest works of this period is the neo-Renaissance National Theatre (1883) by Josef Zítek.

As in the rest of Europe, Czech architecture in the early 20th century was under the spell of **Art Nouveau**, with its sinuous, 'botanical' lines. The term came from the French *l'art nouveau* and was known as *secese* in Bohemia, *Sezessionstil* in Austria and *Jugendstil* in Germany. The most visible Art Nouveau works in Prague are the Municipal House (Obecní dům), the

ARCHITECTURAL STYLES

Romanesque

This style dates from the 10th to the 13th centuries. A typical Romanesque church has thick walls, closely spaced columns and heavy, rounded arches. Of the surviving Romanesque structures in Prague and the Czech Republic, many are simple circular (rotunda) chapels.

Gothic

The Gothic style predominated in the Czech lands from the 13th to 16th centuries. It represented not just a new aesthetic but new engineering that permitted thinner walls and – in churches – taller, more delicate columns and great expanses of stained glass. Distinctive features include pointed arches and ribbed roof-vaults, external 'flying buttresses' to support the thinner walls and elaborate, carved doorway columns.

Right: The Basilica of St George viewed from the Gothic heights of St Vitus Cathedral. The basilica is considered the best preserved Romanesque church in Prague.

RICHARD NEBESKY

Renaissance

The 16th century saw a new enthusiasm for classical forms and an obsession with grace and symmetry. Czech versions of this, especially in houses and chateaux, featured elaborate gables and rooftops and exterior walls covered with sgraffito in which designs such as mythical scenes are cut through the plaster into deeper, darker-coloured layers.

Baroque

This resplendent, triumphal style is closely associated with the rebuilding of Prague (and re-imposition of Catholicism) after the Thirty Years' War. The style's marble columns, emotional sculpture and painting and rich, gilded ornamentation combine to produce extravagant and awe-inspiring interiors. Prague is dominated by baroque façades.

JOHN KING

Left: The baroque splendour of Malá Strana's St Nicholas Church.

RICHARD NEBESKÝ

Rococo

This is essentially late, over-the-top baroque. Florid in the extreme, elaborate and 'lightweight', it was popular with architects in the late 18th century.

Revivalist Styles

Neoclassical, neo-Gothic and neo-Renaissance styles appeared in the late 18th and the 19th centuries. Neoclassicism favoured grand colonnades and pediments and often huge, simple, symmetrical buildings. Renaissance and Gothic revival styles played a part in the National Revival movement in the Czech lands.

Modern

At the turn of the century, the decorative and sensual style called Art Nouveau, *secese, Sezessionstil or Jugendstil* produced some of the Czech Republic's most striking buildings.

Unique to Czechoslovakia was the fruitful development of Cubist architecture. Prague has some surprisingly elegant examples, dating from before WWI.

Art Deco is a latter-day term for an avant-garde 1920s and 1930s style mixing traditional decoration of luxury items with a modern look. The inter-war years also witnessed the Constructivist movement, typified by extreme geometric simplicity and functionalism – less art than an artistic glorification of engineering.

RICHARD NEBESKÝ

JOHN KING

Left: Art Nouveau in Nové Město: an ornate building façade and the elegant décor inside Prague's main train station.

main train station, and structures built for the Terrestrial Jubilee Exposition of 1891 in Bubeneč.

Cubism had a strong influence on architecture before WWI, developing into a striking local style. Some of Prague's finest Cubist façades were designed by Josef Chochol in the neighbourhood just below Vyšehrad. Other appealing examples, by Josef Gočár, are the House of the Black Madonna in Staré Město, and twin houses on Tychonova in Dejvice.

Prague has only a few examples of the inter-war style called **Art Deco**, including the Bank of Czechoslovakian Legions (1923) at Na poříčí 24, and the Adria Palace (1924) at the corner of Národní and Jungmannovo náměstí, both in Nové Město. This period also saw some more avant-garde architecture, most notably the later work of Jan Kotěra, though Prague has few samples. Good examples of the functional, machine-like **Constructivist** style are the Trade Fair Palace in Holešovice, and St Wenceslas Church in Vinohrady.

The architecture of the communist era was heavy-handed and Stalinist, producing many eyesores – including vast, pre-fab residential complexes – and little style or quality. Restoration concentrated on prime tourist sights, neglecting other buildings.

Prague's post-1989 architecture is a mixed bag, some quite out of keeping with its surroundings, some simply ugly, and some surprisingly attractive (see the boxed text above). One of the city's boldest and most controversial new structures is the so-called 'Dancing Building'.

Restoration work, both state-funded and private, has gone into high gear since 1990, though much remains to be done, and some structures are beyond help. Not all restoration work has been in line with the city's poorly enforced laws on preserving the

Post-1989 Architecture in Prague

One of Prague's most idiosyncratic and appealing examples of new architecture is the Dancing Building (Tančící dům), on Rašínovo nábřeží in Nové Město. For its strikingly fluid lines it was initially nick-named the 'Fred & Ginger Building', after the legendary dancing duo of Fred Astaire and Ginger Rogers. Prague law insists that any new structure in the historical centre must be in keeping with its neighbours, and this bumptious, weaving edifice, designed by the Czech Vlado Milunć and the American Frank O Gehry, somehow manages this perfectly.

The Dancing Building (Tančící dům)

RICHARD NEBESKY

By contrast, the bland, glass-and-metal façade of the Myslbek Building, designed by the French firm Caisse des Dépots et Consignations, clashes unpleasantly with its *fin-de-siècle* neighbours on Na příkopě, in Staré Město. On the other hand, the building's rear face, on Ovocný trh, fits in masterfully.

Other recent architecture has tended towards undistinguished commercial/office towers outside the city centre. One with a modicum of shape and personality is the Česká Spořitelna Building on Budějovické náměstí, in Prague 4.

history of the city, and some unique and ir-replaceable structures have been destroyed.

SOCIETY & CONDUCT

Czechs tend to be polite, mild-mannered people with a good sense of humour, not inclined to argue or fight. They can be quite conservative socially. If you're invited to someone's home, you'll find them very hospitable. Do at least bring flowers for your host, and remember to remove your shoes when you enter the house.

It's customary to say *dobrý den* (good day) when entering a shop, café or quiet bar, and to say *na shledanou* (goodbye) when you leave. On public transport, most younger people will give up their seat for the elderly, the sick and pregnant women.

When attending a classical concert, opera, ballet or a play in one of the traditional theatres, men typically wear a suit and tie, and women an evening dress. It's only foreigners who don't, drawing frowns from Czechs. Casual dress is fine at performances of modern music, plays and so on.

RELIGION

Many Czechs were converted to Christianity in the 9th century by the 'Apostles of the Slavs', the monks Cyril and Methodius of Thessaloniki. Christianity became the state religion under Wenceslas, Duke of Bohemia (ruled approximately 925-935) and patron saint of the Czech Republic.

The Church remained loyal to Rome until the end of the 14th century, when reformers including Jan Hus began to argue for the simpler, more accessible practices of early Christianity. Hussites preached in Czech, not Latin, and gave wine as well as bread in the Holy Communion, enraging their conservative colleagues. Hus was excommunicated in 1411 and burned at the stake in 1415, and Bohemia became a hotbed of anti-Catholic nationalism.

Although Hussitism eventually lost its military edge, Bohemia remained a Protestant and independent-minded part of the Holy Roman Empire for two more centuries, until the Protestant Czechs were decisively defeated at the Battle of Bílá Hóra (White Mountain) west of Prague, in 1620. Bohemia was pulled into the Thirty Years' War and the Counter-Reformation, losing both its political and religious independence. The Habsburgs re-Catholicised the nation, though the Czechs never took to Catholicism as they had to Protestantism.

After 1948, communism brought state atheism and the systematic repression of all religion. Most religious institutions were closed and the clergy were imprisoned. Religion, however, was never stamped out; an underground religious network included many priests who secretly performed rites. Full religious freedom returned with the 'Velvet Revolution' of 1989.

The largest church in the country is the Roman Catholic Church, though only about 40% of Czechs call themselves Catholic. Next largest is the reconstituted Hussite Church, with 400,000 members. Of half a dozen Protestant churches, the largest is the Evangelical Church of Czech Brethren with about 180,000 members.

Though church membership is not as strong as in many other European countries, there has been a slight rise in recent years, and a significant rise in the numbers of children attending religious education.

Since WWII the Jewish community in the Czech Republic has shrunk from a prewar total of 120,000 to only about 6000.

LANGUAGE

Naturally enough for the capital of the Czech Republic, the dominant language in Prague is Czech, although you will find that many older Czechs speak some German. Under communism Russian was learned by everybody at school, but this has now been replaced by English. While you'll have little trouble finding English speakers in central Prague, they're scarce in the suburbs and beyond, as are translated menus.

For more information on Czech and a list of useful words and phrases, see the Language chapter at the back of this book.

Facts for the Visitor

WHEN TO GO

While attractions across much of the Czech Republic are closed or keep limited hours outside the summer season, Prague caters for visitors throughout the year. Periods when the tourist crush is especially oppressive are worth avoiding. Favourite European tourist seasons are the Easter and Christmas/New Year holidays, as well as May/June. Czechs tend to go on holiday in July and August, during which time the supply of bottom-end accommodation actually increases, as student hostels are opened to visitors.

If you can withstand the cold and the periodic smog alerts during weather inversions, hotel space is plentiful in winter (outside Christmas/New Year), and Prague is gorgeous under a mantle of snow.

ORIENTATION

Prague sits within the gentle landscape of the Bohemian plateau, straddling the Vltava ('Vl-TA-va'; Moldau in German), the Czech Republic's longest river. At Mělník, 30km downstream (north), the Vltava enters the Labe, which drains northern Bohemia and then crosses Germany (as the Elbe) to the North Sea.

Central Prague consists of five historical towns. On a hill above the west bank of the Vltava is Hradčany, the castle district, dominated by Prague Castle and St Vitus Cathedral, which give the city its trademark skyline. Between the castle and the river is Malá Strana, the 13th century 'Lesser (or Little) Quarter', marked by the green dome of St Nicholas Church. From the open spaces of Petřín Hill, south of and behind

Government Travel Advice

The US State Department's Bureau of Consular Affairs issues periodically updated Consular Information Sheets, which include entry requirements, medical facilities, crime information and other topics. You can receive copies by sending a stamped, self-addressed envelope to Overseas Citizens Services, Room 4800, Department of State, Washington, DC 20520-4818. You'll also find them on the Web at travel.state.gov/index.html. You can listen to recorded travel advice at ☎ 202-647 5225 on a touch-tone phone, or get information via automated fax by dialling ☎ 202-647 3000 from a fax machine.

The Canadian Department of Foreign Affairs & International Trade, 125 Sussex Drive, Ottawa K1A 0G2 (☎ 613-944 6788, toll-free ☎ 800-267 6788, fax-on-demand 613-944 2500, toll-free fax 800-575 2500, Web site www.dfait-maeci.gc.ca/) issues similar Travel Information Reports.

Get British Foreign Office travel advice from the Travel Advice Unit, Foreign & Commonwealth Office, Room 605, Clive House, Petty France, London SW1H 9HD (☎ 0171-238 4503/4, fax 238 4545; from 22 April 2000 ☎ 020-7238 4503/4, fax 7238 4545; Web site www.fco.gov.uk/). Regularly updated Foreign Office travel advice is also displayed on BBC2 Ceefax, from page 470.

Australians can ring the Department of Foreign Affairs advice line in Canberra on ☎ 02-6261 3305 or toll-free ☎ 1300 555 135, for advice on specific countries, or check www.dfat.gov.au/consular/.

Any travel agency linked to the Apollo, Fantasia or Galileo networks can also access this advice directly.

Addresses

Numbers apply to buildings rather than premises. Confusingly, most buildings have *two* numbers. The one on a blue sign is its position on the street, sequentially with odd numbers on one side and even on the other. The one on a red sign is its number in the district, which is part of the old house numbering system and usually bears no relation to its neighbours. Originally, houses were known by their emblems – such as the 'House of Two Suns' (Dům U dvou slunců) – and thus today most old houses in Malá Strana and Staré Město have three identification symbols: emblem, and red and blue numbers.

In this book we use 'blue' numbers; if unavailable, the 'red' one is used. Sometimes both numbers are given, separated by a slash (/), with the red number given first in line with local practice.

Malá Strana, are the finest panoramic views of the city.

On the Vltava's east bank is the 'Old Town', Staré Město, a Gothic and baroque landscape surrounding the immense, central Old Town Square (Staroměstské náměstí). Frozen in time in one corner of Staré Město is Josefov, the former Jewish ghetto, now riven by the Art Nouveau bravado of Pařížská. The 'New Town', Nové Město (new in the 14th century), cradles the Old Town to the south and east, and includes Wenceslas Square (Václavské náměstí), symbol of Bohemia's ancient and modern aspirations.

Within these historical districts – linked by the landmark Charles Bridge over the Vltava – are most of the city's attractions. The whole compact maze is best appreciated on foot, aided by good public transport. Beyond the centre is 19th and 20th century Prague, many of whose districts began as separate towns.

Prague is divided into 10 districts; the relevant district is quoted in all addresses, with the exception of Prague 1, which covers the historical centre (see Map 1 – Greater Prague).

Points of Arrival & Departure

See the Getting There & Away and Getting Around chapters for more details about the following gateways:

Air Ruzyně airport is 17km west of the centre, a 40 minute ride by bus.

Train The main train station, Praha hlavní nádraží (also called Wilsonovo nádraží), is three blocks from Wenceslas Square in north-eastern Nové Město. Other stations served by international trains are Praha-Holešovice, north of the centre, and Praha-Smíchov in the south-west. All three are beside metro stations of the same name.

The most likely stations for long-distance domestic trains are the main station and Masarykovo nádraží, two blocks north of it. Other stations where you might end up include Praha-Dejvice (two blocks to metro station Hradčanská); Praha-Smíchov; Praha-Vysočany, north-east of the centre (bus No 185, 209, 259 or 278 to metro station Českomoravská); or Praha-Vršovice (tram No 24 to Wenceslas Square).

Place Names

In this book we tend to use Czech names for districts, squares, streets and some buildings; this will certainly make it easier for Czechs to understand your queries. Where useful, place names are accompanied by English translations when they first appear.

A few places have become well known among western tourists (and Czech tour guides!) by their English names – such as Charles Bridge (Karlův most), Old Town Square (Staroměstské náměstí) and Wenceslas Square (Václavské náměstí) – and for these we tend to use the English names.

Bus Most international coaches terminate at the bus stand by Želivského metro station (Map 1); one of the international lines uses a stand by Holešovice metro station (Map 4). A few international coaches, all domestic long-distance buses and most of the regional services use Florenc station, beside metro station Florenc (Map 6), or streets nearby. Some regional buses depart from the stands near metro stations Anděl, Hradčanská, Nádraží Holešovice, Palmovka, Radlická, Roztyly, Smíchovské Nádraží and Želivského.

MAPS

PIS (see the following Tourist Offices section) has several free maps. The multilingual *Prague City Map* has transport routes in the centre, and one version has telephone tips, embassy addresses and a street index.

Maps of all kinds are available at newsagents, bookshops and travel agencies for under about 70 Kč. The most precise and readable one of the centre and near suburbs is Kartografie Praha's 1:10,000 *Praha – plán středu města*, which contains transport information, blurbs about major sights and a street index. If you're here for a long stay, Kartografie Praha's 1:20,000 pocket atlas, *Praha – plán města*, covers the whole city.

A public transport map showing all day and night services (metro, tram and bus) is available from any of the four public information offices of Dopravní podnik (DP), the city transport department (see the Getting Around chapter) for a bargain 35 Kč. PIS's free transport map, *Praha doprava*, shows routes out to the city limits, but they're unnumbered.

Serious geo-freaks should check out map specialist Mapis (Map 5; ☎ 57 31 54 59), Štefánikova 63 in Smíchov. It's open on weekdays only, from 9.30 am to 6 pm. MapQuest (www.mapquest.com/) is an online map service that includes an 'interactive atlas'. You can't buy maps from them, but you can customise and print out their online maps.

TOURIST OFFICES

There are only two state tourist organisations in Prague: Prague Information Service (PIS) and the Czech Tourist Authority (ČCCR). Several formerly state-run travel offices are now privatised commercial travel agencies; while staff are sometimes willing to answer questions, they're not there to provide free information to tourists (except at Čedok's headquarters information desk, as noted in the following). See the Getting There & Away chapter for a rundown of the most helpful agencies.

Prague Information Service (PIS)

The municipal tourist office (Pražská informační služba; ☎ 187, fax 24 21 19 89, email info@pis.cz, Web site www.prague-info.cz) has Prague well covered, with good maps and detailed brochures (including on accommodation, historical monuments and monthly entertainment), all free. PIS also publishes a detailed, 20 Kč what's-on guide, *Přehled*, and other general material.

There are four branches, all open weekdays from 9 am to 7 pm (to 6 pm in winter) and weekends from 9 am to 5 pm. Only the chilly one in the Malá Strana Bridge Tower closes in winter, from November to March.

Na příkopě 20, Staré Město (Map 7)
Old Town Hall, Staré Město (Map 7)
Hlavní nádraží (main train station; Map 6)
Malá Strana Bridge Tower, Mostecká 2 (Map 5)

All four offices offer general information, concert and theatre tickets, and the services of the AVE agency for help in finding

---

Info, Info Everywhere

The universal **i** (information) logo is used willy-nilly by anyone keen to attract the attention of Prague's sometimes disoriented visitors. Ironically, the one outfit that offers reliable, generally unbiased aid – PIS – has its own logo: a stylised three-pronged crown.

accommodation. AVE also has a pricey currency exchange at the Old Town Hall branch.

PIS's Pragotur affiliate offers walk-in guide services, boat trips and lower-end restaurant bookings, from a separate desk (☎ 24 48 25 62, fax 24 48 23 80) at the Old Town Hall branch, daily from 9 am to 6 pm (weekends to 4 pm). The Old Town Hall and Na příkopě branches also sell city tours. Refer to the Getting Around chapter for more on organised tours.

Other Tourist Publications *Přehled* is not the only guide to the action in Prague. There are numerous advertiser-supported tourist handbooks sold at travel agencies and newsstands. Best of the lot is probably the *Prague Guide*.

Czech Tourist Authority (ČCCR)
ČCCR (Česká centrála cestovního ruchu; Map 6; ☎/fax 24 25 79 59, fax 24 25 70 91, email cccr-m@mbox.vol.cz, Web site www.czech-tourinfo.cz), Vinohradská 46, Prague 2, once had a good information office here but now appears to be concentrating on helping regional tourist offices market themselves.

ČCCR Offices Abroad Representative offices include:

Austria
   (☎ 01-535 23 61, fax 535 23 60 14)
   Herrengasse 17, 1010 Vienna
France
   (☎ 01 53 73 00 34, fax 01 43 29 57 67)
   Rue Bonaparte 18, 75006 Paris
Germany
   (☎/fax 030-204 47 70)
   Leipzigerstrasse 60, 10117 Berlin
Netherlands
   (☎ 020-575 30 14, fax 575 30 15)
   Strawinskylaan 517, 1077 XX Amsterdam
USA
   (☎ 212-288 0830, fax 288 0971)
   1109-1111 Madison Ave, New York, NY 10028

Čedok
Čedok is the former state tour operator and travel agency, now privatised. The main office (Map 7; ☎ 24 19 71 11, fax 232 16 56) at Na příkopě 18 is a good, if somewhat pricey, one-stop shop for excursions and concert/theatre tickets, as well as travel bookings. It's open weekdays from 8.30 am to 6 pm and Saturday from 9 am to 1 pm. Services at the airport branch are limited to upper-end accommodation and car rental. See under Travel Agencies in the Getting There & Away chapter for a complete list of Čedok branches.

Prague Tourist Center
This cheerful, convenient private office at Rytířská 12 (Map 7; ☎/fax 24 21 22 09) sells maps, guidebooks, souvenirs, concert/theatre tickets, tours and accommodation.

DOCUMENTS
Passport
Check the expiry date of your passport, as you may have trouble getting a visa if it expires less than two months after your proposed visit. Domestic passport offices and many embassies abroad can provide you with a new one, or insert new pages in your present one, fairly quickly.

Visitors with passports in poor condition have apparently been refused entry into the Czech Republic.

Visas
Without a visa, nationals of the UK and Canada can visit the Czech Republic for up to 180 days; all other EU countries and New Zealand for up to 90 days; and the USA and Singapore for up to 30 days. Australians must obtain a visa – 30-day single-entry and 90-day multiple-entry visas cost A$56. Nationals of most other countries, including South Africa, need a visa, good for a stay of up to 30 days. Multiple-entry visas are also available. Visas must be used within six months of the issue date. Don't get a transit visa, which costs as much as a tourist visa and cannot be converted upon arrival.

When applying, you need one or two passport-size photos, and cash or a money order for the fee, which varies according to your nationality. Most Czech embassies in western capitals will accept applications by post if you include a self-addressed envelope with return certified (recorded) postage, and payment by postal money order; get forms from the embassy or a travel agent. Processing is usually immediate for applications in person; mail applications take about two working days.

At the time of writing there were just three Czech border points, plus the arrivals hall at Prague's Ruzyně airport, issuing on-the-spot 30-day tourist visas (for 1500 Kč); see Car & Motorcycle in the Getting There & Away chapter for details.

Within three days of arrival all foreign visitors are expected to register at the local police station. If you're staying in ordinary tourist accommodation, this will be done for you; otherwise it's up to you. This requirement is now rarely enforced, though officials may bring it up if they're feeling bloody-minded.

Visa Extensions

Apply for a visa extension at entrance B of the grim Foreigners' Police & Passport Office (Úřadovna cizinecké policie a pasové služby), Olšanská 2, Žižkov (Map 8; tram No 9 from Wenceslas Square, or a 10 minute walk from Flora metro station). It's open from 7.30 to 11.45 am and 12.30 to 2.30 pm on Monday, Tuesday and Thursday; from 7.30 to 11.30 am and 12.30 to 5 pm on Wednesday; and until noon on Friday.

The telephone number (☎ 61 44 11 19) gives only the office hours, so there's no alternative to fronting up in person. You can ask for six months but you might get less, depending on your citizenship and the number of extensions you've already obtained. An extension costs 200 Kč, payable with special stamps (kolky) sold there or at any post office. The paperwork takes about four working days.

See under Work at the end of this chapter if you intend to stay longer than the statutory tourist visa period, such as to work.

Travel Insurance

A policy that covers theft, loss, flight cancellation and overseas medical treatment is a good idea. For an extended trip, insurance may seem an extravagance but if you can't afford it, you can't afford a medical emergency either. Youth-oriented travel agencies such as Usit Campus, STA Travel, Council Travel and Travel CUTS offer cheaper policies with no baggage cover. See Health in this chapter for information on medical services available in Prague.

Driving Licence & Permits

The Czech Republic recognises any foreign driving licence bearing a photograph of its owner; if yours doesn't, you should get an International Driving Permit. Drivers must also have vehicle registration papers and the 'green card' that shows they carry full liability insurance (for more on drivers' documents, see the Getting There & Away chapter).

Useful Cards

Numerous discounts are available to full-time students and to those who are under 26 years of age or 60 and over.

Hostel Cards The Czech Republic's hostels don't belong to the international HI system, though some hostels do give discounts to HI members.

Student, Youth & Teacher Cards The international student identity card (ISIC) and teacher's card (ITIC) – valid from September to the end of the following year – are aimed at travel-related costs such as airline fares and museum admissions. Youth cards like Euro<26 and Go25 – good for a year from the purchase date – provide more general discounts, for example in shops and cinemas, as well as on some accommodation and travel.

All of these cards are available from youth-oriented travel agencies such as Usit Campus, STA Travel, Council Travel and Travel CUTS. They're also sold at other Prague travel agencies including GTS

International at Ve Smečkách 27 (Map 6; ☎ 22 21 15 04) and Lodecká 3 (Map 7; ☎ 21 81 27 70), and CKM Travel (Map 7; ☎ 26 85 32, fax 26 86 23), Jindřišská 28; and at IPC, the Charles University Information & Advisory Centre (Map 6; ☎ 96 22 80 36), Školská 13a.

You'll need a passport-size photo and solid proof of your age or student status. Prices at the time of research were about 200 Kč. For further information, see the Web sites www.istc.org about ISIC and ITIC; www.euro26.org about Euro<26; and www.ciee.org/idcards/index.htm about ISIC, ITIC and Go25.

Seniors' Cards Some discounts are available to travellers aged 60 and over. The Rail Europe Senior (RES) Card gives you about 30% off on international journeys, and domestic journeys connecting with an international service. To be eligible for this card you must have a local senior citizens' railcard, the availability of which depends on the country you're in. In Britain, railcards (UK£16) and RES Cards (UK£5) are sold at mainline train stations.

Prague Card This is a three-day, tourist-oriented pass good for transport on buses, trams, metro and the Petřín funicular, plus entry to city museums and state-run galleries. It costs 480 Kč (children 380 Kč) at CKM Travel, Čedok, American Express and a few other travel agents (see Travel Agents in the Getting There & Away chapter).

Travellers Cheque Purchase Receipts

You'll need these to replace lost or stolen travellers cheques. Carry them in a separate place from the cheques.

Work-Related Documents

If you're planning to seek work in Prague, bring along your original birth certificate or a notarised copy of it, plus any credentials relevant to the work you want (such as TEFL certificate or diploma). See the Work

section in this chapter for information on what to do with them.

Photocopies

It's wise to carry photocopies of the data pages of your passport and visa, to ease paperwork headaches should they be lost or stolen. Other copies you might want to carry are of your credit card and travellers cheque numbers (plus the telephone numbers for cancelling or replacing them), airline tickets, travel insurance policy, birth certificate and any documents relating to possible employment. Keep the copies in a separate place from the originals.

EMBASSIES & CONSULATES
Czech Embassies & Consulates

Czech embassies and consulates abroad include the following:

Australia
  Embassy:
  (☎ 02-6290 1386, fax 6290 0006)
  38 Culgoa Circuit, O'Malley, Canberra, ACT 2606
  Consulate:
  (☎ 02-9371 8877, visa information ☎ 9371 8878, fax 9371 9635)
  169 Military Rd, Dover Heights, Sydney, NSW 2030; visas are issued only at the consulate
Austria
  Embassy:
  (☎ 01-894 21 25/6)
  Penzingerstrasse 11-13, 1140 Vienna
Canada
  Embassy:
  (☎ 613-562 3875, fax 562 3878)
  541 Sussex Drive, Ottawa, Ontario K1N 6Z6
France
  Embassy:
  (☎ 01 40 65 13 00)
  15 Avenue Charles Floquet, 75343 Paris Cedex 07
Germany
  Embassy:
  (☎ 0228-91 970)
  Ferdinandstrasse 27, 53127 Bonn
Ireland – see UK
Netherlands
  Embassy:
  (☎ 070-346 97 12)
  Paleisstraat 4, 2514 JA The Hague

New Zealand
  Consulate:
  (☎ 04-564 6001)
  48 Hair St, PO Box 43035, Wainuiomata,
  Wellington; visa applications (for stays over
  90 days, or for working or study visas) must
  be made to the Czech consulate in Sydney,
  Australia
Poland
  Embassy:
  (☎ 022-628 7221)
  Koszykowa 18, 00-555 Warsaw
Slovakia
  Embassy:
  (☎ 07-536 12 05)
  29.Augusta 5, 81 000 Bratislava
UK & Irish Republic
  Embassy:
  (☎ 0171-243 1115, fax 727 9654; from 22
  April 2000 ☎ 020-7243 1115, fax 7727 9654)
  26 Kensington Palace Gardens, London W8
  4QY; visa section (☎ 0171-243 7943; from
  22 April 2000 ☎ 020-7243 7943) at No 28
USA
  Embassy:
  (☎ 202-274 9100, fax 363 6308,
  Web site www.czech.cz/washington)
  3900 Spring of Freedom St NW, Washington,
  DC 20008
  Consulate:
  (☎ 310-473 0889)
  10990 Wilshire Blvd, Suite 1100,
  Los Angeles, CA 90024

Embassies & Consulates in Prague

Most embassies are in or around Malá
Strana and Hradčany, and are open for visa-
related business only until 11 am or 1 pm.

Australia
  Honorary Consul:
  (☎ 24 31 07 43)
  Na Ořechovce 38, Prague 6: emergency
  assistance only (such as lost or stolen
  passport); otherwise contact the Australian
  embassy in Vienna or Warsaw
Austria
  Embassy:
  (Map 9; ☎ 57 32 12 82)
  Viktora Huga 10, Prague 5
Canada
  Embassy:
  (Map 3; ☎ 24 31 11 08, fax 24 31 02 94)
  Mickiewiczova 6, Prague 6

France
  Embassy:
  (Map 5; ☎ 57 32 03 52)
  Velkopřerovské náměstí 2, Prague 1
Germany
  Embassy:
  (Map 5; ☎ 57 32 01 90)
  Vlašská 21, Prague 1
Ireland
  Embassy:
  (Map 5; ☎ 57 53 00 61)
  Tržiště 13, Prague 1
Netherlands
  Embassy:
  (Map 3; ☎ 24 31 21 90)
  Gotthardská 6/27, Prague 6
New Zealand
  Honorary Consul:
  (☎ 25 41 98): emergency assistance only (eg
  lost or stolen passport); otherwise contact the
  New Zealand Embassy in Bonn
Poland
  Consulate:
  (Map 6; ☎ 57 32 06 78)
  Václavské náměstí (Wenceslas Square) 49,
  Prague 1
Slovakia
  Embassy:
  (Map 3; ☎ 35 05 21)
  Pod hradbami 1, Prague 6
UK
  Embassy:
  (Map 5; ☎ 57 32 03 55, 24 hours)
  Thunovská 14, Prague 1
USA
  Embassy:
  (Map 5; ☎ 24 21 98 44/6)
  Tržiště 15, Prague 1

CUSTOMS

You can import a reasonable amount of personal effects and up to 6000 Kč worth of
gifts and other 'noncommercial' goods. If
you're over 18 years of age, you can bring
in 2L of wine, 1L of spirits and 200 ciga-
rettes (or equivalent tobacco products).

Before you make a major purchase in
Prague, find out how much it will cost to get
it out of the country. Consumer goods ex-
ceeding 30,000 Kč in value are dutiable at
22%.

You cannot export genuine antiques, and
customs officials are a suspicious lot. If you
have any doubt about what you're taking

out, show it to staff at the National Museum (Wenceslas Square) or the Museum of Decorative Arts (17.listopadu). A certification from them should mean that you don't experience any problems with airport or postal customs. For mailing any such items over 2kg, go to the customs post office (Map 1; Celní pošta; ☎ 57 01 91 11), Plzeňská 139, Smíchov (tram No 4, 7 or 9 to the Klamovka stop, three stops west from Anděl metro station), open Monday and Wednesday from 7 am to 6 pm, and Tuesday, Thursday and Friday until 3 pm.

You can import and export unlimited amounts of Czech or foreign currency. Arriving visitors may occasionally be asked to prove that they have the equivalent of at least 7000 Kč (about US$230) in convertible currency.

MONEY
Currency
The unit of Czech money is the *koruna* or crown, abbreviated Kč (for *koruna česká*). A koruna is divided into 100 *haléřů* or heller (h). Notes come in 5000, 2000, 1000, 500, 200, 100, 50 and 20 Kč denominations, and coins in 50, 20, 10, 5, 2 and 1 Kč and 50, 20 and 10 haléřů sizes.

The Czech Republic has had new currency since 1993; don't accept anything with *korun československých* on it.

Exchange Rates
The koruna has been freely convertible on world currency markets since 1996. When this book went to press, typical exchange rates were:

country	unit		koruna
Australia	A$1	=	19.3 Kč
Canada	C$1	=	19.9 Kč
euro	€1	=	35.5 Kč
France	1FF	=	5.4 Kč
Germany	DM1	=	18.1 Kč
Japan	¥100	=	25.0 Kč
Slovakia	Sk100	=	83.8 Kč
UK	UK£1	=	50.3 Kč
USA	US$1	=	30.4 Kč

US dollars and German Deutschmarks are as welcome as the koruna in touristy parts of Prague, and are the most sensible currencies to bring.

Exchanging Money
The easiest, cheapest way to carry money is in the form of a payment card from your bank, with which you can get cash from your own account, over the counter or from an ATM. Charges are minimal at major Prague banks (typically from zero to about 2%) and some home banks charge nothing at all for the use of these cards. Provided you make withdrawals of at least several thousand koruna at a time, you'll pay less than the assorted commissions on travellers cheques.

The next most convenient method for obtaining currency is a credit card, athough charges will be higher.

ATMs Bank ATMs that accept most major payment/credit cards are common all over Prague, and especially around Wenceslas Square, 28.října, Na příkopě, náměstí Republiky and the airport. Most have limits of around 2000 to 3000 Kč for each individual withdrawal.

Note that some ATMs get locked up when the banks close for the night, though Česká spořitelna banka has 'Bankomat' portable ATMs in metro and bus stations and elsewhere.

Credit Cards Prague's mid-range and upper-end hotels and restaurants, most shops, and Čedok and other travel agents usually accept any major credit card (*platební karta*).

Be careful when you pay for something with a card: complete the 'total' box on the sales slip yourself, add a currency symbol before the amount due with no space in between, and be sure that only one sales slip is imprinted.

Lost Travellers Cheques & Cards If your travellers cheques or cards are lost or stolen, the best way to freeze the accounts

Good Day, Can I Help You with Your Money?

One of Prague's biggest scams is the exorbitant commissions collected by private exchange bureaux (*směnárna*) along tourist routes, and the tricks they use to conceal the fact.

Local bureaux may advertise low commissions but use less favourable exchange rates; or minimum commissions, easily misunderstood as minimum transactions; or selling rates, which look better than the buying rates they'll pay you (incidentally, the high rake-offs are from foreigners: Czechs pay much lower charges, or none at all, at these places).

Outfits such as Chequepoint and Exact Change take commissions of up to 10%, or more. Hotel exchanges are slightly less greedy, charging around 5% and often doing their sums using lower than bank rates. Even American Express and Thomas Cook look pretty hungry unless you're using their travellers cheques.

Whatever you carry, you're best off at one of the major banks (still state-owned at the time of writing), where exchange rates are the most favourable, and typical commissions are from zero to 2%, though their opening hours are limited (weekdays only, from 8 or 9 am to 5 or 6 pm). Čedok and post offices charge 2% at similar rates to the banks.

The following table gives a coarse indication of some over-the-counter commissions and buy rates for US$ and UK£ cash during a three day period at the time of research. It's only for illustrative purposes, since actual numbers change by the day.

source	commission	buy US$1	buy UK£1
IPB	2%	32.5	53.0
Čedok	2%	32.4	52.5
Komerční	2%	32.2	52.5
American Express	4%	31.5	51.7
AVE	5%	32.2	51.7
Hotel Jalta	5%	31.0	50.7
Chequepoint	9 to 10% (for 3000 Kč)	32.5	53.1

There's an automatic exchange machine for foreign banknotes at Československá obchodní banka, Na příkopě 14. It charges 2% (and just 1% from November to May), with no minimum requirement. The Bank of Austria on the corner of Melantrichova and Havelská has a 24 hour machine charging 3%.

Re-Exchange When it's time to go and you want to resell your koruna, they get you again. The best deal we found was with IPB at the airport, which charges just 1% commission to buy back koruna. Private exchanges commonly take around 5%.

There is no legal limit to how much you can sell back, though many banks have their own limits (such as 5000 Kč at Živnostenská, 1000 Kč at Komerční). IPB at the airport buys back any amount. Most do not buy back coins.

and get replacements is to call your home office (or the Prague office in the case of American Express or Thomas Cook). Don't forget to bring the numbers! Local numbers for this purpose include American Express (☎ 24 21 99 78), Visa (☎ 24 12 53 53, Živnostenská banka) and MasterCard/Eurocard (☎ 24 42 31 35, Komerční banka).

Banks & Exchange Offices

Some tourist-zone (Prague 1) offices of the city's main foreign-exchange banks are:

American Express
   (Map 6; ☎ 24 21 99 92, fax 22 21 11 31)
   Wenceslas Square 56
Česká spořitelna banka
   (Map 7; ☎ 24 22 92 68)
   Na příkopě 29
Československá obchodní banka
   (Map 7; ☎ 24 11 11 11)
   Na příkopě 14
Investiční a poštovní banka or IPB
   (Map 7; ☎ 22 04 11 11)
   Senovážné náměstí 32
Komerční banka
   (Map 7; ☎ 24 02 11 11)
   Na příkopě 33
Thomas Cook
   (Map 7; ☎ 21 10 52 72/77) Národní 28
   and (Map 6; ☎ 24 81 71 73)
   Staroměstské náměstí 5
Živnostenská banka
   (Map 7; ☎ 24 12 11 11)
   exchange office to the right of the
   main entrance at Na příkopě 20; even
   if you have no business, it's worth
   looking in at the main hall's lavish Art
   Nouveau interior

Other foreign banks include:

Banque National de Paris
   (☎ 57 00 61 11)
   Vitežná 1, Prague 5
Citibank
   (☎ 24 30 41 11)
   Evropská 178, Prague 6
Crédit Lyonnais
   (☎ 22 07 61 11)
   Ovocný trh 8, Prague 1
Société Générale
   (☎ 24 83 23 00)
   Pobřežní 3, Prague 8

Good for late night transactions is the 24 hour exchange at Hotel Jalta, Wenceslas Square 45 (Map 6).

International Transfers If you're not an American Express or Thomas Cook customer, the fastest way to get emergency money from home is through Western Union, at the office of Sport Turist (Map 6; ☎ 24 22 85 18), Národní 33. It's open weekdays from 9 am to 12.30 pm and 1.15 to 6 pm (Friday to 5 pm) and Saturday from 10 am to 12.30 pm and 1.15 to 4.30 pm. You'll be paid in koruna.

Black Market The koruna became fully convertible in 1996. There is no longer a black market; anyone who approaches you offering such a deal is a thief, and there are plenty of them loitering around Na příkopě and the arcades on Jindřišská near the corner with Wenceslas Square. Common tricks include shortchanging and the substitution of worthless old Czechoslovakian banknotes or those from other former eastern bloc countries.

Costs

Things are still fairly cheap in Prague for western visitors (though not for locals in the historical centre). The big exception is accommodation, where tourist prices are in line with Western Europe.

By staying at cheap hostels or camp sites, sticking to self-catering and stand-up cafeterias, and going easy on the beer, you might get away with US$15 per person a day in summer. If you stay in private accommodation or upmarket hostels away from the city centre, eat at cheap restaurants and use public transport, you can get by on US$25 to US$35. Sharing a double room with bath in a mid-range hotel or pension, and eating in good Czech or western restaurants, will cost US$40 to US$70. These costs don't include extras such as entertainment, souvenirs, postage and tours.

Eating and sleeping near the city centre will cost more, as will having a room to yourself. Rates may drop if you stay for more than one or two nights. Except for the Christmas/New Year and Easter periods, some places drop their prices outside the summer season. In nearby towns, such as those described in the Excursions chapter, prices are consistently lower.

Naturally, Bohemia's splendid beer will increase your costs: half a litre can range from as little as 5 Kč in local shops, or 9 Kč on draught in pubs, to 60 Kč or more in posh restaurants.

An annoying aspect of Czech 'free market economics' is the two-tier price system, in which foreigners pay up to double the local price for most hotel rooms, for international airline and bus tickets, and for museum and concert tickets. Most theatre tickets are snapped up by scalpers and travel agencies and resold to foreigners at several times the original price. Sometimes simply questioning the price difference results in an 'error correction'. With enough charm and enough Czech you can pay local prices by steering clear of 'tourist' rooms and by ordering from the Czech-language menu.

Discounts Many discounts – for transport, for tourist attractions, in hotels and in some restaurants – are available to full-time students and people aged under 26 or 60 and over, and sometimes to their spouses and children. Many bargains are not advertised; the best way to find them is to wave an identity card at every opportunity. See under Documents in this chapter about available cards and how to get them.

Tipping & Bargaining
If you were fairly served in a restaurant, round up the bill to the next 10 Kč (or the next 20 Kč if it's over about 100 Kč). The usual protocol is for them to show you the bill and for you, as you hand over the money, to say how much you're paying with the tip included.

Change is usually counted out starting with the big notes, on down to the littlest coins. In posher restaurants, if you say *děkuji* (thank you) during this process, your waiter may assume the rest is a tip.

There's little scope for bargaining Prague prices down, except possibly at the open-air markets (see the Shopping chapter).

Taxes
Value-added tax (VAT) is only 5% on food but up to 22% on hotel rooms, meals in restaurants and general luxury items. This tax is included in the price and is not added at the cash register, so you won't feel it directly.

POST & COMMUNICATIONS
The main post office at Jindřišská 14 (Map 6), just off Wenceslas Square, is open daily from 7 am to 8 pm for basic postage and parcel services. Most other services – and all services at the city's 115 other post offices – are available weekdays from 8 am to 6 or 7 pm and Saturday until noon.

At the time of research, the main post office was in the midst of renovations, with services scattered in temporary locations, as noted in the following sections. The main telephone bureau, including fax, telegram and telex services (all open 24 hours a day), was around the corner at Politických vězňů 4, though there are also public telephones in the main atrium of the post office. There was no visible information window.

Postal Rates
Rates are modest in the Czech Republic, and you should always use air mail. Mail to Europe – automatically air mail – is 8 Kč for a letter or 6 Kč for a postcard (1 Kč less to Slovakia). To anywhere else by air, a letter is 11 Kč and a postcard 7 Kč. Express service is 15 Kč extra, recorded delivery 15 Kč and registration 20 Kč. We've never seen any aerogrammes, although stamp counters will sell you an envelope and a few sheets of air-mail paper for a few koruna.

Parcels up to 2kg can go at small-packet rates; 2kg by surface/air is 235/250 Kč to Europe, or 250/560 Kč to anywhere else. Books and other printed matter go for reduced rates in bundles up to 5kg; if you're persistent you can send up to 15kg of them (ask for M-pytel service). Fast, secure Express Mail Service (EMS) is also available (such as 2kg to the UK for 710 Kč or to Australia for 1226 Kč).

Sending Mail

At the time of writing, stamps were sold at windows 3 to 8 (with prettier special issues at windows 12 and 13), as well as by street vendors and PNS newsagents. Letters go in the orange boxes outside post offices and around the city.

Parcels could be sent from window 17 on the ground floor, though small-packet services and EMS close at noon on Saturday, and all day Sunday. Always get a receipt (*paragon*) when sending anything larger than a letter by air mail or a more expensive service: postal workers have been known to charge for such services and then send the item by surface mail.

See the earlier Customs section if you want to post out antiques (though it's best to carry anything of value out of the country yourself, as some postal workers do have sticky fingers). In principle, anything else can be posted internationally from any major post office. In practice, many postal employees still suffer from Communist-era anxieties about 'regulations', and may send you off to the customs post office if you want to send anything over 2kg, no matter what it is.

Parcels containing glass and crystal will not be accepted by the US, Australian and New Zealand postal systems.

Receiving Mail

At the time of writing, poste restante (*uložené zásilky*) was to the right of the entrance and upstairs in room A214, open weekdays from 7 am to 8 pm and Saturday to 1 pm. Mail is held here for about one month. You must present your passport to claim mail, and you should remember to check under your first name too. Mail should be addressed to Poste Restante, Hlavní pošta, Jindřišská 14, 110 00 Praha 1, Czech Republic.

Holders of American Express cards or travellers cheques can have letters and faxes held for up to one month at the Prague office (see the boxed text under Money, earlier in this chapter, for the co-ordinates). The British and Canadian embassies will hold letters for their citizens for a few months. None of these offices will accept registered letters or parcels.

Telephone

All calls in and from the Czech Republic are charged according to the number of *impulsů* (impulses or units), the size of which depends on the receipient of the call, the time of day its made and how you make the call.

Old blue coin telephones, which accept 2, 5, 10 and 20 Kč coins, are adequate for local calls, but you need a bag of coins and a lot of patience to make long-distance or international calls from them. Certain counter-top coin telephones, for example in some bars and restaurants, have an extra red button that you must push after your party answers, causing the money to drop and you to be connected; if you don't, your party will hear nothing.

More convenient, especially if you want to make international calls, are newer blue or grey public telephones that accept telecards. They're increasingly common, and cards are sold in post and telephone offices, newsagents, tobacconists, department stores, some hotels and travel agencies, and at PIS branches. Cards storing 50 (150 Kč), 80 (240 Kč), 100 (300 Kč), 120 (360 Kč) and 150 units (450 Kč) are available.

Changing Numbers

Since 1993, the Prague telephone system has been undergoing a complete overhaul. New local numbers are being put into effect across the board, a process that will continue for some time. Although efforts have been made to use new numbers in this book, you may well find that some numbers don't work. If so, talk to PIS, check the latest telephone book, or ring directory assistance on ☎ 120 (for numbers in Prague) or ☎ 121 (for numbers elsewhere in the Czech Republic).

Telephone-Speak

The various signal-tones in Prague's telephones don't always sound like the ones back home. Here are the useful ones to know:

- Ready to dial: long tone, very short pause (– – –)
- Ringing: short tone, long pause (-   -   -)
- Engaged (Busy): equal tone/pause, shorter than in the UK (- - -)
- Trying to connect: very short pips (······)

The simplest and cheapest option is to pay a deposit at the telephone bureau and make your call in a soundproof booth, where a little meter ticks off your money. Charges are about 25% less than in coin or cardphones. The main drawback is the foul attitude of many telephone bureau staff.

Calls from hotel or restaurant telephones tend to cost at least twice as much as those from a public telephone. Calls to mobile telephones are more expensive than those to stationary ones.

Local Calls A call within Prague costs 3 Kč per three-minute impuls at a coin or card telephone, or 2.40 Kč from the telephone bureau. During off-peak periods, from 7 pm to 7 am on weekdays and all day on weekends and holidays, an impuls lasts six minutes.

For information about Prague numbers (including new telephone numbers) dial ☎ 120.

Regional & Long-Distance Calls To call another city in the Czech Republic, dial 0, plus the telephone code, plus the number. An intercity call costs 3 Kč per 20 to 30-second impuls (40 to 60 seconds during off-peak periods) at a coin or card telephone, or 2.40 Kč from the telephone bureau.

The telephone bureau has directories for Prague and other major cities. For information about non-Prague numbers, dial ☎ 121. For help with any domestic call, dial ☎ 0 102.

International Calls To call out of the Czech Republic, dial 00 followed by the country code for your target country, the area code for your target city (you'll probably have to drop the first zero) and then the number. Dialling is done for you at the telephone bureau.

International direct dialling (IDD) calls are charged by the second or thereabouts, so there's no minimum call duration. At the time of writing, approximate sample IDD rates for a one-minute call from the telephone bureau, during off-peak/peak times, were 17/23 Kč to the UK, 28/42 Kč to the USA and 38/63 Kč to Australia. Calls from coin or card phones are charged at 3 Kč/impuls, that is, 25% more than at the bureau. Operator assistance adds about 50 Kč a minute. Check the rates before placing your call, and ask for a receipt.

For international directory enquiries, which has some multilingual operators, dial ☎ 0 149. For information on international rates and services, dial ☎ 0 139. For operator assistance with most international calls, call ☎ 0 132.

Reverse-Charges Calls You can place an international collect (reverse-charges) call from the telephone bureau without putting down any cash, or from a public telephone for the price of a local call. Tell the operator *účet volaného*.

However, since Czech Telecom prices are higher than in Western Europe, it may be cheaper to use so-called 'country-direct'

FACTS FOR THE VISITOR

Country-Direct Numbers

Many countries have arrangements for direct connections to an operator in that country for collect, account or credit-card calls. To do this in Prague, dial ☎ 00 420 plus:

Australia/Optus:	06110
Australia/Telstra:	06101
Canada:	00151
France:	03301
Ireland:	35301
Netherlands:	03101
Singapore:	06501
UK/BT:	04401
UK/Mercury:	04450
USA/AT&T:	00101
USA/MCI:	00112
USA/Sprint:	87187

numbers for collect, account or credit-card calls; see the boxed text above.

Calls to Prague To call Prague from another country, dial that country's international access code, plus 420 (Czech Republic), plus 2 (Prague) and then the number.

Fax & Telegram

Faxes and telegrams can be sent and received 24 hours a day at the telephone bureau. Fax rates are the same as telephone rates, with an A4-sized page taking about 1½ minutes. Many hotels and agencies have fax services too, but rates are around twice the post office rate. American Express members can receive (but not send) faxes at the Wenceslas Square office (for address details see the boxed text 'Banks & Exchange Offices' in the Money section earlier in this chapter), for 5 Kč per page.

Telegrams cost 21 Kč per word to the UK and other EU countries, and 31 Kč to the USA and Australia, though delivery can sometimes take two or three days.

Email & Internet Access

Many cybercafés in Prague now offer public access to computers with Internet connections. Following is a selection of those near the centre, along with their co-ordinates, hours and on-line rates. Most have subscription rates that are lower, and some have email boxes for rent (though a Web-based email account like Hotmail or Yahoo! Mail is more versatile and can be accessed anywhere).

Cybeteria (Map 6; ☎ 24 23 50 20, fax 26 09 62, email info@cream.cybeteria.cz), Štěpánská 18; weekdays 10 am to 8 pm, Saturday noon to 6 pm; 50 Kč per half-hour
Internet Café (Map 6; ☎ 21 08 52 84, fax 21 08 52 48, email internetcafe@highland.cz), Palác Metro arcade, Národní 25; weekdays 9 am to 9 pm, weekends 3 to 10 pm; 2 Kč per minute
Internet Lounge (email kavarna@oasanet.cz), Kavárna, Obecní dům (Map 7) daily 8 am to 11 pm; 40 Kč for the first 10 minutes, then 3 Kč per minute
Pl@neta (Map 8; ☎/fax 67 31 11 82, email info@planeta.cz), Vinohradská 102, Prague 3; daily 8 am to 10 pm; 1.50 Kč per minute
Terminal Bar (Map 7; ☎ 21 87 16 66, fax 231 17 74, email terminal@terminal.cz), Soukenická 6; weekdays 9 am to 2 am, weekends 10 am to 2 am; 25 Kč per quarter-hour

If you have your own laptop and modem, and an account with a server with PoPs (local access points) in the Czech Republic, you might be able to log on from your hotel room for the cost of a local or long-distance call. Most newer, upper-end hotels will have Internet facilities for business customers, and rooms may have telephone jacks, usually USA standard (RJ-11). Adapters for older Czech jacks can be found in electronic supply shops.

Be sure the hotel doesn't have a digital telephone exchange, which can blow your modem. You can always plug safely into an analogue data line such as the hotel's fax line. Get on and off quickly; calls from hotels are expensive.

Smaller hotels may know nothing about the Internet and may simply refuse the

Czech Internet Jargon

If you surf the Web at a Prague cybercafé you may have to do it in Czech. Following is a bit of useful Czech cyber-speak:

File	Soubor
New	Nový
Open	Otevřít
Close	Zavřít
Save	Uložit
Save As ...	Uložit jako...
Print	Tisk
Exit	Konec
Edit	Upravit
Cut	Vyjmout
Copy	Kopírovat
Paste	Vložit
Help	Nápověda
Bookmark	Záložka, Odkaz
Search	Hledat

use of their lines. Even if they agree, many hotel-room telephones are hard-wired into the wall, in which case you'd need a little tool kit and, preferably, a line tester, available from Web-based dealers such as Magellan's (www.magellans.com) and Konexx (www.konexx.com).

A problem with ordinary lines in the Czech Republic is the faint 7MHz 'beeps' that mark units of calling time, which can interfere with modems bought outside the country. The solution is an in-line filter, available from many computer shops, or the Web-based shops mentioned above. Cybercafé data lines don't have this problem.

Even if everything else works, however, Prague's chaotic telephone system and the ongoing conversion to a digital system (see the boxed text under Telephone in this section) may thwart you. For the moment, a cybercafé looks like the best bet.

INTERNET RESOURCES
Three Web sites with useful, wide-ranging Prague information are:

Anděl 3W (www.andel3w.dk/prague/)
Martin Gregor's Web site (members.aol.com /mpgregor/private/prague.htm)
Sunsite (sunsite.mff.cuni.cz/prague/)

The Czech Ministry of Foreign Affairs has an English-language site (www.czech.cz) packed with Czech Republic information and lots of links. Czech Happenings, a Czech News Agency (ČTK) Web site with current reports, is at www.ctknews.com.

The Lonely Planet Web site has up-to-the-minute travel information, as well as a Czech Republic profile (www.lonelyplanet .com).

Note that Web site addresses, though correct at press time, are particularly prone to change.

BOOKS
For information on Prague bookshops, see the Shopping chapter.

Lonely Planet
If you're doing any further travelling in the region, pick up Lonely Planet's *Czech & Slovak Republics* or the wider-ranging *Central Europe* or *Eastern Europe* guidebooks. Lonely Planet's *Central Europe* and *Eastern Europe* phrasebooks have extensive sections on the Czech language.

Guidebooks
Nothing to Do in Prague is a thorough, and thoroughly enjoyable, self-published guide to over 100 bars, clubs and cafés in Prague – locations, prices, clientele, plus deadpan reviews and shaggy-dog anecdotes – by two expats, Conor Crickmore and Nigel Robinson. It's sold, for about 150 to 200 Kč, at bigger hostels and most bookshops in the centre.

History
The Oxford historian Timothy Garton Ash's *We the People: the Revolutions of 1989* features gripping I-was-there accounts of the revolutions that swept away the region's old guard in 1989. William Shawcross's *Dubček & Czechoslovakia* is a

biography of the late leader of the Prague Spring, with a hasty post-1989 update. Another biography is Michael Simmons' *The Reluctant President: A Political Life of Václav Havel*.

Essays & Memoirs

The essays and memoirs of the dissident-turned-president Václav Havel offer a revealing 'inside' view. *Disturbing the Peace* is a collection of recent historical musings. *Letters to Olga* is a collection of letters to his wife from prison in the 1980s. *Living in Truth* is a series of absorbing political essays.

Patrick Leigh Fermor's *A Time of Gifts* is the luminous first instalment of his trek through Europe, including Czechoslovakia, in the early 1930s.

Fiction

Bruce Chatwin's *Utz* is a quiet, absorbing novella about a porcelain collector in Prague's old Jewish quarter. For information on fiction by Czech authors, refer to Literature in the Arts section of the Facts about Prague chapter.

NEWSPAPERS & MAGAZINES

Prague has no English-language daily newspaper, but *The Prague Post*, which is weekly, is very good value for visitors at 45 Kč. Along with local news and features, it has a summertime 'facts for the visitor' pull-out, travel tips, concert and restaurant reviews, and day-by-day arts and entertainment listings. It also has an on-line edition (www.praguepost.cz).

The New Presence (subtitled The Prague Journal of Central European Affairs) is a translation of the Czech monthly *Nová Přítomnost*, with features and essays on current affairs, politics and business. For business-oriented newspapers and magazines, see Doing Business, later in this chapter.

Major European (including British and French) and American newspapers and magazines are on sale at kiosks in tourist zones and at the main train station. Many of these are also stocked at the newspaper reading room of the City Library (see Libraries, later in this chapter).

RADIO & TV
Radio

English-language news and cultural programming of the BBC World Service is broadcast locally at 101.1MHz FM, on the hour, weekdays from 1 to 5 and 9 to 11 am, 5 and 10 pm, and midnight; and weekends from 1 to 6 am, 10 am to 5 pm, 7 and 10 pm, and midnight.

The former Czechoslovakia was the second European nation after Britain to start its own radio station: Czech Radio (Český rozhlas) has been broadcasting since May 1923. Czech Radio 2, also called Prague Radio (92.6MHz and 102.7MHz FM), has a daily English-language news programme called 'Radio Prague Calling' at 5.30 pm (Radio Prague also puts daily transcripts of its news bulletins on the Web at www.radio.cz).

Radio 1 (91.9MHz FM) features a good news programme, 'Central Europe Today', weekdays from roughly 7 to 7.15 am, and the daily 'Demon Sounds' music programme from 7 to 8 pm, along with other alternative music throughout the day. The FM dial is in fact full of Czech DJs playing western pop and rock. For current listings, see the 'On Radio' section in *The Prague Post*.

The former Czechoslovak National Assembly building beside the National Museum is now the world headquarters for Radio Free Europe, which broadcasts its propaganda from a transmitter in the suburbs.

TV

The only regular English-language programming on the two state-run TV channels is 'Euronews' on ČT 2, with one-hour segments on weekdays at 8 am and half-hour slots on weekends at 7 am. Of the two private channels, TV Nova and Prima TV, Nova shows lots of old American flicks and dubbed sitcoms. Anyone with a satellite dish can choose from a big menu of European stations.

PHOTOGRAPHY & VIDEO

Forty-five years of secret police lurking behind every shrub have made some people uneasy about being photographed, so ask first. 'May I take your photograph?' is *Mohu si vás vyfotit?*

Film & Equipment

The Old Town and Malá Strana have numerous small shops with western print film and processing services. Some Kodak franchises also have Ektachrome (but not Kodachrome) slide film. Some shops stock 8mm video cassettes (but be careful: the Czech Republic itself uses the French PAL system, which is incompatible with SECAM and NTSC systems; know what your home system uses).

Reliable shops can be found in the Kotva (Old Town) and Krone (Nové Město) department stores. There are large labs at Národní 39 and Celetná 3 (both Map 6). Fototechnika, Vodičkova 36, and the ČTK photo-developing counter in the passage at Opletalova 6-7 (both Map 6) have moderately priced professional slide and print films.

Avoid Czech colour and slide film, as you may not be able to process it outside the country. You can get prints developed in Prague, but some photo shops deal with substandard labs and you may end up with damaged goods. We have found ČTK to be trustworthy.

For passport/visa photos, try Fotolab at Wenceslas Square 50, or Exkod at Tržiště 3, Malá Strana. A Polaroid mini-studio in the Můstek metro station lobby, below Wenceslas Square, does Polaroid passport photos (enter via Krone department store).

For camera repairs, try Fototechnika, or Foto Jan Pazdera in the passage at Vodičkova 28 (Map 6). Video cameras can also be repaired at BS Foto, Betlémské náměstí (Map 6).

TIME

The Czech Republic is on Central European Time, ie GMT/UTC plus one hour. Clocks are reset to daylight-saving time in the summer, that is, forward one hour on the last weekend in March and back one hour on the last weekend in October.

Czechs tend to use the 24 hour clock and there's no equivalent of am and pm, though they can commonly add *ráno* (morning),

---

Film-Damaging Airport X-Rays

If you carry unprocessed film in your checked-in baggage, even in a lead-lined 'filmsafe' pouch, you're inviting trouble. Several international airports now use 'smart' CTX 5000 scanners for checked-in baggage. These scan first with a mild beam, then zero in ferociously on anything suspicious. A lead pouch would not only be ineffective but would invite further scans, and film inside is virtually certain to be ruined. Even tests by the manufacturer have confirmed this.

For obvious reasons there's no list of airports using the scanner, though they allegedly include some in the USA, the UK, France, the Netherlands, Belgium, Israel, South Africa and several Asian countries.

On the other hand, scanners for hand luggage at most major airports are relatively harmless, at least for slow and medium-speed films. There are no plans yet to use the CTX 5000 for hand luggage. The moral of the tale is obvious: always carry unprocessed film in your hand luggage, and if possible get officials to hand-inspect it. They may refuse, though having the film in clear plastic bags (and preferably clear canisters) can help to persuade them.

dopoledne (before noon), *odpoledne* (afternoon) or *večer* (evening).

ELECTRICITY

Electricity is 220V, 50Hz AC, and quite reliable in Prague. Nearly all the outlets have the two small round holes common throughout continental Europe; some also have a protruding earth (ground) pin. If you have a different plug or want to use the earth pin, bring an adaptor, as they are difficult to find in the Czech Republic. North American appliances will also need a transformer if they don't have built-in voltage adjustment.

WEIGHTS & MEASURES

The metric system is in use. A comma is used instead of a decimal point, and full stops are used at thousands, millions etc. A dash is used after prices rounded to the nearest koruna. Thus, for example, 3000 koruna would be written 3.000,–.

LAUNDRY

Prague's original self-service laundry (*samoobslužná prádelna*) is Laundry Kings (☎ 312 37 43), open daily from 8 am to 10 pm. A 6kg load takes about two hours and costs around 125 Kč to wash and dry. There's also a good bulletin board, snacks and newspapers, and a drop-off service. From metro station Hradčanská, take the 'Praha Dejvice' exit, turn left into Dejvická and it's at No 16 (Map 3).

Laundryland (Map 10; ☎ 25 11 24, delivery service ☎ 0603 41 10 05), Londýnská 71, is open daily from 8 am to 10 pm, and also has branches at Táboritská 3, Prague 3 (Map 8; to 8 pm) and in the Pavilon shopping centre, Vinohradská 50 (Map 6).

Another self-service laundrette is Astera (☎ 24 23 73 35), Jindřišská 5 (Map 6). The self and full-service Prague Laundromat (☎ 25 55 41), Korunní 14, Prague 2 (Map 10) is open daily from 8 am to 8 pm and has a children's play area. The 5 à Sec Laundrette is at Dlouhá 20 (Map 7).

All of these laundries also have dry-cleaning services.

Locally run laundries are hard to find, and a load can take up to a week; find them in the Yellow Pages under *prádelny* (laundries). Hotels sometimes offer pricey services.

If you'd rather do yours in the hotel sink, bring along a universal sink plug and a bit of line. Detergent is easy to find in the shops.

TOILETS

Public toilets are free in state-run museums, galleries and concert halls. Most cafés and restaurants don't seem to mind non-guests using theirs – ask for *záchod*, *vé cé* (WC) or *toalet* – but some in tourist areas charge 2 or 3 Kč.

Elsewhere, such as in train, bus and metro stations, toilets are staffed by mostly burly attendants who ask for 2 Kč for use of the toilet (their only pay) and may sell a few sheets of toilet paper (*toaletní papír*) if you need it. Most places are fairly clean. Men's are marked *muži* or *páni*, women's *ženy* or *dámy*.

HEALTH

No vaccinations are required for the Czech Republic. Public hygiene in Prague, while not at Western European levels, is quite good. For people with respiratory problems, Prague can be an unpleasant place to be in mid-winter, when vehicle emissions turn the air dangerously foul during periodic weather inversions.

Precautions

Prague's tap water is drinkable, though it's an unpleasant chlorinated brew. There have been isolated instances of contamination in outer districts in the past, though this is unlikely to affect most visitors. Bottled water is available almost everywhere, as many Czechs prefer it to tap water.

Bottled milk is pasteurised, and yoghurt is always hygienic. Note that some perishable supermarket food items bear a date of manufacture (*datum výroby*) as well as a firm 'consume-within' (*spotřebujte do ...*) period, while others (such as long-life milk) have a minimum-shelf-life (*minimální třanlivost*) date (after which freshness is not guaranteed).

Most restaurants and takeaway food outlets are as hygienic as anywhere in Europe, though you're safest with hot, freshly made items.

Medical Services

Emergency treatment and non-hospital first aid are free for all visitors to the Czech Republic. EU citizens may get cheap or free treatment under reciprocal health-care treaties (check before you leave home). Others must pay for treatment, normally in koruna, and at least some must be paid up front. Everyone must pay for prescribed medications.

A travel insurance policy that covers medical treatment abroad is a good idea; those offered by various youth-travel agencies are good value.

The best hospital in Prague, equipped and staffed to western standards, is Na Homolce, Roentgenova 2, Motol, Prague 5 (Map 1); take bus No 167 from Anděl metro station. The foreigners' polyclinic and emergency entrance are on the north side, 5th level. The telephone number from 7.30 am to 4 pm daily is ☎ 52 92 21 46; after hours, call ☎ 52 92 25 22 or ☎ 52 92 11 11. A separate children's clinic (☎ 52 92 20 43, after hours ☎ 95 92 20 25) is on the 1st floor.

For eye treatment and emergencies, the 24 hour Second Eye Clinic (*oční klinika*) is in pavilion B of Všeobecná fakultní nemocnice (Hospital), U nemocnice 2, Nové Město (Map 9).

Several pricey but professional private clinics have English-speaking doctors, some of them western-trained, and a range of both in and out-patient services. One is the Canadian Medical Centre (Map 1; ☎ 316 55 19, weekdays from 8 am to 6 pm; ☎ 0601-21 23 20 at other times), Veleslavínská 30/1; take tram No 20 or 26 from Dejvice metro station. The American

Medical Center (Map 4; ☎ 87 79 73, 24-hours ☎ 80 77 56/58), Jankovského 48, Prague 7, is open weekdays from 8.30 am to 6 pm, and at any time for an emergency; take tram No 5 or 17 from Nádraží Holešovice metro station.

The drop-in Fakultní poliklinika (Map 9; ☎ 24 90 41 11, ext 311), Karlovo náměstí 32, is geared for foreigners and has English-speaking staff and an ambulance service. It's open weekdays from 7.30 am to 3 pm (Friday to 2 pm).

District clinics have after-hours emergency services (from 7 pm to 7 am, and all weekend). The city's biggest polyclinic (Map 1; ☎ 692 89 70) is at Antala Staška 80 in Prague 4, south-west of Budějovická metro station. The Prague 1 clinic (Map 6; ☎ 24 94 91 81) is at Palackého 5, off Jungmannova in southern Nové Město.

Dental Services

There are dental clinics at Na Homolce Hospital, the Fakultní poliklinika and the Prague 4 polyclinic. For after-hours emergencies in Prague 1 go to the district clinic at Palackého 5. See under Medical Services earlier for the locations of all of these.

Medicines & Pharmacies

Pharmacies (*lekárna*) are plentiful, and most city districts have one that stays open 24 hours a day. In Prague 1 it's at the district clinic at Palackého 5 (see Medical Services). Prague 2's is Lékárna U sv Ludmily (Map 10; ☎ 25 81 89 or 24 23 72 07), Belgická 37. But over-the-counter and prescription medicines are not always available, so it's wise to bring what you need.

Ticks

Ticks (*klíště*) are a common nuisance in forests, and even in suburban gardens, from May to September. About 5% of them carry encephalitis, a cerebral inflammation that can cause death, and about 25% carry lyme disease, a potentially serious bacterial infection that affects the nervous system, joints and skin.

The Křivoklátsko region, south-west of Prague (see the Excursions chapter), has one of the country's highest rates of tick-borne encephalitis (TBE). In the Czech Republic and in other European countries you can get a tick-borne-encephalitis vaccine as a series of two or three injections. The injections give good protection against TBE and can be administered quickly: it takes about 10 days to get the three shots. The vaccination is not expensive (400 Kč per injection in the Czech Republic) and there are no side effects. TBE vaccinations are not available in Australia or the USA.

With lyme disease, red blotches, sometimes several centimetres or more across, sometimes pale in the centre, may appear – though a tick bite can also cause blotches without lyme disease, and vice versa – accompanied by tiredness, weakness and/or flu-like symptoms. There's no widely available vaccine, but if it's detected early it can be treated with antibiotics, so immediate medical attention is obviously in order. Lyme disease can also be transmitted by mosquitoes and gadflies.

Avoid ticks by wearing socks and long trousers when walking in woods and tall grass. If a tick buries itself in your skin, *don't* pick it off, but coax it out by covering it in vaseline or oil.

HIV & AIDS

Infection with HIV, the Human Immuno-deficiency Virus, may develop into the usually fatal AIDS, Acquired Immune Deficiency Syndrome. Any exposure to blood, blood products or bodily fluids may put an individual at risk. The major route of HIV transmission is via unprotected sex; apart from abstinence, the most effective preventative is always to practise safe sex using condoms. HIV can also be spread by dirty needles, so acupuncture, tattooing and body piercing are potentially as dangerous as intravenous drug use if the equipment is not clean.

In 1997, 368 people in the Czech Republic were registered as HIV positive, though the true number may be 10 times higher. Neither HIV testing nor any other medical checks are required for entry visas, or work or residency permits.

It's impossible to detect the HIV-positive status of an otherwise healthy-looking person without a blood test. Organisations in Prague offering confidential HIV testing include the following:

The National AIDS Prevention Centre (Národní linka prevence AIDS; Map 9; toll-free ☎ 0801 444 44), KHS, Dittrichova 17, Nové Město, Prague 2; weekdays from 8 am to noon for blood samples, 1 to 6 pm for consultations

AIDS Centrum (☎ 66 08 26 28) at Bulovka hospital (Map 1; fakultní nemocnice s poliklinikou), Budínova 2, Prague 8; take tram No 14 or 24 from Wenceslas Square

Drug Problems

Drop In (Map 6; ☎ 26 57 30), Karoliny Světlé 18 (enter from ulice Boršov), Staré Město, is an easygoing and informal drug-counselling centre, open weekdays from 9 am to 3.30 pm (Friday to 4 pm).

Spas

The Czech Republic has dozens of mineral-spring spas where Czechs and foreigners come for a cure or a rest. A spa visit – typically about three weeks – must be booked at least two months in advance through Balnea (Map 6; ☎ 21 10 53 06, fax 24 21 42 11), Národní 28, 110 01 Prague 1, or a Čedok office abroad. Room, board and treatment start at about US$60 per person per day in summer, less in winter.

The closest spa town to Prague is Poděbrady, convenient but not very exciting. The most famous, attractive and touristy ones are at Karlovy Vary and Mariánské Lázně in western Bohemia, within reach of Prague as excursions.

WOMEN TRAVELLERS

To many westerners the Czech Republic seems to be picking up, sexually speaking, where it left off in 1948. Newsstands groan under porno rubbish. The expatriate press teems with arguments about whether this is sexism or freedom of expression, while on the whole Czechs seem to be less fussed about the matter than foreigners are.

The darker side is that sexual violence has been on the rise since 1989. Although the number of attacks is still low in comparison with the west, and although many expat women go out alone at night, it's probably not a good idea, even in Old Town Square and Wenceslas Square.

Women (especially solo) may find the atmosphere in most non-touristy pubs a bit raw, as they tend to be male territory. *Kavárny* (coffee shops) often dispense beer and wine too, and are more congenial, as are *vinárny* (wine bars).

Among Prague's few refuge or crisis centres for women is the White House of Safety (Bílí dům bezpečí; ☎ 43 88 33), though the phone line is open only on Tuesday from 5 to 7 pm.

GAY & LESBIAN TRAVELLERS

Homosexuality is legal in the Czech Republic (the age of consent is 15), but the marriage or de facto status of gay and lesbian couples is not legally recognised. Czechs are not accustomed to seeing homosexuals show affection for each other in public, though they are unlikely to object overtly.

There are several monthly magazines aimed at homosexuals, though all are in Czech: *SOHO Revue*, gay-oriented *Prince* and lesbian-oriented *Promluv* and *Alia*. *Amigo*, sold in gay and lesbian establishments and at some newsstands, is a kind of gay/lesbian tourist guide to Prague; it also has a Web site (www.amigo.cz) that has an English-language guide to the Czech and Slovak Republics.

SOHO, the Union of Homosexual Organisations (☎ 24 22 38 11, email soho@bbs .infima.cz, Web site jidas.pm.cesnet.cz /~bobrik/soho), offers information on events, venues and resources and runs a gay/lesbian crisis line on ☎ 0602-33 80 92. The local gay press lists other resources, though many are Czech-language discussion groups.

Christian gay men and women can contact one of the volunteers at ☎ 25 46 50 on Wednesday from 9 am to 7 pm for information on upcoming gatherings. Two groups, the Lesbian Christian Association and Ecumenical Gays, meet on the first Sunday of each month at 2 pm, at Logos (☎ 24 22 03 27 on Wednesday from 10 am to 10 pm only), U školské zahrady 1, Prague 8 (from Palmovka metro station take tram No 12, 14 or 24).

A good Web site listing gay/lesbian-friendly cafés, bars, accommodation and resources in Prague is maintained by Macromedia Solutions (www.macromedia-solutionsltd.com/glprague.html).

DISABLED TRAVELLERS

Increasing, but still limited, attention is being paid to facilities for the disabled in Prague. Wheelchair ramps are becoming more common, especially at major street intersections and in upper-end hotels (in the text we identify hotels with facilities for the disabled). For the blind or poorly sighted, most pedestrian-crossing lights in central Prague emit a ticking sound when the light is green. McDonald's and KFC entrances and toilets are wheelchair-friendly.

The Stavovské Theatre is equipped for the hearing-impaired, and this and several other theatres are wheelchair-accessible. The monthly what's-on booklet *Přehled* (see Tourist Offices earlier in this chapter) indicates venues with wheelchair access.

Few buses and no trams have wheelchair access, but special wheelchair-accessible buses operate on weekdays on certain routes, including between Florenc bus station and náměstí Republiky, and between Holešovice train station and náměstí Republiky (contact one of the four DP information centres listed in the Getting Around chapter for more information).

The main train station (hlavní nádraží), Holešovice train station and a handful of metro stations (Hlavní Nádraží, Hůrka, Luka, Lužiny, Nádraží Holešovice, Stodůlky and Zličín) have self-operating lifts.

Other metro stations (Chodov, Dejvická, Florenc C line, Háje, IP Pavlova, Opatov, Pankrác, Roztyly and Skalka) have modified lifts that can be used with the help of station staff. Czech Railways (ČD) claims that every large station in the country has wheelchair ramps and lifts, but in fact the service is poor.

When flying, disabled people should inform the airline of their needs when booking, and again when reconfirming, and again when checking in. Most international airports (including Prague's) have ramps, lifts, accessible toilets and telephones. Aircraft toilets, on the other hand, present problems for wheelchair travellers, who should discuss this early on with the airline and/or their doctor.

Organisations

The Prague Wheelchair Users Organisation (Pražská organizace vozíčkářů; Map 7; ☎ 232 58 03 or 24 81 62 31, email pov@ server1gts.cz), Benediktská 6, Josefov, has information about travelling in Prague and the Czech Republic. They can arrange transport at about half the cost of a taxi, as well as guides.

Czech Blind United (Sjednocená unie nevidomých a slabozrakých v ČR; Map 6; ☎ 24 81 83 98/73 93, email sons_zahr@ braillnet.cz), Karlínské náměstí 12, Karlín, Prague 8, has information for the blind, but no services.

Two Prague travel agencies advertising themselves as offering tours or support for disabled travellers are Fertour (☎/fax 24 31 60 94 or 53 05 95, email fertour@m.box .vol.cz), Mostecká 3, 118 00 Prague 1, and Best Tour (☎ 87 89 47, fax 87 08 04), U Uranie 17, 170 00 Prague 7. Also see the following section on Senior Travellers.

SENIOR TRAVELLERS

While senior residents of Prague get many concessions, such as on museum admission and public transport, there are no formal discounts for senior travellers here. But a senior card (see Documents, earlier in this chapter) will get you sizeable knockdowns

on international travel, similar to those for under-26s, as noted throughout the Getting There & Away chapter.

A Prague travel agency advertising itself as a specialist in tours for senior travellers, including foreign visitors, is CK Srdce Evropy or Heart of Europe (☎ 24 16 24 86, fax 24 16 24 82), V jámě 1, Prague 1.

Travellers aged over 50 can check out tours and bargain fares offered by senior specialists SAGA Holidays (toll-free ☎ 800-343 0273 in the USA and ☎ 0800 300 500 in the UK; Web site www .saga.co.uk/) and Mundi Color Holidays (☎ 0171-828 6021, fax 834 5752; from 22 April 2000 ☎ 020-7828 6021, fax 7834 5752) in the UK.

PRAGUE FOR CHILDREN

Czechs are generally family oriented and there are plenty of activities for children around the city.

Museums of possible interest to children include the Toy Museum (p86) – though it's frustratingly hands-off; the National Technology Museum (p119), especially the vast hall full of trains, cars and aeroplanes; the Museum of Military History (p86); and the Museum of Aircraft & Space Exploration (p124).

For outdoor activity, try the Zoo (p120) or Petřín Hill (p90), a large park where parents and kids alike can take a break from sightseeing. In the park itself you can enjoy the funicular railway, the mirror maze, Petřín Tower (with terrific views of Prague if the weather is clear), the Štefánik Planetarium and a playground. For the best views of all, go to the TV Tower (p121).

In summer there are boats and paddleboats for hire on the river. Take one to the aptly named Children's Island (Dětský ostrov), which has a playground (p124). Older children might enjoy horse riding, tennis or bowling (p127). In winter there are plenty of ice rinks (p128).

March is the time of the spring fair, when the Fairgrounds in Bubeneč (p118) turn into a large entertainment park full of rides, shooting galleries and candy floss. If there's a circus in town it will most likely be on Letná Plain, opposite the AC Sparta Praha Stadium in Bubeneč.

On weekends and holidays between April and October, vintage tram cars trundle along a special sightseeing route, No 91, around the historical centre; see the Tram & Bus section in the Getting Around chapter. And don't miss the changing of the guard at Prague Castle (p80) – but get in position before the crowds do, or the kids won't see a thing.

Several theatres cater for children, but nearly everything is in Czech. Two good ones are the Divadlo Minor or Minor Children's Theatre (Map 7; ☎ 24 22 96 75), Senovážné náměstí 28; and the Divadlo Spejbla a Hurvínka (a marionette theatre named after Spejbl and Hurvínek, Josef Skupa's famous puppet duo of the early 20th century; Map 3; ☎ 31 21 24 13), Dejvická 38, Prague 6. The Říše loutek or Puppet Kingdom, the National Marionette Theatre (Map 7; ☎ 232 34 29), Žatecká 1, is aimed at adults too, with its long-running production of the famous Mozart's opera *Don Giovanni*. Programmes for these and many other theatres are provided in PIS's *Přehled* and in other cultural monthlies.

Czech restaurants do not specifically cater for children in the western sense, like McDonald's with its playgrounds etc. Some restaurants have a children's menu (*dětský jídelníček*), but even if they don't, they can usually provide smaller portions for a lower price.

Daycare

Baby Studio Dáda (Map 7; ☎ 21 10 72 78, ☎/fax 21 10 71 15), Hybernská 8, is a good school and care centre for children, to which you can bring your two to 12-year-old, even for just a few days. It's open weekdays from 8 am to 6 pm (office 9 am to noon and 1 to 5 pm), and fees at the time of writing were 53 Kč per hour for the nursery (games, exercises, free play) or 79 Kč per hour for classes (dance basics, art, music etc).

Two reliable babysitting agencies are Affordable Luxuries (☎ 21 66 13 19), Štepanská 15, Prague 2, and Babysitting (☎ 301 17 64/65), Vondroušova 1194, Prague 6. Typical rates at the time of writing were 50 to 80 Kč per hour.

LIBRARIES

The newly renovated, barrier-free City Library (Městská knihovna; Map 7; ☎ 22 11 33 71) on Mariánské náměstí in Staré Město is bulging with foreign-language material, including periodicals (to the left), fiction (to the right) and newspapers (in the basement). It's open daily except Sunday: the main library from 10 am to 8 pm (except from 1 pm Monday and until 5 pm Saturday), and the basement reading room from 9 am to 8 pm (except to 5 pm Saturday). A library card costs 55/80 Kč for six/12 months, plus a refundable 1000 Kč deposit for non-residents.

See the later section on Cultural Centres for more reading rooms. Through a side entrance to the library on Valentinská is a branch of the Prague Municipal Gallery, with occasional exhibitions of contemporary Czech art.

UNIVERSITIES

The Czech Republic's oldest and most distinguished university is Charles University, founded in 1348 by Charles IV in the single building called the Karolinum, at Železná 9 (Map 7). Today it has 13 faculties and several research centres, in about 160 buildings scattered all over the city (plus two faculties in Hradec Králové and one in Plzeň).

To find out about courses, student cards or student hangouts, go to IPC, the university's Information & Advisory Centre (Informačně-poradenské centrum; Map 6; ☎ 96 22 80 36) at Školská 13a. It's open weekdays from 10 am to noon and 1 pm to 6 pm (to 4 pm Tuesday and Friday).

For details of Czech-language courses at the university, see the Courses section in the Things to See & Do chapter.

CULTURAL CENTRES

If you're looking for foreign-language newspapers or information about other cultures, try these centres:

France
> Institut Français de Prague (Map 6; ☎ 24 21 66 30), Štěpánská 35, with a French media and book library; open Tuesday to Friday from 10 am to 6 pm and Saturday to 1 pm, and a pleasant café, open weekdays from 9 am to 6 pm

Germany
> Goethe Institut (Map 6; ☎ 24 91 57 25), Masarykovo nábřeží 32

Poland
> Polish Cultural Centre (Map 6; ☎ 24 21 47 08), Wenceslas Square 51

UK
> British Council (Map 6; ☎ 24 91 21 79), Národní 10 (enter on Voršilská), with British papers and magazines and satellite Sky TV news; the British embassy, Thunovská 14 in Malá Strana, also has a reading room

USA
> American Center for Culture and Commerce (USIS; Map 7; ☎ 24 23 10 85), Hybernská 7a, has American newspapers, magazines and reference books, plus a business reference service and occasional events

The City Library is also well stocked with foreign-language periodicals; see the earlier section on Libraries.

DANGERS & ANNOYANCES

Following are Prague's main emergency telephone numbers, though you cannot count on getting through to an English speaker:

Ambulance	☎ 155
Automobile Emergencies	☎ 123 or 154 (ÚAMK), ☎ 124 (ABA)
Fire	☎ 150
Municipal Police	☎ 156
National Police	☎ 158

For information on taxi rip-offs, see the Getting Around chapter. Double pricing in hotels is noted in the Places to Stay chapter, overcharging in restaurants in the Places to Eat chapter. Tourists are charged two or three times as much as Czechs in commissions at independent exchange offices, for admission into some museums and for some theatre tickets.

Theft

Tourism and heady commercialism have spawned an epidemic of petty (and not-so-petty) crime. Where tourists are concerned, this mainly means pickpockets. Naturally, the prime trouble spots are where tourists gather in crowds. These include Prague Castle (especially at the changing of the guard), Charles Bridge, Old Town Square (especially in the crowd watching the astronomical clock mark the hour), the entrance to the Old Jewish Cemetery, Wenceslas Square, Ruzyně airport, in the metro and on trams (especially getting on and off the crowded Nos 9 and 22). People who lean over to look at your menu may be more interested in your wallet.

There's no point in being paranoid, but it makes obvious sense to keep valuables well out of reach, such as inside your clothing. Be alert in crowds and on public transport.

Lost or Stolen Belongings

It's usually helpful to go to your embassy first. The staff ought to give you a letter to take to the police, preferably in Czech, asking for a police report, without which you cannot collect on insurance. Try to get the embassy to provide its own report in your language too.

The British embassy has this down to an art and will also help you get in touch with a relative or the bank to get more money. For British and unrepresented Commonwealth citizens, it may even arrange an emergency passport to get you home.

For a police report, go to the Prague 1 police station at Konviktská 14 (Map 6), unless the theft occurred in another district, in which case you must go to that district's main police station. Problems at the main train station should be reported to the police station on Šafaříková 12 (Map 10). Unless you speak Czech, forget about telephoning the police, as they rarely speak English.

If your passport has been stolen, apply for a replacement visa at the Foreigners' Police & Passport Office at Olšanská 2 in Žižkov (see Visa Extensions under Documents earlier in this chapter). On the subject of lost or stolen cards or travellers cheques, see Money earlier in this chapter.

For anything except travel documents, you might get lucky at the city's lost & found office (ztráty a nálezy; Map 6; ☎ 24 23 50 85) at Karoliny Světlé 5, east of the National Theatre. It's open weekdays from 8 am to noon and 12.30 to 5.30 pm (except Tuesday to 4 pm and Friday to 2 pm). There's also a 24 hour lost & found office (☎ 20 11 42 83) at the airport.

Racism

You may be surprised at the level of casual prejudice directed at Romanies (Gypsies), whom people are quick to blame for the city's problems. Dark-skinned visitors may encounter low-level discrimination. Overt hostility towards visitors is rare, though there have recently been some assaults by skinheads on dark-skinned people.

LEGAL MATTERS

It's an unwritten rule that you should carry your passport at all times. Even Czechs are required to carry identification. If you can't prove your identity to police, you can be detained for up to 48 hours.

Many older police officers retain a Communist-era mistrust of foreigners. Younger officers are easier to deal with, but almost nobody speaks enough English to be pleasant. See the preceding Dangers & Annoyances section about where to go for a police report. The Foreigners' Police & Passport Office (see Visa Extensions under Documents earlier in this chapter) is the place for visa-related problems.

Possession of any soft drug, including marijuana, is punishable by up to two years in prison.

If you fall foul of Czech law, your embassy may have a list of Czech lawyers who might help, though the help is unlikely to be free of charge.

In general your embassy is the best first stop in any emergency, but there are some things it cannot do for you. These include: getting local laws or regulations waived because you're a foreigner; investigating a crime; providing legal advice or representation in civil or criminal cases; getting you out of jail; and lending money or paying your bills (though the British embassy might pay emergency travel costs in certain special circumstances).

BUSINESS HOURS

Shops tend to open from 8.30 or 9 am to 5 or 6 pm on weekdays and to 11 am or 1 pm on Saturday, closing on Sunday. Department stores close at 8 pm on weekdays, an hour or two earlier on Saturday, and at 6 pm on Sunday. Touristy shops in central Prague are open later at night and on weekends.

Restaurant hours vary, but most places operate from at least 11 am to 11 pm daily (some close on Monday). You will find almost no places open during the Christmas holiday.

Major banks are open weekdays at least from 9 am to 5 pm. Many money-exchange offices carry on daily until 11 pm or later (see the earlier Money section).

Government office hours are weekdays from 8.30 am to 5 pm, though some tourist offices operate later and on weekends. The main post office at Jindřišská 14 is open from 7 am to 8 pm daily for some, but not all, services (see Post & Communications earlier in this chapter). Other post offices are open from about 8 am to 6 pm weekdays and until noon on Saturday.

Most museums and galleries are open daily year-round from 9 or 10 am to 5 or 6 pm, but many close on Monday and sometimes the first working day after a holiday. You can visit Prague's bigger churches during similar hours.

Castles, chateaux and other historical monuments outside the city are open in summer (daily except Monday and the first working day after a holiday) from 8 or 9 am to 5 or 6 pm, except for a lunch break. Most shut down from November to March, with some limited to weekends in October and April. But Karlštejn and Křivoklát castles are open seven days a week year-round (except Christmas Eve and New Year's day) from at least 9 am to 4 pm. If you plan to take a guided tour, remember that ticket offices close an hour or so before the official closing time, depending on the length of the tour.

PUBLIC HOLIDAYS & SPECIAL EVENTS
Public Holidays

On the following public holidays, banks, offices, department stores and some shops close. Restaurants, museums and tourist attractions tend to stay open.

1 January
New Year's Day (*Nový rok*)
March or April
Easter Monday (*Pondělí velikonoční*) – the country collapses in a mirthful rite of spring: Czech men of all ages swat their favourite women on the legs with willow switches, and the women respond with gifts of hand-painted eggs, after which everybody parties; the culmination of several days of serious spring-cleaning, cooking and visiting
1 May
Labour Day (*Svátek práce*) – once the communist 'holy' day, it's now just a chance for a picnic or a day in the country. To celebrate the arrival of spring, many couples lay flowers at the statue (Map 5) of the 19th century poet, Karel Hynek Mácha, author of *Máj* (May), a poem about unrequited love (President Havel has been known to pay homage here); also see the boxed text 'Majáles' on the next page
8 May
Liberation Day (*Den osvobození*) – anniversary of the liberation of Prague by its citizens in 1945; under communism this was celebrated on 9 May, the day the Red Army marched in
5 July
SS Cyril & Methodius Day (*Den Cyrila a Metoděje*) – recalls the Slavs' introduction to literacy and Christianity by the two missionary monks from Thessaloniki
6 July
Jan Hus Day (*Den Jana Husa*) – commemo-

rates the 1415 burning at the stake of the great Bohemian religious reformer; kicked off by low-key celebrations and bell-ringing at Prague's Bethlehem Chapel the evening before
28 October
Independence Day (*Den vzniku Československa*) – the anniversary of the founding of the Czechoslovak Republic in 1918, now celebrated as the day of independence from the Austro-Hungarian Empire
24 December
'Generous Day', Christmas Eve (*Štědrý den*) – the big day for evening family meals and gift-giving
25 December
Christmas Day (*Vánoce*) – the day for visiting friends and relatives, and a turkey and dumpling lunch
26 December
St Stephen's Day (*Štěpána*) – equivalent to Boxing Day

Special Days

The following are not public holidays but special days (*významné dny*) for remembrance or celebration:

6 January
Three Kings' Day (*Tři králové*) – formal end of the Christmas season, sometimes celebrated with carol singing, bell ringing and gifts to the poor
19 January
Anniversary of Jan Palach's Death – in memory of the Charles University student who in 1969 burned himself to death in protest against the Soviet occupation
7 March
Birthday of Tomáš Garrigue Masaryk – commemorates Czechoslovakia's father-figure and first president

Saints' Days

Practically every day of the year is the day of a particular saint, something Roman Catholics will be familiar with. To Czechs, a person's 'name day' (the day of the saint whose name that person bears) is very much like a birthday, and a small gift or gesture on that day never goes amiss.

Majáles

Until WWII, students regularly celebrated 1 May as Majáles, a spring festival dating back to at least the early 19th century. Banned by the Nazis and later under communism, it was revived during the 'Prague Spring' of the mid-1960s, only to disappear once more in 1969. Nobody got it together again until 1997.

Majáles 1998 coincided with a visit by Beat Generation writer Lawrence Ferlinghetti for the Prague Writers Festival, recalling the crowning of Allen Ginsburg as king of the 1965 Majáles. Ginsburg was allowed into the country on the strength of his anti-US government views, but he made his distaste for authoritarianism quite clear and was quickly thrown out. The secret service documents surrounding his expulsion were published in a booklet in 1998.

Today's Majáles starts with an early-afternoon parade – with bands, students in fancy dress, and a float with the king of Majáles – from náměstí Jana Palacha, via Kaprova to the Old Town Square and the Karolinum. From there everybody moves on to Střelecký ostrov for an all-night bash, including live bands, student theatre and non-stop sausages and beer.

30 April

Burning of the Witches (*Pálení čarodějnic*) – Czech version of a pre-Christian festival for warding off evil, featuring burning brooms at the Fairgrounds at Bubeneč, and all-night, end-of-winter bonfire parties on Kampa island and in suburban backyards

1 May

Majáles (see the boxed text above)

5 May

Czech Uprising (*České povstání*) – anniversary of Prague's 1945 anti-Nazi uprising preceding liberation

17 November

Start of the 'Velvet Revolution' – anniversary of the 1989 beating of student demonstrators by security police, triggering the fall of the communist regime

24 December to 1 January

Christmas/New Year – while many Czechs celebrate an extended holiday, stuffing themselves with carp (sold live from big tubs in the streets), Prague is engulfed by revellers from all over Europe and the tourist season is on again, briefly and furiously

Festivals

Among Prague's better annual events are the following; for updates, check the PIS Web site (www.prague-info.cz).

January
Febiofest

International Festival of Film, Television & Video – new works by international film-makers, shown throughout the Czech Republic and Slovakia

February to October
AghaRTA International Jazz Festival

AghaRTA Jazz Centrum and a few other venues

Early April
Musica Ecumenica

International Festival of Spiritual Music, in major venues around the city

Mid-April & October
Musica Sacra Praga

Festival of Sacred Music, in various concert halls and churches

May
Festival of Chamber Music

Czech composers, at Bertramka

12 May to 4 June
Prague Spring (Pražské jaro) International Music Festival

Prague's most prestigious event, with classical music concerts in theatres, churches and historic buildings; kicked off on the anniversary of Smetana's death with a procession from his grave at Vyšehrad to the Obecní dům (Municipal House), for a performance of his *Má vlast* (My Country); for more information, see the Entertainment chapter

June
Jam
Rock festival at Autokemp Džbán camp site, Vokovice (see North-West Outskirts in the Places to Stay chapter)
Tanec Praha
International festival of modern dance

July to August
Open-Air Opera Festival
Various venues, such as Wallenstein Garden

July to September
Prague Folk Festival
At the theatre of the City Library

August to September
Verdi Festival
Verdi's works, at the State Opera House

September
Prague Autumn
International music festival, mainly at the Rudolfinum
Svatováclavské slavnosti
St Wenceslas Festival of spiritual art (music, painting, sculpture)

October
Mozart v Praze
Mozart Festival, at Bertramka and other major venues around town; runs for most of the month
Lucerne International Jazz Festival
Lucerne Music Bar in Lucerne Passage, Staré Město

October to November
Musica Iudaica
Festival of Jewish Music, especially the composers of Terezín (see the Excursions chapter), at various venues

December
Festival Bohuslava Martinů (Bohuslav Martinů Music Festival)
Rudolfinum and other venues

DOING BUSINESS
A free-market economy has been evolving, haphazardly, in the Czech Republic since 1989. Laws and regulations have been written from scratch; some have worked, some have failed and all are full of loopholes. It's not unusual for locals to take advantage of innocent newcomers, or to renege on agreements. It's essential that a reliable Czech partner be found for any venture: someone to deal with complex procedures and steer clear of crooked deals.

Lawsuits can take years, and many judges have not yet grasped the meaning of a free society. Entrenched bureaucratic habits remain in place. Another big obstacle is the not-yet-privatised banking sector, with its overemphasis on cash as the basis of the economy.

Foreign lawyers who have passed the bar exam in their own country can work for foreign-owned firms, but in theory only as advisers on law in their home country. They must first take a fairly basic test (not a bar exam) on general information about the Czech Republic, administered two or three times a year.

The growing expatriate business community in Prague is well informed by a glossy monthly magazine, *The Prague Tribune*, and two weekly newspapers, the *Central European Business Weekly* and the *Prague Business Journal*, with business-oriented regional news plus a few entertainment and restaurant listings. *The Prague Post* also has an extensive business section.

Useful Organisations
If you want to do business, talk to the commercial section of your embassy in Prague, or the American Chamber of Commerce (AmCham; Map 7; ☎ 24 81 42 80, fax 24 81 80 67, email amcham@telecom.cz), Malá Štupartská 7, Staré Město, about work permits and other matters. AmCham has lots of useful resources; some that are on sale in bookshops and kiosks are free here:

Prague Expatriate Guide (240 Kč in shops), updated at least annually, with a wide range of information for expatriates and their families, from business to kids to entertainment
Prague Post Book of Business Lists (450 Kč in shops), an annual with graded lists of accountants, lawyers, hotels, moving companies, printers, security firms, banks and so on
Prague Phone Book, a specialised 'yellow pages'

Also check out Resources, a massive, quarterly-updated subscriber directory of co-ordinates for ministries, companies, associations, services etc. Trade Links (☎ 24 21 06 92, fax 24 21 86 92), PO Box 131, 110 01 Prague 1, publishes translations of Czech commercial, accounting and bankruptcy laws.

The Economic Chamber of the Czech Republic (Map 4; ☎ 66 79 48 45, fax 80 48 94) is at Argentinská 38, Prague 2. Two organisations with information for investors are Czechinvest, the Czech Agency for Foreign Investment (☎ 24 06 24 46, fax 24 06 22 08), Politických vězňů 20, and the Confederation of Czech Industries (Map 6; ☎ 24 91 56 91), Mikulandská 7.

Of many translating and interpreting firms, one of the most professional is Artlingua (Map 6; ☎ 29 37 41), Myslíkova 6, Prague 2.

The four largest Czech commercial banks are Komerční banka, Česká spořitelna, Investiční a poštovní banka (IPB) and Československá obchodní banka. Leading foreign banks are Citibank, Société Générale, Banque National de Paris and Crédit Lyonnais. For further details on these banks, see the boxed text under Money earlier in this chapter.

WORK

You can find short or long-term work teaching English (or other languages) at numerous language schools in Prague. If you can prove your qualifications to them, they'll take care of the paperwork for a work permit. Major, trustworthy schools include:

Angličtina Expres
(☎ 24 25 14 28, fax 24 23 81 86)
Berlitz
(☎ 22 12 55 50)
London School of Modern Languages
(☎ 21 00 16 02, fax 21 00 16 05)
Státní jazyková škola
(State Language School; ☎ 24 91 41 14)

You might find employment in the expat-run restaurants and bars springing up like mushrooms around Prague. Possibilities also exist in many foreign-owned businesses. Investment, banking, real estate and management firms need experienced staff and often employ non-Czech speakers, but the odds of getting such a job are better from home than in Prague. The *Prague Post* usually has a few advertisements for such positions.

Permits

There are a million routes through the permits maze, depending on circumstances. Following is a summary of the process for those aiming to be hired by a local company to do something like teaching English or tending a bar.

From the relevant local labour office, your prospective employer will already have obtained a permit to employ foreigners in specific categories of work (this means demonstrating that there aren't enough Czechs to do the job).

Then you must get a work permit, specific to the job in question, from the main labour office (Pracovní úřad pro hlavní město), Zborovská 11, Smíchov, Prague 5 (Map 9). Your prospective employer will probably get this for you, or at least help (and sign) at appropriate points. You must present a completed application form; proof of any educational requirements for the job (such as a TEFL certificate or other credentials if you want to teach English beyond the level of conversational practice); Czech translations of the application and credentials; and your passport. There's no fee. The process takes about 12 weeks. The permit is good for a year, and can be renewed a year at a time.

The next step is to apply for a residence permit, but first you'll need a criminal-record check by the city crime registry (Trestní rejstřík), náměstí Hrdinů 1300, Pankrác, Prague 4 (Map 1). For this you must present a completed form, an original birth certificate, and translations of both. This can be done in half a day if you're prepared to wait around, or in about 10 days if you aren't. The fee is 50 Kč, paid with special stamps (*kolky*) sold at the office or at any post office.

Then it's off to the Foreigners' Police & Passport Office (Úřadovna cizinecké policie a pasové služby), Olšanská 2, Žižkov, Prague 3 (Map 8), to apply for your 'green card' or residence permit. You must show your work permit; the crime-registry certificate; a completed, translated application form; proof of a permanent address (normally a standard form for your landlord to sign and notarise); three passport-size photos; and 1000 Kč in kolky. This takes about two months. A residence permit is good for a year and can be renewed annually.

All documents must be translated by a registered translating service, of which there are many in Prague.

If you want to set up your own business in Prague (see the preceding Doing Business section), the process is a lot more complex. It's easy to see why most people get help from their employers or from specialist agencies. One reliable Prague agency specialising in work and residency permits is RZP (Map 6; ☎/fax 697 50 48), U vodárny 14, Prague 3. It makes sense to arrange your job in advance so that much of the paperwork is done before you arrive.

Of course a great many expats work without permits. You can usually extend a tourist visa once or twice before the Foreigners' Police & Passport Office gets suspicious and starts giving you smaller and smaller extensions. But be careful: police are gradually increasing the frequency of their identity checks, and employers who hire workers without permits can, if caught, be nailed with crippling fines.

When and if the Czech Republic becomes a member of the EU, EU citizens will no longer need to apply for a work permit, though they'll still need a residence permit.

Other Help

If you're settling in and looking for flatmates, Czech lessons, work, a haircut etc, there are good notice boards at Laundry Kings and Prague Laundromat (see Laundry in this chapter); The Globe and Big Ben bookstores (see the Shopping chapter); and FX Café, Bělehradská 120, Vinohrady.

Volunteer Work

KMC (Klub mladých cestovatelů or Young Travellers' Club; Map 6; ☎ 90 00 15 18, ☎/fax 24 23 06 33), Karolíny Světlé 30, organises international work camps from June to August. Projects in the Prague region at the time of writing included work in a centre for handicapped children, renovation work at the zoo, and gardening at Průhonice park. Contracts are for a minimum of three weeks with no pay, but room and board are provided. The registration fee varies from nothing to US$100, depending on the work. You're expected to reserve months ahead, through Hostelling International or a volunteer organisation in your home country.

Getting There & Away

Students and people aged under 26 or 60 and over can get some big travel discounts. See under Useful Cards in the Documents section of the Facts for the Visitor chapter for information about student, youth and senior ID cards.

AIR

Prague Ruzyně, on the western outskirts of the city, is the Czech Republic's only international airport. It's served by about two dozen international carriers, including ČSA (České aerolinie), the state airline.

The high season for travel to Prague is roughly June or July to September, plus the Easter and Christmas/New Year periods. Advance booking is essential at these times.

Buying Tickets

World aviation has never been so competitive, making air travel better value than ever. But you have to research the options carefully to make sure you get the best deal. The Internet is a useful resource for checking air fares: many travel agencies and airlines have a Web site.

Discounted tickets are released by airlines through selected travel agencies, and these are often the cheapest deals going. Some airlines now sell discounted tickets direct to the customer, and it's worth contacting airlines anyway for information on routes and timetables. Sometimes, there is nothing to be gained by going direct to the airline – specialist discount agencies often offer fares that are lower and/or carry fewer conditions than the airline's published prices. You can expect to be offered a wider range of options than a single airline would provide, and, at worst, you will just end up paying the official airline fare.

The exception to this rule is the new breed of 'no-frills' carriers, which mostly sell direct. At the time of writing none of the leading players (easyJet and Go of the UK, Ryanair of Ireland and Virgin Express

of Belgium) had established links to the Czech Republic, but Prague is sure to be on the wish-lists of several of them.

Unlike the 'full-service' airlines, the no-frills carriers often make one-way tickets available at half the return fare – meaning that it is easy to stitch together an open-jaw itinerary, where you fly in to one city and out of another. Regular airlines may offer open-jaws, particularly if you are flying in from outside Europe.

Some single (one-way) air tickets, such as from Prague to London, are cheapest when bought at the Prague end, but if you're going only to the Czech Republic, you'll save even more with a return (round-trip) ticket from home.

Fares quoted here are approximate high-season return fares, based on advertised rates at the time of writing. None of them constitutes a recommendation for any airline.

Other Parts of the Czech Republic

Air Ostrava (☎ 24 88 93 83) is a growing Czech airline that flies from Prague to Ostrava two to four times a day, and onward to points in the Slovak Republic and Germany.

Other Countries

The Slovak Republic To Bratislava, ČSA flies two to three times a day, and the Slovak airline Tatra Air has services three times each weekday. To Košice, ČSA flies twice a day and Air Ostrava goes six days a week.

The UK Discount air travel is big business in London. Check out the travel sections in the weekend broadsheets – such as *The Independent* on Saturday and *The Sunday Times* – and their 'bucket-shop' adverts, and the travel classifieds in London's

Air Travel Glossary

Baggage Allowance This will be written on your ticket and usually includes one 20kg item to go in the hold, plus one item of hand luggage.

Bucket Shops These are unbonded travel agencies specialising in discounted airline tickets.

Bumped Just because you have a confirmed seat doesn't mean you're going to get on the plane (see Overbooking).

Cancellation Penalties If you have to cancel or change a discounted ticket, there are often heavy penalties involved; insurance can sometimes be taken out against these penalties. Some airlines impose penalties on regular tickets as well, particularly against 'no-show' passengers.

Check-In Airlines ask you to check in a certain time ahead of the flight departure (usually one to two hours on international flights). If you fail to check in on time and the flight is overbooked, the airline can cancel your booking and give your seat to somebody else.

Confirmation Having a ticket written out with the flight and date you want doesn't mean you have a seat until the agent has checked with the airline that your status is 'OK' or confirmed. Meanwhile you could just be 'on request'.

Courier Fares Businesses often need to send urgent documents or freight securely and quickly. Courier companies hire people to accompany the package through customs and, in return, offer a discount ticket which is sometimes a phenomenal bargain. In effect, what the companies do is ship their freight as your luggage on regular commercial flights. This is a legitimate operation, but there are two shortcomings – the short turnaround time of the ticket (usually not longer than a month) and the limitation on your luggage allowance. You may have to surrender all your allowance and take only carry-on luggage.

Full Fares Airlines traditionally offer 1st class (coded F), business class (coded J) and economy class (coded Y) tickets. These days there are so many promotional and discounted fares available that few passengers pay full economy fare.

ITX An ITX, or 'independent inclusive tour excursion', is often available on tickets to popular holiday destinations. Officially it's a package deal combined with hotel accommodation, but many agents will sell you one of these for the flight only and give you phoney hotel vouchers in the unlikely event that you're challenged at the airport.

Lost Tickets If you lose your airline ticket an airline will usually treat it like a travellers cheque and, after inquiries, issue you with another one. Legally, however, an airline is entitled to treat it like cash and if you lose it then it's gone forever. Take good care of your tickets.

MCO An MCO, or 'miscellaneous charge order', is a voucher that looks like an airline ticket but carries no destination or date. It can be exchanged through any International Association of Travel Agents (IATA) airline for a ticket on a specific flight. It's a useful alternative to an onward ticket in those countries that demand one, and is more flexible than an ordinary ticket if you're unsure of your route.

No-Shows No-shows are passengers who fail to show up for their flight. Full-fare passengers who fail to turn up are sometimes entitled to travel on a later flight. The rest are penalised (see Cancellation Penalties).

On Request This is an unconfirmed booking for a flight.

Air Travel Glossary

Onward Tickets An entry requirement for many countries is that you have a ticket out of the country. If you're unsure of your next move, the easiest solution is to buy the cheapest onward ticket to a neighbouring country or a ticket from a reliable airline which can later be refunded if you do not use it.

Open Jaw Tickets These are return tickets where you fly out to one place but return from another. If available, this can save you backtracking to your arrival point.

Overbooking Airlines hate to fly empty seats and since every flight has some passengers who fail to show up, airlines often book more passengers than they have seats. Usually excess passengers make up for the no-shows, but occasionally somebody gets bumped. Guess who it is most likely to be? The passengers who check in late.

Point-to-Point Tickets These are discount tickets that can be bought on some routes in return for passengers waiving their rights to a stopover.

Promotional Fares These are officially discounted fares, available from travel agencies or direct from the airline.

Reconfirmation At least 72 hours prior to departure time of an onward or return flight, you must contact the airline and 'reconfirm' that you intend to be on the flight. If you don't do this the airline can delete your name from the passenger list and you could lose your seat.

Restrictions Discounted tickets often have various restrictions on them – such as needing to be paid for in advance and incurring a penalty to be altered. Others are restrictions on the minimum and maximum period you must be away, such as a minimum of 14 days or a maximum of one year.

Round-the-World Tickets RTW tickets give you a limited period (usually a year) in which to circumnavigate the globe. You can go anywhere the carrying airlines go, as long as you don't backtrack. The number of stopovers or total number of separate flights is decided before you set off and they usually cost a bit more than a basic return flight.

Stand-by This is a discounted ticket where you only fly if there is a seat free at the last moment. Stand-by fares are usually available only on domestic routes.

Transferred Tickets Airline tickets cannot be transferred from one person to another. Travellers sometimes try to sell the return half of their ticket, but officials can ask you to prove that you are the person named on the ticket. This is less likely to happen on domestic flights, but on an international flight tickets are compared with passports.

Travel Agencies Travel agencies vary widely and you should choose one that suits your needs. Some simply handle tours, while full-services agencies handle everything from tours and tickets to car rental and hotel bookings. If all you want is a ticket at the lowest possible price, then go to an agency specialising in discounted tickets.

Travel Periods Ticket prices vary with the time of year. There is a low (off-peak) season and a high (peak) season, and often a low-shoulder season and a high-shoulder season as well. Usually the fare depends on your outward flight – if you depart in the high season and return in the low season, you pay the high-season fare.

weekly *Time Out* and *TNT* entertainment magazines.

British Airways (☎ 0345-222 111) and ČSA (☎ 0171-255 1898; from 22 April 2000 ☎ 020-7255 1898) fly twice daily between London Heathrow and Prague. British Midland (☎ 0345-554 554) flies the route once or twice daily. ČSA also flies four times weekly from London Stansted and five times a week from Manchester. The journey time for all these flights is about two hours.

In peak season, fares are around UK£200 return – usually a little less from Stansted, a little more from Manchester. At other times of the year you could find something for up to UK£50 less. The lowest fares are not usually through the airlines direct; discount agents such as Hamilton Travel (☎ 0171-344 3333; from 22 April 2000 ☎ 020-7344 3333) or Trailfinders (☎ 0171-937 5400, fax 937 9294; from 22 April 2000 ☎ 020-7937 5400, fax 7937 9294), or specialists such as Regent Holidays (☎ 0117-921 1711, fax 925 4866) can normally come up with something cheaper.

Students, and travellers under 26 years of age, qualify for even better fares through companies such as STA Travel (☎ 0171-361 6161; from 22 April 2000 ☎ 020-7361 6161; Web site www.statravel.co.uk) and Usit Campus (☎ 0171-730 3402; from 22 April 2000 ☎ 020-7730 3402; Web site www.usitcampus.co.uk).

Elsewhere in Europe From most Continental cities, routes to and from Prague are sewn up between the main airline from the home country and ČSA. Usually fares are agreed between the two airlines on a route, and revenue divided, so there is no real competition and fares are high.

From Charles de Gaulle, ČSA flies once or twice a day and Air France twice. At the time of research the best summer fare was about 1270FF. Amsterdam connections include two a day with ČSA and three with KLM-Royal Dutch Airlines. A typical summer fare is about f408. From Frankfurt, ČSA has one or two daily flights, and

Lufthansa two or three. A summer fare with ČSA is about DM320.

Paris travel agencies specialising in bargain flights include Usit Voyages (☎ 01 42 44 14 00), Go Voyages (☎ 01 49 23 26 86, Minitel 3615 GO) and Council Travel (☎ 01 44 55 55 44). STA Travel's Paris agent is Voyages Wasteels (☎ 01 43 25 58 35). A reliable source of bargain tickets in the Netherlands is NBBS Reizen (☎ 020-620 50 71).

The USA & Canada The *Los Angeles Times*, *San Francisco Examiner*, *Chicago Tribune*, *New York Times*, Toronto *Globe & Mail* and *Vancouver Sun* have big weekly travel sections with lots of travel-agency ads. The monthly newsletter *Travel Unlimited* (PO Box 1058, Allston, MA 02134) publishes the cheapest courier air fares from the USA for destinations worldwide.

The only direct flights from the USA to Prague are the daily Delta Air Lines/Swissair (toll-free ☎ 800-241 4141) codeshare service from New York JFK and the four times a week ČSA/Continental (toll-free ☎ 800-231 0856) codeshare flight from Newark. Fares for these are likely to be high – around US$700 return for the cheapest and most restrictive ticket. A much wider range of departure points, and lower fares, are available on airlines that stop in a third country en route: Air France via Paris, British Airways via London and Lufthansa Airlines via Frankfurt are the main ones. Low-season fares from the east coast may be available for as little as US$500, while flights from the west coast start around the US$700 mark.

From Canada, ČSA has a flight two or three times a week from Toronto via Montreal to Prague. The minimum fare is around C$1000; again, flying via an intermediate point may save you money.

In the USA, two reliable sources of cheap tickets are STA Travel (toll-free ☎ 800-777 0112, Web site www.sta-travel.com) and Council Travel (toll-free ☎ 800-226 8624, Web site www.counciltravel.com). Canada's best bargain-ticket agency is Travel

CUTS (☎ 416-979 2406, fax 416-979 8167, Web site www.travelcuts.com). All have offices throughout their respective countries.

Australia & New Zealand Check the travel agencies' ads in the Yellow Pages, and the Saturday travel sections of the *Sydney Morning Herald* and the Melbourne *Age*.

The best available high season return fare from east-coast Australia is about A$2150 with Lauda Air (about A$500 less in the low season). Qantas/ČSA have seasonal special air fares that can be almost as low.

An efficient dealer in discount air fares is Flight Centre, headquartered in Melbourne (☎ 03-9650 2899, fax 9650 3751). STA Travel has central offices in Sydney (☎ 02-9212 1255, fax 9281 4183, Fast Fare Hotline ☎ 1300 360 960, Web site www .statravel.com.au) and Auckland (☎ 09-309 0458, fax 309 2059, Fast Fare Hotline ☎ 366 6673). Both agencies have branch offices throughout both Australia and New Zealand.

Airline Offices
Reliable sources of discounted air tickets in Prague include CKM Travel, GTS International, Čedok and ČD (see Travel Agencies later in this chapter). ČSA's Service Centre (Map 7; ☎ 20 10 46 20), V celnici 5, just off náměstí Republiky, offers flight information and ticket sales on weekdays only, from 8.30 am to 6 pm. Other airline offices in Prague include:

Aeroflot
  (☎ 24 81 26 83) Pařížská 5
Air Canada
  (☎ 24 89 27 30) Revoluční 17
Air France
  (☎ 24 22 71 64) Wenceslas Square 10
Air India
  (☎ 24 21 24 74) Wenceslas Square 15
Alitalia
  (☎ 24 81 00 79) Revoluční 5
Austrian Airlines
  (☎ 231 18 72) Revoluční 15
British Airways
  (☎ 22 11 44 44) Ovocný trh 8

British Midland
  (☎ 20 11 44 95) Ruzyně Airport
Delta Air Lines
  (☎ 24 23 22 58) Národní 32
El Al Israel Airlines
  (☎ 24 21 73 49) Wenceslas Square 48
Finnair
  (☎ 24 21 19 86) Španělská 2
KLM-Royal Dutch Airlines
  (☎ 24 21 69 50) Na příkopě 13
LOT Polish Airlines
  (☎ 20 11 45 35) Pařížská 18
Lufthansa Airlines
  (☎ 24 22 91 53) Pařížská 28
MALEV-Hungarian Airlines
  (☎ 24 81 26 71) Pařížská 5
Sabena
  (☎ 24 81 21 11) Pařížská 11
Scandinavian Airlines (SAS)
  (☎ 24 21 47 49) Rytířská 13
Swissair
  (☎ 24 81 21 11) Pařížská 11

Departure Tax
The 390 Kč international departure tax is invariably included in the ticket price.

BUS
Other Parts of the Czech Republic
The state bus company is ČSAD (Czech Automobile Transport). Its long-distance coaches tend to be faster, more frequent and marginally more expensive than trains. Foreigners and Czechs pay the same fares. There are also several private domestic carriers.

All domestic long-distance buses and most regional services (such as those for excursions around Prague) use Florenc station (Map 6). Some regional buses depart from stands near metro stations Anděl, Hradčanská, Nádraží Holešovice, Palmovka, Radlická, Roztyly, Smíchovské Nádraží and Želivského.

Agencies don't book seats on domestic buses, but they can tell you which stand is best for a particular trip – or indeed whether you're better off taking the train. You might get some help from ČSAD's information line (☎ 1034, 6 am to 8 pm), though little English is spoken. Florenc also has an information window (No 8, open daily from 6 am to 9 pm); if you get no joy there, try the friendly Tourbus travel agency upstairs.

At Florenc there is a formidable maze of charts on the walls, though they're not impossible to figure out. One gives route numbers and departure platforms for each major destination. Others give all departure times for each route number. Then there are timetables for every route. To figure out when the next bus leaves, you'll probably have to look at timetables for more than one route number. The footnotes may drive you crazy (crossed hammers means workdays, ie weekdays, only). You can buy your own regional timetables from the Nadatur bookshop, Hybernská 5 (Map 7).

Short-haul tickets are sold on the bus. Long-distance domestic tickets are sold at the station. Since ticketing is computerised at Florenc, you can often book ahead.

There are generally more departures in the morning. Buses, especially if full, sometimes leave a few minutes early, so be there about 10 minutes before departure time. Many services don't operate on weekends, so trains are a better bet then.

Florenc has a left-luggage office (*úschovna zavazadel*) upstairs, open daily from 5 am to 11 pm.

Other Countries

Eurolines With the increase in availability of low air fares, buses no longer offer the cheapest public transport around Europe. But if you can't find a cheap flight or prefer to stay on the ground, buses are a good deal. The easiest way to book tickets is through Eurolines, a consortium of coach operators with offices all over Europe. Coaches are as fast as the trains and fairly comfortable, with on-board toilets, reclining seats and sometimes air conditioning. They stop frequently for meals, though you'll save a bit by packing your own munchies. Book at least a few days ahead in summer.

Peak season is from mid-June to the end of September. At that time Eurolines goes to Prague from London (Victoria Coach Station) daily for UK£95 return (UK£85 for people under 26 years or 60 years and over); the 1277km trip takes about 23 hours. Eurolines buses run to Prague from Paris (1066km, 16½ hours) daily, and on a roundabout route from Amsterdam via Rotterdam, Antwerp and Brussels (1133km, 19 hours) four times a week.

Discounts depend on the route, but children from four to 12 years old typically get 30 to 40% off, and under-26s and seniors about 10%. For coach junkies, a Eurolines Pass gives you unlimited travel to 36 major European cities for 30/60 days for a peak-season price of UK£229/279 (under-26s and seniors UK£199/249).

Among some 200 Eurolines offices in Europe are the following:

Eurolines
(☎ 01 49 72 51 51, fax 01 49 72 51 61, Minitel 3615 EUROLINES, Web site www.eurolines.fr) Gare Routière Internationale de Paris, 28 Avenue de Général de Gaulle, Bagnolet, Paris
Deutsche Touring/Eurolines
(☎ 069-790 353, fax 706 059, Web site www.deutsche-touring.com) Am Romerhof 17, Frankfurt
Eurolines Nederland
(☎ 020-560 8787, fax 560 8766) Rokin 10, Amsterdam
(same ☎ and fax) Amstel Bus Station, Julianaplein 5, Amsterdam
Eurolines UK
(☎ 0990-143 219, fax 01582-400 694, email welcome@eurolines.uk.com, Web site www.eurolines.co.uk/euro1.htm) 52 Grosvenor Gardens, London

Eurolines' USA agent is British Travel International (toll-free ☎ 800-327 6097).

Busabout This UK-based budget alternative to Eurolines is aimed at younger travellers, but has no upper age limit. It runs coaches along three interlocking European circuits: the 'North Zone' runs from Paris through Brussels and Amsterdam to Berlin and Prague. It continues to Munich, where it links up with the 'South Zone' (to Italy and southern France) and, in winter, the

'Snow Zone' around the Alps. Pick-up points are usually convenient for hostels and camping grounds. In Prague, Busabout stops at the Pension Sunshine-Vysočany, Drahobejlova 17.

Each circuit costs UK£109 (UK£99 for youth and student card holders) for two weeks, with the add-on from London to Paris an extra UK£30 return. You can buy Busabout tickets directly from the company (☎ 0181-784 2816; from 22 April 2000 ☎ 020-8784 2816; Web site www .busabout.com) or from suppliers such as Usit Campus and STA Travel. The Eurobus company, which used to offer a similar service, went out of business in 1998.

Other Coach Lines Independent operators that go to Prague for a bit less than Eurolines – and have Prague offices – include Kingscourt Express and Capital Express (London only), Bohemia Euroexpress International (BEI) and Bohemian Express; see Travel Agencies later in this chapter. Typical London-Prague return fares for all these are about UK£85 (UK£79 for under-26s and seniors); other sample BEI fares include Amsterdam f225, Berlin DM100 and Hamburg DM160.

Another European line serving Prague is Tourbus (see Travel Agencies later in this chapter).

Coach Stands Most international coaches use the stand beside Želivského metro station (Map 1). Some – such as those of Capital Express and Tourbus, and a few of BEI's – use Florenc station (Map 6). Kingscourt Express goes to/from Ke Štvanici (opposite McDonald's) near Florenc. Bohemian Express uses a stand at Nádraží Holešovice metro station (Map 4).

Although Florenc has international ticket windows (Nos 5 and 5a, open daily), buying your bus ticket from a travel agency gives you the widest choice and usually the best price. Reliable ones include CKM Travel, GTS International, Bohemiatour, Čedok and the ČD branch at the main train station. Operators with their own agencies include

Eurolines, BEI, Bohemian Express, Capital Express, Kingscourt Express and Tourbus, though their tickets are also sold at other agencies. For addresses see Travel Agencies later in this chapter.

TRAIN
Other Parts of the Czech Republic

Czech Railways (ČD) provides cheap, efficient train services throughout the country, though many services are being cancelled for lack of passengers. Travel in 2nd class costs about 53 Kč per 100km.

Services include SuperCity (SC on timetables; only for 1st class international trains), EuroCity (EC), Intercity (IC), Express (Ex), Rapid (R), Fast (Sp) and Ordinary (Os). You cannot book a place on a Fast or Ordinary train; for the others, 'R' in the timetable indicates that reservations are recommended, and a boxed or circled 'R' means they're mandatory.

You can buy just a ticket (*jízdenka*), or a ticket with a reservation (*místenka*) for a seat (*místo*), couchette (*lehátkový vůz*) or sleeper (*spací vůz*). You cannot get a reservation without a ticket.

Tickets can be purchased up to 30 days ahead. Once validated, tickets for distances over 50km are valid for 24 hours, those for under 50km only until 6 am the next day. Surcharges include 60 Kč for Intercity tickets and 30 Kč for Express. A 1st class ticket costs 50% more than 2nd class.

Finding out when trains depart requires some ingenuity: services are not always daily, timetable footnotes are incomprehensible, and clerks seldom speak English. Write down your destination and proposed travel date (month in Roman numerals), point to your watch and cross your fingers. Since the system is computerised, you should get a print-out of departure times.

If you'll be in the Czech Republic for any length of time, consider getting your own regional or national timetables from the ČD travel agency outside level 3 of the main station, or from the Nadatur bookshop, Hybernská 5 (Map 7).

There's no need to book domestic rail travel before you arrive in the Czech Republic.

Other Countries

Trains go daily to Prague from most major European cities. Paris, Amsterdam, Munich and Vienna are major western European rail hubs. Trains are cheaper than flying, but still expensive without a rail pass (see the next section). In summer you should book at least a few weeks ahead.

From the UK, the cheapest route is across the Channel by ferry, hovercraft or Seacat to Paris, and from there to Prague. Connex Southeastern (☎ 0870-603 0405, fax 603 0505) handles this London-Paris route, and can sell you tickets for the onward journey to Prague too. A 2nd class return ticket from London via Cologne – the cheapest and most direct of half a dozen routes – is UK£252 (UK£197 if you stay away for at least one Saturday; UK£164 for under-26s),

plus about UK£10 for a couchette or from UK£25 to 40 for a sleeper. Tickets are good for two months and you can break your journey anywhere en route. London-Prague takes 25 to 30 hours.

For speed and convenience, the best route is from London Waterloo to Brussels via the Channel Tunnel. You must change trains in Brussels, and possibly also in Cologne, Frankfurt or Munich. The fastest journey time is about 22 hours. Services are run by the Eurostar passenger train service (☎ 0990-186 186) or the Eurotunnel vehicle-carrying service (☎ 0990-353 535). These operators do not sell tickets to Prague. Instead, you should consult Rail Europe (☎ 0990-848 848); this company is part of French Railways (SNCF), but arranges rail travel between the UK and many European countries. The adult return fare is UK£288 if your trip includes at least one Saturday night away, with supplements for couchettes.

For travellers under 26, special fares are available through youth travel specialists such as Usit Campus (☎ 0171-730 3402; from 22 April 2000 ☎ 020-7730 3402; Web site www.usitcampus.co.uk).

In France SNCF has a nationwide telephone number (☎ 08 36 35 35 35 in French, ☎ 08 36 35 35 39 in English), a Minitel address (3615 SNCF) and a Web site (web.sncf.fr). Contact Rail Europe in the USA at ☎ 800-4EURAIL, fax 432-1FAX; and in Canada at ☎ 800-361-RAIL, fax 905-602 4198.

Rail Passes

If you plan to travel widely in Europe, the following special tickets or passes may be good value for getting to/from the Czech Republic, though at the time of writing, travel within the country was cheaper at local fares than with a pass. Even with a pass you must still pay for seat and couchette reservations, and supplements on express trains.

You can get most of the following passes through Rail Europe (see the preceding Other Countries section for contact details).

Headaches on the Rails

Overnight trains running the Berlin-Prague, Budapest-Prague and other major routes have experienced some bold thefts from sleeping passengers, so keep a grip on your bags.

Some Czech train conductors may claim there's something wrong with your ticket, usually in the hope of a bribe. Ensure that you have the right ticket for your train and don't pay any 'fine', 'supplement' or 'reservation fee' without a written receipt (*doklad*). If the conductor won't provide this, you shouldn't pay anything extra.

Some conductors may take your ticket, promise to return it later, and not do so. A conductor may only hold your ticket if you board a train on which you've reserved a couchette or sleeper, in which case the attendant keeps your ticket overnight so you don't have to be woken up for ticket controls. Don't forget to get it back.

The soaring Gothic façade of St Vitus Cathedral.

Time for reflection: Petřín Hill's mirror maze.

Romanesque glory: Basilica of St George.

Jumble of rooftops from Old Town Hall Tower.

St Wenceslas rides again on Štorch House mural.

The magic of the Old Town Square and Týn Church by night

Inter-Rail Pass This pass entitles you to 22 consecutive days' 2nd class rail travel in one of eight western and central European 'zones' (excluding your own country), for UK£229 (UK£159 for under-26s). Multizone passes are valid for one month's travel and are better value, allowing two zones for UK£279/209, three zones for UK£309/229, and all eight zones for UK£349/259. You'd need a three-zone pass to travel from the UK to Prague. You must have been resident in Europe for at least six months before starting your travels.

Euro Domino Pass If you don't plan to be on the move all that much, this pass – called a Freedom Pass in the UK – allows a few days per month of unrestricted train travel within a particular country. For 2nd class travel in the Czech Republic, the cost is UK£39 for three days (UK£29 for under-26s), UK£59/39 for five days or UK£89/69 for 10 days.

Czech Explorer Pass This Usit Campus pass is UK£23 for a week's unlimited 2nd class travel within the Czech and Slovak republics (UK£15 for the Czech Republic only). It's available only to holders of youth, ISIC or ITIC cards and their spouses and children.

Rail Europe Senior Card This card, available to travellers aged 60 and over, is good for discounts of around 30% on international tickets, including to and from the Czech Republic. To be eligible for it you must have a local senior citizens' railcard. In Britain you can get these and Rail Europe Senior Cards from mainline train stations.

Eurailpass This is the Inter-Rail counterpart for non-European residents. It's valid for unlimited rail travel (1st class for those over 26, 2nd class for under-26s) in 17 European countries. It's meant to be purchased before you get to Europe, although you can buy it from Rail Europe for about 10% more, provided your passport shows

> ## You're Going Where?
>
> Rail travel in the Czech Republic tends to be cheaper per kilometre than in Western European countries, so you'll save money on any train journey to/from Western Europe by buying a ticket that terminates at a Czech border town (for example, Děčín, Cheb, Plzeň, České Budějovice or Břeclav) and then getting another from there. When buying a ticket out of the Czech Republic, write 'Praha → (name of the frontier station)' on a piece of paper for the clerk.

you've been in Europe for less than six months. Although not valid in the UK or the Czech Republic, it may still be worth getting for travel elsewhere in Europe. To use it on a journey to/from the Czech Republic, you will have to buy separate tickets beyond/to the Czech border.

Arriving in Prague by Train

Most international trains arrive at Prague's main station (Praha hlavní nádraží; Map 6). A few go to Praha-Holešovice (Map 4) or Praha-Smíchov (Map 9). All these stations are beside metro stations. Masarykovo nádraží, two blocks north of the main station, is the primary domestic station.

Main Train Station You disembark at level 3 into a swarm of currency exchange desks, accommodation offices and people offering places to stay. Get your bearings and a map at the helpful PIS booth on level 2 (open daily from 9 am to 4 pm).

Up on level 4 is the original (and mostly abandoned) Art Nouveau station; levels 3, 2 and 1 are the modern extension beneath Wilsonova třída. Buses are outside the northern (right) end of level 3 and out front on Opletalova. Taxis are outside the southern end, and there's a metro station entrance on level 2. Public-transport information is available at the DP booth beside the metro entrance. Level 1 has a 24 hour left-luggage office (*úschovna*) and day-use lockers.

If you arrive in the middle of the night without a hotel booking, store your bags and take a long walk until the sun rises. This station is a magnet for pickpockets, crazies and urine-soaked drunks, and at night it's a bad place to hang out. Most of the station's currency exchange and accommodation offices close from about 11 pm to 6 am. The closest hostel with a night desk is Kolej Jednota, just north of the station at Opletalova 38.

Leaving Prague by Train

You can buy international train tickets out of the Czech Republic in advance from main train stations or from ČD, GTS International or Čedok travel agencies (see later in this chapter). ČD and its agency branches also sell Inter-Rail passes. Credit cards are accepted at the ČD agency outside level 3, but not at train station ticket windows.

Information about connections is available at ☎ 24 22 42 00. Station lobbies have timetables on rotating drums. The main station has an information office at the northern end of level 3. The international windows at the main station are Nos 12, 16, 18, 20, 22 and 24.

Tickets are valid for two months, with unlimited stopovers. See the Other Parts of the Czech Republic section for information on ČD services.

CAR & MOTORCYCLE

See Car & Motorcycle in the Getting Around chapter for details about car rental, breakdown support and driving in Prague itself.

Czech Border Crossings

The following are border posts that can issue 30-day tourist visas or 48-hour, nonextendable transit visas on the spot. Fees for on-the-spot visas (either type) are around 1500 Kč; approval is at the officials' discretion; and although these border posts are open round the clock, visas are normally issued only during daytime business hours.

Dolní Dvořiště, South Bohemia (Wullowitz, Austria)
Hatě (Znojmo), South Moravia (Kleinhaugsdorf, Austria)
Rozvadov, West Bohemia (Waidhaus, Germany)

You can often save hours by detouring away from popular crossings to smaller ones nearby. Rozvadov is a notorious bottleneck on weekends; other busy ones are Cínovec, Strážný and Dolní Dvořiště.

Documents

The Czech Republic recognises any foreign driving licence bearing a photograph of its owner; if yours doesn't, you should get an International Driving Permit. Drivers must also have their passport, vehicle registration papers and the 'green card' that shows they carry full liability insurance (see your domestic insurer about this). Without proof of insurance, you'll be forced to take out insurance at the border, for around 3000 Kč a month for a car or 600 Kč a month for a motorcycle. If the car isn't yours, avoid potential headaches by carrying a notarised letter from the owner saying you're allowed to drive it.

You must pay a tax to use most motorways and express roads in the Czech Republic; those sections that are free of the tax requirement are signposted *bez poplatku* (free of charge). A tax sticker, valid for the calendar year, is available at border posts, post offices, petrol stations and offices of ÚAMK (the Czech automobile and motorcycle club; see the Getting Around chapter). At the time of research the price of a sticker was 800 Kč for any vehicle (including towed trailer or caravan) up to 3500kg. The fine for not having a sticker is 5000 Kč.

Road Rules

As in the rest of Continental Europe, you drive on the right in the Czech Republic. The legal driving age is 18. Don't drink any alcohol if you'll be driving – regulations

Road Signs

Standard European signs are in common use. Intersections are frequently marked with only a small black-and-white sign showing which direction has the right of way. A yellow diamond on a white background indicates that you are on a main road and have the right of way; when the yellow diamond has a black slash across it you must give way to vehicles on your right, or to both left and right.

In cities and towns, watch out for *Pěší zóna* signs, which indicate pedestrian-only zones; there may be few other clues that you're not meant to be driving there.

Some signs that don't conform with international conventions include:

Průjezd zakázán – closed to all vehicles
Objížďka – detour
Jednosměrný provoz – one way
H or *Nemocnice* – hospital

permit no alcohol in the blood, and penalties are severe.

Speed limits vary in built-up areas from 40 to 50km/h between 5 am and 11 pm, up to 90km/h outside these hours. On major roads the maximum speed is 90km/h, and on motorways (freeways) 130km/h. Although the official speed limit at the country's many rail crossings is 30km/h, it's better to stop and look for coming trains, as many well used crossings have no barriers and some don't even have flashing lights.

If the car has seat belts, they must be worn by all passengers. Children under 12 years old aren't allowed in the front seat. Each vehicle must be equipped with a first-aid kit and two red-and-white warning triangles (to be set up behind and in front of your car if you break down). You must also display a sticker on the rear indicating the country of registration.

Riders of motorcycles over 50cc must wear helmets and goggles, and their passengers must wear helmets. Headlights must be switched on day and night. The maximum speed for motorcycles is 90km/h, and police make a point of booking foreign motorcyclists who keep up with cars on the motorways.

You may not overtake a tram, trolleybus or bus if it is stationary and there is no passenger island. In Prague you may only overtake trams on the right; anywhere else, you can do so on the left if it is not possible on the right.

Driving Offences On-the-spot fines for driving offences can run as high as 2000 Kč. Fines for foreigners are commonly inflated; if no docket/receipt (*paragon*) is given, it's possible you're being overcharged, so politely demand one.

Fuel

Petrol or gasoline (*benzín*) is widely available, but not all stations are open on Sunday (and after 6 pm on weeknights). Leaded petrol (*special* at 91 octane, *super* at 96 octane), unleaded petrol (*natural* at 95 and 98 octane) and diesel (*nafta*) are stocked by most petrol stations. At the time of writing, unleaded petrol was about 23 Kč per litre, diesel about 18.50 Kč. LPG (liquefied petroleum gas; about 12 Kč per litre) is available in every region but at a limited number of outlets.

See the Getting Around chapter for details about fuel in Prague.

HITCHING

Hitching is never entirely safe in any country in the world, and we don't recommend it. Travellers who decide to hitch should understand that they are taking a small but potentially serious risk. People who do choose to hitch will be safer if they travel in pairs and let someone know where they are planning to go.

TRAVEL AGENCIES

Following are the co-ordinates of some of the better Prague travel and sales agencies connected with international transportation. For packaged arrangements, see the Organised Tours section at the end of this chapter.

Čedok

Čedok, the former state tour operator and travel agency, is a good – if rather pricey and very busy – one-stop shop for excursions, and domestic and international travel bookings of all sorts (except the airport office, which is limited to upper-end accommodation and car rental). The main office is open weekdays from 8.30 am to 6 pm and Saturday from 9 am to 1 pm; and the others on weekdays from 9 am to 6 pm and Saturday from 9 am to noon.

Main Office, Na příkopě 18, Staré Město (Map 7; ☎ 24 19 71 11, fax 232 16 56, email overseas.incoming@cedok.cz)
Pařížská 6, Josefov (Map 7; ☎ 232 72 16)
Rytířská 16, Staré Město (Map 7; ☎ 26 09 74)
Malostranské náměstí 7, Malá Strana (Map 5; ☎ 57 17 59 59)
Ruzyně airport (☎ 36 78 02)

Representative offices abroad include:

France
(☎ 01 44 94 87 50) 32 Ave de l'Opéra, 75002 Paris
Netherlands
(☎ 020-622 48 88, fax 638 54 41) Kleine Gartmanplatzonen 21, 1017 RP Amsterdam
UK
(☎ 0171-839 4414, fax 839 0204; from 22 April 2000 ☎ 020-7839 4414, fax 7839 0204) 53-54 Haymarket, London SW1Y 4RP

CKM Travel

The former state-run youth-travel office, CKM, is now a series of unrelated (but co-operating) private agencies across the country. CKM Travel (Map 7; ☎ 26 84 31 for air tickets, ☎ 26 85 32 for other services, fax 26 86 23), Jindřišská 28, Nové Město, is a good place for youth, student and teacher cards, bus tickets, cheap air tickets and budget accommodation. It's open weekdays from 9 am to 1 pm and 1.30 to 6 pm, and on Saturday morning.

GTS International

GTS International, with a branch (Map 6; ☎ 22 21 15 04) at Ve Smečkách 27, and another (Map 7; ☎ 21 81 27 70) at Lodecká 3, sells youth and student cards, Eurolines and Busabout bus tickets, and train and air tickets.

ČD

The Czech Railways (ČD) agency (☎ 24 21 48 86) outside level 3 at the main train station, and a branch (☎ 24 61 70 66) at Holešovice train station, does domestic and international train bookings and tickets, and sells rail passes. The branch at the main station sells bus tickets and youth-price air tickets too, and accepts credit cards; there's also a glum, cash-only ČD office down in the main hall. All are open daily.

Eurolines Czech Republic

This agency, also called JUDr Jan Hofmann after the next-door parent agency, is the main Prague agent for the Eurolines bus consortium. The office (Map 7; ☎ 24 21 34 20, fax 24 21 08 35) is at Opletalova 37, opposite the main train station. A kiosk at the eastern end of the international coach stand (Map 1) – terminus for most Eurolines coaches – is open at least when Eurolines coaches are due in or out for the sale of any remaining tickets, though not for advance bookings.

Bohemiatour

Low-overhead Bohemiatour (Map 7; ☎ 231 25 89, fax 231 38 06), Zlatnická 7, Nové Město, sells international bus tickets and package tours.

Bohemia Euroexpress International

BEI (Map 1; ☎/fax 27 74 51), Koněvova 126, Prague 3 (take tram No 9 from Wenceslas Square), is the local outlet for a Czech coach line with services to and from the UK, the Netherlands, Germany, Italy and elsewhere in Europe. BEI's London affiliate is the Czech & Slovak Tourist Centre (☎ 0171-794 3263/4, fax 794 3265; from 22

April 2000 ☎ 020-7794 3263/4, fax 7794 3265; email cztc@cztc.demon.co.uk, Web site www.czech-slovak-tourist.co.uk).

Bohemian Express

This low-cost domestic and international coach line has its own agency (Map 8; ☎ 684 21, fax 684 09 97 48) at Sokolská 93, but Čedok, GTS, CKM and other travel agencies sell its tickets too. Don't confuse it with the Bohemian Lines agency a few doors down at No 103. Bohemian Express has a London office (☎ 0171-828 9008; from 22 April 2000 ☎ 020-7828 9008), as well as services to Belgium and Sweden.

Capital Express

Capital Express is a coach line with frequent London-Prague services, and a sales agency (Map 4; ☎ 87 03 68, fax 87 03 92, email capital@comp.cz) at U Výstaviště 3, Prague 7. Other travel agencies also sell its tickets. Its UK office (☎ 0171-243 0488, fax 727 3024; from 22 April 2000 ☎ 020-7243 0488, fax 7727 3024) is at 57 Princedale Rd, Holland Park, London W11 4NP.

Kingscourt Express

Kingscourt Express is another London-Prague coach line with a sales agency (Map 7; ☎ 24 23 45 83, fax 24 23 52 45) at Havelská 8, Staré Město. Its London office (freephone ☎ 0800-496 0001, ☎ 0181-673 7500, fax 673 3060; from 22 April 2000 ☎ 020-8673 7500, fax 8673 3060) is at 15 Balham High Rd, London SW12 9AJ.

Tourbus

Cheerful Tourbus (☎ 24 21 02 21), upstairs at Florenc bus station (Map 6), is open daily until 8 pm for domestic and international bus tickets, city travel passes, tours, telephone cards and some accommodation assistance. Tourbus is also an international coach line.

ORGANISED TOURS
From the Czech Republic

Čedok has the widest range of short trips and package tours of the Czech Republic, though generally at the highest prices. Their offices abroad (see Tourist Offices in the Facts for the Visitor chapter) can make the arrangements or identify local agencies who sell their packages. A local operator who does many of the same ones for a bit less money is Prague Sightseeing Tours (☎ 231 46 61).

Among Bohemia's more appealing destinations, Čedok and Prague Sightseeing Tours manage several on very long day trips by coach from Prague, for about 2000/1600 Kč each. They include trips west to the handsome spa town of Karlovy Vary; south to the home of the original Budvar (Budweiser) beer, České Budějovice; and to truly beautiful Český Krumlov, whose old centre is a UNESCO World Heritage Site, with a castle second only to Prague's. Čedok also offers golf and spa holidays, and escorted driving tours around the Czech and Slovak republics.

For offerings by Čedok and other operators in and around Prague, see the Getting Around chapter. For tour operators offering help to travellers with special requirements, see the Senior Travellers and Disabled Travellers sections in the Facts for the Visitor chapter.

From the UK

New Millennium (☎ 0121-711 2232, fax 711 3652) runs coach holidays to Prague starting at UK£154 per person for 10 days' bed & breakfast, and air holidays from UK£284 for eight days. Travelsphere (☎ 01858-410456, fax 432202) offers an eight day trip (three nights in Vienna and four in Prague) including flights, transfers and accommodation from UK£379.

Short breaks from Travelscene (information ☎ 0181-427 8800, reservations ☎ 427 4445, fax 861 3674; from 22 April 2000 information ☎ 020-8427 8800, reservations ☎ 8427 4445, fax 8861 3674) start at UK£299 for three nights or UK£367 for seven nights, with flight supplements of up to UK£144, depending on airport, airline and season. Another agency offering

Prague and multi-city breaks is Danube Travel (☎ 0171-493 0263, fax 493 6963; from 22 April 2000 ☎ 020-7493 0263, fax 7493 6963). Other short-break operators that are worth considering include Time Off (☎ 0990-846 3633) and Thomson Breakaway (☎ 0181-210 4500; from 22 April 2000 ☎ 020-8210 4500).

The cheerful, well connected Czech & Slovak Tourist Centre (☎ 0171-794 3263/4, fax 794 3265; from 22 April 2000 ☎ 020-7794 3263/4, fax 7794 3265; email cztc@cztc.demon.co.uk, Web site www .czech-slovak-tourist.co.uk) offers a wide range of travel packages, as well as various transport, accommodation, tour and other options.

Prague-related offerings from Martin Randall Travel (☎ 0181-742 3355, fax 742 7766; from 22 April 2000 ☎ 020-8742 3355, fax 8742 7766; email info@ martinrandall.co.uk) include a five to six day art tour guided by an art historian for around UK£900, and lecturer-accompanied music tours to the Prague Spring Festival for around UK£1300.

From the USA

American-International Homestays (☎ 303-642 3088, fax 642 3365, email ash@igc .apc.org, Web site www.commerce.com /homestays) organises multi-city homestays in which host families act as de facto guides to their city. The 17-day programmes (Prague plus Budapest, Kraków or Berlin) are US$2449 (including the air fare to/from New York) or US$1699 (without the air fare). Homestay tours with guides, local

transport, accommodation and dinner can also be arranged, as well as ordinary bed and breakfast accommodation.

From Australia

An agency in Australia organising Prague tours is Eastern Europe Travel Bureau (Sydney ☎ 02-9262 1144, fax 9262 4479, email eet@ausemail.com.au; Melbourne ☎ 03-9600 0299, fax 9670 1793). Packages start at A$438 for two, for five nights, including guided tours. They can also book homestays and apartments.

WARNING

The information in this chapter is particularly vulnerable to change: prices for international travel are volatile, routes are introduced and cancelled, schedules change, special deals come and go, and rules and visa requirements are amended. Airlines and governments seem to take a perverse pleasure in making price structures and regulations as complicated as possible. You should check directly with the airline or a travel agency to make sure you understand how a fare (and any ticket you may buy) works. In addition, the travel industry is highly competitive and there are many lurks and perks.

The upshot of this is that you should get opinions, quotes and advice from as many airlines and travel agencies as possible before you part with your hard-earned cash. The details given in this chapter should be regarded as pointers and are not a substitute for your own careful, up-to-date research.

Getting Around

Prague's compact historical centre (Hradčany, Malá Strana, Staré Město and Nové Město) is best appreciated on foot, with the help of cheap, widespread public transport. Pollution, traffic congestion and traffic vibration damage to old buildings have led to the creation of pedestrian-only zones, and restrictions on vehicle traffic.

THE AIRPORT

Just before passport control is a small currency exchange window of the commercial bank IPB, open daily from 8 am to 5 pm with the best terms of any bank in Prague at the time of writing. In the baggage claim hall are more exchanges, and an AVE accommodation agency. In the arrivals hall are numerous ATMs, a 24 hour left-luggage office, a ČSA lost & found (☎ 20 11 42 83) – supposedly open 24 hours but closed when we arrived – and several pricey car rental agencies.

Alas, information is scarce at the airport. A Čedok desk (☎ 36 78 02) offers little apart from upper-end accommodation and car rental. Several other 'Information' windows mainly dispense flight information. PIS, the Prague Information Service, is conspicuously absent.

TO/FROM THE AIRPORT

City bus No 119 runs about every 10 minutes all day (less often on weekends) between the airport and Dejvická metro station; bus No 254 also makes the trip, but less often. It takes about 45 minutes, including the metro trip, to/from the city centre. At the airport, buy a 12 Kč bus ticket from the lobby newsstand or from machines at the bus stand, in the third rank in front of the arrivals hall. Tickets are not sold on the bus. Buses Nos 179 and 225 link the airport with Nové Butovice metro station, in the south-west outskirts.

Minibuses of the private operator Welcome Touristic Praha depart on the hour and half-hour between 7.30 am and 6.30 pm from in front of the ČSA Service Centre (Map 7; ☎ 20 10 46 20) at V celnici 5 (from the airport from 8.30 am to 7 pm). The fare is 95 Kč; buy tickets on board. They also stop at the Hotel Diplomat, near Dejvická metro station.

Microbuses of Cedaz (☎ 20 11 42 96) depart on the hour and half-hour from 5.30 am to 9.30 pm from náměstí Republiky (6 am to 9 pm from the airport), also collecting passengers on Evropská, near Dejvická metro station. The fare is 90 Kč, with tickets from the driver. Cedaz also runs vans to specific addresses, taxi-style – a good deal if there are enough of you: 360 Kč for up to four or 720 Kč for five to eight people to the centre, or 720 Kč for up to eight people to more distant points.

A private taxi company, Fix Car (☎ 20 11 38 92, and with a desk in the terminal), runs officially sanctioned taxis with polite drivers. A carload (up to four people) is 500 Kč to hotels around Malá Strana and Old Town Square, or higher fixed fares to more distant points. They charge 20% less for the return trip to the airport.

Prague's notoriously unscrupulous ordinary taxis will also take you to the airport, for perhaps 20% less if you're lucky. They cannot collect passengers at the airport arrivals hall.

PUBLIC TRANSPORT

Big-city transport is rarely a joy to travel on, but Prague's system is cheap, extensive and increasingly user-friendly, with detailed information at well marked stops, recorded next-stop information on many buses and trams, and good maps.

Information

The city transport department (Dopravní podnik, or DP; ☎ 96 19 31 32, 96 19 31 29 or 96 19 20 33) has information offices in four metro stations: Muzeum and Můstek

GETTING AROUND

(open daily from 7 am to 9 pm) and Karlovo Náměstí and Nádraží Holešovice (to 6 pm only). Here you can get tickets, directions, a multilingual system map (35 Kč), a map of night services (*Noční provoz*), and a detailed and useful guide to the whole system.

PIS (see Tourist Offices in the Facts for the Visitor chapter) has an English-language *Transport* brochure with much the same information as DP's, plus a transport map showing metro, bus and tram lines (but unnumbered) out to the city limits.

Tickets & Passes

A ticket (*jízdenka*) for one journey by metro, tram, bus or the Petřín funicular (see the Things to See & Do chapter) is 12 Kč, or half-price for six to 15-year-olds, as well as for large luggage and bicycles. Kids under six years ride free. Validate (punch) your ticket by sticking it in the little yellow machine in the metro station lobby or on the bus or tram. Once validated, tickets can be used for 60 minutes on weekdays from 5 am to 8 pm, and for 90 minutes from 8 pm to midnight and on weekends. Unlimited transfers are allowed on all types of public transport.

There's also a short-hop 8 Kč ticket, good for 15 minutes on buses and trams, or for up to four metro stations. No transfers are allowed with these, and they're not valid on the Petřín funicular nor on night trams or buses.

Tickets are sold from machines in metro stations, individually or in discounted books at newsstands, Trafiky snack shops, PNS and other tobacco kiosks, all metro station ticket offices, and DP information offices.

Passes Various DP travel passes are good for unlimited travel on the entire system – though you may find they aren't very good value unless you hate walking or are staying outside the centre. A short-term season ticket (*jízdenka síťová*), good for one/three/ seven/15 days, is 70/180/250/280 Kč from ticket outlets and PIS offices. It's not valid

until you fill in your name and birthdate, and punch it in the machine at its first use.

Long-term visitors can get a one/three/ 12 calendar month season pass (*měsíční jíz-denka*) for 380/1000/3400 Kč. To get one, bring your passport and a passport-size photo to DP headquarters at Na bojišti 5, near metro station IP Pavlova (Map 8); any DP information office; or any of about half the city's metro stations (ideally up to the 8th or from the 25th of any month).

Prague Card This three day pass, geared toward tourists, is valid for transport on the whole DP system, plus entry to most of the city's museums and state-run galleries. It costs 480 Kč (children 380 Kč) at CKM Travel, Čedok, American Express and a few other travel agencies (see Travel Agencies in the Getting There & Away chapter).

Inspectors Inspectors pounce frequently and will fine you 200 Kč on the spot if you don't have a signed pass or a validated ticket. A dumb-foreigner act rarely cuts any ice with them. At such miniscule prices, cheating is pretty silly in any case.

Tram & Bus

The metro is quickest over the territory it covers, but trams are much more relaxed, and buses cover all the areas that trams miss. Most trams and buses operate daily from 4.30 am to 12.15 am. Routes and

Vintage Trams

On weekends and holidays between April and October, vintage tram cars trundle around a special sightseeing route, No 91. Starting from Malostranské náměstí every hour from 1.10 to 7.10 pm, they loop round via the National Theatre, Wenceslas Square, Masarykovo train station and the Fairgrounds (Výstaviště), for 15 Kč (kids 7 Kč). Ordinary tickets and passes cannot be used on this line. Call ☎ 312 3349 for more information.

schedules are posted at each stop. Tram-line numbers have one or two digits, buses three (suburban bus numbers start with '3').

There is a limited night service (at 40-minute intervals) on certain lines from midnight to 5 am: tram Nos 51 to 58 all pass the corner of Lazarská and Spálená (north of Karlovo náměstí; Map 6) so you can transfer from one tram to another, or to any of bus Nos 501 to 512, which connect with the trams here. Night services are indicated by reverse-colour signs at stops.

Metro (Map 2)

Like other Soviet-designed underground systems, Prague's 43 station, 44km network is reliable, efficient and clean. Trains run from 5 am to midnight daily. User-friendly maps and diagrams make the system easy to understand for non-Czech-speakers.

A polite recorded voice announces each station. At the station, it warns: *Ukončete výstup a nástup, dveře se zavírají* (Finish getting on and off, the doors are closing). As the train pulls away, it says: *Příští stanice ...* (The next station is ...), perhaps noting that it's a *přestupní stanice* (transfer station). When you disembark, signs point you towards the *výstup* (exit) or to a *přestup* (connecting line).

At the time of research, a three station extension of the B-line (in the north-eastern outskirts, Prague 9 and 14) was on the verge of opening.

CAR & MOTORCYCLE

Driving in Prague is no fun. Trying to find your way around – or to park legally – while coping with trams, buses, other drivers, cyclists and pedestrians, and police on the lookout for a little handout, can make you wish you'd left the car at home.

You can ease the trauma by avoiding weekday peak-traffic hours: in central Prague from 4 pm onwards (on Friday from as early as 2 pm). Try not to arrive in or leave the city on a Friday or Sunday after-noon or evening, when half the population

seems to head to/from their *chaty* (weekend houses).

Most Old Town streets are narrow, and many are cobbled. Central Prague has many pedestrian-only streets, including parts of Wenceslas Square, Na příkopě, 28.října, most of Old Town Square and some streets leading into it. Most are marked with *Pěší zóna* (Pedestrian Zone) signs, and only service vehicles and taxis have special permits to drive in these areas.

PIS's *Transport* brochure has much useful information for drivers, including emergency breakdown services, where to find car repair shops (according to make) and all-important parking tips. For general information about driving in the Czech Republic, including border crossings, documents and road rules, see Car & Motorcycle in the Getting There & Away chapter.

Parking

Parking in most of Prague 1 is regulated with permit-only and parking-meter zones. Meter fees are around 30 to 40 Kč per hour, with time limits from two to six hours. Traffic inspectors willingly hand out fines, clamp wheels or tow away vehicles. Parking in one-way streets is normally only allowed on the right-hand side.

There are several parking lots at the edges of the Old Town and around the outer city (most are marked on the 1:20,000 Kartografie Praha and Žaket city maps). On average the fee is around 30 Kč for the first hour or 340 Kč for 24 hours. Public transport between these lots and the centre is good.

Underground parking lots include:

Main train station (Bolzanova; Wilsonova)
Kotva department store (náměstí Republiky)
Hotel Inter-Continental (Pařížská)
State Opera Theatre (Wilsonova)
Konstruktiva (under náměstí Jana Palacha)
Tržnice Smíchov (náměstí 14.října, Prague 5)

Guarded parking lots include:

Masarykovo railway station (Na Florenci)
Náplavka (corner of Na Františku and Revoluční)

National Theatre (Divadelní)
Hotel Opera (Těšnov)
Malostranské náměstí (Malá Strana)

Car Theft

A western car with foreign plates is a prime target for thieves, especially in central Prague, though the chances of theft are no higher than in the west. Older Czech cars are also getting popular, for the domestic spare-parts market, as are smaller items such as windscreen wipers, antennas and car emblems. Of course, don't leave your possessions visible in the vehicle.

Passing Trams

In Prague you may overtake a tram only on the right, and only if it's in motion. You must stop for any tram taking on or letting off passengers where there's no passenger island. A tram has the right of way when making any signalled turn across your path. For more road rules, see the Getting There & Away chapter.

Fuel

Leaded and unleaded fuel are available from all Prague petrol stations, and diesel at most of them. There is at least one round-the-clock station on every major highway and road in and out of Prague. LPG gas is more of a problem: we found 25 stations selling it, but only five (see Map 1) are legal operations. These are:

(☎ 684 81 13) corner of Habrová and Na Jarově, Jarov, Prague 3
(☎ 683 00 51) Voctářova (behind the tennis courts), Libeň, Prague 8
(☎ 82 91 63) Novovysočanská 2740/28, Na krejcárku, Prague 9 (open 24 hours)
(☎ 66 03 58 81) Českomoravská (near the intersection with Sokolovská), Na Balabence, Prague 9
(☎ 66 03 56 28) Na Harfě 14 (off Českomoravská opposite the Praha-Libeň train station), Vysočany, Prague 9 (open 24 hours)

Emergencies

In case of an accident the police should be contacted immediately if damage exceeds about 1000 Kč (US$30). Even if damage is slight, if you're driving your own car it's a good idea to report the accident to the police, who can issue a certificate that will help you avoid headaches when you take the car out of the country.

For emergency service ÚAMK, the Czech automobile and motorcycle club (also called Automoto-klub), provides nationwide assistance. Its 24-hour service numbers for the so-called 'Yellow Angels' (Žlutý anděl) are ☎ 123 from Prague or ☎ 0 123 from the rest of the Czech Republic. The ÚAMK Prague office (Map 1; ☎ 61 10 43 33) is on Na strži 9, Nusle, Prague 4. Autoturist (Map 7; ☎ 24 22 59 18), náměstí Republiky 6, is a travel agency that promotes ÚAMK and its services.

ÚAMK has agreements with numerous national auto and tourist clubs, the Alliance Internationale de Tourisme and the Fédération Internationale de l'Automobile. If you're a member of any of these, ÚAMK will help you on roughly the same terms as your own club would. If not, you must pay for all services.

The emergency number ☎ 154 is for a towing and road assistance service, to which several private towing companies belong. The ☎ 123 and ☎ 154 numbers normally go through the same switchboard.

Another outfit offering round-the-clock repair services is Autoklub Bohemia Assistance or ABA, also known as Autoklub české republiky (☎ 124 from Prague, ☎ 0 124 from outside Prague). Their information centre (Map 6; ☎ 26 14 91) is at Opletalova 29.

Repairs

Spare parts (other than for Škodas) can be hard to find, but most well known models can be repaired at a basic level by at least one garage in Prague. Repair shops for major foreign brands include:

Daewoo, Subaru
    Avanti Car (☎ 54 61 26)
    Nádražní 54, Smíchov, Prague 5
Fiat
    Autocentrum Dojáček (☎ 72 03 47)
    U seřadiště 7, Vršovice, Prague 10

Ford
    Ford Charouz (☎ 70 65 40)
    Černokostelecká 116, Prague 4
Peugeot
    (☎ 782 15 00) Novostrašnická 46, Prague 10
Nissan, Ford
    (☎ 76 67 53) Severní XI-1/2458, Prague 4
Renault
    (☎ 88 73 03) Ďáblická 2, Prague 8
Volkswagen, Audi
    Verold-Autocentrum (☎ 57 21 16 48)
    Mezi lány 22, Jinonice, Prague 5
Most models
    Uni Car Service (☎ 0602 31 76 86)
    Dudkova 187, Prague 9

Car Rental

Some local car-hire companies with similar selections are as follows. Typical rates for a Škoda Felicie at the time of writing were 400 to 600 Kč per day plus 2 to 3 Kč per kilometre; or 700 to 750 Kč per day plus about 2 Kč per kilometre beyond 200km; or 13,000 to 15,000 Kč per month plus about 2 Kč per kilometre beyond 4000km.

Autopůjčovna Mostex
    (☎ 627 84 26) Pražská 16, Prague 10
Discar Marcel Vlasák
    (☎ 687 05 23) Hovorčovice 192, Prague 9
Josef Stašek – Půjčovna osobních automobilů
    (☎ 20 97 20 49 or 0602-30 82 21)
    Horoměřice 194, Prague 6
Secco Car
    (☎ 80 06 47 or 684 34 03) Přístavní 39,
    Prague 7; deposit required

Mainstream agencies range from A-Rent Car/Thrifty and Europcar at 2000 Kč per day to Avis and Hertz at 3000 Kč and up per day (all with unlimited mileage). All have airport pick-up points (where you pay an extra 300 Kč surcharge) as well as central offices:

A-Rent Car/Thrifty
    (Map 6; ☎ 24 22 98 48) Washingtonova 9
Avis
    (Map 7; ☎ 21 85 12 25) Klimentská 46
Budget
    (Map 7; ☎ 24 88 99 95) Hotel Inter-
    Continental, Pařížská

CS-Czechocar
    (Map 7; ☎ 21 63 74 23/24 or 61 17 32 08)
    Na příkopě 23, Rathova passage
Europcar
    (Map 7; ☎ 24 81 05 15) Pařížská 28
Hertz
    (Map 6; ☎ 42 12 28 42) Karlovo náměstí 28

TAXI

Prague is plagued with unscrupulous cabbies, weakly regulated. Hailing a taxi on the street, at least in a tourist zone, is inviting trouble, and the taxi stands around Wenceslas Square, Národní (Národní třída) and Old Town Square are notorious for rip-offs; even Czechs are not safe. Getting a driver to use his meter is like getting blood from a stone. It's a pity, because an honest taxi fare is good value.

The city government mounted a major effort to regulate the trade, but it foundered when taxi companies filed suit, crying that their rights were being trampled. Only on the matter of taxis *from* the airport did the city prevail, so that while disoriented new arrivals still pay over the odds, the drivers are fairly honest. Elsewhere it's still a jungle, and fresh paint, roof lights and checker stripes are no guarantee of honesty.

You're much better off calling a radio-taxi, as they're better regulated and more responsible. From our experience the following companies, all with 24 hour service, have honest drivers, some of whom speak a little English:

AAA Radio Taxi   (☎ 1080 or 32 24 44)
Cedaz   (☎ 20 11 42 96)
Fix Car   (☎ 20 11 38 92)
Profitaxi   (☎ 1035 or 61 31 41 11)

If you insist on flagging a taxi, ask the approximate fare in advance and ask the driver to use the meter (*zapněte taximetr, prosím*). If it's 'broken', find someone else. If you get the rare driver who willingly turns on the meter, he probably deserves a tip just for that.

At the time of writing, the maximum rate was 25 Kč flag fall plus 17 Kč per kilometre, or 4 Kč per minute while it's stalled in traffic or waits while you enjoy the view. On this basis, some honest fares from Wenceslas Square are: main train station, 65 Kč; Malostranské náměstí, 100 Kč; Vyšehrad, 110 Kč; and the city zoo, 160 Kč. Journeys outside Prague are not regulated.

Regulations say the meter must be zeroed when you get in, and fares must be displayed. At the end of the journey the driver must give you a meter-printed receipt showing company name, taxi ID number, date and times of the journey, end points, rates, the total, the driver's name and his signature. Get one before you pay, and make sure it has all these things in case you want to make a claim.

There's no telephone number you can use for complaints. To complain, go to the Revenue Department at City Hall (Map 7), Platnéřská 19. The city publishes *Taxi Service in Prague*, a multilingual and annually updated brochure with useful tips for both visitors and residents alike. Unfortunately it's not available at the airport, but you can get one from PIS.

BOAT

From April to October, water level and weather permitting, cruise boats of Prague Passenger Shipping or PPS (☎ 29 83 09 or 90 00 08 22) chug up and down the Vltava from the central quay (*centrální přístaviště*; Map 9), near Karlovo náměstí metro station.

Most photogenic is a two hour jaunt north to Hradčany and south to Vyšehrad, daily at 3.30 pm, for 200 Kč. A one hour, 150 Kč trip runs hourly from the National Theatre to Vyšehrad, from 10 am to 8 pm from May to September, and from 2 to 6 pm in April and October. On weekends and holidays (plus Friday from early June to mid-September) at 9 am, a boat goes 37km south (upstream) through a wild, green landscape to Štěchovice, almost to the big dam at Slapy, arriving back at 6.30 pm. This fine escape is 150 Kč return.

Other sailings go up and down the river while you lunch, snack or dine expensively on board.

Shorter trips to the zoo and Troja chateau (10km, 1¼ hours each way, 40 Kč return) depart at 9.30 am and 1.30 pm, on weekends and holidays in April, and daily from May to September. Morning departures can be choked with school groups, and a more peaceful alternative is bus No 112 from Nádraží Holešovice metro station, and the boat back at 11 am or 5 pm. The boats also stop at Kampa, Čechův most, Nádraží Holešovice and Císařský ostrov.

PPS has a longer season from the Kampa landing next to Charles Bridge, with 50-minute, 200 Kč cruises every hour: from 11 am to 8 pm, June to September; from 11 am to 6 pm in May; and from noon to 5 pm, March to April and October to December.

Excursions of Evropská vodní doprava or EVD (Map 7; ☎ 231 02 08), which leave from a landing behind the Hotel Inter-Continental, include a one hour tour (200 Kč) each hour from 10 am to 6 pm daily, a two hour tour including lunch and music (550 Kč) and an evening tour with dinner and music (650 Kč).

All river transport stops in winter.

Boat Rental

If you just want a quiet float on the river, rent a rowing boat (about 40 Kč an hour) or pedal-boat (50 Kč) from one of three places on the north end of Slovanský ostrov (Map 6); from another north of Charles Bridge at the end of Platnéřská (Map 7); or at the back of Klub Lávka on Novotného lávka (Map 7). You can't take these boats beyond the upstream and downstream weirs.

From the Posezení na řece café on Slovanský ostrov you can tootle between the weirs for 45 minutes in a 12 seat cruise boat, if there are enough people to fill it. The price is 80 Kč per person, and trips can be booked through Beta-tour (☎ 0602 26 78 40 or 24 91 81 35).

BICYCLE

Prague is not a brilliant place to ride a bike. Traffic is heavy, pollution can be choking and there are no bicycle lanes. The cobblestones in older streets will loosen your teeth, and tram tracks are treacherous, especially when wet.

You'll need a good lock for wheels and frame: western bikes are a popular target. Spare parts are available in the city's many bike shops, but scarcer outside Prague.

If you're at least 12 years old you can take your bicycle on the metro for an extra 6 Kč. You must keep it near the last door of the rear carriage, and only two bikes are allowed in. You can't do it from 5.30 to 8.30 am and from 2.30 to 5.30 pm on working days, nor at any time when the carriage is full, nor if there's already a pram in the carriage.

Bicycle Rental

The only place we could find that rents bicycles to the public is A Landa (Map 10; ☎ 24 25 61 21), Šumavská 33, Prague 2. Mountain bikes are around 150 Kč per day or 100 Kč per day for more than three days. Some major hotels occasionally rent bicycles to their guests.

Resources

For its members, the Cyclists' Touring Club in the UK (CTC; ☎ 01483-417217, fax 426994, email cycling@ctc.org.uk, Web site www.ctc.org.uk) publishes a free information pack on cycling in the Czech and Slovak republics. CTC also offers tips on bikes, spares, insurance etc, and can put you in touch with others who've cycled there.

ORGANISED TOURS

Čedok has a selection of foreign-language city tours and out-of-city excursions, which can be arranged at any of its city-centre offices (see Travel Agencies in the Getting There & Away chapter). Many of the tours offered by upper-end hotels and travel agencies are just Čedok's with extra fees added on.

The Old Town Hall and Na příkopě branches of PIS (see Tourist Offices in the Facts for the Visitor chapter) also sell tours and excursions, and the operators – including Premiant City Tour (☎ 24 23 00 72) and

Prague Sightseeing Tours (☎ 231 46 61) – also hawk them directly on the street.

All the tours look the same: such as a basic two hour bus tour for about 350 Kč, a 3½ hour combined bus and walking tour for about 650 Kč, or a three hour Old Prague on Foot tour for 300 Kč. All the operators offer river cruises too – though you can do these more cheaply on your own (see the earlier Boat section). Čedok's packages are consistently more expensive than the others. Best Tour, based at the Hotel Meran, Wenceslas Square 27, runs a three hour city tour for 530 Kč.

PIS's Pragotur affiliate provides walk-in guide services from a desk (☎ 24 48 25 62, fax 24 48 23 80) at the Old Town Hall PIS office, weekdays from 9 am to 6 pm (by telephone from 8 am) and weekends from 9 am to 4 pm. At the time of research, rates for a three hour spin were 800 Kč for one or two people, plus 300 Kč per additional person. From its office (Map 6; ☎ 24 81 61 20, fax 24 81 61 72) at Za Poříčskou branou 7, open on weekdays, Pragotur also offers pre-booked tours.

Another PIS affiliate, Prague History (Pražská vlastivěda; ☎ 231 11 27 or 24 81 61 84), offers a monthly 'menu' of first-rate tours of historical places often skipped by other operators or off-limits to the public. The tours are in Czech but a translator can be arranged. They're based at the Pragotur office.

Another vendor of unconventional tours is Prague Walks (☎ 61 21 46 03). Look for their flyers in hotels and at the PIS offices, announcing meeting points for 1½ to two-hour jaunts like Velvet Revolution Walk, Žižkov Pub Walk and Ghost Tour, each for about 250 Kč.

Excursions

The same agencies that do city tours also run half and full-day coach excursions outside Prague on selected days; such as Konopiště (four hours, about 800 Kč), and Karlštejn or Kutná Hora (4½ hours, 850 Kč). Best Tour (see the preceding section)

offers a four hour afternoon bus tour to Karlštejn for 790 Kč.

Central European Adventures has one-day guided bicycle tours around Karlštejn and Koněprusy (daily except Monday, 680 Kč) and guided canoe tours on the Beroun-ka River (weekends, 810 Kč). Buy tickets at PIS offices, and meet them by the astronomical clock on the Old Town Square at 8.30 am.

On a more serious mission is the Matana travel agency (Map 7; ☎ 232 19 54, ☎/fax 232 10 49, email matana@ms.anet.cz, Web site www.tours.cz/matana), Maiselova 15, with historical tours to places of interest to Jewish visitors, including Prague's Josefov district and Terezín (see the Excursions chapter). All revenues go towards supporting the activities of Prague's small Jewish community, including social work and the reconstruction of property returned after 1989.

Things to See & Do

THINGS TO SEE & DO

Prague's prime attraction is its physical face. The city centre is a haphazard museum of some 900 years of architecture – stodgy Romanesque, sublime Gothic, handsome Renaissance, dazzling baroque, 19th century revivals of all of them, and mouthwatering Art Nouveau – all amazingly undisturbed by the 20th century and folded into a compact network of lanes, passages and culs-de-sac.

Also on offer is a heady menu of entertainment: classical music, from world-class festivals to tourist concerts in every other church; opera and ballet; avant-garde

Highlights

The historical core of the city – Hradčany (the Castle District) and Malá Strana (the Small Quarter) west of the river, Staré Město (the Old Town) and Václavské náměstí (Wenceslas Square) to the east, and Charles Bridge between – covers only about 3 sq km and is pedestrian-friendly, so you can see a lot even on a short visit.

Concerts
The finest places to see a classical music concert are the Rudolfinum, and Smetana Hall in the Obecní dům. In summer, chamber concerts are held in many halls and churches; equally impressive are organ recitals, for which St James Church is said to have the best acoustics.

Museums
If you like museums, don't miss the amazing model of 19th century Prague at the Museum of the City of Prague in northern Nové Město. The best of the permanent collections of the National Gallery are those of modern Czech art and 19th and 20th century French art at the Trade Fair Palace in Holešovice; of 19th century Czech painting and sculpture at the Convent of St Agnes in Staré Město; and of Gothic and Renaissance art at the Convent of St George in Prague Castle.

Architectural Highlights
The city's best standing Romanesque structure is the Basilica of St George in Prague Castle. The eastern wing of St Vitus Cathedral, one of Europe's finest churches, is the clear winner in the Gothic category. The Summer (or Belvedere) Palace at Hradčany is certainly the finest Renaissance building.

Of Prague's many baroque masterpieces, one of the most elegant exteriors is the almost rococo façade of the Kinský Palace on Old Town Square, while St Nicholas Church in Malá Strana draws fans of baroque from all over Europe.

The city has a high concentration of fine Art Nouveau buildings; top of the line, inside and out, is the Obecní dům (Municipal House).

Cubism found its architectural voice in Prague; there are more Cubist buildings here than in any other city in the world. Some striking façades are at Celetná 34 in Staré Město, at Neklanova 30 near Vyšehrad, and Tychonova 4-6 in Dejvice.

Rising above Prague's mostly humdrum modern architecture is the extraordinary (and controversial) Dancing Building on Rašínovo nábřeží in Nové Město.

79

drama; jazz and rock; a few excellent museums; and dozens of art galleries. There are some good restaurants, and plenty of ordinary ones full of good cheer and world-famous Czech beer. Within reach as day trips are a dozen medieval chateaux and castles.

Prague's greatest *dis*traction is that it's now one of Europe's most popular tourist destinations, and choked with summer crowds.

Most (but not all) state-run museums and galleries are closed on Monday, while the Old Jewish Cemetery and the synagogues of Josefov are closed to the public on Saturday. Most museums and some sights charge a nominal admission fee of around 30 to 40 Kč, and galleries typically charge about 100 Kč, except where noted in this chapter. Youth and student discounts are often available if you ask; though there are some reductions for seniors, they're for residents only.

SUGGESTED ITINERARIES

If you're on a weekend break, a walk down the Royal Way (Královská cesta) – the route of ancient coronation processions – takes in the best of the city's architectural treasures, beginning with Prague Castle and St Vitus Cathedral. From the castle, descend to St Nicholas Church, the centrepiece of Malá Strana. After lunch, make your way across Charles Bridge and through the backstreets of Staré Město to Old Town Square. Next day, see the Old Jewish Cemetery and return to Old Town Square – the view from the Old Town Hall tower and a look inside Týn Church are recommended. Don't miss the striking of the town hall's Astronomical Clock. Complete the Royal Way down Celetná to the Powder Tower, stopping to look inside St James Church and the beautiful Obecní dům (Municipal House). Return along Na příkopě to historic Wenceslas Square.

On a longer stay, linger in Hradčany to see Strahov Monastery, the Loreta and the Summer Palace, and climb Petřín Hill for a splendid view over the city. In Josefov, go inside the Old-New Synagogue; in Nové Město, stroll down Národní (Národní třída) to the National Theatre; and take a few hours to lose yourself in Staré Město's backstreets. It's also worth riding a tram or the metro south to the ancient stronghold of Vyšehrad.

Prague Castle

Prague Castle (Pražský hrad, or just *hrad* to Czechs) is the most popular and visited sight in Prague. According to the *Guinness Book of Records*, it's the largest ancient castle in the world – 570m long, an average of 128m wide and occupying 7.28 hectares.

Its history starts in the 9th century when Prince Bořivoj founded a fortified settlement here. It grew as rulers made their own additions, which explains its mixture of styles. The castle has always been the seat of Czech rulers, as well as the official residence, although the current president, Václav Havel, has chosen to live in his own house on the outskirts of the city.

Prague Castle has had four major reconstructions, from that of Prince Soběslav in the 12th century to a classical facelift under Empress Maria Theresa. In the 1920s President Masaryk hired a Slovene architect, Josef Plečnik, to renovate the castle.

FIRST COURTYARD

On either side of the main gate are the *Battling Titans* by Ignác Platzer (1767-70). Below them stand the castle guards, who are posted at the main gate and the east gate. President Havel hired the costume designer for the film *Amadeus* to replace their Communist-era khaki uniforms with the present ones, reminiscent of the early Czechoslovak Republic. A favourite sport of younger tourists is to get them to crack a smile, which they do now and then.

Knots of castle guards march across the grounds from time to time. At the main gate, the guard is changed on the hour. The longest and most impressive display is at noon, with an exchange of banners, while a

The night lights of Prague Castle and Charles Bridge from across the Vltava

Pastel façades on the southern side of the Old Town Square

Malá Strana in winter: icy quiet on Čertovka ...

... and snow-sprinkled rooftops

Castle Hours, Services & Approaches

In some ways Prague Castle is a mini-town, with many services within its walls. The grounds are open year-round, daily from 5 am to midnight (from 6 am to 11 pm from November to March). The gardens are open daily from 10 am to 6 pm (the Royal Gardens and those south of the castle buildings are closed in winter). Admission to the grounds and gardens is free. Most sights inside are open from 9 am to 5 pm (in winter to 4 pm), and most exhibition halls from 10 am to 6 pm, though hours vary.

Arrive early or late to beat the crowds and the heat. Courtyards are hot and shadeless on a summer day, so a hat and water are recommended too.

Orientation & Information

The castle's own information centre (☎ 24 37 33 68 or 24 37 24 34, concert information ☎ 24 37 23 64) is in the third courtyard, opposite the main entrance to St Vitus Cathedral. It's open daily from 9 am to 5 pm (in winter to 4 pm). Here you can get a free castle map and buy a 100 Kč ticket (50 Kč for children aged six to 15 and students), good for entry to all the castle's attractions except the Lobkowicz Palace (National Museum) and Burgrave's Palace (Toy Museum). You can also buy this general ticket at major buildings within the castle. It's valid for three days, so you don't have to cram everything into a single visit.

Guides speaking English or other languages are available for an extra fee, or you can rent your own 'Audio Guide' cassette.

The information office has a free multilingual quarterly programme with mini-features and information on exhibitions and other events at the castle. At the Chapel of the Holy Cross in the second courtyard is a box office, open daily from 9 am to 4.45 pm. For further information on concerts in the castle, call ☎ 24 37 23 64.

A post office is next to the information office. Česká Spořitelná banka has an ATM in the information office. Chequepoint exchange bureaux in the box office and near the post office take a very stiff 10% commission.

Emergency

The castle police station is at Vikářská, though its main function is to look after the president and the castle. For other matters (such as theft on the castle grounds) you must visit the main city police station at Konviktská 14 in Staré Město.

Food

See the Places to Eat chapter for eating options in and near the castle.

Approach Routes

The main approaches to the castle are from the trams in Malostranské náměstí – up Nerudova and Ke Hradu, or up Thunovská and the Castle Steps (Zámecké schody) – to the main gate; and from Malostranská metro station, up the Old Castle Steps (Staré zámecké schody) and through the eastern gate.

All are hard work on a hot day, and none is suitable for a wheelchair. An entrance with almost no climbing is from the north, along U Prašného mostu from the Pražský hrad stop of tram No 22. Catch this tram (northbound) at Malostranské náměstí or at Malostranská metro station.

PRAGUE CASTLE

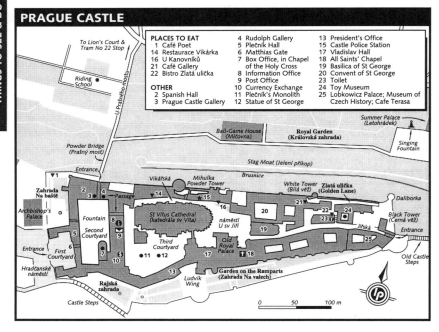

PLACES TO EAT
1 Café Poet
14 Restaurace Vikárka
16 U Kanovníků
21 Café Gallery
22 Bistro Zlatá ulička

OTHER
2 Spanish Hall
3 Prague Castle Gallery

4 Rudolph Gallery
5 Plečník Hall
6 Matthias Gate
7 Box Office, in Chapel of the Holy Cross
8 Information Office
9 Post Office
10 Currency Exchange
11 Plečník's Monolith
12 Statue of St George

13 President's Office
15 Castle Police Station
17 Vladislav Hall
18 All Saints' Chapel
19 Basilica of St George
20 Convent of St George
23 Toilet
24 Toy Museum
25 Lobkowicz Palace; Museum of Czech History; Cafe Terasa

six piece brass band plays a fanfare from the windows of Plečník Hall (Plečníkova síň).

The pointy flagpoles in the first courtyard are among Plečník's controversial 1920s additions.

SECOND COURTYARD

The second courtyard is entered through the baroque **Matthias Gate** (Matyášova brána; 1614). The Spanish Hall (Španělský sál) and Rudolf Gallery (Rudolfova galérie) are among the castle's finest buildings, but like all the others in the western end of the castle they're only for state use.

The **Chapel of the Holy Cross** (kaple sv Kříže; 1763) on the right was once the treasury of St Vitus Cathedral. In the middle of the courtyard is a baroque fountain and a 17th century well with Renaissance lattice work.

At the northern end of the courtyard is the **Prague Castle Gallery** (Obrazárno Pražského hradu), which is open daily from 10 am to 6 pm. Exhibits include examples of 16th and 17th century European and Czech paintings and sculpture.

The **Imperial Stables** (Cisařská konírna), opposite the passage leading to the Prague Castle Gallery, has good temporary art exhibits. It's open Tuesday to Sunday from 10 am to 6 pm.

Powder Bridge Street (U Prašného Mostu)

A detour past the gallery crosses the Powder Bridge (Prašný most), built in 1540. The Stag Moat (Jelení příkop) below it was later used for raising game animals, hence the name. Today it's open to the public. On the outer north wall, overlooking the moat, is a gate into a bomb shelter started by the

Communists in the 1950s but never completed. Its tunnels run under most parts of the castle.

Royal Garden (Královská Zahrada)

This garden, on the far side of the Stag Moat, started as a Renaissance garden built by Ferdinand I in 1534. To the left of the entrance from U Prašného mostu is the Lion's Court (Lví dvorek), named after the lions and other animals that were once kept here, in Prague's first private zoo.

The most beautiful of the garden's buildings is the **Ball-Game House** (Míčovna; 1569), but it's only open for exhibitions. The Habsburgs played an early version of badminton here. Eastwards is a well kept park popular for its azaleas and tulips – it was from here, Europe's first tulip garden, that tulips went to the Netherlands – and the bronze Singing Fountain (Zpívající fontána).

Beyond this is the **Summer Palace** (Letohrádek), sometimes (although incorrectly) called the Belvedere Palace. Built from 1538 to 1564, this is the most authentic Italian Renaissance building outside Italy, with arcades and a copper roof that looks like an inverted ship's hull. It houses temporary modern art exhibitions (open daily except Monday, from 10 am to 6 pm).

West of the Royal Garden is the former **Riding School** (Jízdárna), built in 1695, now a venue for temporary modern art exhibitions. Exhibitions in all these venues have separate admission prices.

THIRD COURTYARD

Entering from the second courtyard brings you straight to the main entrance of St Vitus Cathedral, the country's largest cathedral, with the main steeple 97m high.

St Vitus Cathedral (Katedrála Sv Víta)

This Gothic cathedral, now blackened by age and pollution, occupies the site of a 10th century Romanesque rotunda built by Duke Wenceslas.

The cathedral's foundation stone was laid in 1344 by Emperor Charles IV. His architect, Matthias of Arras, began work in the French Gothic style but died eight years later. His German successor, Peter Parler, completed much of the structure in a freer, late-Gothic style before he died in 1399. Renaissance and baroque details were added over the following centuries, but it was only in 1861, during the Czech National Revival, that a concerted effort was made to finish the cathedral. Many architects were involved, most notably Josef Mocker, and the job was completed in 1929.

You Mean There Are More?

Mention cathedrals in Prague and St Vitus springs to mind. Although it is the city's Roman Catholic cathedral, it does not belong to the Church, and never has. Ever since Charles IV dreamed the idea up in the 14th century, it has been state property. Heated discussions on the issue accompanied the restitution of Church property after 1989, but history prevailed.

You might be surprised to know that Prague has four other cathedrals (a cathedral is the principal church of a bishopric or equivalent), though all are called churches. Atop Petřín Hill is the Old Catholics' Church of St Lawrence (kostel sv Vavřince; Map 5). On Karlova in Staré Město is the cathedral of the Greek Orthodox Church, St Clement Church (kostel sv Klimenta; Map 7). The Church of SS Cyril & Methodius (kostel sv Cyrila a Metoděje; Map 9) on Resslova is home to the Russian Orthodox bishop. And Malá Strana's St Nicholas Church (kostel sv Mikuláše; Map 5) belongs to the Hussite Church.

ST VITUS CATHEDRAL (KATEDRÁLA SV VÍTA)

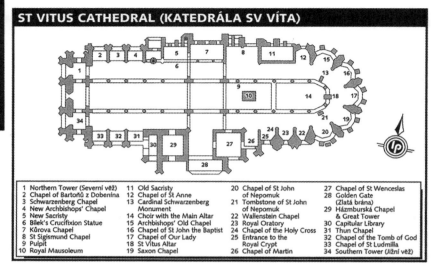

1 Northern Tower (Severní věž)
2 Chapel of Bartoňů z Dobenína
3 Schwarzenberg Chapel
4 New Archbishops' Chapel
5 New Sacristy
6 Bílek's Crucifixion Statue
7 Kůrova Chapel
8 St Sigismund Chapel
9 Pulpit
10 Royal Mausoleum

11 Old Sacristy
12 Chapel of St Anne
13 Cardinal Schwarzenberg
   Monument
14 Choir with the Main Altar
15 Archbishops' Old Chapel
16 Chapel of St John the Baptist
17 Chapel of Our Lady
18 St Vitus Altar
19 Saxon Chapel

20 Chapel of St John
   of Nepomuk
21 Tombstone of St John
   of Nepomuk
22 Wallenstein Chapel
23 Royal Oratory
24 Chapel of the Holy Cross
25 Entrance to the
   Royal Crypt
26 Chapel of Martin

27 Chapel of St Wenceslas
28 Golden Gate
   (Zlatá brána)
29 Házmburská Chapel
   & Great Tower
30 Capitular Library
31 Thun Chapel
32 Chapel of the Tomb of God
33 Chapel of St Ludmilla
34 Southern Tower (Jižní věž)

The doorways are richly decorated with carvings of historical and biblical scenes, the most beautiful of which is the mosaic of the *Last Judgment* (1370-71) on the south doorway, the **Golden Gate** (Zlatá brána). Its wrought-iron gate has scenes of people at work: blacksmith, shoemaker, butcher.

The interior is enhanced by traditional and modern **stained-glass windows**. Of its numerous side chapels, the most beautiful is Parler's **Chapel of St Wenceslas** (kaple sv Václava), adorned with frescoes and 1345 semiprecious stones. On the southern side of this chapel, a small door – locked with seven locks – hides a staircase to the Coronation Chamber, above the Golden Gate, where the Czech **crown jewels** are held. Rarely exhibited to the public (you can see replicas at the museum in the Lobkowicz Palace), they include the gold crown of St Wenceslas, which Charles IV had remade from the original Přemysl crown in 1346.

A **wooden relief** by Caspar Bechterle (1623) beside the Chapel of St Anne shows the escape from Prague of Frederick of the Palatinate after the Battle of Bílá Hora

(White Mountain). One of the best modern sculptures is the wooden *Crucifixion* by František Bílek, which has been in the cathedral since 1927.

The **choir** includes the ornate Royal Mausoleum with images of Ferdinand I, his wife Anna Jagellonská and son Maxmilián II. In the **Royal Crypt** are the remains of Charles IV, Wenceslas IV, George of Poděbrady and Rudolf II. On a clear day, views from the **Great Tower** are great, and you get a close look at the 1597 clockworks. The tower's Sigismund Bell, made by Tomáš Jaroš in 1549, is Bohemia's largest.

In the courtyard facing the cathedral's south entrance is Plečník's 16m granite **monolith** (1928) dedicated to the victims of WWI. At the south-eastern end of the courtyard, a gate leads to the **Garden on the Ramparts** (Zahrada Na valech), an elegant manicured space with fine views over the city.

Old Royal Palace (Starý Královský Palác)

This is one of the oldest parts of the castle.

Dating from 1135, it was originally for Czech princesses; from the 13th to the 16th century it was the king's palace.

At its heart is **Vladislav Hall** (Vladislavský sál), one of Prague's best examples of late-Gothic architecture. It was used for banquets, councils and coronations – and in bad weather, jousting! Hence the **Riders' Staircase** (Jezdecké schody) leading in from one side. The presidents of the republic have all been sworn in here.

In one corner of the hall is the entrance to the **Ludvík Wing**. On 23 May 1618, nobles rebelling against Emperor Rudolf II threw two of his councillors and their secretary out of the window of the chancellery here. They survived, their fall broken by the moat that was there in those days, but the event triggered off the Thirty Years' War.

Across the hall from the Ludvík Wing is the **New Land Rolls Room**, the old map repository for land titles, where the walls are covered with clerks' old coats of arms. At the eastern end of Vladislav Hall is **All Saints' Chapel** (kaple Všech svatých), and to its right a terrace with great city views.

ST GEORGE SQUARE (NÁMĚSTÍ U SV JIŘÍ)

This is the plaza behind the cathedral, and the heart of the castle.

Convent of St George (Klášter Sv Jiří)

This very ordinary-looking building was Bohemia's first convent, established in 973 by Boleslav II. It was closed and converted to an army barracks in 1782. It's now a branch of the National Gallery, with an excellent collection of Czech Gothic, Renaissance and baroque art, including the jewel of 14th century Czech Gothic art, a trio of panels by the Master of the Třeboň Altar.

Basilica of St George (Bazilika Sv Jiří)

The striking church adjoining the convent was established in the 10th century by Vratislav I (the father of St Wenceslas), and is the Czech Republic's best-preserved Romanesque structure. What you see is mostly the result of attempts from 1887 to 1908 to give it back a pure Romanesque look. Přemysl royalty are buried here.

Inside are some fine, partially preserved frescoes. Beside the altar is what is probably the tomb of St Ludmilla, grandmother of Duke Wenceslas. In the left wall is a hole through which nuns from the convent next door communicated with the rest of the world. The basilica's acoustics make it a good venue for classical concerts.

MIHULKA POWDER TOWER (PRAŠNÁ VĚŽ)

This tower on the northern side of St Vitus was built at the end of the 15th century as part of the castle's defences. Later it was the workshop of the cannon and bell-maker Tomáš Jaroš, who cast the bells of St Vitus. Alchemists employed by Rudolf II worked here. It's thought to have gotten its name in the 19th century, from *mihule* (lamprey eels) bred in the area. Today it's a museum of alchemy, bell and cannon-forging, and Renaissance life in Prague Castle (information is in Czech only).

On the wall opposite the entrance is a spherical clock inscribed with the days of the month, the days of the week, hours and minutes, though it hasn't worked for years.

ZLATÁ ULIČKA

Off Jiřská, along the northern wall of the castle, is **Golden Lane** (Zlatá ulička), also called Goldsmiths' Lane (Zlatnická ulička). Its tiny, colourful cottages were built in the 16th century for the sharpshooters of the castle guard, and later used by goldsmiths. In the 18th and 19th centuries they were occupied by squatters, and later by artists such as the writer Franz Kafka (who stayed at No 22 from 1916 to 1917) and the Nobel-laureate poet Jaroslav Seifert. Today, most are souvenir shops.

At the western end of the lane is the **White Tower** (Bílá věž), where the Irish trickster alchemist Edward Kelley was imprisoned by Rudolf II. At the eastern end is the **Daliborka** tower, named after the knight Dalibor of Kozojedy, imprisoned here in 1498 for supporting a peasant rebellion, and later executed. According to an old tale, he played a violin during his imprisonment, which could be heard throughout the castle. Smetana based his 1868 opera *Dalibor* on the tale.

JIŘSKÁ ULICE

On Jiřská Ulice, just inside the east gate of the castle with its **Black Tower** (Černá věž), is **Lobkowicz Palace** (Lobkovický palác), built in the 1570s. Inside is a branch of the National Museum (☎ 53 73 64), with a good collection on Czech history from the arrival of the Slavs until 1848. Exhibits include replicas of the Czech crown jewels, the sword of executioner Jan Mydlář (who lopped off the heads of 27 rebellious Protestant nobles in Old Town Square in 1621) and some of the oldest marionettes in the Czech Republic. The museum is not covered by the castle ticket; admission is 20 Kč, and it's open daily except Monday from 9 am to 5 pm.

Opposite is the **Burgrave's Palace** (Purkrabství), in whose tower is a private **Toy Museum** (Muzeum hraček), claiming to be the second largest of its kind in the world, with exhibits going back to Greek antiquity. It's an amazing collection, but sure to be frustrating for kids since everything is hands-off except a few pushbuttons. This too is not covered by the castle ticket; admission is 40 Kč (20 Kč for children aged six to 15 and students), and it's open daily from 9.30 am to 5.30 pm (but closed Friday in winter).

Hradčany

Hradčany is the residential area around the west gate of Prague Castle. In 1320 it was made a town in its own right. Before it became a borough of Prague in 1598, it twice suffered heavy damage: in the Hussite wars, and in the Great Fire of 1541. After this, palaces were built in place of the older

town houses, some by Habsburg nobility in the hope of cementing their power at Prague Castle.

Today Hradčany district reaches as far as Pohořelec and the Strahov Monastery. There are a few government offices around Hradčanské náměstí and along Loretánská, but the rest is still basically residential.

HRADČANSKÉ NÁMĚSTÍ (Map 5)

Hradčanské náměstí has kept its shape since the Middle Ages. At its centre is a plague column by Ferdinand Brokoff (1726). Several former canons' residences (Nos 6 to 12) have richly decorated façades.

The **Schwarzenberg Palace** (Schwarzenberský palác) sports a sgraffito façade as startling as a Hawaiian shirt. The Schwarzenbergs acquired it in 1719. Inside is a glum **Museum of Military History** (Vojenské historické muzeum) and an adjacent room full of miscellaneous 'antiquities', including a big collection of tin soldiers. It's open from May to October, daily except Monday from 10 am to 6 pm.

Opposite is the rococo **Archbishop's Palace** (Arcibiskupský palác), bought and remodelled by Archbishop Antonín Bruse of Mohelnice in 1562, and the seat of archbishops ever since. Its wonderful interior, including a chapel with frescoes by Daniel Alexius (1600), is only open to the public on the day before Good Friday.

Diagonally behind is the baroque **Sternberg Palace** (Šternberský palác; 1707), home to the National Gallery's collection (☎ 20 51 45 99) of 14th to 19th century European art. It's open daily except Monday from 10 am to 6 pm.

LORETÁNSKÉ NÁMĚSTÍ (Map 5)

From Hradčanské náměstí it's a short walk west to Loretánské náměstí, created early in the 18th century when the **Černín Palace** (Černínský palác) was built. This palace today houses the foreign ministry.

In 1948, the foreign minister Jan Masaryk, son of the founding president of Czechoslovakia, fell to his death from a bathroom window here, allegedly while trying to escape from his Czech secret service tormentors. The new communist government, which at the time claimed he committed suicide, would have had good reason to get rid of this democrat and staunch anti-communist, but the true facts may never be known.

At the northern end of the square is a **Capuchin Monastery** (klášter kapucínů; 1600-02), Bohemia's oldest operating monastery.

The Loreta

The square's main attraction is the Loreta, an extraordinary baroque place of pilgrimage founded by Benigna Kateřina Lobkowicz in 1626, and meant to resemble the house of the Virgin Mary (Santa Casa), which legend says was carried by angels to the Italian town of Loreto as the Turks were advancing on Nazareth. The duplicate **Santa Casa** (Svatá chýše), with fragments of its original frescoes, is in the centre of the courtyard.

Behind it is the **Church of the Nativity of Our Lord** (kostel Narození Páně), built in 1737 to a design by Kristof Dientzenhofer. The claustrophobic interior includes two skeletons – of the Spanish saints Felicissima and Marcia – dressed in nobles' clothing with wax masks over their skulls.

Finally there's the startling **Chapel of Our Lady of Sorrows** (kaple Panny Marie Bolestné) at the corner of the courtyard, featuring a crucified bearded lady: St Starosta, pious daughter of a Portuguese king who promised her to the king of Sicily against her wishes. After a night of tearful prayers, she awoke with a beard, the wedding was called off, and her father had her crucified. She was later made patron saint of the needy and godforsaken.

Most eye-popping is the **treasury** on the 1st floor. It's been ransacked at least four times over the centuries, but some amazing items were left behind. Most over-the-top is a 90cm-tall monstrance called the **Prague Sun** (Pražské slunce), made of solid silver with plenty of gold and 6222 diamonds.

Above the Loreta's entrance 27 bells, made in Amsterdam in the 17th century, play *We Greet Thee a Thousand Times* every hour.

The Loreta is open daily except Monday from 9 am to 12.15 pm and 1 to 4.30 pm. Foreigners pay a stiff 80 Kč (students 60 Kč). Photography is not allowed, the rule enforced with a 1000 Kč fine by persons who could pass for former Czech secret service agents.

STRAHOV MONASTERY (STRAHOVSKÝ KLÁŠTER) (Map 5)

This former monastery complex was founded in 1140 by Vladislav II to house the Premonstratensians. Today's structure, completed in the 17th and 18th centuries, functioned until the communist government closed it and imprisoned most of the monks, who have recently returned.

Inside is the 1612 **Church of St Roch** (kostel sv Rocha), now an exhibition hall. The **Church of the Assumption of Our Lady** (kostel Nanebevzetí Panny Marie) was built in 1143, and heavily decorated in the 18th century in baroque style. Mozart allegedly played the organ here.

The monastery's biggest attraction is the **Strahov Library** (Strahovská knihovna), the largest monastic library in the country. You can look through the door, but you can't go into the two storey Philosophy Hall (Filozofický sál), with its carved floor-to-ceiling shelves lined with beautiful old tomes. Covering the ceiling is the *Struggle of Mankind to Gain Real Wisdom*, a fresco by Franz Maulbertsch. Down the hall is the Theology Hall, with a ceiling fresco by Siard Nosecký. At the entrance is the grandly named **Museum of Czech Literature** (☎ 20 51 66 95), a small exhibit of miniature books. The library is open from 9 am to noon and 1 to 5 pm, daily except Monday.

In the second courtyard is the **Strahov Picture Gallery** (Strahovská obrazárna), with a valuable collection of Gothic, baroque, rococo and Romantic monastery art on the 1st floor, and temporary exhibits on the ground floor. It's open from 9 am to noon and 12.30 to 5 pm, daily except Monday.

Malá Strana

Malá Strana (the Small Quarter) clusters around the foot of Prague Castle. Most tourists climb up to the castle along the Royal Way, along Mostecká and Nerudova, but the narrow side streets of this baroque quarter have plenty to offer. Almost too picturesque for its own good, the district is now a favourite movie and commercial set.

Malá Strana started in the 8th or 9th century as a market settlement. In 1257 Přemysl Otakar II granted it town status. Fortifications (the so-called 'Hunger Wall'; see the later section on Petřín Hill) were built by Charles IV.

Malá Strana was twice almost destroyed: during battles between Hussites and the Prague Castle garrison in 1419, and in the Great Fire of 1541. Renaissance buildings and palaces replaced destroyed houses. The baroque churches and palaces that give Malá Strana its present charm date from the 17th and 18th centuries. The largely residential quarter is a historical preserve.

NERUDOVA ULICE (Map 5)

Nerudova, part of the Royal Way, is architecturally the quarter's most important street. Most of its old Renaissance façades were later 'baroquefied'. Many still have their original shutter-like doors.

At No 47 is the **House of Two Suns** (Dům U dvou slunců), an early baroque building where the Czech poet Jan Neruda lived from 1845 to 1891. The **House of the Golden Horseshoe** (Dům U zlaté podkovy) at No 34 is named after the relief, above the doorway, of St Wenceslas, whose horse was said to be shod with gold. In 1749, the first pharmacy in Hradčany opened here, and still operates next door.

From 1765 Josef of Bretfeld made his **Bretfeld Palace,** on the corner with Janský

vršek, a centre for social gatherings; among his guests were Mozart and Casanova.

The baroque **Church of Our Lady of Unceasing Succour** (kostel Panny Marie ustavičné pomoci, also called kostel Panny Marie U kajetánů) at No 24 was, from 1834 to 1837, a theatre, the divadlo U Kajetánů, which featured Czech plays during the Czech National Revival.

Most houses bear emblems of some kind. No 18, built in 1566, is named after **St John of Nepomuk,** patron saint of the Czechs, whose image was added in about 1730. The **House of the Three Fiddles** (Dům U tří housliček), a Gothic building rebuilt in Renaissance style in the 17th century, once belonged to a family of violin makers.

Úvoz, Nerudova's uphill extension, takes you to Strahov Monastery, with fine views over the city.

MALOSTRANSKÉ NÁMĚSTÍ (Map 5)

This is really two squares, with St Nicholas Church (kostel sv Mikuláše) – Malá Strana's primary landmark – between them. It has been the hub of Malá Strana since the 10th century, though it lost some of its personality when Karmelitská was widened at the turn of this century. Today it's a mixture of official buildings and touristy restaurants, with a tram line through the middle.

What is today a nightclub and a restaurant called Malostranská beseda, at No 21, was the **old town hall,** where in 1575 non-Catholic nobles wrote the so-called *České konfese* (Czech Confession), a pioneering demand for religious tolerance addressed to the Habsburg emperor and eventually passed into Czech law by Rudolf II in 1609. On 22 May 1618, Czech nobles gathered at the Smiřický Palace at No 18; the next day they flung two Habsburg councillors out of a window in Prague Castle, setting off the Thirty Years' War.

St Nicholas Church (Kostel Sv Mikuláše)

This beautiful, heavily decorated church with a huge green cupola that dominates

Malá Strana is one of central Europe's finest baroque buildings (don't confuse it with the other St Nicholas Church on Old Town Square). It was begun by Kristof Dientzenhofer; his son Kilian continued the work and Anselmo Lurago finished the job in 1755.

On the ceiling, Johann Kracker's 1770 *Life of St Nicholas* is Europe's largest fresco. In the first chapel on the left is a mural by Karel Škréta, into which he has painted the church official who kept track of him as he worked; he is looking out through a window in the upper corner.

The church is open daily, for 30 Kč. From May to September it's open from 9 am to 6 pm (to 4.30 pm on concert days); in winter it closes earlier.

BELOW THE CASTLE TO KLÁROV (Map 5)

The **Castle Steps** (Zámecké schody) were originally the main route to the castle; the houses around them were built later. The steps merge into Thunovská street. Around the corner on Sněmovní, in the Thun Palace (Thunovský palác), is the Czech **Parliament House** (Sněmovna), seat of the lower house of today's parliament and also of the national assembly that on 14 November 1918 deposed the Habsburgs from the Czech throne.

The **House of the Golden Stag** (Dům U zlatého jelena) at Tomášská 4 has a 1726 statue, by Ferdinand Brokoff, of St Hubert and a stag with a cross between its antlers.

Wallenstein Palace (Valdštejnský Palác)

On Valdštejnské náměstí is the first of the monumental baroque structures built by Albrecht of Wallenstein, generalissimo of the Habsburg armies. The vast palace, which in 1630 displaced 23 houses, a brickworks and three gardens, was financed by Wallenstein's confiscation of properties from Protestant nobles who lost the Battle of Bílá Hora (White Mountain) in 1620. It's now occupied by the Senate of the Czech Republic.

Parks & Gardens

Beside the palace is the enormous **Wallenstein Garden** (Valdštejnská zahrada), open daily from 10 am to 6 pm; enter from Letenská. At the eastern end of the garden is the **Wallenstein Riding School** (Valdštejnská jízdárna), home to changing exhibitions of modern art, open daily except Monday, from 10 am to 6 pm.

The quiet **Vojan Park** (Vojanovy sady), entered from U lužického semináře, is all that remains of Prague's oldest park, established in 1248. Up the hill towards Dejvice is **Chotek Park** (Chotkovy sady), Prague's first public park, established in 1833.

SOUTH OF NERUDOVA TO KAMPA (Map 5)

The buildings in Vlašská and Tržiště suffered serious neglect under the communists, but lower Tržiště has recently had a total face-lift. Vlašská has another Lobkowicz Palace, this one home to the **German embassy**. In summer 1989, it was besieged by thousands of East Germans trying to get into West Germany.

The fine baroque **Vrtbov Garden** (Vrtbovská zahrada), entered through house No 25 on the corner of Karmelitská and Tržiště, has statues and vases by Matthias Braun and a terrace with good views of Prague Castle and Malá Strana. At the time of writing it was under restoration.

The unimposing 1613 **Church of Our Lady Victorious** (kostel Panny Marie Vítězné) in Karmelitská has on its central altar a waxwork figure of the baby Jesus brought from Spain in 1628, the so-called **Infant of Prague** (Pražské jezulátko, also known by its Italian name of Bambino di Praga). Among miracles it's said to have worked are protection of Prague from the plague and from the destruction of the Thirty Years' War. It's visited by a steady stream of pilgrims, especially from Italy, Spain and Latin America. The 18th century German prior ES Stephano wrote about the miracles, kicking off what eventually became a worldwide cult of worship. The Infant's wardrobe consists of 60 costumes donated from all over the world, changed in accordance with a religious calendar.

Maltézské Náměstí

This quiet square gets its name from the Knights of Malta, who in 1169 established a monastery beside the **Church of Our Lady Below the Chain** (kostel Panny Marie pod řetězem). Only a few sections of the church remain. Beyond the statue of St John the Baptist is a music school; listen for classical melodies drifting from the windows.

A short way east is Velkopřevorské náměstí, and opposite the **French embassy** is the **John Lennon Wall** (Lennonova zeď), a kind of political focus for Prague's pre-1989 youth. Most western pop music was banned by the Communists, and some Czech musicians who played it went to jail. Beatles lyrics began appearing on the wall in the 1980s, and the secret police never managed to keep it clean. After his death on 8 December 1980, Lennon became a pacifist hero in the Czech subculture. Decay and lightweight graffiti ate away at the political messages, until little remained of Lennon but his eyes. In August 1998 the wall was

repaired and whitewashed, but artists have since painted new graffiti on it.

Kampa

Lying off the Malá Strana bank, with Charles Bridge passing over its northern end, this is the most picturesque of Prague's islands. It was once used as farmland, and was home to a popular pottery market. In the 13th century the town's first mill, the Sovovský mlýn, was built on Čertovka (Devil's Stream), which separates Kampa from the mainland, and other mills followed.

The area along the stream and under Charles Bridge is sometimes called 'Prague's Venice'. Cafés beckon from **Na Kampě** square, below the bridge, though the summer sun is ferocious here.

The southern part of Kampa is a park with views across to the Old Town. Near the tip of the island is another graffiti wall. For more on Kampa, see the Islands of Prague section later in this chapter.

AROUND ÚJEZD (Map 5)

On Říční is one of Malá Strana's oldest Gothic buildings, the **Church of St John at the Laundry** (kostel sv Jana Na prádle), built in 1142 as a local parish church. Inside are the remains of 14th century frescoes. The arresting name refers to its 1784 conversion into a laundry. In 1935 it was reconsecrated by the Czechoslovak Hussite Church.

PETŘÍN HILL (PETŘÍNSKÉ SADY) (Map 5)

This 318m hill, called simply Petřín by Czechs, is actually a network of eight parks (Strahovská, Lobkovická, Schönbornská, Vrtbovská, Seminářská, Růžový and Petřínské, plus Kinského in Smíchov) comprising Prague's largest single green space. It's great for cool, quiet walks and fine views of the 'city of 100 spires'. Once there were vineyards here, and a quarry that provided the stone from which most of Prague's Romanesque and Gothic buildings were assembled.

Every year, on the anniversary of his death, the John Lennon Wall has acted as a hippy shrine.

RICHARD NEBESKÝ

Petřín is easily accessible from Hradčany and Strahov, or you can ride the **funicular railway** (*lanová dráha*) from Újezd (at U lanové dráhy) up to Růžový sad (Park). It runs every 10 to 20 minutes from 9.15 am to 8.45 pm, for the same price as a bus ride (you can use ordinary city transit tickets and passes). You can also get off halfway up and dine with a great view at the Nebozízek Restaurant (see the Places to Eat chapter).

Just south of the cable-car terminus is **Štefánik Observatory** (Štefánikova hvězdárna; ☎ 57 32 05 40), a 'people's observatory' where you can view the stars if it's clear, or look at photos and old instruments if it's not. It's open Tuesday to Friday from 2 to 7 pm and 9 to 11 pm, and weekends from 10 am to noon, 2 to 7 pm and 9 to 11 pm, from April to August; and shorter hours during the rest of the year.

North of the terminus on the summit is **Petřín Tower** (Petřínská rozhledna), a 62m Eiffel Tower lookalike built in 1891 for the Prague Exposition. You can climb its 299 steps for 30 Kč (kids and students 20 Kč). It's open from 9.30 am to 6.30 pm (weather permitting): daily from April to October, and on weekends only the rest of the year. Some of the best views of Prague are from here, and on clear days you can see the forests of central Bohemia.

On the way to the tower you cross the **Hunger Wall** (Hladová zeď), running from Újezd to Strahov. These are the fortifications completed in 1362 under Charles IV, and are so named because they were built by the poor of the city in return for food.

Below the tower is **The Maze** (Bludiště), also built for the 1891 Prague Exposition and later moved here. Inside is a mirror maze that's good for a laugh, and a diorama of the 1648 battle between Praguers and Swedes on Charles Bridge. From April to October it's open daily from 10 am to 6.30 pm; the rest of the year it's open only on weekends, from 10 am to 5 pm. Admission costs 30 Kč (20 Kč for kids and students).

Opposite is the **Church of St Lawrence** (kostel sv Vavřince), with a ceiling fresco depicting the founding of the church in 991 at a pagan site with a sacred flame. In the Middle Ages executions took place in the area.

In the peaceful Kinský Gardens (Kinského zahrada) on the southern side of Petřín (Map 5; technically in Smíchov) is the 18th century wooden **Church of St Michael** (kostel sv Michala), transferred here, log by log, from the village of Medveďov in Ukraine. Such structures are rare in Bohemia, though still common in Ukraine and north-eastern Slovakia.

Staré Město & Josefov

A settlement and marketplace existed on the eastern bank of the Vltava by the 10th century. In the 12th century this was linked to the castle district by the forerunner of the Charles Bridge, and in 1231 Wenceslas I honoured it with a town charter and the beginnings of a fortification. This 'Old Town' – Staré Město – has been Prague's working heart ever since. The town walls are long gone, though their route is still traced by Národní, Na příkopě and Revoluční streets.

Staré Město shared in the boom when Charles IV gave Prague a Gothic face befitting its new status as capital of the Holy Roman Empire. Charles founded the Karolinum (Charles University) in Staré Město in 1348, and began Charles Bridge in 1357. When Emperor Joseph II amalgamated Prague's towns into a single city in 1784, the Old Town Hall became its seat of government.

Many of Staré Město's buildings have Gothic insides and Romanesque basements. To ease the devastation of frequent flooding by the Vltava, the level of the town was gradually raised, beginning in the 13th century, with new construction simply rising on top of older foundations. (You can see an example of this at Můstek metro station – at the corner of Na můstku and Na příkopě, go down the stairs, and as you enter the station – on the left just before the escalators – there are some of the arches of

The Jews of Prague

Prague's Jewish community was first moved into a walled ghetto in about the 13th century, in response to directives from Rome that Jews and Christians should live separately. Subsequent centuries of pogroms and official repression culminated in Ferdinand I's threat, only grudgingly withdrawn, to throw all Jews out of Bohemia.

The reign of Rudolf II saw honour bestowed on Prague's Jews, a flowering of Jewish intellectual life and prosperity in the ghetto. Mordechai Maisel (or Maisl), mayor of the ghetto, Rudolf's finance minister and Prague's wealthiest citizen, bankrolled some lavish redevelopment. Another major figure was Judah Löw ben Bezalel, or Rabbi Löw, prominent theologian, chief rabbi, student of the mystical teachings of the qabbala, and nowadays best known as the creator of the mythical *golem* – a kind of proto-robot made from the mud of the Vltava.

When they helped to repel the Swedes on Charles Bridge in 1648, Prague's Jews won the favour of Ferdinand III – to the extent that he had the ghetto enlarged. But a century later they were driven out of the city for over three years, to be welcomed back only because Praguers missed their business.

In the 1780s Emperor Joseph II outlawed many forms of discrimination, and in 1848 the ghetto walls were torn down, and the Jewish quarter – named Josefov in honour of Joseph II – was made a borough of Prague.

The demise of the quarter (which had slid into squalor as its population fell) came between 1893 and 1910 when it was cleared, ostensibly for public health reasons, divided down the middle by Pařížská třída and lined with new Art Nouveau housing.

The community itself was all but eliminated by the Nazis, with nearly three-quarters of the city's Jews dying in camps from 1941. The communist regime slowly strangled what remained of Jewish cultural life and thousands emigrated. Today only about 6000 Jews live in Prague, compared with an estimated pre-WWII total of 120,000.

---

the stone bridge that spanned the moat.) A huge fire in 1689 contributed to an orgy of rebuilding in the re-Catholicised 17th and 18th centuries, giving the formerly Gothic district a heavily baroque face.

The only intrusions into Staré Město's medieval layout have been appropriation for the Jesuits' massive college, the Klementinum, in the 16th and 17th centuries, and the 'clearance' of Josefov, the Jewish quarter, at the end of the 19th century.

At the centre of everything is Old Town Square. If the maze of alleys around it can be said to have an 'artery', it's the so-called Royal Way, the ancient coronation route to Prague Castle; in this part of the city, it runs from the Powder Tower, down Celetná to Old Town Square, along Karlova and over Charles Bridge.

JOSEFOV (THE OLD JEWISH QUARTER) (Map 7)

The slice of Staré Město within Kaprova, Dlouhá and Kozí streets contains the remains of the once-thriving mini-town of Josefov, Prague's former Jewish ghetto: half a dozen old synagogues, the town hall, a ceremonial hall and the powerfully melancholy Old Jewish Cemetery. In a grotesquely ironic act, the Nazis spared these to be a 'museum of an extinct race' – thanks to which they have instead survived as a memorial to seven centuries of oppression.

The Old-New Synagogue is still used for religious services; the others have been converted to exhibition halls holding what is probably the world's biggest collection of sacred Jewish artefacts, many of them saved from demolished Bohemian synagogues. All rooms are open from 9 am to 5.30 pm, but are closed to the public on Saturday.

Sadly, tourist tickets to the so-called Jewish Museum (cemetery, ceremonial hall and Maisel, Pinkas and Klaus synagogues) and to the Old-New Synagogue (plus the Jubilee Synagogue in Nové Město) are a major tourist rip-off at 250 Kč (50 Kč for Czechs) and 200 Kč (20 Kč for Czechs), respectively. The Czech rate is printed in words, so most tourists can't read it. Tickets are sold at Klaus Synagogue, U hřbitova 3a; at Pinkas Synagogue, on Široká just outside the cemetery; and at the Matana travel agency, around the corner at Maiselova 15.

Old-New Synagogue (Staronová Synagóga)

Completed about 1270, this is Europe's oldest 'working' synagogue and one of Prague's earliest Gothic buildings. You step down into it because it predates the raising of Staré Město's streets against floods.

Men must cover their heads (a hat or bandanna serves as well as the 5 Kč paper yarmulkes sold at the entrance). Around the central chamber are an entry hall, a winter prayer hall and the room from which women watch the men-only services. The interior, with a pulpit surrounded by a 15th century wrought-iron grille, looks much as it would have 500 years ago. The 17th century scriptures on the walls were recovered from beneath a later 'restoration'. On the eastern wall is the Holy Ark that holds the Torah scrolls. In a glass case at the rear, little light bulbs beside the names of the prominent deceased are lit on their death days.

With its steep roof and 'crowstep' gables, this looks like a place with secrets, and at least one version of the golem legend (see the boxed text 'The Jews of Prague' on the previous page) ends here: the creature, left alone on the Sabbath, runs amok; Rabbi Löw rushes out in the midst of a service, removes its magic talisman and carries the lifeless body into the synagogue's attic, where some insist it still lies.

The synagogue is open until 6 pm, except on Friday when it closes at 5 pm.

High Synagogue (Vysoká Synagóga)

Opposite the Old-New Synagogue is the elegant 16th century High Synagogue, so called because its prayer hall (closed to the public) is upstairs. On the ground floor is a Jewish Museum shop.

Jewish Town Hall (Židovská Radnice)

Built by Maisel in 1586 and given its rococo façade in the 18th century, the Jewish Town Hall is closed to the public, except for the Kosher Eatery on the ground floor (see the Places to Eat chapter). It has a clock tower with one Hebrew face whose hands, like the Hebrew script, run 'backwards'.

Klaus Synagogue (Klauzová Synagóga)

In this 1694 baroque building by the cemetery entrance is a good exhibit of Jewish artefacts and ceremonies of birth, death, worship and special holy days.

Ceremonial Hall (Obřadní Síň)

This was built around 1906 beside the cemetery entrance. Inside is an exhibit on Jewish traditions, similar to what's in Klaus Synagogue.

Pinkas Synagogue (Pinkasova Synagóga)

This handsome synagogue on Široká was built in 1535 and used for worship until 1941. After WWII it was converted into a powerful memorial, with the names, birth dates and dates of disappearance of the 77,297 Bohemian and Moravian victims of the Nazis inscribed across wall after wall. It also has a collection of paintings and drawings by children held in the Terezín concentration camp during WWII (see the Excursions chapter).

Maisel Synagogue (Maiselova Synagóga)

This neo-Gothic synagogue at Maiselova 10 replaced a Renaissance original built by Maisel and destroyed by fire. It houses another exhibit of synagogue silver, textiles, prints and books.

Spanish Synagogue (Španělská Synagóga)

Named after its striking Moorish interior, this 1868 building has an exhibit on Jews in the Czech Republic from emancipation to the present day.

Old Jewish Cemetery (Starý Židovský Hřbitov)

Founded in the early 15th century, this is Europe's oldest surviving Jewish cemetery, truly a monument to dignity in the face of great suffering. It has a palpable atmosphere of mourning even after two centuries of disuse (it was closed in 1787).

Some 12,000 crumbling stones (some brought from other, long-gone cemeteries) are heaped together, but beneath them are perhaps 100,000 graves, piled in layers because of space limitations. Most contain the name of the deceased and his/her father, the date of death (and sometimes of burial), and poetic texts. Elaborate markers from the 17th and 18th centuries have bas-relief and sculpture, some of it indicating the deceased's occupation and lineage. The oldest standing stone (now replaced by a replica), dating from 1439, is that of Avigdor Karo, a chief rabbi and court poet to Wenceslas IV.

The most prominent graves, marked by pairs of marble tablets with a 'roof' between them, are near the main gate. They include those of Mordechai Maisel and Rabbi Löw.

You enter the cemetery through the Pinkas Synagogue on Široká and exit through a gate between Klaus Synagogue and the Ceremonial Hall on U starého hřbitova. This is one of Prague's most popular sights, and the chattering tour groups tend to break its spell.

Since the cemetery was closed, burials have taken place at the Jewish Cemetery in Žižkov. Remnants of another old Jewish burial ground are at the foot of the TV tower in Žižkov (Map 8).

Pařížská Třída

Despite their association with the demise of the Jewish quarter, Pařížská třída (Parisian Avenue) and the adjacent streets are themselves a kind of museum. The ghetto was cleared at a time of general infatuation with the French Art Nouveau style, and its old lanes were lined with courtly four and five-storey residential buildings – their stained glass and sculptural flourishes are now slipping into disrepair. Pařížská třída's many trees give it a Parisian flavour.

Just off the northern end of Pařížská, beside the Hotel Inter-Continental at Elišky Krasnohorské 10-14, is a Cubist building by Otakar Novotný dating from 1921, though its striking façade is unfortunately starting to disintegrate.

Museum of Decorative Arts (Umělecko-průmyslové Muzeum)

This wonderful museum of European and Czech 'applied art' arose as part of a European movement to encourage a return to aesthetic values sacrificed to the Industrial Revolution. Its four halls full of 16th to 19th century artefacts including furniture,

Haven't We Been Here Before?

The street leading into Jan Palach Square from the north is 17.listopadu (17 November), which now has a dual meaning. It originally honoured students killed in an anti-Nazi demonstration in 1939. Exactly 50 years later, students marching in memory of that day were clubbed by police in Národní třída, triggering the national outrage that brought down the communist government.

tapestries, porcelain and a fabulous trove of glasswork area feast for the eyes. Don't miss the rococo grandfather of all grandfather clocks in room No 3.

Labels are in Czech but detailed English and French texts are available in each room. What you see is only a fraction of the collection; other bits appear now and then in single-theme exhibitions.

The museum's French neo-Renaissance quarters, built in 1890, are at 17.listopadu 2, opposite the Rudolfinum. It's open daily except Monday and holidays, from 10 am to 6 pm, for 40 Kč.

Rudolfinum & Jan Palach Square

Jan Palach Square (náměstí Jana Palacha) is a memorial to the young Charles University student who in January 1969 set himself alight in Wenceslas Square in protest against the Soviet invasion. Across the road, on the philosophy faculty building, where Palach was a student, is a plaque with a spooky death mask.

Presiding over the square is the Rudolfinum, home of the Czech Philharmonic. This and the National Theatre, both designed by the architects Josef Schulz and Josef Zítek, are considered Prague's finest neo-Renaissance buildings. Completed in 1884, the Rudolfinum served between the wars as the seat of the Czechoslovak parliament. On the top floor is the Rudolfinum Gallery, with temporary art exhibitions; it's open daily except Monday from 10 am to 6 pm, for 40 Kč.

OLD TOWN SQUARE (STAROMĚSTSKÉ NÁMĚSTÍ) (Map 7)

The huge 1.7 hectare Old Town Square (also called Staromák) has been Prague's heart since the 10th century, and was its main marketplace until the beginning of the 20th century.

Despite the over-the-top commercialism and the crowds of tourists that swarm around the square, it's impossible not to

---

Czech History in Old Town Square

The Old Town Square has been the scene of some momentous events in Czech history:

1338 John of Luxembourg grants Staré Město the right to a town hall, and a private house is purchased for the purpose

1422 Execution of Jan Želivský, the Hussite preacher who led Prague's first defenestration, touching off the Hussite Wars

1437 Execution of 57 more Hussites

1458 Election of the Hussite George of Poděbrady as King of Bohemia, in the Town Hall

21 June 1621 Beheading of 27 Protestants after the Battle of Bílá Hora (White Mountain)

1784 The Town Hall becomes the governmental seat of a newly unified Prague city

6 July 1915 Unveiling of the statue of Jan Hus on the 500th anniversary of his martyrdom

2 November 1918 The 270-year-old column commemorating the end of the Thirty Years' War (and a symbol of Austrian rule) is toppled

8 May 1945 Nazi SS units try to demolish the Old Town Hall as German troops begin pulling out after three days of fighting against Prague residents; the following day, the Red Army marches in

21 February 1948 Klement Gottwald proclaims a communist government from the balcony of the Kinský Palace

21 August 1968 Warsaw Pact tanks roll across the square as the 'Prague Spring' comes to an end; the Jan Hus statue is draped in black

THINGS TO SEE & DO

Charles Bridge (Karlův Most)

Charles Bridge (Maps 5 & 7) was begun by Charles IV to replace an earlier bridge that had been washed away by floods. Designed by Peter Parler, it was completed about 1400, though it only got Charles' name in the 19th century. Despite occasional flood damage, it withstood wheeled traffic for 600 years – thanks, legend says, to eggs mixed into the mortar – until it was made pedestrian-only after WWII.

Crossing it is everybody's favourite Prague activity. By 9 am it's a 500m-long fairground, with an army of tourists squeezing through a gauntlet of hawkers and buskers, beneath a rank of imposing baroque statuary.

In the crush, don't forget to look at the bridge itself and the grand views up and down the river. In the summer you can climb up into the towers at either end, built originally for its defence. Admission to each is 30 Kč. They're normally open from 10 am to 6 pm; the Malostranská Bridge Tower (with a PIS branch office inside) is closed from November to March. Each tower has a small exhibit.

Gangs of pickpockets work the bridge day and night, so keep track of your purse or wallet.

St John of Nepomuk,
the patron saint of Czechs,
was canonised in 1729.

Towers & Statues

The bridge's first monument was the crucifix near the eastern end, erected in 1657. The first and still most popular statue – the Jesuits' 1683 monument to St John of Nepomuk – inspired other Catholic orders, and a score more went up, like ecclesiastical billboards, over the next 30 years. New ones were added in the mid-19th century, and one (plus replacements for some lost to floods) in the 20th century.

As most statues were of soft sandstone, several weathered originals have been replaced with copies. Some of the originals are in an exhibit in the casemates (kasematy) under the walls at Vyšehrad, while others are in the Lapidárium at the Fairgrounds in Holešovice.

There are actually two Malá Strana bridge towers (Malostranské mostecké věže). The lower one was originally part of the long-gone 12th century Judith Bridge. The taller tower was built in the mid-15th century in imitation of the one at the Staré Město end.

From the western (Malá Strana) end, the monuments are:

1 SS Cosmas and Damian, charitable 3rd century physician brothers (1709)
2 St Wenceslas (1858)
3 St Vitus (1714)
4 SS John of Matha and Félix de Valois, 12th century French founders of the Trinitarian order, for the ransom of enslaved Christians (represented by a Tatar standing guard over a group of them), with St Ivo (1714)
5 St Philip Benizi (sv Benicius, 1714)

Charles Bridge (Karlův Most)

6 St Adalbert (sv Vojtěch), Prague's first Czech bishop, canonised in the 10th century (1709, replica)

7 St Cajetan, Italian founder of the Theatine order in the 15th century (1709)

8 *The Vision of St Luitgard*, agreed by most to be the finest piece on the bridge, in which Christ appears to the blind saint and allows her to kiss his wounds (1710)

9 St Augustine (1708, replica)

10 St Nicholas of Tolentino (1706, replica)

11 St Jude Thaddaeus, Apostle and patron saint of hopeless causes (1708); further along on the right, beyond the railing, is a column with a statue of the eponymous hero of the 11th century epic poem, the *Song of Roland* (*Bruncvík*)

12 St Vincent Ferrer, a 14th century Spanish priest, and St Procopius, Hussite warrior-priest (1712)

13 St Anthony of Padua, 13th century Portuguese disciple of St Francis of Assisi (1707)

14 St Francis Seraphicus (1855)

15 St John of Nepomuk, patron saint of Czechs: according to the legend illustrated on the base of the statue, Wenceslas IV had him trussed up in a suit of armour and thrown off the bridge in 1393 for refusing to divulge confessions by the queen, though the real reason had to do with the bitter conflict between church and state; the stars in his halo allegedly followed his corpse down the river (bronze, 1683)

16 St Wenceslas as a boy, with his grandmother and guardian St Ludmilla, patroness of Bohemia (about 1730)

17 St Wenceslas with St Sigismund (son of Charles IV and Holy Roman Emperor) and St Norbert, 12th century German founder of the Premonstratensian order (1853)

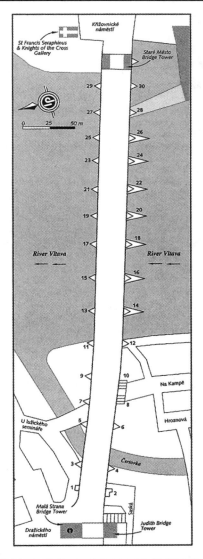

Charles Bridge (Karlův Most)

18 St Francis Borgia, 16th century Spanish priest (1710)

19 St John the Baptist (1857); further ahead on the right, a bronze cross on the railing marks the place where St John of Nepomuk was thrown off (see No 15 earlier)

20 St Christopher, patron saint of travellers (1857)

21 SS Cyril and Methodius, who brought Christianity and a written language to the Slavs in the 9th century (the newest statue, 1938)

22 St Francis Xavier, 16th century Spanish missionary celebrated for his work in the Orient (1711, replica)

23 St Anne with Madonna and Child (1707)

24 St Joseph (1854)

25 Crucifix (gilded bronze, 1657), with an invocation in Hebrew saying 'holy, holy, holy Lord', funded by the fine of a Jew who had mocked it (in 1696); the stone figures date from 1861

26 Pietá (1859)

27 Madonna with St Dominic, Spanish founder of the Dominicans in the 12th century, and St Thomas Aquinas (1709, replica)

28 St Barbara, 2nd century patron saint of miners; St Margaret, 3rd or 4th century patron saint of expectant mothers; and St Elizabeth, a 13th century Slovak princess who renounced the good life to serve the poor (1707)

29 Madonna with St Bernard, founder of the Cistercian order in the 12th century (1709, replica)

30 St Ivo, 11th century bishop of Chartres (1711, replica)

The elegant Old Town Bridge Tower (Staroměstská mostecká věž) was, like the bridge, designed by Peter Parler. Here, at the end of the Thirty Years' War, a Swedish army was finally turned back by a band of students and Jewish ghetto residents. Looking out from the eastern face of the tower are SS Adalbert and Procopius, and below them Charles IV, St Vitus and Wenceslas IV. The tower also features a bit of 'Gothic porno': below these worthies on the left side of the arch is a stone relief of a man with his hand up the skirt of what appears to be a nun.

---

enjoy the place – the cafés spilling onto the pavement, the omnipresent buskers and performing dogs and the silly horse-drawn beer wagons. This is also a venue for *alfresco* concerts, political meetings, and even fashion shows. Its pastel gingerbread baroque and neo-Renaissance façades reveal nothing of their crumbling interiors, and there's hardly a hint of the harrowing history that the square has witnessed (see the boxed text 'Czech History in Old Town Square' on page 95).

Jan Hus Statue

Ladislav Šaloun's brooding Art Nouveau sculpture of Jan Hus dominates the square in the same way that Hus's mythic memory dominates Czech history (see the boxed text 'Jan Hus' under History in the Facts about Prague chapter). It was unveiled on 6 July 1915, the 500th anniversary of Hus's death at the stake, to patriotic noises but less than unanimous artistic approval. The steps at its base – being just about the only place in the square where you can sit down without having to pay for something

– act as a magnet for footsore Praguers and visitors.

The brass strip on the pavement nearby is the so-called **Prague Meridian**. Until 1915 the square's main ornament was a 17th century column (commemorating Habsburg victory in the Thirty Years' War), whose shadow used to cross the meridian at high noon. Three years after the Hus statue went up, and five days after Czechoslovakia's declaration of independence, the column was toppled by jubilant Praguers.

Old Town Hall
(Staroměstská Radnice)

Staré Město's ancient town hall, founded in 1338, looks like a row of private buildings with a tower at the end – the result of its having been gradually assembled from existing buildings by a medieval town council short of funds.

The arcaded building at the corner, called **Dům U minuty,** is covered with Renaissance sgraffito. Franz Kafka lived in it as a child just before it was bought for the town hall.

A Gothic chapel and a neo-Gothic north wing were destroyed by Nazi shells in 1945, on the day before the Soviet army marched into Prague. The chapel has been laboriously reconstructed.

A plaque on the tower's eastern face contains a roll-call of the 27 Czech Protestant nobles beheaded in 1621 after the Battle of Bílá Hora (White Mountain); crosses on the ground mark the spot where the deed was done. Another plaque commemorates a critical WWII victory by Red Army and Czechoslovak units at Dukla Pass in Slovakia.

It's *de rigueur* to wait for the hourly show by the hall's splendid **Astronomical Clock**, or *orloj* (see the boxed text on the following page). You can also see selected rooms of the town hall, the Gothic chapel and the Apostles from behind the scenes for 30 Kč. But, apart from the clock, the hall's best feature is the **view** from the 60m tower, open from 9 am to 6 pm (on Monday from 11 am to 5 am), which is certainly

worth the additional fee of 30 Kč. The hall also has an **art gallery** (☎ 24 81 07 58), left of the main entrance, open daily except Monday, from 9 am to 6 pm.

Opposite the Old Town Hall at No 27 is the **Museum of Czech Glass** (Muzeum českého skla), open daily from 10 am to 9 pm. For 50 Kč you can watch a man making kitschy glass items before your eyes, and then buy some to take home.

St Nicholas Church
(Kostel Sv Mikuláše)

The baroque wedding cake in the northwestern corner of the square is St Nicholas Church, built in the 1730s by Kilian Dientzenhofer (not to be confused with at least two other St Nicholas churches in Prague, including Kilian's and his father's masterwork in Malá Strana). Considerable grandeur has been worked into a very tight space; originally the church was wedged behind the Old Town Hall's north wing (destroyed in 1945). Chamber concerts are often held beneath its stucco decorations, a visually splendid (though acoustically mediocre) setting.

Franz Kafka was born next door, at what is now a privately run **Franz Kafka Exhibition** (Expozice Franze Kafky), at U radnice 5. The mediocre, 20 Kč photo exhibit is open Tuesday to Friday from 10 am to 6 pm, and Saturday to 5 pm.

Kinský Palace (Palác Kinských)

Fronting the late-baroque Kinský or Goltz-Kinský Palace at No 12 is probably the city's finest rococo façade, completed in 1765 by the redoubtable Kilian Dientzenhofer.

Alfred Nobel, the Swedish inventor of dynamite, once stayed here; his crush on pacifist Bertha Kinský may have influenced him to establish the Nobel Peace Prize. Many living Praguers have a darker memory of the place, for it was from its balcony in February 1948 that Klement Gottwald proclaimed communist rule in Czechoslovakia.

The Astronomical Clock

The Old Town Hall tower was given a clock in 1410 by the master clockmaker Mikuláš of Kadaně; this was improved in 1490 by one Master Hanuš, producing the mechanical marvel you see today. Legend has it that Hanuš was afterwards blinded so he could not duplicate the work elsewhere, and in revenge crawled up into the clock and disabled it. (Documents from the time suggest that he carried on as clock master for years, unblinded, although the clock apparently didn't work properly until it was repaired in about 1570.)

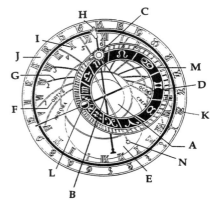

Four figures beside the clock represent the deepest civic anxieties of 15th century Praguers: Vanity, Greed (originally a Jewish moneylender, cosmetically altered after WWII), Death and Pagan Invasion (represented by a Turk). The four figures below these are the Chronicler, Angel, Astronomer and Philosopher.

On the hour, Death rings a bell and inverts his hourglass, and a parade of Apostles passes two windows, nodding to the crowd: on the left side, Paul (with a sword and a book), Thomas (lance), Jude (book), Simon (saw), Bartholomew (book) and Barnabas (parchment); on the right side, Peter (with a key), Matthew (axe), John (snake), Andrew (cross), Philip (cross) and James (mallet). At the end, a cock crows and the hour is rung.

On the upper face, the disk (**A**) in the middle of the fixed part depicts the world known at the time – with Prague (**B**) at the centre, of course. The gold sun (**C**) traces a circle through the blue zone of day, the brown zone of dusk (*CREPUSCULUM* in Latin) in the west (*OCCASUS*, **D** on the diagram), the black disc (**E**) of night, and dawn (*AURORA*) in the east (*ORTUS*, **F** on the diagram). From this the hours of sunrise and sunset can be read. The curved lines (**G**) with black Arabic numerals are part of an astrological 'star clock'.

The sun-arm (**H**) points to the hour (adjusted for daylight-saving time) on the Roman-numeral ring (**I**); the top XII is noon and the bottom XII is midnight. The outer ring (**J**), with Gothic numerals, reads traditional 24 hour Bohemian time, counted from sunset; the number 24 (**K**) is always opposite the sunset hour on the fixed (inner) face.

The moon (**L**), with its phases shown, also traces a path through the zones of day and night, riding on the offset moving ring (**M**). On the ring you can also read which houses of the zodiac the sun and moon are in. The hand with a little star at the end of it (**N**) indicates stellar time.

The calendar-wheel beneath all this astronomical wizardry, with 12 seasonal scenes in praise of rural Bohemian life, is a duplicate of one painted in 1866 by the Czech Revivalist Josef Mánes. You can have a close look at the beautiful original in the Museum of the City of Prague (see the Nové Město section). Most of the dates around the calendar-wheel are marked with the names of their associated saints; 6 July honours Jan Hus.

The National Gallery rooms at the palace are undergoing long-term reconstruction.

House of the Stone Bell (Dům U Kamenného Zvonu)

Next door at No 13, its 14th century Gothic dignity rescued in the 1960s from a second-rate baroque renovation, is the House of the Stone Bell, named after the house sign at the corner of the building. Inside, two restored Gothic chapels now serve as a branch of the Prague Municipal Gallery (☎ 24 28 75 26), open daily except Monday, from 10 am to 6 pm, for 30 Kč, with changing modern art exhibits, and as a chamber-concert venue.

Church of Our Lady Before Týn (Kostel Panny Marie Před Týnem)

The spiky-topped 'Týn church' is early Gothic, though it takes some imagination to visualise the original in its entirety because it's strangely hidden behind the four storey Týn School (not a Habsburg plot to obscure this 15th century Hussite stronghold, but almost contemporaneous with it). Inside it's smothered in heavy baroque.

The entrance is up a passage beside the Café Italia. Two of the church's most striking features are a huge rococo altar on the northern wall, and the beautiful north-eastern entrance. On the lower south wall are two tiny windows that once looked in from the house at Celetná 3 – one from the bedroom of the teenage Franz Kafka (1896-1907). See the boxed text on the next page.

The Danish astronomer Tycho Brahe, one of Rudolf II's most illustrious 'consultants' (who died in 1601 of a burst bladder during a royal piss-up), is buried near the chancel.

The Týn church is an occasional concert venue and has a very grand-sounding pipe organ, but at the time of writing the church was being renovated.

Týnský Dvůr

The Týn church's name comes from a medieval courtyard for foreign merchants, the Týnský dvůr or just Týn, behind it on Štupartská. One side of the courtyard complex has been renovated as the Hotel Ungelt (see the Places to Stay chapter).

On another corner, in the restored Renaissance **House at the Golden Ring** (Dům U zlatého prstenu), Týnská 6/630, is a branch of the Prague Municipal Gallery, with a fine collection of 20th century Czech art. In the basement is an exhibit of 1990s free expression, including audiovisual, digital photography and computer art. Note the original painted ceiling beams in some rooms. The gallery is open daily except Monday, from 10 am to 6 pm, for 100 Kč (free on the first Tuesday of each month).

ST JAMES CHURCH (KOSTEL SV JAKUBA) (Map 7)

This long, tall Gothic church, behind the Týnský dvůr on Malá Štupartská, began in the 14th century as a Minorite monastery church. It had a beautiful baroque face-lift in the early 18th century. Pride of place goes to the over-the-top tomb of Count Jan Vratislav of Mitrovice, an 18th century lord chancellor of Bohemia, on the northern aisle.

In the midst of the gilt and whitewash is a grisly memento. Hanging to the left of the main door is a shrivelled human arm. In about 1400 a thief apparently tried to steal the jewels off the statue of the Virgin. Legend says the Virgin grabbed his wrist in such an iron grip that his arm had to be lopped off. (The truth may not be far behind: the church was a favourite of the guild of butchers, who may have administered their own justice.)

It's well worth a visit to enjoy St James' splendid pipe organ and famous acoustics. Recitals – free ones at 10.30 or 11 am after Sunday Mass – and occasional concerts are not always noticed by ticket agencies, so check the notice board outside.

ALONG THE ROYAL WAY (Map 7)

The lanes from the Powder Tower to Charles Bridge are part of the original route

THINGS TO SEE & DO

of coronation processions held right into the 19th century. Nearly all of this Royal Way in Staré Město is pedestrianised.

We follow the coronation route in reverse direction from Charles Bridge.

The Klementinum

To boost the power of Rome in Bohemia, Ferdinand I invited the Jesuits to Prague. Selecting one of the city's choicest bits of real estate, they set to work in 1578 on

Kafka's Prague

Literary Prague at the onset of the 20th century was a unique melting pot of Czechs, Germans and Jews. Though he wrote in German, Franz Kafka is a son of Prague; he lived here all his life, haunting the city and haunted by it, needing it and hating it. One could look at *The Trial* as a metaphysical geography of Staré Město, whose Byzantine alleys and passages break down the usual boundaries between outer streets and inner courtyards, between public and private, new and old, real and imaginary.

Most of Kafka's life was lived around Josefov and Old Town Square. He was born on 3 July 1883 in an apartment beside St Nicholas Church; only the stone portal remains of the original building. As a boy, he lived at: Celetná 2 (1888-89); 'U minuty', the Renaissance corner building that's now part of the Old Town Hall (1889-96); and Celetná 3 (1896-1907), where his bedroom window looked into Týn Church. He took classes between 1893 and 1901 at the Old Town State Gymnasium in the Kinský Palace on the square, and for a time his father Hermann ran a clothing shop on the ground floor there.

On the southern side of the square, at No 17, Berta Fanta ran an intellectual salon in the early part of this century to which she invited fashionable European thinkers of the time, including Kafka and fellow writers Max Brod (Kafka's friend and biographer), Franz Werfel and Egon Erwin Kisch.

After earning a law degree from the Karolinum in 1906, Kafka took his first job from 1907 to 1908, an unhappy one as an insurance clerk with the Italian firm Assicurazioni Generali, at Wenceslas Square 19 (on the corner of Jindřišská). At Na poříčí 7 in northern Nové Město is the former headquarters of the Workers' Accident Insurance Co, where he toiled on the 5th floor from 1908 until his retirement in 1922.

The last place where he lived with his parents (1913-14) – and the setting for his horrific parable *Metamorphosis* – was a top-floor flat across Pařížská from St Nicholas Church, facing Old Town Square. At the age of 33 he finally moved into a place of his own at Dlouhá 16 (at the narrow corner with Masná), where he lived from 1915 to 1917, during which time he also spent a productive winter (1916-17) at a cottage rented by his sister at Zlatá ulička (Golden Lane) 22, inside the Prague Castle grounds. By this time ill with tuberculosis, he took a flat for a few months in 1917 at the Schönborn Palace at Tržiště 15 in Malá Strana (now the US embassy).

Kafka died in Vienna on 3 June 1924 and is buried in the Jewish Cemetery at Žižkov.

Prague's flagship of the Counter-Reformation, the Church of the Holy Saviour on what is now Karlova (there is another Holy Saviour church just north of Old Town Square, and a Sanctuary of the Holy Saviour in the Convent of St Agnes).

After gradually buying up most of the adjacent neighbourhood, the Jesuits started building their college, the Klementinum, in 1653 – by the time of its completion a century later, it was the largest building in the city after Prague Castle. When the Jesuits fell out with the pope in 1773, it became part of Charles University.

The western façade of the **Church of the Holy Saviour** (kostel Nejsvětějšího Spasitele (Salvátora)) faces Charles Bridge, its sooty stone saints glaring down at merrymakers and the traffic zipping through Křižovnické náměstí. Alongside the church, Karlova ulice takes a bend at the little round **Assumption Chapel** (Vlašská kaple Nanebevzetí Panny Marie), completed in 1600 for the Italian artisans who worked on the Klementinum (it's still technically the property of the Italian government).

Eastwards on Karlova you can look inside **St Clement Church** (kostel sv Klimenta), lavishly rehabilitated in baroque style from 1711 to 1715 to plans by Kilian Dientzenhofer. It's now Greek Orthodox, with services on Sunday at 8.30 and 10 am, to which conservatively dressed visitors are welcome. (There is another St Clement Church in northern Nové Město.)

The three churches form most of the south wall of the Klementinum, a vast complex of beautiful rococo halls now occupied by the Czech National Library. Tragically, it's closed to the public. From gates on Křižovnická, Karlova and Seminářská you can detour through several courtyards. In a courtyard at the centre of the complex is an 18th century observatory tower.

A room you might be able to see is the **Chapel of Mirrors** (Zrcadlová kaple), frequently a concert venue (see the notices posted outside). One architectural handbook suggests that this over-the-top room with mirrors on the ceiling looks more like a boudoir than a chapel!

Near the Klementinum

Beside the Staré Město tower of Charles Bridge is the 17th century **Church of St Francis Seraphinus** (kostel sv Františka Serafinského), its dome decorated on the inside with a fresco of the Last Judgment. The church belongs to the Order of Knights of the Cross, the only Bohemian order of Crusaders still in existence.

Beside the church, in the **Knights of the Cross Gallery** (Galérie Křižovníků), are the Order's ecclesiastical treasures, an arch from the long-gone Judith Bridge, a tacky chapel decorated with stalactites, and occasional changing exhibitions. The gallery is open daily except Monday, from 10 am to 5 pm, for 30 Kč.

Just south of the bridge, at the site of the former Old Town mill, is Novotného lávka, a pedestrian lane full of sunny, overpriced *vinárny* (wine bars) with smashing views of the bridge and castle. At No 1, the private **Opera Mozart Theatre** is a venue for chamber concerts and opera (see the Entertainment chapter). Despite a recent renovation, an upstairs **museum** (☎ 26 53 71) devoted to Bedřich Smetana, Bohemia's sentimental favourite composer, remains uninspiring and lacks labels in English. It's open daily except Tuesday, from 10 am to 5 pm, for 40 Kč.

In the cellar at Karlova 12 is the **Museum of Marionette & Puppet Cultures** (Museum loutkářských kultur), showing the evolution of puppets from the late 17th to early 19th centuries, with 315 samples of this wonderful Czech tradition. It's open daily from 10 am to 8 pm, for 100 Kč. The building called **The Golden Snake** (U zlatého hada), at Karlova 18 on the corner of Liliová, was Prague's first coffee house, opened in 1708 by an Armenian named Deomatus Damajan; it's now a Chinese restaurant.

At Husova 19-21, on the corner of Karlova, is a good modern-art gallery, the **Czech Museum of Fine Arts** (České

Hello Spot, What's for Dinner?

One statue decorating the façade of the House at the Golden Well (Dům U zlaté studny), at the corner of Karlova and Seminářská, bears a closer look. A man is lifting his robe to reveal a bloody wound above the knee, while beside him a dog happily munches on something. The statue is of St Roch (sv Roch), who in the 14th century travelled around Europe helping sufferers of the plague, and came to be known as their patron saint.

Local folklore insists that the good man allowed himself to be castrated by a dog, the better to eliminate all temptations from his life of service. Another, only slightly less risible, story is that he himself caught the plague (a bleeding sore on one's thigh was said to be a sure sign of it), and in the interest of public health had his dog fetch his food for him – though the dog seems to have polished off most of that loaf of bread himself.

muzeum výtvarních umění; ☎ 24 22 20 68), open daily except Monday, from 10 am to noon and 1 to 6 pm. Entrance is usually 20 Kč.

At Žatecká 1, a couple of blocks north of Karlova, is an old theatre called **Puppet Kingdom** (Říše loutek), which got a new lease of life when the respected Kladno puppet troupe moved in with a puppet show for adults – Mozart's opera *Don Giovanni* at 490 Kč a throw, a campy sell-out for several years now. The name 'National Marionette Theatre' was a joke that has stuck.

Malé Náměstí

In 'Little Square', the south-western extension of Old Town Square, is a Renaissance fountain and 16th century wrought-iron grille. Here several fine baroque and neo-Renaissance exteriors decorate some of Staré Město's oldest structures. One of the best known is the VJ Rott Building at No 3, now four floors of snack bars and fine-food shops.

Mariánské Náměstí

On the 2nd floor of the newly renovated City Library (Městská knihovna) at Mariánské náměstí 3 (see Libraries in the Facts for the Visitor chapter) is a branch of the Prague Municipal Gallery, open daily except Monday, from 10 am to 6 pm, for 30 Kč. Enter on Valentinská.

Celetná Ulice

This pedestrianised lane from Old Town Square to the Powder Tower is an open-air museum of well groomed, pastel-painted baroque façades over Gothic frames (and Romanesque foundations, deliberately buried to raise Staré Město above the Vltava's floods).

But the most interesting façade dates only from 1912: Josef Gočár's delightful Cubist front (Prague's first), on the so-called **House of the Black Madonna** (Dům U černé Matky Boží) at No 34, at the corner of the Old Fruit Market (Ovocný trh). Its baroque predecessor's Madonna house-marker went to an exhibition in 1997 and didn't come back, allegedly because historians wanted to do tests to determine its age (it could date as far back as the 14th century). Meanwhile, a replica has been promised. The building now houses a branch of the Czech Museum of Fine Arts (☎ 24 21 17 32), with a fairly interesting permanent exhibition on Czech Cubism, open daily except Monday, from 10 am to 6 pm. Entry is 35 Kč.

Powder Tower (Prašná Brána)

The 65m-tall Powder Tower was begun in 1475 during the reign of King Vladislav II Jagiello on the site of one of Staré Město's original 13 gates. After the defenestration of the mayor in 1483, the king moved to Prague Castle and the tower was left unfinished. The name comes from its use as a gunpowder magazine in the 18th century. Josef Mocker rebuilt, decorated and steepled it between 1875 and 1886, giving it its neo-Gothic icing. It's open for great views between April and October, daily from 10 am to 6 pm, with a 30 Kč entry fee. There is also a tiny exhibit about the tower.

Municipal House (Obecní Dům)

Don't miss the 'Dům', Prague's most sensually beautiful building, with an unrivalled Art Nouveau interior and a façade that looks like a Victorian Easter egg.

It's on the site of the royal court, seat of Bohemia's kings from 1383 to 1483 (when Vladislav II moved to Prague Castle) and only demolished at the turn of this century. Between 1906 and 1912 the Obecní dům was built in its place – a lavish joint effort by some 30 of the leading artists of the day, producing a cultural centre that was to be the architectural climax of the Czech National Revival.

The exterior mosaic, *Homage to Prague*, is set between sculptures representing the oppression and rebirth of the Czech people. You enter beneath a wrought-iron and glass canopy an interior that is Art Nouveau down to the doorknobs.

The restaurant and the *kavárna* flanking the entrance are like walk-in museums of design, and even the basement club and restaurant are handsome. Upstairs are half a dozen over-the-top salons – including the Lord Mayor's Hall, done up entirely by Alfons Mucha, whose paintings and posters have made him an international symbol of Art Nouveau. Also here is Smetana Hall, Prague's biggest concert hall, and a gallery with temporary art exhibits (open daily from 10 am to 6 pm, for 60 Kč). On the way to the basement are a snack bar, a souvenir shop and a ticket counter for admission to the gallery.

Symbolic moments here include the proclamation of an independent Czechoslovak Republic on 28 October 1918, and meetings between Civic Forum and the Jakeš regime in November 1989. The Prague Spring music festival always opens on 12 May, the anniversary of Smetana's death, with a procession from Vyšehrad to the Obecní dům, and a gala performance of his symphonic cycle *Má vlast* (My Country) in Smetana Hall.

Around Obecní Dům

Across náměstí Republiky looms **Hibernian House** (Dům U hybernů). In 1810 this monstrous Empire façade was affixed to a 17th century monastery church by the Viennese architect Georg Fischer, and it became the Prague Customs House. It's now an exhibition hall.

At U Obecního domu 1 is another Art Nouveau gem, the **Hotel Paříž**, built in 1907 and now completely restored.

NA PŘÍKOPĚ (Map 7)

The name means 'on the moat'; with Národní, 28.října and Revoluční this street marks the moat (filled in at the end of the 18th century) by the old Staré Město walls.

This was the haunt of Prague's German café society in the 19th century. Today it is (along with Národní) the main upmarket shopping precinct, lined with banks, bookshops, tourist cafés and a few interesting buildings, including the following:

No 20, Živnostenská banka headquarters, with a very grand Art Nouveau interior completed in 1896 by Osvald Polívka, co-architect of the Obecní dům

Nos 19-21, the Myslbek Building (1996), a trendy shopping complex with a bland glass and metal front but a daring back, facing Ovocný trh

No 18, now Čedok headquarters, also designed by Polívka (1912) and linked with No 20 by a bridge over Nekázanka ulice

No 16, the Church of the Holy Cross (Kostel sv Kříže), a leaden Empire-style block by Georg Fischer

No 12, House of the Black Rose (U černé růže); upstairs, in an ornate and charming neo-Renaissance interior by Josef Fanta (1880), is the Moser crystal shop

No 10, the Sylva-Taroucca Palace, a rococo masterpiece by Kilian Dientzenhofer (1751), and the oldest building on the street

Na příkopě runs westwards from Wenceslas Square as 28.října (28 October; Czechoslovak Independence Day), and Wenceslas Square runs northwards as Na můstku (On the Little Bridge; that is, where a footbridge once crossed the moat – you can see an arch of it, on the left just past the ticket machines and the underground entrance to Můstek metro station).

Although developers go giddy over this junction (Map 6) – nicknamed the Golden Cross – it's a charmless spot with postcard vendors, prostitutes and loitering heavies.

Wax museums seem to be *de rigueur* for tourist centres nowadays; leave it to Prague to have two. First to arrive was the **Wax Museum** (Map 6; Muzeum voskových figurín) at 28.října 13, with an overpriced (120 Kč) who's who of barely recognisable Czech historical figures. But check out the clever, multi-media 'Magic Prague in a Storm of History' exhibit. It's open daily from 10 am to 8 pm (the other wax museum is on Národní; see the later West of Wenceslas Square section).

ST GALL'S MARKET AREA (Maps 6 & 7)

In about 1230 a new market quarter, Havelské Město or St Gall's Town (named after the 7th century Irish monk who helped introduce Europe to Christianity), was laid out for the pleasure of the German merchants invited into Prague by Wenceslas I.

Modern-day Rytířská and Havelská were at that time a single plaza, surrounded by arcaded merchants' houses. Specialist markets (*trhy*) included those for coal (Uhelný trh) at the western end and for fruit (Ovocný trh) at the eastern end. In the 15th century an island of stalls was built down the middle.

Havelská Market (Maps 6 & 7)

All that remains of St Gall's market today is the souvenir, flower, fruit and vegetable market on Havelská ulice, and the clothes hawkers in adjacent V kotcích. No match for the original, it's still Prague's most central open-air market.

At the eastern end of Havelská is the **Church of St Gall** (Map 7; Kostel sv Havla), as old as St Gall's Town itself. Jan Hus and his predecessors preached church reform here. The Carmelites took possession of it in 1627, and in 1723 added its present shapely baroque face. The Czech baroque painter Karel Škréta (1610-74) is buried in the church.

At the western end of Havelská is the former coal market (Uhelný trh), and nearby the plain 12th century **Church of St Martin in the Wall** (Map 6; Kostel sv Martina ve zdi), a parish church enlarged and Gothicised in the 14th century. The name comes from its having had the Old Town wall built right round it. In 1414 the church was the site of the first-ever Hussite communion service *sub utraque specie* (with both bread and wine), from which the name 'Utraquist' derives.

The Karolinum (Map 7)

Charles University – central Europe's oldest university, founded by Charles IV in 1348 – took as its original home the so-called Rotlev or Röthlow House at Železná 9. With Protestantism and Czech nationalism on the rise, the reform preacher Jan Hus became rector in 1402 and soon persuaded Wenceslas IV to slash the voting rights of the university's German students – thousands of them left Bohemia when this was announced.

The facilities of the ever-expanding university were concentrated here in 1611, and by the 18th century the old burgher's house had grown into a sizeable complex, known as the Karolinum. After the Battle of Bílá Hora (White Mountain) it was handed over to the Jesuits, who gave it a baroque working-over. When they were booted out in 1773 the university took it back. WWII damage led to remodelling and expansion.

Charles University now has faculties all over Prague, and the Karolinum is used only for some medical faculty offices, the University Club and occasional academic ceremonies. Its finest room is the high-ceilinged assembly hall upstairs.

Among pre-university Gothic traces is the **Chapel of SS Cosmas & Damian**, with its extraordinary oriel protruding from the southern wall. Built around 1370, it was renovated in 1881 by Josef Mocker.

For practical information about the university, see Courses at the end of this chapter and Universities in the Facts for the Visitor chapter.

Estates Theatre (Stavovské Divadlo) (Map 7)

Beside the Karolinum at Železná 11 is Prague's oldest theatre and its finest neoclassical building. Opened in 1783 as the Nostitz Theatre (after its founder, Count Anton von Nostitz-Rieneck), it was patronised by upper-class German Praguers. It came to be called the Estates Theatre (Stavovské divadlo) – the Estates being the traditional nobility – and is still commonly known by this name.

After WWII it was renamed the Tyl Theatre (Tylovo divadlo) in honour of the 19th century Czech playwright Josef Kajetán Tyl, from one of whose plays came the Czech national anthem, *Kde domov můj?* (Where Is My Home?) The early 1990s saw the name revert to Stavovské divadlo. Its Czech-language plays occasionally include simultaneous English translation. The theatre is equipped for disabled and hearing-impaired visitors (see the Entertainment chapter).

Around the corner at Ovocný trh 6 is the 17th century Kolowrat Theatre, now also a National Theatre venue.

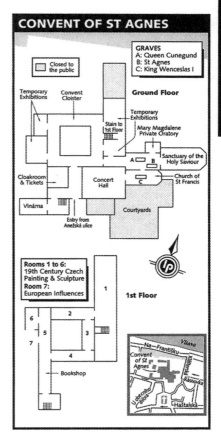

CONVENT OF ST AGNES

GRAVES
A: Queen Cunegund
B: St Agnes
C: King Wenceslas I

Closed to the public

Temporary Exhibitions   Convent Cloister   **Ground Floor**

Temporary Exhibitions

Stairs to 1st Floor

Mary Magdalene Private Oratory

Sanctuary of the Holy Saviour

Cloakroom & Tickets   Concert Hall   Church of St Francis

Vinárna

Entry from Anežská ulice

Courtyards

Rooms 1 to 6:
19th Century Czech
Painting & Sculpture
Room 7:
European Influences

1st Floor

6 2
5 3
7
4
Bookshop

Na—Františku   Vltava
Convent of St Agnes

CONVENT OF ST AGNES (KLÁŠTER SV ANEŽKY) (Map 7)

In the north-eastern corner of Staré Město are the surviving buildings of the former Convent of St Agnes, Prague's oldest standing Gothic structures, now finely restored and used by the National Gallery.

In 1234 the Franciscan Order of the Poor Clares was founded by the Přemysl king Wenceslas I, who made his sister Anežka (Agnes) its first abbess. Agnes was beatified in the 19th century, and with timing that could hardly be accidental, Pope John Paul II canonised her as St Agnes of Bohemia just before the revolutionary events of November 1989.

In the 16th century the buildings were handed over to the Dominicans, and after Joseph II dissolved the monasteries, they became a squatter's paradise. They've only been restored in the last few decades.

The complex consists mainly of the cloister, a sanctuary and a church in French Gothic style. In the Chapel of the Virgin

Mary (kaple Panny Marie), within the **Sanctuary of the Holy Saviour** (svatyně sv Salvatora), are the graves of St Agnes and of Wenceslas I's queen Cunegund. Alongside this is the smaller **Church of St Francis** (Kostel sv Františka), in whose chancel Wenceslas I is buried. Part of its ruined nave and other rooms have been rebuilt as a chilly concert and lecture hall.

The 1st floor of the **cloister** now holds the National Gallery's good permanent collection (☎ 24 81 06 28) of 19th century Czech paintings and sculptures, and in the last room a shifting show of works by other European artists who influenced them. Included is an eclectic selection from Josef Mánes, the foremost painter of the Czech National Revival. Don't miss the luminous little landscapes of Josef Navrátil.

Everything is open daily except Monday, from 10 am to 6 pm. Normal admission is 70 Kč (free for the disabled). It's at U milosrdných 17, on the corner of Anežská (take any tram along Revoluční, or bus No 207 from Jan Palach Square).

The winding lanes around St Agnes and Haštalské náměstí retain a feeling of earlier times. Only furious lobbying by residents and Prague intellectuals saved the area from the same clearance that ravaged Josefov at the turn of the century.

SOUTH-WEST STARÉ MĚSTO (Maps 6 & 7)

The meandering lanes and passageways in the quarter from Karlova ulice south to Národní are Prague's best territory for aimless wandering. When the crowds thin out early or late in the day, this area can cast such a spell that it's a surprise to return to the 20th century outside its borders.

Bethlehem Chapel (Betlémská Kaple) (Map 6)

On Betlémské náměstí is one of Prague's most important churches, the real birthplace of Hussitism.

Reformist Praguers won permission to build a chapel where services could be held in Czech instead of Latin, and in 1391

proceeded to construct the biggest chapel Bohemia had ever seen, for some 3000 worshippers. Architecturally it was a radical departure, with a simple square hall focused on the pulpit rather than the altar. Jan Hus preached here from 1402 to 1412, marking the emergence of the church-reform movement from the sanctuary of Charles University (where he was rector).

In the 18th century the chapel was torn down. Remnants were discovered around 1920 and – because Hussitism had official blessing as an antecedent of communism – the whole thing was painstakingly reconstructed from 1948 to 1954 in its original form, based on old drawings, descriptions, and traces of the original work in outer walls that were still standing. It's now a National Cultural Monument.

Only the street-facing wall is brand new. You can still see some original bits in the eastern wall: the pulpit door, several windows and the door to the preacher's quarters. These quarters, including rooms used by Hus and others, are apparently original too; they're now used for exhibits. The wall paintings are modern, based on old Hussite tracts. The indoor well predates the chapel.

It's open daily from 9 am to 6 pm, with an English text available at the door; admission is 30 Kč. Every year on the night of 5 July, the eve of Hus' burning at the stake in 1415, a commemorative celebration is held here, with speeches and bell-ringing.

Náprstek Museum (Náprstkovo Muzeum) (Map 6)

At the western end of Betlémské náměstí is a small museum founded by Vojta Náprstek, a 19th century industrialist with a passion for both anthropology and modern technology. His ethnographical collection, also known as the Museum of Asian, African & American Cultures, is open daily except Monday, from 9 am to noon and 12.45 to 5 pm, for 30 Kč (his technology exhibits are now part of the National Technology Museum in Holešovice).

St Giles Church (Kostel Sv Jiljí) (Map 7)

With stocky Romanesque columns, tall Gothic windows, and oozing baroque inside, this is a good place to appreciate the religious dimension to Prague's past architectural fortunes. The church, on the corner of Zlatá and Husova, was founded in 1371. The proto-Hussite reformer Jan Milíč of Kroměříž preached here before the Bethlehem Chapel was built. The Dominicans gained possession during the Counter-Reformation, built a cloister next door and 'baroquefied' it in the 1730s. Václav Reiner, the Czech painter who did the ceiling frescoes a few years before his death, is buried here.

Chapel of the Holy Cross (Kaple Sv Kříže) (Map 6)

A tiny Romanesque rotunda at the western end of Konviktská is one of Prague's oldest buildings. It started out as a parish church in about 1100. Saved from demolition and restored in the 1860s by a collective of Czech artists, it still has the remnants of some 600-year-old wall frescoes, though you may have to attend Mass to see them (Sunday and Tuesday at 5 pm, with an English-language Mass on the first Monday of each month at 5.30 pm).

Police & Secret Police (Map 6)

Staré Město's charm goes a bit cold along Konviktská and Bartolomějská, and not just because the block between them is full of police offices. Before November 1989, the block was occupied by the StB (Státní bezpečnost, or State Security), the hated secret police. Czechs are still understandably twitchy about police of any shade and it's a common suspicion that a few former StB officers are still around, but now in new uniforms.

Backing onto Bartolomějská is an old convent and the once-lovely 18th century **St Bartholomew Church** (Kostel sv Bartoloměje), for a time part of the StB complex and recently returned to the Franciscans. The church is closed to the public,

but the enterprising Unitas Penzion has rented space from the nuns, and guests can now spend the night in refurbished StB prison cells, including one where Václav Havel spent a night (see the Places to Stay chapter).

Nové Město

Nové Město means 'New Town', although the crescent of the city east and south of Staré Město was only 'new' when it was founded by Charles IV in 1348. Its outer fortifications were knocked down in 1875. The layout has been essentially preserved, although most surviving buildings are from the 19th and early 20th centuries. Many blocks are honeycombed with dark, pedestrian-only passages, some of which are lined with shops, cafés and theatres.

Nové Město extends from Revoluční and Na příkopě out to Wilsonova and the main railway line, and south of Národní almost to Vyšehrad. Its focus is Wenceslas Square, a broad, 750m-long boulevard lined with *fin-de-siècle* buildings, sloping down from the National Museum towards Staré Město. Náměstí Republiky, which falls on Revoluční, the dividing line between Staré and Nové Město, is described in the earlier Staré Město section.

POSTAGE STAMP MUSEUM (MUZEUM POŠTOVNÍ ZNÁMKY) (Map 7)

Philatelists will enjoy this little museum (☎ 231 20 60) at Nové mlýny 2, near the northern end of Revoluční, with old postal signs and an exhibit on how stamps are drawn and printed; others may enjoy the scenes of 19th century rural Bohemia on the walls. It's open daily except Monday, from 9 am to 4.30 pm, for 25 Kč.

Across the street is the stone **Petrská vodárenská věž** or waterworks tower, built around 1660 on the site of earlier wooden ones. From here, wooden pipes once transported river water to buildings in Nové Město.

MUSEUM OF THE CITY OF PRAGUE (MUZEUM HLAVNÍHO MĚSTA PRAHY) (Map 6)

At Na poříčí 52 near the Florenc metro station is an excellent museum of the city's history. Built between 1896 and 1898, the ground floor is devoted to the period up to the Battle of Bílá Hora (White Mountain) in 1620. Upstairs are knick-knacks including the Old Town Hall clock's 1866 calendar-wheel with Josef Mánes' beautiful panels.

But what everybody comes to see is Antonín Langweil's astonishing 1:480 scale model of Prague as it looked between 1826 and 1834. It's most rewarding after you've got to know Prague a bit, so you can spot the changes. Other drawings, paintings and woodcuts offer earlier 'snapshots' of the city.

The museum is open daily except Monday from 10 am to 6 pm, for 30 Kč. There's a good English text if you ask.

AROUND JINDŘIŠSKÁ ULICE (Maps 6 & 7)

Squarely at the end of Jindřišská is the **Jindřišská Tower** (Map 7; Jindřišská věž), a former watchtower or bell tower built in the 15th century (another, more run-down, tower is Petrská věž, on Petrské náměstí at the northern end of Nové Město).

Around the corner, at Jeruzalémská 7, is the **Jubilee Synagogue** (Map 7; Jubilejní synagóga), also called the Great (Velká) Synagogue, dating from 1906. Its elaborately decorated Moorish-style interior is now open to the public. Note the names of donors on the colourful stained-glass windows, and the grand organ above the entrance. It's open daily except Saturday and holidays, from 1 to 5 pm, for 30 Kč.

A good **Mucha Museum** (Map 6), at Panská 7, features the sensuous poster art of Alfons Mucha as well as sketches, photographs and other memorabilia. There's also a video on his life (available in English or Czech, just ask). It's open daily from 10 am to 6 pm, for 120 Kč (Czechs pay 50 Kč).

MAIN TRAIN STATION (HLAVNÍ NÁDRAŽÍ) (Map 6)

Have a look at the fading Art Nouveau elegance of the original, above-ground section of the station, designed by Josef Fanta and built between 1901 and 1909. The exterior and vaulted interior are full of bas-relief women's faces from around the world. Under the central dome a plaque says *Praga: mater urbium* (Prague: Mother of Cities). See the Train section of the Getting There & Away chapter for a practical tour of the station.

A statue at the northern end of the park in front of the station was meant to celebrate the Soviet liberation of Prague at the end of WWII but has always been vaguely insulting, with its submissive Czech soldier embracing his bigger Soviet comrade. Now stripped of its plaque, it looks more like a celebration of gay love in the military.

NATIONAL MUSEUM (NARODNÍ MUZEUM) (Map 6)

Looming above Wenceslas Square is the neo-Renaissance bulk of the National Museum, designed in the 1880s by Josef Schulz as an architectural symbol of the Czech National Revival.

The museum was founded in 1818 as a regional natural history museum by several Czech aristocrats. However it was Caspar Sternberg who originally conceived the idea of a national museum and who is credited with most of the work of establishing it. Its first home was at the Sternberg Palace in Hradčany, but in 1846 it was moved to a building on Na Příkopě where the Živnostenská bank now stands. Today's National Museum building was built from 1885 to 1891 on the site of the former Horse Gate.

The museum's rocks, fossils and coins are pretty routine, and devoid of English labels. The changing exhibits – usually about a theme or person in Czech history – are normally much more interesting than the permanent exhibits.

Perhaps most appealing is the building itself, especially the grand stairwell, and the upper gallery of the 'pantheon' with (strangely womanless) murals of Czech legend and history by František Ženíšek and Václav Brožík, and pink-bottomed cherubs by Vojtěch Hynais.

Light-coloured areas on the façade of the museum are patched-up bullet holes. In 1968, Warsaw Pact troops apparently mistook the museum for the former National Assembly or the radio station, and raked it with gunfire.

The museum (☎ 24 49 71 11) is open daily (except the first Tuesday of each month), from 10 am to 6 pm. The 60 Kč admission (students 30 Kč) is waived on the first Monday of each month.

Across the road to the north-east is the former **National Assembly** building (1973), built on the site of the former Stock Exchange (1936-38; parts of its walls can be seen inside). It's now the world headquarters for Radio Free Europe. Next beyond it is the **Smetana Theatre** or State Opera (Statní opera).

WENCESLAS SQUARE (VÁCLAVSKÉ NÁMĚSTÍ) (Map 6)

A horse market in medieval times, Wenceslas Square (also called Václavák) got its present name during the nationalist upheavals of the mid-19th century. It has been the scene of a great deal of Czech history ever since. A giant Mass was celebrated in the square in 1848. In 1918 the new Czechoslovak Republic was celebrated here.

In January 1969, in protest against the Warsaw Pact invasion, university student Jan Palach set himself on fire on the steps of the National Museum, staggered into the square and collapsed. The next day some 200,000 people showed up to honour him. It was four agonising days before he died.

Following the 17 November 1989 beating of students by police on Národní, thousands gathered here in anger, night after night. A week later, in a stunning mirror-image of Klement Gottwald's 1948 proclamation of communist rule, Alexander Dubček and Václav Havel stepped onto the balcony of the **Melantrich Building** to a

In 1989 Alexander Dubček greeted jubilant crowds in Wenceslas Square, 21 years after the Prague Spring.

thunderous, tearful ovation, and proclaimed its end.

At the top of the square is Josef Myslbek's muscular equestrian **statue of St Wenceslas** (sv Václav), the 10th century pacifist Duke of Bohemia, 'Good King Wenceslas' of the Christmas carol – never a king but decidedly good. Flanked by other patron saints of Bohemia – Prokop, Adalbert, Agnes and Wenceslas' grandmother Ludmilla – he has been plastered with posters and bunting at every one of the square's historic moments. Near the statue, where Jan Palach fell, a small memorial to the victims of communism bears photographs and handwritten epitaphs for Palach and other stubborn rebels.

In contrast to the solemnity of this shrine, the square beyond it has become a monument to the capitalist urge, a gaudy gallery of cafés, shops, greedy cabbies and pricey hotels. Noteworthy buildings (from the top of the square, even numbers on the west side, all on Map 6 unless noted) include:

Grand Hotel Evropa (1906), No 25: the most beautiful building on the square, Art Nouveau inside and out; have a peep at the French restaurant at the rear of the ground floor, and at the 2nd floor atrium

Melantrich Building, No 36: from its balcony Havel and Dubček spoke in November 1989

Wiehl House (1896; named after its designer, Antonín Wiehl), **No 34**: with a façade decorated with neo-Renaissance murals by Mikuláš Aleš and others

Peterkův dům (Peterka House), **No 12**: Jan Kotěra's 1901 Art Nouveau building

Baťa shoe store, No 6: designed by Ludvík Kysela in 1929 for Tomáš Baťa, art patron, progressive industrialist and founder of the worldwide shoe empire

Lindt Building, next door at **No 4**: also designed by Ludvík Kysela, finished the year before the Baťa store and one of the republic's first constructivist buildings

Koruna palác (Map 7; 1914), **No 1**: an Art Nouveau design by Antonín Pfeiffer, this is the building with a tower on the north-eastern corner of the square; and note its charming tiny façade around the corner on Na příkopě

At the bottom, Wenceslas Square intersects the upmarket shopping street of Na příkopě at the so-called 'Golden Cross' (described under Staré Město).

WEST OF WENCESLAS SQUARE (Map 6)
Lucerna Passage

The most elegant of Nové Město's many passages runs beneath the Lucerna Palace, bounded by Štěpánská, Vodičkova and V jámě. It was designed by Václav Havel, the president's grandfather (and is still owned by the president's sister-in-law). The Art Nouveau Lucerna complex includes theatres, cafés, a cinema and a nightclub-cum-restaurant.

Of numerous entrances to the complex, the handsomest is beneath the 1902 **U Nováků** building at Vodičkova 30, which itself has one of Prague's finest Art Nouveau façades, complete with mosaics of country life.

Church of Our Lady of the Snows (Kostel Panny Marie Sněžné)

The most sublime attraction in the neigh-bourhood is this Gothic church at the bottom of Wenceslas Square. It was begun in the 14th century by Charles IV but only the chancel was ever completed, which accounts for its proportions: seemingly taller than it is long. Charles had intended it to be the grandest church in Prague; the nave is higher than that of St Vitus, and the altar is the city's tallest. It was a Hussite stronghold, ringing to the sermons of Jan Želivský, who led the 1419 defenestration that touched off the Hussite Wars.

The church is entered past the Austrian Cultural Institute (temporary art exhibitions are held here), Jungmannovo náměstí 18. Have a look at the church's fine Gothic entryway (now locked) and the bizarre Cubist streetlamp by Emil Králíček (1913), at the western corner of Jungmannovo náměstí 14. Beside the church is the **Chapel of the Pasov Virgin** (kaple Panny Marie Pasovské), now a venue for temporary art exhibitions.

Rest your feet in the **Františkánská zahrada**, former monastery gardens built beside the church by the Franciscans, and now a peaceful park in the middle of the block.

Along Národní

Národní is central Prague's 'high street', a stately gauntlet of mid-range shops and grand government buildings – topped off by the National Theatre at the Vltava end. Following are some attractions on a stroll west from Jungmannovo náměstí.

Fronting Jungmannovo náměstí at Národní 40 is an age-blackened, imitation Venetian palace known as the **Adria Palace**. Beneath it is the Adria Theatre, original home of Laterna Magika (the Magic Lantern Theatre) and meeting place of Civic Forum in the heady days of the Velvet Revolution. From here, Dubček and Havel walked through the Lucerna Passage to their 24 November 1989 appearance on the balcony of the Melantrich Building. The black-light Theatre Animato now uses the theatre (see under Theatre in the Entertainment chapter).

Details of central Prague: Malá Strana sgraffito (top right), House of the Black Sun (middle left), Koruna palàc (middle right), Old Town Hall (bottom left), St James Church (top left & bottom right)

RICHARD NEBESKÝ

RICHARD NEBESKÝ

RICHARD NEBESKÝ

RICHARD NEBESKÝ

RICHARD NEBESKÝ

JONATHAN SMITH

Modern Prague: striking graffiti (top, middle & bottom left), artistic house emblem in Hradčany (top right), the Myslbek building rear gate (middle right) and Franz Kafka's silhouette (bottom right)

Prague's second wax museum, **Pražské panoptikum**, in the Palác Metro passage at No 25, includes a mock-up of a 19th century Josefov alley, deserted except for two figures, one of whom is Franz Kafka. It's open daily from 10 am to 8 pm, for 119 Kč.

The **plaque** with hands making a V-symbol and reading '17.11.89', on the wall near No 16, is in memory of the students clubbed on that date, an event that pushed the communist government towards its final collapse a few days later.

West of Voršilská, the lemon-yellow walls of the **Convent of St Ursula** (klášter sv Voršila) frame a pink church whose lush baroque interior includes a battalion of Apostle statues. Out front is St John of Nepomuk, and in the building's lower right niche is a gruesome statue of St Agatha holding her severed breasts.

Across the road at No 7 is the fine Art Nouveau façade (by Osvald Polívka) of the **Viola Building**, former home of the Prague Insurance Co, with huge letters spelling out 'Praha' around five circular windows, and mosaics spelling out *život, kapitál, důchod, věno* and *pojišťuje* (life, capital, income, dowry, insurance). The building next door, a former publishing house, is also a Polívka design.

On the southern side at No 4, looking like it has been bubble-wrapped by Christo, is Nová Scéna, the 1983 New National Theatre building, home of **Laterna Magika**. This pioneering, multi-media theatre, combining projected images, music and live actors, was humbly born at the other end of the street in the Adria Theatre, but has here become a permanent, pricey tourist attraction.

Finally, facing the Vltava across Smetanovo nábřeží, is the **National Theatre** (Národní divadlo), neo-Renaissance flagship of the Czech National Revival, funded entirely by private donations and decorated inside and out by a roll-call of prominent Czech artists. Architect Josef Zítek's masterpiece burned down within weeks of its 1881 opening but, incredibly, was re-funded and restored under Josef Schulz in less than two years. It's now mainly used for ballet and opera performances.

Across Národní from the theatre is the **Kavárna Slavia**, known for its river views and comically awful service, and once *the* place to be seen or to grab an after-theatre nosh. After several changes of ownership and a face-lift, it's now *the* place for tourists.

MASARYKOVO NÁBŘEŽÍ (MASARYK EMBANKMENT) (Map 6)

About 200m south of the National Theatre along Masarykovo nábřeží is a grand Art Nouveau building at No 32, once the East German embassy, now occupied by the **Goethe Institut**.

Opposite is **Slovanský ostrov** (Slav Island or Žofín; Map 6), a sleepy, dog-eared sandbank with river views and gardens. For more about this and Prague's other islands, see the Islands of Prague section later in this chapter. For more on renting a boat here, see the Getting Around chapter.

At the south end of the island is the Mánes Building, with a restaurant, disco and the **Mánes Gallery**. The gallery was founded in the 1920s by a group of artists headed by painter Josef Mánes, as an alternative to the Czech Academy of Arts. It still has one of Prague's better displays of contemporary art, with changing exhibits, open daily except Monday, from 10 am to 6 pm (admission 25 Kč).

KARLOVO NÁMĚSTÍ (Maps 6 & 9)

At over seven hectares, Charles Square is Prague's biggest square, although it's more of a park. Presiding over it is **St Ignatius Church** (Kostel sv Ignáce; Map 9), a 1660s baroque *tour de force* designed by Carlo Lurago for the Jesuits. It's worth a look for its huge stone portal and lavish interior.

The square's historical focus is the **New Town Hall** (Novoměstská radnice; Map 6) at the north-eastern end, built when 'New Town' was new. From its windows two of

Wenceslas IV's Catholic councillors were flung to their deaths in 1419 by followers of the Hussite preacher Jan Želivský, giving defenestration (throwing out of the window) a new political meaning and Czechs a new political tactic, and touching off the Hussite Wars.

The 203m **tower**, added 35 years later, is open from April to September, daily except Monday, from 10 am to 6 pm. For 20 Kč you can climb its 221 steps, and see the town hall's Gothic Hall of Justice, site of the defenestration. The town hall also has an art gallery with temporary exhibits.

The baroque palace at the south end of the square belongs to Charles University. It's known as Faustův dům (Faust House; Map 9) because, according to a popular story, Mephisto took Dr Faust to hell through a hole in the ceiling here; and because of associations with Rudolf II's Irish court alchemist, Edward Kelley, who toiled here in the 16th century trying to convert lead to gold.

Resslova to the west, and Žitná and Ječná to the east, are central Prague's cross-town arteries. The intersection of Resslova with the square is the city's nocturnal transport hub; all eight night-time tram routes pass through here (see the Getting Around chapter).

RESSLOVA ULICE (Map 9)

The baroque **Church of SS Cyril & Methodius** (Kostel sv Cyril a Metoděj), a 1730s work by Kilian Dientzenhofer and Paul Bayer at the corner of Resslova and Na Zderaze, was the hiding place of seven Czechoslovak paratroopers who took part in the assassination of Reinhard Heydrich, the Nazi governor of Bohemia and Moravia, in May 1942. During the German siege of the church, attempts were made to fire through a gap in the wall into the crypt where they were holed up, and to flood it using fire hoses. In the end all seven were killed or committed suicide. See the boxed text on the assassination of Heydrich under History in the Facts about Prague chapter,

and the section on Lidice in the Excursions chapter, for more on this and the aftermath.

You can see the crypt, and an exhibit and video about Nazi persecution of the Czechs, daily except Monday, from 10 am to 5 pm (in winter to 4 pm), for 30 Kč. Enter at a side door on Na Zderaze. On the Resslova side of the church is a plaque (where fresh flowers are sometimes placed) at the gap in the wall, still bearing bullet marks.

On the other side of Resslova is the 14th century Gothic **Church of St Wenceslas in Zderaz** (Kostel sv Václava na Zderaze), the former parish church of Zderaz, a village that predates Nové Město. On its western side are bits of a wall and windows from its 12th century Romanesque predecessor.

RAŠÍNOVO NÁBŘEŽÍ (RAŠÍN EMBANKMENT) (Map 9)

President **Václav Havel's flat**, where he first chose to live in preference to Prague Castle, faces the river from the top floor of a nondescript building at Rašínovo nábřeží 78; this is surely the world's least pompous presidential residence. Today he lives in a house on the outskirts of Prague 6.

On the corner of Rašínovo nábřeží and Resslova is the arresting **Dancing Building** (Tančící dům), whose daring, curvy outlines led its architects, Vlado Milunć and the American Frank O Gehry, to name it at first the 'Astaire & Rogers Building', after the legendary dancing duo. It's surprising how well it fits in with its ageing neighbours. It was completed in 1996.

From here the Vltava is lined in both directions with *fin-de-siècle* apartment houses. Two blocks south, in Palackého náměstí, is Stanislav Sucharda's extraordinary **monument to František Palacký** – an Art Nouveau swarm of haunted bronze figures around a stodgy statue of the 19th century historian and giant of the Czech National Revival.

EMMAUS MONASTERY (KLÁŠTER EMAUZY) (Map 9)

A block inland from Palackého náměstí, at Vyšehradská 49, is Emmaus Monastery, originally called Na Slovanech Monastery. It was completed in 1372 for a Slavonic order of Benedictines by order of Charles IV, who persuaded the pope to allow the Old Church Slavonic liturgy here, possibly in the hope of undermining the Orthodox Church in neighbouring Slavonic states. These un-Roman Catholic beginnings probably saved it from later Hussite plundering. Spanish Benedictines later renamed it Emmaus.

The monastery's Gothic **St Mary Church** (Kostel Panny Marie) was damaged by Allied bombs in February 1945. A few ceiling frescoes are still visible. The asymmetrical spires, added in the 1960s, look vaguely out of place. The attached cloisters have some fine, faded original frescoes, salted with bits of pagan symbolism. Unfortunately the whole complex was under restoration at the time of writing.

Across Vyšehradská is the 1739 **Church of St John of Nepomuk on the Rock** (Kostel sv Jana Nepomuckého na Skalce), one of the city's most beautiful Dientzenhofer churches. Just south on Na slupi is a large, peaceful **botanical garden**, open every day.

EAST OF KARLOVO NÁMĚSTÍ (Maps 6 & 9)

Though full of hospitals, the area east of Karlovo náměstí has a few delights. Wedged between Žitná and Ječná (Map 9) is the 14th century **St Stephen Church** (Kostel sv Štěpána), with a 15th century tower, 17th and 18th century chapels, and a neo-Gothic face-lift carried out by Josef Mocker in the 1870s.

Behind it on Na Rybníčku is one of Prague's three surviving round Romanesque chapels, the **Rotunda of St Longinus** (Rotunda sv Longina; Map 6), built in the early 12th century. It's unfortunately closed to the public.

The most striking building in the quiet neighbourhood south of Ječná, and one of the city's finest non-church baroque structures, is **Vila Amerika** (1720) at Ke Karlovu 20 (Map 9). This French-style summer house designed by Kilian Dientzenhofer is

now a museum (☎ 29 82 14) dedicated to the composer Antonín Dvořák, open daily except Monday from 10 am to 5 pm, for 30 Kč.

From April to October, the Original Music Theatre of Prague can be seen performing Dvořák's vocal and instrumental works in period costume in the villa's salon, at 8 pm on Tuesday and Friday. Tickets, at a whopping 490 Kč, are available only from the museum.

Around the corner at Na bojišti 12 (Map 9) is the **U kalicha** (At the Chalice) pub. Here the hapless Švejk is arrested at the beginning of Jaroslav Hašek's comic novel of WWI, *The Good Soldier Švejk* (which Hašek cranked out in instalments from his own local pub). U kalicha is milking the connection, as you'll see from all the tour buses outside.

At the southern end of Ke Karlovu (Map 9) is a little church with a big name, **Church of the Assumption of the Virgin Mary & Charlemagne** (Kostel Nanebevzetí Panny Marie a Karla Velikého), founded by Charles IV in 1350 and modelled on Charlemagne's burial chapel in Aachen. In the 16th century it acquired its fabulous ribbed vault, whose revolutionary unsupported span was attributed by some to witchcraft. The monastery buildings next door house a humdrum **Police Museum** (Muzeum policie), open daily except Monday, from 10 am to 5 pm, for a mere 10 Kč.

Below the church you can find some of Nové Město's original fortifications, and look out at the Nusle Bridge (Nuselský most) leaping the valley of Botič Creek to Vyšehrad, with six lanes of traffic on top and the metro inside.

Inner Suburbs

VYŠEHRAD (Map 9)

Archaeologists know that various early Slavonic tribes set up camp near Hradčany and at Vyšehrad (High Castle), a crag above the Vltava south of Botič Creek, which passes through the Nusle valley. But Vyšehrad alone is regarded as Prague's *mythical* birthplace. According to legend, the wise chieftain Krok built a castle here in the 7th century. Libuše, the cleverest of his three daughters, prophesied that a great city would rise here. Taking as her king a ploughman named Přemysl, she founded Praha and the Přemyslid line of Czech rulers.

Vyšehrad may in fact have been settled as early as the 9th century. Boleslav II (ruled 972-99) may have lived here for a time. There was a fortified town by the mid-11th century. Vratislav II (ruled 1061-92) moved here from Hradčany, beefing up the walls, and adding a castle, the St Lawrence Basilica, the Church of SS Peter & Paul and the Rotunda of St Martin. His successors stayed until 1140, when Vladislav II returned to Hradčany.

Vyšehrad then faded until Charles IV, aware of its symbolic importance, repaired the walls and joined them to those of his new town, Nové Město. He built a small palace, and decreed that coronations of Bohemian kings should begin with a procession from here to Hradčany.

Nearly everything was wiped out during the Hussite Wars. The hill remained a ruin – except for a township of artisans and traders – until after the Thirty Years' War, when Leopold I re-fortified it.

The Czech National Revival generated new interest in Vyšehrad as a symbol of Czech history. Painters painted it, poets sang about the old days, Smetana set his opera *Libuše* there. Many fortifications were dismantled in 1866 and the parish graveyard was converted into a national memorial cemetery.

Vyšehrad retains a place in Czech hearts. Since the 1920s the old fortress has been a quiet park, with splendid views of the Vltava valley. It's a great place to stroll, shake off the urban blues, and take in a bit of Prague's mythical flavour.

A good booklet about Vyšehrad's buildings is available from the Casemates, St Lawrence Basilica and the Vyšehrad Gallery.

The Vyšehrad Complex

Orientation From Vyšehrad metro station, head west past the Palace of Culture (Palác kultury) to the Tábor Gate (Táborská brána). Inside are the remains of another gate (brána Špička), an information office (open daily from 9.30 am to 6.30 pm), a café, and the Leopoldova brána, the most elegant of the fort's gates. The Táborská and Leopoldova gates were erected, and the Gothic Špička gate pulled down, in the course of refortification after the Thirty Years' War.

A steeper entrance is up from the No 18 or 24 tram on Na slupi or the No 7 tram on Svobodova, through the 1842 Brick Gate (Cihelná brána, also called Pražská or Vyšehradská brána). Check out the fine views of the Nusle valley from the northeastern bastion.

A more demanding route is up the long stairs from tram No 3, 16, 17 or 21 on the riverside drive, to Vyšehrad Cemetery.

Rotunda of St Martin Vratislav II's little chapel (Rotunda Sv Martina) is Prague's oldest standing building. In the 18th century it was used as a powder magazine. The door and frescoes date from a renovation in about 1880.

Nearby are a 1714 plague column and the baroque St Mary Chapel in the Ramparts (kaple Panny Marie v hradbách), dating from about 1750, and behind them the remains of the 14th century Church of the Beheading of St John the Baptist (kostelík Stětí sv Jana Křtitele).

Stone Cluster In the park across the road from the former New Archdeaconry (Nové děkanství) is a cluster of three phalli, made of a stone not found in this region. It's believed these may have been part of a prehistoric sundial or solstice marker.

Vyšehrad Cemetery For Czechs this cemetery (Vyšehradský Hřbitov) may be the hill's main attraction. In the late 19th century, the parish graveyard was made into a memorial cemetery for the cultural good of the land. For the real heroes, an elaborate pantheon called the Slavín (loosely, Hall of Fame), designed by Antonín Wiehl, was added along the northern side in 1894.

The Slavín's 50 or so graves and some 600 in the rest of the cemetery include those of Smetana and Dvořák, writers Karel Čapek, Jan Neruda and Božena Němcová, painter Alfons Mucha and sculptor Josef Myslbek; a directory of big names is at the entrance. Some of the most beautiful headstones bear names few foreigners will recognise. It's open daily from 8 am to 7 pm in summer, to 6 pm in spring and autumn and from 9 am to 4 pm in winter.

The Prague Spring music festival kicks off every 12 May, the anniversary of Smetana's death, with a procession from his grave to the Obecní dům.

Church of SS Peter & Paul Vratislav II's church (Kostel Sv Petra a Pavla) has been built and rebuilt over the centuries, culminating in a neo-Gothic work-over by Josef Mocker in the 1880s. The towers were added in 1903, and most of the interior frescoes only in the 1920s. It's open daily except Monday, from 9 am to noon and 1 to 5 pm (except morning only on Friday, and from 11 am on Sunday).

What's Love Got to Do with It?

Šárka was one of a renegade army of women who fled across the Vltava after the death of Libuše, mother of the Přemysl line. She was chosen as a decoy to trap Ctirad, captain of the men's army. Unfortunately she fell in love with him, and after her cohorts did him in, she threw herself into the Šárka Valley (see North-West Outskirts later in this chapter) in remorse. The women were slaughtered by the men of Hradčany in a final battle.

Beside the church are the **Vyšehrad Gardens** (Vyšehradské sady), with four statues by Josef Myslbek, based on Czech legends. Libuše and Přemysl are in the north-western corner; in the south-east are Šárka and Ctirad (see the boxed text 'What's Love Got to Do with It?'). On Sunday from May to August, open-air concerts are held here at 2.30 pm, with anything from jazz to oompah to chamber music.

Casemates (Kasematy) Within Vyšehrad's ramparts there are many vaulted casemates. At the Cihelná or Pražská gate, 20 Kč will buy you a guided tour through several of these chambers, now used as a historical exhibit and for storing four of Charles Bridge's original baroque statues (other originals are at the Lapidárium in Holešovice).

Other Attractions For 5 Kč you can look at the foundations of the 11th century Romanesque **St Lawrence Basilica** (bazilika sv Vavřince), daily from 11 am to 6 pm. Ask for the key in the snack bar by the Old Archdeaconry.

In front of the south-western bastion are the foundations of a small **palace** built by Charles IV, and then dismantled in 1655. Perched on the bastion is the **Vyšehrad Gallery** (Galérie Vyšehrad), with temporary exhibitions, open from 9.30 am to 5.30 pm, for 5 Kč. Below the bastion are some ruined guard towers poetically named 'Libuše's Bath'.

In the north-western corner is the former **New Provost's House** (Nové proboštství; 1874). In the adjacent park is an open-air **Summer Theatre** (Letní scéna) where you can catch a concert or cultural show on most Thursdays from 6 pm or the odd children's performance on Tuesday afternoon (usually around 2 pm).

Places to Eat There are mediocre *cafés* inside the Špička Gate and by St Lawrence Basilica, and *Penguin's* near the Tábor Gate. *Vinárna Na Vyšehradě*, opposite the

Church of SS Peter & Paul, is adequate but a bit pricey.

Cubist Architecture

If you've taken the trouble to come out to Vyšehrad, don't miss a clutch of Prague's famous Cubist buildings in the streets north of the Brick Gate. Cubist architecture, with its eye-catching use of elementary geometric forms, is more or less unique to the Czech Republic, particularly Prague.

Best of the lot is a simple, striking façade by the dean of Czech Cubist architects, Josef Chochol, at Neklanova 30. Others by Chochol are at Libušina 3, and a villa on Rašínovo nábřeží, just before it tunnels beneath Vyšehrad rock. All date from around 1913. Other works by lesser lights are scattered around the neighbourhood.

BUBENEČ & HOLEŠOVICE (Maps 1, 3 & 4)

This patch of Prague at the Vltava's 'big bend' sprang from two old settlements, Holešovice and the fishing village of Bubny. Both remained small until industry arrived in the mid-19th century and the Hlávkův Bridge (1868) linked it to Nové Město. Close behind came a horse-drawn tram line, a river port and the Fairgrounds. The area was made part of Prague in 1884.

Strictly speaking, the boundary between Bubeneč (to the west) and Holešovice (to the east) is the eastern edges of Stromovka and Letná, and Čechova ulice between them.

Fairgrounds (Výstaviště) (Maps 3 & 4)

This vast exhibition area (general information ☎ 20 10 32 04) grew up around several buildings erected for the 1891 Terrestrial Jubilee Exposition. These include the Prague Pavilion (Pavilón hlavního města Prahy), which houses the Lapidárium, and the Palace of Industry (Průmyslový palác).

This is the venue for the big spring and autumn fairs. Though a bit dreary on weekdays if there are no fairs, it's a popular weekend destination just about any time, if only for a sausage, a beer and a taste of traditional *dechovka* (Bohemian brass-band music).

Admission is free, or 60 Kč in the warm months if you've come to see the **Křižík Fountain** (Křižíkova Fontána; Map 3) do its thing: a computer-controlled dance to recorded classical, rock or electronic music. Sometimes the show is accompanied by songs and music; when we were there, performances included 'The Music of Freddie Mercury' and highlights from the musical *Hair*, prices hovering around 160 Kč. Normal times are 8, 9 and 10 pm daily (plus 3 and 5 pm on weekends, and 11 pm daily except Friday); ☎ 20 10 32 80 for information. It's best after sunset, lit with coloured lights.

In late August the Slovak dance ensemble Lúčnica performs at the fountain (☎ 24 21 11 80 or 21 61 01 73 for information).

Behind the fountain building is the **Spiral Theatre** (divadlo Spirála), a venue for Czech-language musicals (see the Entertainment chapter). **Dětský svět** is a children's theatre with regular weekend performances. The **Maroldovo Panorama** is an impressive 360° diorama of the 1434 Battle of Lipany (in which the Hussite Taborites lost to the Hussite Utraquists); it's open Tuesday to Friday from 2 to 5 pm, and weekends from 10 am to 5 pm. All these are shown on Map 3.

The **Lapidárium** (Map 4; ☎ 37 31 58) is a repository of some 400 sculptures from the 11th to the 19th centuries, removed from Prague's streets and buildings to save them from demolition or pollution. They include bits of the Old Town Square's Marian column, torn down by a mob in 1918, and at least three of Charles Bridge's original statues (others are in the Casemates at Vyšehrad). It's open Friday from noon to 6 pm, and weekends and holidays from 10 am to 12.30 pm and 1 to 6 pm.

Get to the Fairgrounds on westbound tram No 12 from Nádraží Holešovice metro station.

Stromovka (Map 3)

Stromovka, west of the Fairgrounds, is Prague's largest park, at over a million square metres. In the Middle Ages it was a royal hunting preserve, which is why it's sometimes called the Royal Deer Park (Královská obora). Rudolf II had rare trees planted and several lakes dug (fed by the Vltava via a canal that still functions).

Stromovka has a **Planetárium**, just outside the Fairgrounds. If there are at least 20 people, sky-shows (in Czech) are presented on weekends and, in July and August, daily except Friday, for 25 Kč. There are also periodic slide, film and video shows on weekday evenings or you can just wander through the exhibits in the main hall for 10 Kč. The building is open Monday to Thursday from 8 am to noon and 1 to 6 pm, and weekends from 9.30 am to 6 pm (closed Friday).

Centre for Modern & Contemporary Art (Map 4)

The National Gallery's Centre for Modern & Contemporary Art (☎ 24 30 11 11) was opened in 1996 at the northern end of the yawning Trade Fair Palace (Veletržní palác) in Holešovice. The splendid collection includes 20th century European and Czech art, and 19th and 20th century French art. Not everybody finds that the constructivist-style venue (completed in 1928) appeals as much as the contents: one visitor said it looks like a state-of-the-art prison block.

It's open daily except Monday, from 10 am to 6 pm (Thursday to 9 pm). Admission is 80 Kč for the permanent collection, 40 Kč for short-term exhibitions; youth and student discounts apply, and entry is free for children. It's at Dukelských hrdinů 47; take tram No 12 west from Nádraží Holešovice metro station, two stops to Veletržní.

National Technology Museum (Národní Technické Muzeum) (Map 3)

This fun museum has a huge hall full of locomotives, aeroplanes, motorcycles and 1920s and 1930s Czech Škoda and Tatra cars. You can take a tour down a mineshaft or learn about photography, astronomy or timepieces. The museum (☎ 37 36 51), at Kostelní 42, is open daily except Monday, from 9 am to 5 pm, for 25 Kč. From Vltavská metro station, take tram No 1 or 25 west, three stops to Letenské náměstí, and walk down Nad štolou and Muzejní streets. Admission costs 30 Kč.

Letná (Map 3)

Letná is a vast open area between Hradčany and Holešovice, with a parade ground

The Pink Tank

Smíchov meets Malá Strana at náměstí Kinských (Map 5), formerly náměstí Sovětských tankistů – the Square of Soviet Tank Crews – in memory of the Soviet soldiers who marched into Prague on 9 May 1945. Here for many years stood tank No 23, allegedly the first to enter the city (in fact it was a later Soviet 'gift').

In 1991, artist David Černý decided that the tank, being a weapon of destruction, was an inappropriate monument to the Soviet soldiers and painted it pink. The authorities had it painted green again, and charged Černý with a crime against the state. This infuriated many parliamentarians, 12 of whom painted the tank pink again. Their parliamentary immunity saved them from arrest and secured Černý's release.

After complaints from the Soviet Union, the tank was removed. Only a grassy patch remains, where every 9 May a few die-hard communists celebrate their own version of Liberation Day.

to the north and a peaceful park, the **Letná Gardens** (Letenské sady), descending to the Vltava with postcard views of the city and its bridges. In 1261 Přemysl Otakar II held his coronation celebrations here.

The present layout dates from the early 1950s, when a 30m-high, 14,000 tonne statue of Stalin, the biggest monument to the man in the eastern bloc, was erected here by the Czechoslovak Communist Party, only to be blown up in 1962 by the same sycophants when Stalin was no longer flavour of the decade. Today in its place stands a peculiar **giant metronome**. Skateboarders make good use of the area.

Letná was once the site of Moscow-style May Day military parades. In 1989, 750,000 people gathered in support of the 'Velvet Revolution'. In 1990 Pope John Paul II gave an open-air Mass here to over a million people.

Hanavský Pavilón in the south-western corner is a charming but pricey Art Nouveau restaurant built by Otto Prieser for the 1891 Terrestrial Jubilee Exposition. It also makes a handy starting point for a wider walk in Letná; take tram No 18 from Malostranská metro station, one stop to Chotkovy sady.

SMÍCHOV (Maps 1, 5 & 9)

The suburb of Smíchov became part of Prague in 1838 and grew into an industrial quarter full of chimney stacks, railway yards and a large brewery known for the popular Staropramen beer.

Bertramka (Map 9)

Mozart stayed at this elegant 17th century villa during his visits to Prague in 1787 and 1791, as guest of composer František Dušek. Here he finished his opera *Don Giovanni*. Today the house, at Mozartova 169, is a modest Mozart museum (☎ 54 38 93). Summer concerts and other events are also held here. It's open daily from 9.30 am to 6 pm. Take tram No 4, 7 or 9 from Anděl metro station.

TROJA (Map 1)

Facing the Vltava north of the 'big bend' is **Troja Castle** (Trojský zámek; ☎ 689 07 66), a 17th century baroque chateau with a gang of stone giants on the balustrade above its French gardens. On the walls and ceiling of the main hall is a vast, obsequious mural depicting the Habsburgs in full transcendental glory. The chateau houses part of the Prague Municipal Gallery's collection of 19th century Czech painting. From April to October it's open daily except Monday, from 10 am to 6 pm; in winter it's open on weekends only, to 5 pm. You must go on a tour, for a stiff 100 Kč (50 Kč for student and youth-card holders). The last tour starts one hour before closing time.

Across the road is the city **zoo**, in 60 hectares of wooded grounds. You may find the 2300 flea-bitten creatures depressing, but kids love them. Pride of place, at the top of the hill, goes to a herd of Przewalski's horses, little steppe-dwellers that still survive in the wilds of Mongolia and are successfully bred here. A rackety funicular climbs the hill for a few koruna in the summer. The zoo is open year-round, daily from 9 am to 7 pm, for 40 Kč (20 Kč for kids aged three to 15 and students). Outside the entrance is a *pivnice*, **Restaurace U Lišků** – open daily to 10 pm with modestly priced specials – and several pricier places.

From here it's a short walk north to one of Prague's **botanical gardens**, open from April to October, daily from 9 am to 6 pm.

From Nádraží Holešovice metro station it's a 10 minute trip to the zoo and chateau, at the end of the line on bus No 112; buses depart four or five times hourly. Or – on weekends and holidays in April, and daily from May to September – take the boat: excursions leave from the pier by Palackého most (Map 9) at 9.30 am and 1.30 pm and return at 11 am and 5 pm; Troja is the final stop. The round trip is 40 Kč.

VINOHRADY (Maps 6, 8 & 10)

Vinohrady is south-east of the National Museum and main train station. The name refers to vineyards that grew here centuries ago; even as recently as 200 years ago there was little urbanisation.

Náměstí Míru (Map 10)

Vinohrady's physical and commercial heart is náměstí Míru (Peace Square), dominated by the brick neo-Gothic **St Ludmilla Church** (Kostel sv Ludmily). Right behind it at No 9 is the neo-Renaissance **National House** (Národní dům, also called the Kulturní dům), with exhibition and concert halls. On the north side of the square is the 1909 **Vinohrady Theatre** (Divadlo na Vinohradech), a popular drama venue.

Though relatively close to the centre of Prague, the genteel, tree-shaded neighbourhood south from the square to Havlíčkovy sady, with its *fin-de-siècle* mansions in every 'neo' style, has a peaceful, Parisian feel.

Church of the Most Sacred Heart of Our Lord (Kostel Nejsvětějšího Srdce Páně) (Map 8)

With its perforated brickwork, outsize clock tower and ultra-simple interior, this is probably Prague's most original church, brash and lovely at the same time. Completed in 1932, it's the work of Josef Plečnik, the Slovenian architect who also raised a few eyebrows with his additions to Prague Castle. It's in náměstí Jiřího z Poděbrad, by the metro station of the same name.

St Wenceslas Church (Kostel Sv Václava) (Map 1)

Another surprise from the same period is Josef Gočár's 1930 constructivist church, with its fragile-looking tower, climbing a hillside at náměstí Svatopluka Čecha (take tram No 4 or 22 from Karlovo náměstí).

ŽIŽKOV (Maps 1, 6 & 8)

Named after the one-eyed Hussite hero and military commander, Jan Žižka, who whipped Holy Roman Emperor Sigismund and his army on a hill here in 1420, Žižkov has always been a rough-and-ready neighbourhood, working-class and full of revolutionary fizz well before 1948. Streets from the beginning of the 20th century near the centre are slowly getting a face-lift but many are run-down and glum. There's little for visitors except numerous pubs, some nightclubs, views from Žižkov Hill and Prague's futuristic TV Tower, and several melancholy cemeteries.

Žižkov (or Vítkov) Hill (Maps 6 & 8)

The famous battle of 1420 took place on this long mound separating Žižkov and Karlín districts. From beside the colossal 1950 equestrian **statue** of the general you can enjoy superior views across Staré Město to Prague Castle.

Behind you is the grandiose **National Memorial** (Národní památník), completed around 1930 as a memorial to the Czechoslovak 'unknown soldier' but later hijacked as a mausoleum for communist leader Klement Gottwald, who has since been buried elsewhere. The memorial is now closed, weedy and neglected.

From Florenc or the main train station, walk along Husitská; after the first railway bridge, climb to the left up U památníku. On the way up, battle freaks can stop at the run-down **Army Museum**, with a courtyard full of rusting tanks, and exhibits on the history of the Czechoslovak army and the resistance movement. It's open daily except Monday and Friday, from 9.30 am to 6 pm in summer; and the rest of the year on weekdays from 9 am to 5 pm.

TV Tower (Televizní Věž) (Map 8)

Prague's tallest, ugliest landmark is the 216m TV Tower (☎ 67 00 57 66), erected in the 1970s. For 30 Kč (kids under 10 years old get in free) you can ride a high-speed elevator up for views right out past the edges of the city. But you're actually *too* high to see the city skyline or much detail, so it's a bit of a disappointment. The viewing area is open daily from 10 am to 11 pm; there's also a restaurant (at 63m).

The tower is built on the site of a **Jewish cemetery** that operated until 1890, after Josefov's was shut. What's left of the cemetery is just north of the tower. The area, called Mahlerovy sady (Mahler Park), is about four blocks north-east of Jiřího z Poděbrad metro station, or about the same distance south-west from the Lipanská stop on tram No 9 from Wenceslas Square.

Olšany Cemetery & the Grave of Jan Palach (Map 8)

Jan Palach, the university student who set himself on fire in January 1969 as a protest against the Soviet invasion, was buried in Olšany Cemetery (Olšanské hřbitovy), Prague's main cemetery. When his grave became a focus for demonstrations, the remains were moved in 1974 to his home village, but were re-interred here in 1990.

The cemetery was founded in 1680 during a plague epidemic. Its oldest stones are in the north-western corner, near the 17th century **St Roch Chapel** (kaple sv Rocha).

There are several entrances along Vinohradská, east of Flora metro station. Enter at the main gate, turn right and go about 50m to Palach's grave. The cemetery is open May to September from 8 am to 7 pm; to 6 pm in March, April and October; and from 9 am to 4 pm in winter.

Jewish Cemetery (Map 1)

Franz Kafka is buried in this sad, overgrown graveyard (Židovské hřbitovy), opened around 1890 when the previous Jewish cemetery – now at the foot of the TV Tower – was closed. The entrance is beside Želivského metro station, and the grave of Kafka and his parents is to the right, about two-thirds of the way along the front wall. Men should cover their heads (yarmulkes are available at the gate).

The cemetery is open year-round, daily except Saturday and Jewish holidays, from 9 am to 5 pm (from 9 am to 2 pm on Friday); last admissions are half an hour before closing.

Outer Suburbs

NORTH-WEST OUTSKIRTS (Maps 1 & 3)

This area stretches from eastern Dejvice out to the vast, ugly housing estates in the north. It also takes in the green Šárka valley, the great battleground at Bílá hora (White Mountain), the Star Summer Palace and Břevnov Monastery.

Dejvice (Maps 1 & 3)

Near the north-eastern edge of Hradčany, at Mickiewiczova 1, is the striking, red-brick **Bílkova vila** (Bílek Villa; Map 3), designed by the sculptor František Bílek in 1911 as his own home, and now a museum of his unconventional stone and wood reliefs, furniture and graphics. A sign in front also calls it František Bílek Sochařský Atelier (Sculpture Studio). From mid-May to mid-October the villa is open daily except Monday from 10 am to 6 pm, and the rest of the year on weekends only to 5 pm; admission is 60 Kč. Take tram No 18 one stop north from Malostranská metro station.

Nearby at Tychonova 4-6 (Map 5) is a marvellous matching pair of **Cubist houses** designed by the architect Josef Gočár as his residence.

In the north of Dejvice, the unusual villa suburb of **Baba** was a 1933 to 1940 project by a team of Cubist artists and designers to build cheap, attractive, single-family houses. The **Hanspaulka** suburb to the south (Map 1) was a similar project, built between 1925 and 1930.

Šárka Valley (Map 1)

The valley of the Šárecký potok (Šárka Creek) is one of Prague's best-known and most valuable nature parks. It's named after the warrior Šárka, who threw herself off a cliff here (see the earlier Vyšehrad section for more about the legend).

From metro station Dejvická, catch tram No 20 or 26 to its western terminus, at Divoká Šárka. The most attractive area is nearby, among the rugged cliffs near the

Džbán Reservoir. You can swim in the reservoir.

From there it's about a 7km walk north-east down the valley on a red-marked trail to the suburb of Baba, where the creek empties into the Vltava. There's a bus stop by the Vltava at Podbaba, for the trip back to the centre, or you can walk south about 1.5km to the northern terminus of trams No 20 and 25, opposite the Holiday Inn in Dejvice (Map 3). Buses also run the full length of the Šárka valley, should you want to cut your walk short.

Břevnov Monastery (Břevnovský Klášter) (Map 1)

This is the Czech Republic's oldest Benedictine monastery, founded back in 993 by Boleslav II and Bishop St Vojtěch Slavníkovec. The men, from opposing and powerful families intent on dominating Bohemia, met at Vojtěška spring, each having a dream that this was the place to found a monastery. The name comes from *břevno* (beam), after the beam laid across the spring where they met.

The present monastery building and the nearby baroque **Church of St Margaret** (bazilika sv Markéty) were completed in 1720 by Kristof Dientzenhofer. In 1993, the 1000th anniversary of the monastery's founding, the restored 1st floor, with its fine ceiling frescoes, and the crypt, with the original foundations and a few skeletons, were opened to the public for the first time.

The monastery was used as a secret-police archive until 1990. Jan Patočka (1907-77), a leading figure of the Charter 77 movement who died after interrogation by the secret police, is buried in the **cemetery** behind the monastery.

The church, crypt and parts of the monastery can be seen with a guided tour on Saturday and Sunday only. From mid-April to mid-October walk-in visitors can join tours at 10.30 am and 1, 2.30 and 4 pm; the rest of the year they're at 10 am and 2 pm only. The price is 30 Kč for foreigners. Visits at other times are only by prior arrangement (☎ 35 15 20, fax 35 08 87).

The monastery gardens are open free of charge on Sunday from 10 am to 6 pm.

Take tram No 8 from Hradčanská metro station, or tram No 22 from náměstí Míru, Karlovo náměstí or Malostranská metro station, to the Břevnovský klášter stop.

Star Summer Palace (Letohrádek Hvězda)

In 1530 Ferdinand I established a hunting reserve on a verdant hill east of Bílá hora (White Mountain). There, in 1556, Archduke Ferdinand of Tyrol built a Renaissance summer palace, in the shape of a six-pointed star.

Inside is a museum (☎ 36 79 38) dedicated to two leading lights of the Czech National Revival: Alois Jirásek (1851-1930), who wrote powerful stories based on Czech legends, and the artist Mikuláš Aleš (1852-1913). It's open year-round, daily except Monday, from 10 am to 5 pm, although at the time of writing it was closed for restoration.

Take one of the same trams as for Břevnov Monastery, but three stops further to Malý Břevnov.

White Mountain (Bílá Hora)

The 381m White Mountain, on the western outskirts of Prague, was the site of the 1620 Protestant military collapse that ended Czech independence for almost 300 years. The only modern reminder of the battle is a small monument in the middle of the field.

Take one of the same trams as for Břevnov Monastery, but to the end of the line.

SOUTH-WEST OUTSKIRTS (Map 1)

This corner of Prague has few accessible sights, though the **Barrandov Cliffs** (Barrandovské skály) – named after a French geologist, Joachim Barranda, who explored the area – are a unique geological formation. Nearby are the well known Barrandov film studios.

Good for a pleasant hike are the scenic **Prokopské** and **Dalejské údolí** (valleys), along Dalejský potok between the suburbs of Hlubočepy and Jinonice. An 8km trail starts near the corner of Novoveská and Pod Vavřincem in southern Jinonice (from Jinonice metro station, take bus No 130 or 149 one stop to Sídliště Jinonice). It ends at Haladova Garden in Hlubočepy, from where you can catch bus No 104 or 120 from Hlubočepská to Smíchovské Nádraží metro station.

Zbraslav

This town 10km south of Prague was only incorporated into Greater Prague recently, although as early as 1268 Přemysl Otakar II built a hunting lodge and a chapel here, later to be rebuilt as a Cistercian monastery. In 1784 this was turned into a castle. The castle, temporarily closed at the time of writing, should have reopened by the time you read this with a National Gallery permanent collection of oriental and Asian art, and some Czech sculpture in the garden. For information ☎ 57 92 16 38/39.

Take bus No 243 from Smíchovské Nádraží metro station.

SOUTH-EAST OUTSKIRTS (Map 1)

Several huge, unkempt woodlands lie at the edges of the city. Two of the biggest are **Michelský les** and adjoining **Kunratický les**, straight out of Roztyly metro station. Michelský les has a mini-zoo and a snack bar with beer and sausages.

NORTH-EAST OUTSKIRTS (Map 1)

At the **Museum of Aircraft & Space Exploration** (Muzeum letectví a kosmonautiky; ☎ 20 20 75 04), on Mladoboleslavská in the Kbely district, Prague 9, you can have a close look at a Russian MiG fighter plane or at a host of exhibits on aeronautics and space flight, including the exploits of Russian cosmonauts. It's open from May to October, daily except Monday and Friday, from 10 am to 6 pm, for 40 Kč. Take bus Nos 185 or 259 from Českomoravská metro station.

The Islands of Prague

Over the centuries islands have appeared and disappeared in the Vltava as it deposited silt or washed it away. Today there are eight islands, and since the river was dammed they have remained fairly stable. Landfilling has now joined two others, located between Holešovice and Libeň, to the mainland.

Veslařský ostrov (Regatta Island; Map 1), south of Vyšehrad, has been around since 1420. Once owned by, and named after, a wealthy German prince, it was renamed by the Communists in 1952. Today it has a sports ground and a yacht club.

Císařská louka (Imperial Meadow; Maps 1 & 9), opposite Vyšehrad, is a favourite place for picnics. It was once a royal playground (Wenceslas II held his coronation celebrations on the island) and gold was panned there in the 19th century. On the northern tip is a camp site with a fine view of Vyšehrad.

Dětský ostrov (Children's Island; Map 5), north of Jiráskův most, is the smallest island. It appeared in 1355, and has washed away and returned several times since. It has a children's playground.

Slovanský ostrov (Slav Island; Map 6), also known as Žofín, south of the National Theatre, is the 'youngest', first mentioned in 1610. Its banks were reinforced with stone in 1784, and a spa and a dye works were built in the early part of the next century. Bohemia's first train had a demonstration run here in 1841, roaring down the island at 11km/h. The island got its present name in 1925, after Slav conventions held here since 1848. In the middle of the island is a 19th century meeting hall and a new restaurant. At the southern end is Šitovská věž, a 15th century water tower (once part of a mill) with an 18th century onion-dome roof.

Střelecký ostrov (Marksmen's Island; Map 5) is crossed by Most Legií. The name originates from its use in the 16th century as a cannon and rifle target for the Prague garrison. Prague students held their 1998 Majáles festival here (for details see the boxed text in the Public Holidays & Special Events section of the Facts for the Visitor chapter).

Kampa (Map 5) lies off Malá Strana, across the Čertovka channel. It's the only artificial island, formed when ditches were dug to get the Vltava to run mill-wheels. Kampa was settled in the 16th century after being raised above flood level. In 1939 the river was so low that it was again joined to the mainland, and many coins and items of jewellery were found in the dry channel. For more on Kampa, see the earlier section on Malá Strana.

Ostrov Štvanice (Chase Island; Map 4), between Holešovice and Karlín, was first mentioned in 1118. The name derives from times when Praguers gathered around a wooden corral to watch bull, bear or boar chases. Czechoslovakia's first artificial ice rink was built here between 1930 and 1932. The Czech Tennis Open is held annually on its clay courts and Davis Cup ties have been played here. Beneath Hlávkův most, the bridge linking the island to Nové Město, are river locks through which excursion boats pass now and then. To get to the island, take tram No 3 from Wenceslas Square.

Císařský ostrov (Imperial Island; Map 1), between Troja and Bubeneč, is the northernmost island and the longest, at 1250m. The name refers to an imperial pheasant-breeding centre maintained here by Rudolf II. Today the island is home to several sports clubs, a racecourse and a horse-riding school.

Museums & Galleries

If you're pursuing special interests, the following list of museums and galleries should help you plan your explorations and locate the relevant places.

MUSEUMS

Museum admission charges are typically from 30 to 40 Kč, except where noted. Youth and student discounts are often available if you ask; those for seniors are for residents only.

Army Museum (p121; Map 6), U památníku 2, Žižkov

Czech Museum of Fine Arts (p103; Map 7; ☎ 24 22 20 68), Husova 19-21, Staré Město: changing exhibitions

Czech Museum of Fine Arts (p104; Map 7; ☎ 24 21 17 32), House of the Black Madonna, Celetná 34, Staré Město: permanent collection on Czech Cubism

Dvořák Museum (p115; Map 9; ☎ 29 82 14), Vila Amerika, Ke Karlovu 20, Nové Město

Jewish Museum (p92; Map 7), Josefov, Staré Město: Old Jewish Cemetery, synagogues and other buildings in Josefov

Lapidárium (p118; Map 4; ☎ 37 31 58), Výstaviště (Fairgrounds), Bubeneč

Mozart Museum at Bertramka (p120; Map 9; ☎ 54 38 93), Mozartova 2/169, Smíchov

Mucha Museum (p110; Map 6), Panská 1, Nové Město

Museum of Aircraft & Space Exploration (p124; Map 1; ☎ 20 20 75 04), Mladoboleslavská, Kbely, Prague 9

Museum of the City of Prague (p110; Map 6), Na poříčí 52, Nové Město

Museum of Czech Glass (p99; Map 7), Old Town Square 27, Staré Město

Museum of Czech History (p86; Prague Castle map; ☎ 53 73 64), Lobkowicz Palace, Prague Castle: Czech history until 1848

Museum of Czech Literature (p87; Map 5; ☎ 20 51 66 95), Strahov Monastery, Hradčany: exhibit of miniature books

THINGS TO SEE & DO

Museum of Decorative Arts (p94; Map 7), 17.listopadu 2, Josefov

Museum of Marionette & Puppet Cultures (p103; Map 7), Karlova 12, Staré Město

Museum of Military History (p86; Map 5), Schwarzenberg Palace, Hradčanské náměstí, Hradčany: up to 1918

National Museum (p110; Map 6; ☎ 24 49 71 11), Wenceslas Square 68

National Technology Museum (p119; Map 3; ☎ 37 36 51), Kostelní 42, Holešovice

Náprstek Museum of Asian, African & American Cultures (p108; Map 6; ☎ 24 21 45 37), Betlémské náměstí 1, Staré Město

Police Museum (p115; Map 9), Ke Karlovu 453/1, Prague 2

Postage Stamp Museum (p109; Map 7; ☎ 231 20 60), Nové mlýny 2, Nové Město

Pražské panoptikum (p113; Map 6), Národní 25, Staré Město: wax museum

Smetana Museum (p103; Map 7; ☎ 26 53 71), Novotného lávka 1, Staré Město

Wax Museum (p106; Map 6), 28.října 13, Staré Město

STATE-RUN GALLERIES

Galleries generally charge around 100 Kč (except as noted). Most state galleries are closed on Monday.

Knights of the Cross Gallery (p103; Map 7), Křižovnické náměstí 3: over-the-top ecclesiastical miscellany and changing exhibitions

Summer Palace (Letohrádek; p 83; Map 5): changing exhibitions

National Gallery, Centre for Modern & Contemporary Art (p119; Map 4; ☎ 24 30 11 11), Trade Fair Palace, Dukelských hrdinů 47, Holešovice: permanent collection of 20th century European and Czech art, and 19th and 20th century French art, as well as changing exhibitions

National Gallery, Convent of St Agnes (p107; Map 7; ☎ 24 81 06 28), U milosrdných 17, Staré Město: 19th century Czech painting and sculpture

National Gallery, Convent of St George (p85; Prague Castle map), Prague Castle: Czech Gothic and Renaissance art

National Gallery, Rudolfinum Gallery (p95; Map 7), Alšovo nábřeží 12, Josefov: changing exhibitions

National Gallery, Kinský Palace (p99; Map 7), Old Town Square 12, Staré Město, under renovation at time of writing: changing exhibitions

National Gallery, Riding School (p83; Map 5; ☎ 24 37 32 32), U Prašného mostu 55, Prague Castle: changing exhibitions

National Gallery, Sternberg Palace (p86; Map 5; ☎ 20 51 45 99), Hradčanské náměstí 15, Hradčany: permanent collection of 14th to 19th century European art

National Gallery, Zbraslav Castle (p124; Map 11; ☎ 57 92 16 38/39), Zbraslav: permanent collection of oriental and Asian art, some Czech sculpture

Obecní Dům (Municipal House; p105; Map 7), náměstí Republiky 5, Staré Město

Prague Municipal Gallery, Bílkova Vila (p122 Map 3), Mickiewiczova 1, Malá Strana: permanent collection of the works of František Bílek

Prague Municipal Gallery, City Library (p104; Map 7), Valentinská, Mariánské náměstí 1, Staré Město: changing exhibitions

Prague Municipal Gallery, House at the Golden Ring (p101; Map 7), Týnská 6, Staré Město

Prague Municipal Gallery, House of the Stone Bell (p101; Map 7; ☎ 24 28 75 26), Old Town Square 13: changing exhibitions

Prague Municipal Gallery, Old Town Hall (p99; Map 7; ☎ 24 81 07 58), Old Town Square, Staré Město: changing exhibitions

Prague Municipal Gallery, Troja Castle (p120; Map 1; ☎ 689 07 66), Troja: permanent collection of 19th century Czech painting

Strahov Picture Gallery (p87; Map 5), Strahov Monastery, Hradčany: monastery art from Gothic to Romantic, plus various temporary exhibitions

Vyšehrad Gallery (p117; Map 9): changing exhibitions

Wallenstein Riding School (Valdštejnská jízdárna; p89; Map 5), Wallenstein Garden, Malá Strana: modern art exhibitions

PRIVATE GALLERIES

The following galleries display works for both exhibition and sale. Some may be closed for weeks at a time, so call ahead, especially in the case of the more distant ones. Numerous other small galleries come and go.

Behémót Gallery (☎ 231 78 29), Elišky Krásnohorské 6 (Map 7), Josefov: Czech avant-garde art

Franz Kafka Gallery (Map 7; ☎ 24 22 74 54), Old Town Square 22: modern art

Gambra Surrealist Gallery (Map 5), Černínská 5, Hradčany

Hollar Gallery (Map 6), Smetanovo nábřeží 6, Staré Město: contemporary graphics, daily except Monday, 10 am to 1 pm and 2 to 6 pm, admission just 5 Kč

Josef Sudek Gallery, U radnice 5 (Map 7), Staré Město: photographic exhibitions

Mánes Gallery (p113; Map 6; ☎ 29 55 77), Masarykovo nábřeží 250, Nové Město: contemporary art

MXM Gallery (Map 5; ☎ 53 15 64), Nosticova 6, Malá Strana

Nová síň (Map 6), Voršilská 3, Nové Město: contemporary Czech art, open daily except Monday, from 11 am to 6 pm

Pyramid Gallery (Map 6; ☎ 22 07 56 52), Národní 11, Staré Město: modern glass, sculpture, paintings

U prstenu Gallery (☎ 26 28 58), Jilská 14 (Map 7), Staré Město: humour, grotesquerie, phantasmal art, and a café; admission just 5 Kč

Václav Špála Gallery (Map 6; ☎ 24 21 30 00), Národní 30: contemporary Czech art

Via Art Gallery (Map 9; ☎ 29 25 70), Resslova 6, Nové Město

Activities

For a full list of Prague's sports halls and complexes, contact PIS or consult the *Culture in Prague*, *Prague Cultural Events* or *Přehled* magazines.

SWIMMING

The pool at Sport Centrum, at the YMCA (Map 7; ☎ 24 87 58 11), Na poříčí 12, is open to visitors daily from 8 am to 11 pm, for 60 Kč per hour (18 Kč per hour for kids under 140cm tall); multi-visit visitor cards are also available. Esquo Relax Club, by Strahov Stadium (see the following Tennis & Squash section) also has a swimming pool. The pool and sauna at the Hotel Čechie in Karlín (Map 1; see the Places to Stay chapter) is 200 Kč for unlimited time. The Olšanka Hotel in Žižkov (Map 8; see the Places to Stay chapter) has a fitness centre with a pool.

Year-round Olympic-size indoor and outdoor pools at the Plavecký stadión (Swimming Stadium) in Podolí, Prague 4 (Map 1), are open weekdays from 6 am to 9.45 pm and weekends from 8 am to 7.45 pm, at 40/50/60 Kč for one/two/three hours. The complex is on Podolské nábřeží. Take the No 3 tram from Wenceslas Square to the Dvorce stop, from where it's a five minute walk. Bring flip-flops for the grotty shower. Theft is a problem, even from lockers, so leave your valuables at the desk free of charge.

TENNIS & SQUASH

Budget-rate indoor courts are available at a Tenisová hala (tennis hall; Map 5) behind (west of) Strahov stadium, Prague 6; take bus No 143, 149 or 217 from Dejvická metro station or No 176 from Karlovo náměstí. The prestigious Štvanice club (TJ Slavoj Praha; Map 4; ☎ 231 51 83) on ostrov Štvanice also has courts; take tram No 3 from Wenceslas Square.

Outdoor/indoor courts can be rented, for 300/600 Kč per hour, at the Hotel Čechie (Map 1; see the Places to Stay chapter) in Karlín. The Olšanka Hotel (Map 8; see the Places to Stay chapter) in Žižkov has a fitness centre with tennis courts. Another option is TJ Sokol Žižkov (☎ 77 35 24), Saratovská 2, Prague 10, near Strašnická metro station.

Esquo (☎ 20 51 36 09) runs two squash centres by Strahov Stadium (Map 5): Relax Club at Vaníčkova 2, on the eastern side, and Squashcentrum, just to the north. Courts cost from 160 to 333 Kč per hour, depending on the time of day. Squash courts at the Hotel Čechie are from 240 to 320 Kč per hour. The Olšanka Hotel has a fitness centre with a gym, weight room and tennis courts.

FITNESS CENTRES

The weight room (*posilovna*) at Sport Centrum, at the YMCA (Map 7; ☎ 24 87 58 11), Na poříčí 12, is open to visitors daily from 8 am to 11 pm, for about 45 Kč per hour; multi-visit visitor cards are also available. Esquo Squashcentrum (see the previous Tennis & Squash section) has a

THINGS TO SEE & DO

fitness centre, open daily until 11 pm for just 35 Kč per hour. Another one is in the same building as the Hotel Axa (Map 6; ☎ 24 81 25 80), Na poříčí 40.

The centre at the Hotel Čechie (Map 1; see the Places to Stay chapter) in Karlín is 100 Kč for unlimited time. Centrum Krásy Dlouhověkosti (Map 6; ☎ 24 23 56 09), in the passage at Wenceslas Square 43, is open daily for 90 Kč per hour. The Olšanka Hotel (Map 8; see the Places to Stay chapter) in Žižkov has a centre with gym and weight room.

One of the city's biggest fitness centres is Sportovní Centrum Masospol (☎ 61 91 01 23) at Libušská 320, Prague 4; take bus No 113 or 171 from Kačerov metro station.

CYCLING & ROWING

See the relevant sections in the Getting Around chapter for details on where to hire bicycles and rowing boats.

ICE-SKATING

Indoor rinks at several winter-sports complexes (*zimní stadióny*) are open to the public during certain hours from September to March or April. One is on ostrov Štvanice (Map 4), open Friday evening, early on Saturday afternoon, and Sunday evening; take tram No 3 from Wenceslas Square. Others are the HC Sparta Sport Hall (Map 4) by the Fairgrounds in Bubeneč, and beside SK Slavia Praha stadium (Map 1) in Vršovice.

If you're a guest at the Hotel Hasa (Map 10; see the Places to Stay chapter) in Vinohrady and have your own skates, you can use the adjacent all-seasons rink free of charge. In winter, when it's below freezing, parts of certain parks are sprayed with water and turned into rinks.

GOLF

Prague has one nine-hole golf course, the Golf Club Praha (☎ 651 24 64), which is at Na Moráni 4, behind the Hotel Golf in Motol, Prague 5 (Map 1; see the Places to Stay chapter).

The closest 18-hole course is Karlštejn Golf Course (☎ 0311-68 47 16), overlooking Karlštejn Castle. It's several kilometres from Karlštejn village, on the southern bank of the Berounka River; from the village head south-west up a steep hill towards Liteň. A day's play costs 1100 Kč on weekdays, rising to 1500 Kč on weekends and holidays.

BILLIARDS & BOWLING

Pool and billiards are popular, and the city has many clubs. A popular place is the Louvre Billiard Club on Národní 22, in the same entrance as Gany's Café (Map 6). Tables are 100 Kč per hour. For American-style ten-pin bowling, go to the Hotel Forum (Map 10), by Vyšehrad metro station, Prague 4, where a lane costs from 125 to 290 Kč per hour, depending on the time of day (from noon). Lanes at the Hotel Čechie in Karlín (Map 1; see the Places to Stay chapter) cost 250 Kč per hour.

HORSE RIDING

Year-round horse riding is offered at Hucul klub (☎ 57 96 00 14), Zmrzlík 3, Řeporyje, Prague 5; take bus No 256 from Nové Butovice metro station to the Zmrzlík stop. It's open daily except Tuesday, from 9 am to 5 pm. Rates are about 260 Kč per person. Booking ahead is essential.

Riding lessons (and horse racing) are on offer at the TJ Žižka Praha racecourse (Map 1; ☎ 87 84 76) on Císařský ostrov, but transport is awkward. Take bus No 112 from Holešovice metro station to the Kovárna stop and walk south on Pod Havránkou, across the bridge to the racecourse; or get off the PPS ferry to Troja (see the Boat section in the Getting Around chapter).

PRAGUE INTERNATIONAL MARATHON

If you'd like to participate in Prague's own International Marathon, see Spectator Sports in the Entertainment chapter for details of how to register.

The magnificent irregular towers of Týn Church frame the eastern side of the Old Town Square.

JONATHAN SMITH

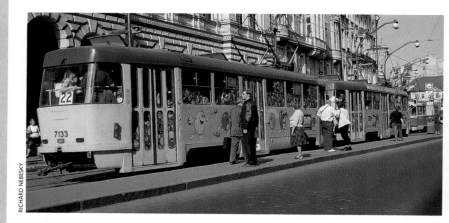

Since 1891 Prague's electric tram network has provided a relaxed and efficient way to get around.

Courses

The Charles University Information & Advisory Centre (Map 6; ☎ 96 22 80 36), Školská 13a, Nové Město, is the place to go for general information on university courses.

The Institute of Linguistics & Professional Training of Charles University (Map 7; ☎ 24 23 00 27, fax 24 22 94 97), Jindřišská 29, 110 00 Praha 1, runs three-week Czech courses for foreigners from mid-July to early August, at Prague or at the spa town of Poděbrady, 50km east of Prague. The application deadline is mid-June. No prior knowledge of the Czech language is required.

The university also offers regular 10-month courses from September to June, for those interested in further study at Czech universities or specialisation in Slavonic studies at a foreign university (students wishing to have credits transferred to their home university must obtain written approval from the head of their department before enrolling). You can also opt for one or two four-month semesters. The university also offers special six-week language courses from time to time, in Prague, Dobruška, Mariánské Lázně, Poděbrady or Teplice.

Angličtina Express (Map 10; ☎ 24 25 14 82), Korunní 2, offers four-week spring and summer courses, running daily for 90 minutes, plus room and board in an adjacent dormitory. The office is open on weekdays from 8 am to 8 pm.

WALKING TOURS

The following walking tours are not so much a way to get your bearings, but a suggestion for how to arrange your entire visit. Take your time: Prague is a pleasure on foot.

Walk 1: The Royal Way (Královská Cesta)

(For the start of this walk, refer to Map 7)

The Royal Way is the ancient coronation route to Prague Castle. That part of it through Staré Město and Malá Strana takes you past some of the city's most inspiring sights. From Wenceslas Square, walk up Na příkopě to náměstí Republiky, from where this tour starts.

Facing náměstí Republiky is the Art Nouveau façade of Prague's most delicious building, the **Municipal House** (Obecní dům). Next door is the 15th century **Powder Tower** (Prašná brána).

Go under the tower and west into Celetná. On the corner with Ovocný trh, the former Fruit Market, is one of the earliest Cubist façades in a city famous for them, on the **House of the Black Madonna**; inside is a museum on Czech Cubism. West towards Old Town Square, Celetná is an open-air museum of pastel baroque façades.

Backtrack a bit and turn off the Royal Way, north into Králodvorská. This area, the Royal Court (Králův dvůr), was once the royal stables. On U Obecního domu is the Art Nouveau **Hotel Paříž**, built in 1907 and recently restored. Just before reaching the Kotva department store, turn left into Jakubská. At the western end of Jakubská is **St James Church**, famous for its pipe organ and acoustics.

The entire block across from the church was once a medieval inn, the **Týn Court**, and has now been renovated. Turn right and go around it by way of quiet Týnská passage. Admire the beautiful north door of the **Týn Church** and turn left behind it to return to Celetná and the Royal Way. Pass No 3, Franz Kafka's boyhood home from 1896 to 1907, and No 2, where his family lived from 1888 to 1889, and you're in Old Town Square. See Walk 2 for a tour round the square.

Left and beyond the Old Town Hall tower, the corner building covered in Renaissance sgraffito is **Dům U minuty**, another Kafka home. Beyond this is Malé náměstí (Little Square), with a Renaissance fountain and fine baroque and neo-Renaissance façades.

Bear left, then right into Karlova. All along the right side of Karlova is the **Klementinum**, once a Jesuit college and now part of the Czech National Library. Along the wall on Karlova are three churches: the Greek Orthodox **St Clement Church**, the little **Assumption Chapel** and the grand **Church of the Holy Saviour**, facing the Vltava.

Inset: Detail of the Astronomical Clock's seasonal calendar-wheel (photograph by John King).

You're now looking at the Old Town tower of **Charles Bridge**. Cross the bridge, through the crowds and past the rows of baroque statues, and drink in the views of Prague Castle.

(From here on, refer to Map 5)
The western end of Charles Bridge crosses Kampa Island, separated from Malá Strana by the Čertovka channel. Just before the Malá Strana bridge towers, look right to the **Hotel U tří pštrosů**, one of Prague's posher establishments; the 16th century house still has traces of its painted façade.

Walk beneath the towers and you're on Mostecká. The upper façades of some of the houses are worth noting, especially the rococo **Kounický Palace** at No 277, now the Yugoslav embassy.

At the top of Mostecká is Malostranské náměstí, bisected by trams and centred on one of Prague's finest baroque structures, **St Nicholas Church**. Cross the square to picturesque Nerudova, named after the poet Jan Neruda, who lived at No 42 in the **House of Two Suns**. On many of the street's mostly baroque façades are colourful emblems that have given these buildings their popular names.

Continue along Úvoz to the **Strahov Monastery**, and head back east, via Loretánská, to Hradčanské náměstí (or go back down Nerudova and climb the stairs at Ke Hradu). At the eastern end of the square is the entrance to **Prague Castle**. Before going in, check out the royal view of the city from the corner of the square. On your right is Petřín Hill, below you the rooftops of Malá Strana. Looking across the Vltava to Staré Město, it's easy to see why Prague is called the 'city of 100 spires'.

Right: From the Old Town Bridge Tower, you can take in the magical atmosphere of Prague's historic centre.

RICHARD NEBESKÝ

Walk 2: Wenceslas Square to Old Town Square

(Refer to Map 6)

This tour starts at Prague's media-famous landmark, the equestrian **statue of St Wenceslas**, the 10th century 'good King Wenceslas' of the Christmas carol. Just below it is a modest memorial to those who died for their resistance to communism. Looming above the statue is the neo-Renaissance **National Museum**.

Below the statue stretches Wenceslas Square, a focal point of Czech history since the 19th century. On 24 November 1989 the obituary of Czech communism was pronounced by Alexander Dubček and Václav Havel from the balcony of the Melantrich building at No 36. Among the square's many late-19th century buildings, the finest is the 1906 Art Nouveau **Grand Hotel Evropa** at No 25.

Two-thirds of the way down the square, Jindřišská ulice, a major tram thoroughfare, enters from the east. Visible at the end of this street is the **Jindřišská Tower**, a 15th century watchtower.

At the bottom of Wenceslas Square is the 'Golden Cross', the inter-section with Na příkopě. The latter is one of the city's premier shopping streets, and marks part of the ancient moat around Staré Město, the Old Town. Detour west from the intersection to Jung-mannovo náměstí and the beautiful 14th century **Church of Our Lady of the Snows**. Back at the Golden Cross, the onward extension of Wenceslas Square is Na můstku, where a footbridge once crossed the moat into Staré Město.

(From here on, refer to Map 7)

Na můstku ends at Rytířská, and a one-block detour east takes you to Prague's oldest theatre and finest neoclassical building, the **Estates Theatre**, where Mozart's opera *Don Giovanni* premiered in 1787. Next door is the **Karolinum**, the first home of Charles University, central Europe's oldest university.

Na můstku then crosses Prague's most central open-air market on Havelská. Now squeeze on into Melantrichova. If you're feeling peckish, pause at Prague's *primo* vegetarian stand-up eatery, Country Life, at No 15.

Then emerge into pastel-painted Old Town Square and join the crowd waiting for the hourly performance of the **Astronomical Clock** on the 14th century Old Town Hall. You can climb the tower for post-card views of the city.

The square's centrepiece is an Art Nouveau bronze **statue of Jan Hus**. Across to the right (east) is the spiky-topped Gothic Týn Church, and next to it, behind Jan Hus, is **Kinský Palace**, probably the city's finest rococo façade. In the north-western corner of the square is the wedding-cake baroque St Nicholas Church.

TOURS

Walk 3: Josefov

(Refer to Map 7)

Prague's Jewish community was confined to a walled ghetto in Staré Město in about the 13th century, and it was not until 1848 that the walls came down. A drastic clearance at the turn of the century meant the end of the ghetto as a community.

At the bottom of Maiselova, on Old Town Square's north-western corner, is the **birthplace of Franz Kafka** (though the building is not the same one). Maiselova runs north into the heart of Josefov. In the second block is the neo-Gothic **Maisel Synagogue**. Beyond the **Jewish Town Hall** in the third block is the **Old-New Synagogue**, Europe's oldest active synagogue, completed about 1270. Beside it is the 16th century **High Synagogue**.

Left down U starého hřbitova are the walls of the melancholy **Old Jewish Cemetery**, Europe's oldest surviving Jewish burial ground – spared, ironically, by a Nazi plan for a memorial to an 'extinguished race'. Continuing along the cemetery wall, a left turn into Břehová brings you to 17.listopadu, across which is the Charles University Law Faculty. The street's name (17 November) refers to the date on which students were killed in a 1939 anti-Nazi demonstration, and to the clubbing of students exactly 50 years later. The latter event triggered the fall of Czechoslovakia's communist government.

Right: With an estimated 100,000 graves, the Old Jewish Cemetery is an evocative reminder of the ghetto.

JOHN KING

Turn left to reach No 2, the **Museum of Decorative Arts**, with a trove of eye-popping 16th to 19th century furnishings (and a good coffee shop). Across the road is the **Rudolfinum**, inter-war seat of the Czechoslovak Parliament and now home of the Czech Philharmonic. From náměstí Jana Palacha (Jan Palach Square) beside the Rudolfinum, you catch your first views of Prague Castle.

Turn left (east) into Široká, with the 16th century **Pinkas Synagogue**, now a memorial to Bohemian and Moravian victims of the Nazis. The eponymous 'hero' of Bruce Chatwin's *Utz* had his fictional home in this street, overlooking the cemetery.

Two blocks on, in a sudden change of atmosphere, you come to Pařížská, testament to Prague's late-19th century infatuation with Art Nouveau architecture. Look left, across the river to the **Letná Gardens**, where a gigantic metronome tick-tocks on the spot once occupied by a 14,000 tonne statue of Stalin.

If your feet are sore, head back to Old Town Square. If you're game for more, go a block north along Pařížská and turn right into Bílkova. At the end, turn left into Kozí and right into U milosrdných, to Prague's oldest Gothic structure, the former **Convent of St Agnes**, home to the National Gallery's fine collection of 19th century Czech art.

Return to Old Town Square via Haštalské náměstí, Kozí and Dlouhá.

Walk 4: Vltava & Petřín Hill

(Refer to Map 5)
A convenient place to start this walk is Malostranská metro station. Head south along Klárov and right into Letenská to the **Wallenstein Garden**. Returning to Klárov, continue south, bearing right into U lužického semináře. On the right is leafy **Vojan Park**, descendant of Prague's oldest park, established in 1248.

Head towards Kampa Island on a small bridge beneath Charles Bridge, with a good view of Prague's most photographed **water wheel**. Continue to Na Kampě, once a pottery market. Detour into one of the little lanes on the right and cross the Čertovka channel to Velkopřevorské náměstí and the John Lennon Wall.

Return to Kampa and continue south either through the park or along the river, enjoying the views of the Old Town. Pass the popular, riverside Rybářský klub fish restaurant.

Leave the island on Říční and turn right at the **Church of St John at the Laundry**. Continue along Všehrdova to Újezd. Turn left and then right into U lanové dráhy for your ascent of Petřín Hill, either on foot through lush gardens or by cable car.

From the top, cross through the **Strahov Gardens** towards Strahov Monastery, enjoying fine views of Hradčany, Malá Strana and the Old Town. Climb **Petřín Tower** for the best views of all. From Strahov Monastery, continue on the final stretch of the Royal Way to Prague Castle, or catch a tram or bus at Pohořelec.

Places to Stay

You can find something habitable in Prague in any season without booking ahead, though it may not be just what you were hoping for. To find a place near the centre, in any price range, in the high season – roughly April to October, plus the Christmas/New Year and Easter holidays – or on a weekend or public holiday even in winter, you should book ahead if you can, preferably by at least a few weeks. Busy public holidays here include those of neighbouring Germany, when day-trippers and weekenders come in their thousands. At the height of summer, roughly July and August, the crowding eases off a bit, and some prices may drop.

Many places in the budget and middle ranges charge foreigners up to three times as much as they do Czechs; hostels, top-end hotels and, increasingly, camping grounds charge everyone the same. We give high-season prices asked of foreigners.

TYPES OF ACCOMMODATION
Camping Grounds
Pitching your own tent is the cheapest way to stay, but don't expect wide open spaces: sites are cheek-by-jowl. Camping grounds differ mainly in attitude and amenities.

Prices include a per-person rate (from 80 to 140 Kč, with discounts for kids) plus charges per car (about 80 to 120 Kč), van (around 120 to 270 Kč), caravan (from 150 to 170 Kč), small tent (about 70 Kč), big tent (from 80 to 120 Kč) and electrical hookup (from 60 to 90 Kč). Some camping grounds have unheated huts or bungalows starting at 140 Kč per bed.

All have showers (with hot water unless stated) and most have communal kitchens and at least a snack bar. Most are on the outskirts of the city, and are open from March to October. Camping gas and Coleman fuel (both called *technický benzín*) and methylated spirits (*líh*) are available.

Camping on public land is prohibited.

Hostels
A 'hostel' can be anything from a dorm full of folding beds in a school gymnasium to a double room with shower – the common factor being that filling the other beds is up to them, not you.

The number of hostel beds explodes from late June to September when the schools are closed, especially in student dorms and sports clubs. Most sports clubs have TJ (*Tělovýchovní jednota*, physical education association) or Sokol (the name of a youth sports movement) in their names. Student hostels with *kolej* (college) in the name are usually of a decent standard, and some have mini-suites.

We list year-round hostels, plus places through which other summer beds can be found. Typical per-bed prices are from 300 to 500 Kč, but they can be as low as 200 Kč and as high as 800 Kč. Few have places to eat on the premises. Except where noted, most don't have curfews.

Among Prague's many hostels is a chain of 'Travellers' Hostels' dotted around the centre. The main one, Pension Dlouhá (Map 7; ☎ 231 13 18, fax 231 61 61, email hostel@terminal.cz) at Dlouhá 33, is open year-round; beds in the others, open only from June to September, can be booked at the Dlouhá location. Other organisations that manage several hostels are Hostel SPUS (see the Malá Strana section) and the BITA agency (see the Accommodation Agencies section).

Czech hostels are not part of the worldwide HI (Hostelling International) system, though many hostels give discounts to HI card-holders. An ISIC, ITIC, Go25 or Euro<26 card may also get you a discount.

Book ahead if you can. KMC or Klub mladých cestovatelů (Young Travellers' Club; ☎/fax 24 23 06 33), Karoliny Světlé 30 (Map 6), is the closest thing to a national co-ordinating body for hostelling. GTS International travel agency (☎ 96 22 43 00),

Ve Smečkách 27, can also help. Many hostels can be booked from abroad through the computerised IBN booking network, linked to the HI booking service.

Pensions

Once upon a time, a pension (*penzion*) meant a boarding house – a home or apartment block fitted out with locking doors, washbasins, extra toilets and sometimes a café – but the term has been hijacked by high-rise hotels that want to sound homy. Real pensions are a nice compromise between hotel comforts and the personal touches of a private home. They're not cheap, and are often out on the fringes of the city. In the centre they start at about 1500/2000 Kč for a single/double.

Private Rooms

A booming sector of small-scale capitalism in Prague is the renting of rooms in private homes. Touts swarm on the arrival platforms of the main and Holešovice train stations; most (but not all) are honest amateurs with good deals and pure motives. Check the location and the transportation: some are right out in the suburbs. If you fancy a particular neighbourhood, go there

and look for *privát* or *Zimmer frei* (rooms for rent) signs.

Away from the city centre, prices per person with bath and toilet shared with the family are about 500 to 1000 Kč per night. For a private entrance and bath, figure about 30% more, and for something near the centre, anywhere from 50 to 100% more. Many people offer discounts for longer stays, but put their prices up for Easter, Christmas and some European holidays.

Hotels

Hotels nowadays tend to rate themselves, using stars: a two star hotel usually offers reasonable comfort for about 600/900 Kč for a single/double with shared bath or 800/1300 Kč with private bath; three stars means around 1600/2100 Kč. Four and five-star hotels are what we call top-end in this book.

Unless noted, prices are for a room with attached shower and toilet. If a hotel claims to be full, ask if there's anything with shared facilities. In addition to being cheaper, these can be quite grand: the 'common bath' down the hall is often a private room with a bathtub. Some refurbished hotels have mini-suites, with two or three rooms (each with its own lock)

A Place of Your Own in Prague

A few travellers have discovered the pleasures of renting their own flat. This doesn't have to be hideously expensive, but you need to shop around. Before you scoff at the idea, consider that the extra cost of a very basic self-catering flat near the centre means minimal transportation costs, access to cheap local food, and the freedom to come and go as you like.

Some Prague agencies will find a flat for you (see the Accommodation Agencies section on the next page), or you can spend a bit more and set it up in advance. The travel classifieds of UK papers list a growing number of agencies whose speciality is accommodation, with typical per-night prices for two people of around UK£20 to UK£70, and appreciable long-stay discounts. Following are a few reputable ones:

- Auto Plan Holidays   (☎ 01543-257 777, fax 419 217)
- Czechbook   (☎/fax 01503-240 629)
- Czechscene   (☎ 01386-442 782)
- TK Travel   (☎ 0208-699 8065, fax 291 9221)

sharing toilet and shower. Not many hotels have air-conditioning. We note those hotels that offer barrier-free, wheelchair-friendly rooms.

Nearly all hotels at mid-range and above have a restaurant, and usually a snack bar, night bar or café as well. 'Hotel Garni' in some hotel names means they're equipped only for a simple breakfast – that is a 'B&B hotel'. Prices given here are without breakfast, unless noted.

Prices separated by a slash are for single/double or single/double/triple rooms, except as noted. Hotels usually have few singles, but the ones they have are often available when larger rooms aren't. Major credit cards are accepted by all top-end hotels; the few mid-range hotels that take them are noted.

ACCOMMODATION AGENCIES

Following are some reputable agencies. Some can arrange private rooms, and most can get cheaper rooms in pensions and hotels. Some have offices at the airport and the main train station. Prices quoted at budget agencies in the train stations are sometimes lower than those asked at the end of your stay, so check in advance with the owner too.

Even the better agencies naturally don't want you dealing directly with the owner, so they usually won't give you the address before you put your money down, which can be maddening if all you want to do is go and have a look at the place.

We found that few respond quickly to queries from abroad. For some UK agencies that arrange accommodation in advance, see the boxed text 'A Place of Your Own in Prague' on the previous page.

American Express (Map 6; ☎ 24 21 99 92), Wenceslas Square 56 – hotel rooms from about 3000 Kč

AVE (reservations ☎ 57 31 51 91/92, fax 57 31 51 93/94, email avetours@avetours.anet.cz), with on-arrival booking offices at the main train station (☎ 24 22 32 26), Holešovice train station (☎ 66 71 05 14), the airport, and PIS branches; efficient and helpful, with hostel,

pension and hotel rooms and a few private rooms

Bohemiatour (Map 7; ☎ 231 25 89, fax 231 38 06), Zlatnická 7, Nové Město – pensions and private rooms

BITA (Berhanu Incoming Travel Agency; Map 3; ☎ 24 31 12 58, fax 24 31 11 07), Terronská 28, Dejvice, Prague 6 – hostels

ČD (☎ 24 21 48 86), outside level 3, main train station, and a branch (☎ 24 61 70 66) at Holešovice train station – glum and unhelpful

Čedok (Map 7; ☎ 24 19 71 11, fax 232 16 56, email overseas.incoming@cedok.cz), Na příkopě 18, Staré Město, plus other branches (see Travel Agencies in the the Getting There & Away chapter) – pensions and pricier hotels

CK Intercity (Map 7; ☎ 24 61 71 68/24 23 06 39), Masarykovo train station (Hybernská side) – open 24 hours, mostly private rooms

CKM Travel (Map 7; ☎ 26 85 32, fax 26 86 23), Jindřišská 28, Nové Město – anything from hostels to top-end hotels

ESTEC Travel Agency (Map 5; ☎ 57 21 04 10, fax 57 21 52 63, email estec@jrc.cz), block 5, Vaníčkova 1, Strahov, Prague 6 – accommodation in all categories, and summer/winter hostels

Intercontact (Map 5; ☎ 57 31 37 93, fax 53 07 88, email intercon@mbox.vol.cz), Karmelitská 27 – private rooms in the centre, hotels all over

Pragotur (Map 6; ☎ 231 11 16, fax 24 81 61 72), Za Poříčskou bránou 7, Nové Město – mainly private rooms in the centre

Stop City (Map 6; ☎ 24 22 24 97, fax 24 23 12 33), Vinohradská 24, Vinohrady – private and pension accommodation in the náměstí Míru area, from 700 Kč per person in summer

Top Tour (Map 6; ☎ 232 10 77, fax 24 81 14 00, email topia@serverpha.czcom.cz), Rybná 3, Staré Město – mostly expensive luxury private homes and summer hostels

Universitas Tour (☎ 26 04 26, fax 24 21 22 90), Opletalova 38, near the main train station – hostels, including one upstairs

Wasteels (Map 6; ☎ 24 61 74 54, fax 24 22 18 72), main train station – cheaper hotels, hostels and private homes

Vesta (Map 6; ☎/fax 24 22 57 69, advance reservations ☎ 24 61 74 58), main train station – hostels, including its own Hostel CK Vesta at the station, and Hotel Kafka in Žižkov

WHERE TO STAY
Malá Strana

All accommodation in this section is on Map 5.

PLACES TO STAY

Hostels An easy and congenial place for on-the-spot hostel accommodation is the 11 block Strahov student dormitory complex, just east of the big Strahov Stadium; take bus No 143, 149 or 217 from Dejvická metro station. Each block operates as a separate hostel in July and August, with the three listed below open year-round. The complex also includes several low-overhead cafés, snack shops and bars. But misanthropes and light sleepers take note: in summer, discos pound away into the night in blocks 1, 10 and 11.

Hostel SPUS (☎ 57 21 07 64, email spus@praha .czcom.cz, block 4) – triples/doubles at 250/ 300 Kč per bed, and affiliated, seasonal hostels in Josefov, southern Nové Město and the south-east outskirts
Hostel ESTEC (☎ 57 21 04 10, email estec@jrc.cz, block 5) – beds for 190 Kč in crowded dorms and 290/400 Kč in quads/ triples; ESTEC is also a travel agency, and can book other accommodation and transport
Müller Hostel (block 11) – beds for 240 Kč

Quiet *Kolej JA Komenského (☎ 352 04 15, Parléřova 6)* can be booked through Universitas Tour (see the preceding Accommodation Agencies section). It's a 10 minute walk west of Prague Castle, or take bus No 108, 174 or 235 west from Hradčanská metro station, to the Hládkov stop.

Recommended for its central location is the year-round *Hostel Sokol (☎ 57 00 73 97, entrance via a courtyard on Všehrdova)*. With over 90 beds (at 220 Kč each), walk-in odds are good even in high season. There's also a kitchen.

Private Rooms *Snack U Kiliána (☎ 57 31 09 50, Všehrdova 13)* has just two rooms, at 1350/1750/2250 Kč for 1/2/3 people.

Hotels At the *Hotel Coubertin (☎ 35 28 51/53, fax 20 51 32 08, Atletická 5)*, beside Strahov stadium, rooms are 1630/2160 Kč, with breakfast. Take bus No 176 from náměstí Kinských or No 143, 149 or 217 from Dejvická metro station.

Near the southern end of Kampa island, the *Kampa Hotel (☎ 57 32 05 08, fax 57 32 02 62, Všehrdova 16)* has unexciting rooms with satellite TV and minibar for 2200/3550 Kč, including breakfast.

Two small hotels styled for business people are *U Páva (☎ 57 32 07 43, fax 53 33 79, U lužického semináře 32)*, with deluxe rooms from 4900/5300 Kč, some with magical views of Prague Castle; and *U krále Karla (☎ 53 88 05, fax 53 88 11, Úvoz 4)*, at 5300/5800 Kč.

Concealed in a manicured rock garden in a far corner of Hradčany is *Pension U raka (☎ 20 51 11 00, fax 20 51 05 11, Černínská 10/93)*, with a few elegant doubles from 6200 Kč (with breakfast), and not a thread out of place. In summer you'd have to book a few months ahead.

Hotel U tří pštrosů (☎ 57 32 05 65, fax 57 32 06 11, Dražického náměstí 12) is at the foot of the Malá Strana towers of Charles Bridge. Overpriced rooms with splendid views start at 5050/6900 Kč, breakfast included.

Another 'executive-style' hotel is the *Hoffmeister (☎ 57 31 09 42, fax 57 32 09 06, Pod Bruskou 9)*, with underground parking, and smallish, air-conditioned rooms (one barrier-free) from 5600/6500 Kč, including breakfast.

Staré Město & Josefov

This is the most expensive part of the city for accommodation of any kind. All accommodation in this section is on Map 7, except where indicated.

Hostels A very central (and popular) hostel is *Express (Map 6; ☎ 24 21 18 01, Skořepka 5)*, with beds in doubles, triples and quads for 350 Kč (200 Kč for students in the off-season), and rooms with bath at 800/1200 Kč. *Hostel Týn (Týnská 21)* can only be booked through the AVE agency (see the earlier Accommodation Agencies section). Beds start at 560/760 Kč for single/double occupancy.

The newly renovated *Pension Dlouhá (☎ 231 13 18, email hostel@terminal.cz,*

Dlouhá 33) is the only Travellers' Hostel open year-round, with beds from 350 Kč in dorms or 490 Kč in doubles. Six other Travellers' Hostels, open around the centre in July and August, can be booked here.

Hostel SPUS (see the Malá Strana section) runs *Hostel U synagogy (☎ 24 81 94 56, fax 24 81 94 58, U staré školy 1),* by the Spanish Synagogue in Josefov. The hostel is open from March to October with beds priced from 350 Kč (dorm) to 490 Kč (single).

Hotels – Budget Highly recommended is *Unitas Penzion (Map 6; ☎ 232 77 00, fax 232 77 09, email cloister@cloister-inn.cz, Bartolomějská 9),* in space rented from a convent that was once a Czech secret police jail. Václav Havel was held here for a day, and if it's available you can stay in the very cell (No P6). Quiet but cramped rooms start at 1020/1200/1650 Kč with common toilet and shower or 1200/2000/2350 Kč with their own, breakfast included. Book ahead if possible. In the convent at the rear are larger rooms (see Cloister Inn in the next section).

In the tourist zone is *Pension U Lilie (☎ 26 09 37, Liliová 15),* where rooms with bath and TV are 1500/1800 Kč, including breakfast.

Hotels – Mid-Range Beside the popular Restaurace U medvídků is the small *Pension U medvídků (Map 6; ☎ 24 21 19 16, Na Perštýně 7),* with eight simply furnished, clean, double rooms for 2860 Kč.

The appealing *Accommodation U krále Jiřího (☎ 24 22 20 13, fax 24 22 19 83, Liliová 10),* has clean period rooms for 1500/2600 Kč, with breakfast. Those in the attic have extra charm, with exposed wooden wall beams.

The *Hotel Central (☎ 24 81 27 34/0 41, fax 232 84 04, Rybná 8)* has clean, nicely furnished rooms for 2400/3100/3600 Kč with breakfast. In the same league is *Hotel U klenotníka (Map 6; ☎ 24 21 16 99, fax 26 17 82, Rytířská 3),* where renovated period

rooms with bath make for a romantic stay, at 2500/3600 Kč.

Fancy retiring to a convent? The *Cloister Inn (or Hotel U klášterního dvora; Map 6; ☎ 232 77 00, fax 232 77 09, email cloister@ cloister-inn.cz, Bartolomějská 9)* has fine refurbished convent rooms from 2520/ 3150/3690 Kč, including breakfast. Under the same management is the budget Unitas Penzion.

A hotel with a history going back to the 13th century is *U zlatého stromu (☎ 24 22 13 85, fax 24 22 13 85, Karlova 6),* opposite the Klementinum, at 3790/3990 Kč.

Hotels – Top End The splendid Art Nouveau *Hotel Paříž (☎ 24 22 21 51, fax 24 22 54 75, U Obecního domu 1)* is now a historic monument. Even if you can't afford it (7680/8320 Kč and up, with breakfast), have a look. Almost opposite is the renovated, late-19th century *Grand Hotel Bohemia (☎ 24 80 41 11, fax 232 95 45, email grand-hotel-bohemia@austria-hotels .icom.cz, Králodvorská 4),* where rooms are 5405/7380 Kč.

Just south of the Convent of St Agnes is the comfortable *Maxmilian Hotel (☎ 21 80 61 11, fax 21 80 61 10, email maximil@ mbox.vol.cz, Haštalská 14),* in a 1904 building with comfortable rooms with all the trimmings for 5650/6600 Kč, including breakfast. North across Haštalské náměstí in a former aristocratic residence is the *Hotel Casa Marcello (☎ 231 02 60, fax 231 33 23, Řásnovka 783),* whose renovated rooms, furnished with antiques, have kept their historical charm. A double is 5900 Kč, and there is also a pleasant courtyard where you can enjoy a drink or a snack.

In the Týnský dvůr, a kind of medieval caravanserai, is the *Hotel Ungelt (☎ 24 81 13 30, fax 231 95 05, Štupartská 1),* with eight elegant suites (doubles/quads 6330/ 7510 Kč, including breakfast).

At the northern end of Pařížská are two luxury hotels devoid of any period character. The five star *Hotel Inter-Continental Praha (☎ 24 88 11 18, fax 24 81 00 71, náměstí Curieových 5/43)* has rooms from

9890/10,370 Kč (with just one barrier-free double), including breakfast and free use of the swimming pool and sauna.

Behind it, facing the river at No 100, is the four star **President Hotel** (☎ *231 48 12, fax 231 82 47)*, with rooms for 6320/6695 Kč, including breakfast. In a former life as the Hotel Budovatel, this was a favourite of party and trade-union bigwigs.

Northern Nové Město

These listings include a few places east of Wilsonova in Karlín (Prague 8), which are near Florenc and most easily reached from northern Nové Město. All places in this section are on Map 6, except where indicated.

Hostels *Hostel Jednota (☎ 24 21 17 73, Opletalova 38)*, near the main train station, has beds from 345 Kč (in a pinch they'll fit you in somewhere, for 100 Kč), including breakfast. Its **Pension** at the same address has beds for 455 Kč per person. Pre-booking with Universitas Tour, at the same address (see the Accommodation Agencies section), gets you a 50 to 60 Kč discount.

Another Universitas Tour hostel is **Kolej Petrská** *(Map 7; ☎ 231 64 30, Petrská 3)*, in a dreary neighbourhood but near trams and food on Na poříčí; a hostel bed is 365 Kč, and a single/double (with breakfast) in a mini-suite is 610/1170 Kč.

The Vesta agency (see the Accommodation Agencies section) runs the **Vesta Hostel** in the attic of the train station, with beds for 320 to 370 Kč in three, four or six-bed dorms, and a few doubles with bath for 900 Kč per person. The station might sound like a less-than-ideal spot, but you're so high up it hardly matters, and the views are great.

At the **Libra Q Hostel** (see Hotels – Budget), dorm beds are 310 to 330 Kč.

If you're on a rock-bottom budget, try the year-round **Raketa Hostel** *(Na Florenci 2)*, inside the rail yard at Masarykovo station. Very basic but fairly clean rooms with shared facilities start at 320 Kč per bed. You must book it with CK Intercity or Vesta (see the Accommodation Agencies section).

If this isn't cheap enough, try **TJ Sokol Karlín** (☎ *231 51 32, Malého 1)*, a truly down-and-out place just east of Florenc bus station, in Karlín. Beds start at 260 Kč, and you must clear out from 8 am to 6 pm.

Hotels – Budget Well priced for its location is the **Libra Q Hostel** *(Map 7; ☎ 22 10 55 36, fax 24 22 15 79, Senovážné náměstí 21)*. Rooms are 750/890/1320/1560 Kč with shared facilities, 980/1380/1630 Kč (no quads) with their own. There is only a small 'HOSTEL' sign above the entrance, and reception is at the end of the courtyard and down a passage on the right.

Close to Florenc bus station is **Hotel Merkur** (☎ *232 38 78, fax 232 39 06, Těšnov 9)*, where basic rooms with shower are 1500/1900 Kč and more modern rooms with bath and TV are 2800/3200 Kč.

Hotels – Mid-Range The renovated – and recommended – **Hotel Opera** (☎ *231 56 09, fax 231 25 23, Těšnov 13/1743)* near Florenc has clean, modern rooms with shower and TV for 3500/3870 Kč, including breakfast.

A good off-season bargain is the floating hotel, **Botel Albatros** *(Map 7; ☎ 24 81 05 47, fax 24 81 12 14, nábřeží Ludvíka Svobody)*. Spartan cabins with tiny shower and toilet are 1500/2500 Kč in summer, and 30% less in the low season. It has a restaurant and café, and connections by tram No 3 to Wenceslas Square.

Na poříčí, though noisy, has tram connections and plenty of eating options. Good for the money is the modest **Hotel Harmony** (☎ *232 00 16, fax 231 00 09, Na poříčí 31)*, with huge, clean rooms (including six barrier-free doubles) – the quieter ones face Biskupská – for 2550/3510 Kč including breakfast, and a pleasant, inexpensive restaurant.

Two group-oriented hotels that occasionally have spare rooms are the **Atlantic** *(Map 7; ☎ 24 81 10 84, fax 24 81 23 78, Na poříčí 9)*, good value at 3200/4100/5100 Kč (with three barrier-free rooms); and the plain *Axa* *(☎ 24 81 25 80, fax 22 32 21 72, email axapraha@mbox.vol.cz, Na poříčí 40)* at 2350/3400 Kč.

Hotels – Top End Rooms with TV and bath or shower at the friendly Best Western *Hotel Meteor Plaza (Map 7; ☎ 24 19 21 30, fax 24 21 30 05, Hybernská 6)* are somewhat overpriced at 4950/5500/6490 Kč, with breakfast.

Opposite Masarykovo train station is the *Renaissance (Map 7; ☎ 21 82 21 00, fax 21 82 23 33, V celnici 1)*, with rooms from 8000/8600 Kč, with breakfast. Several rooms are wheelchair-friendly.

Central Europe's biggest hotel is the 788 room, business-oriented *Hilton Atrium (☎ 24 84 11 11, fax 24 84 23 78, Pobřežní 3)* in Karlín, with glass roof, swimming pool, four restaurants – the lot. Rooms (including three barrier-free singles) start at 7920/8820 Kč.

Southern Nové Město & Vyšehrad

Hostels The cheap and central *Hostel Arnošt (Voršilská 1; Map 6)* offers dorm beds in two to five-bed rooms for just 300 Kč, including a simple breakfast. One drawback is that it's all bunk-beds. It's only open from early July to mid-September. Drop in, or book it at the BITA agency (see the Accommodation Agencies section earlier in this chapter).

Near Karlovo náměstí is *Club Habitat (☎ 29 03 15, fax 29 00 98, Na zbořenci 10; Map 6)*, with a hostel with beds for 450 Kč. East of the square is the *Juniorhotel (Map 6; ☎ 29 13 20)*, at Žitná 10, with dorm beds for 500 Kč (400 Kč with an ISIC/ITIC card) and rooms with toilet, shower and TV for 1500/2200/2820 Kč including breakfast. But it tends to get booked out by groups.

The good *Hostel U melouna (Map 9; Ke Karlovu 7)*, a 15 minute walk south on Sokolská from IP Pavlova metro station, was renovated specifically as a hostel. At the time of writing there was no telephone number; book it through Hostel SPUS in Strahov (see the Malá Strana section).

Quiet *Penzion Amadeus (Map 9; ☎ 692 73 21/22, Slavojova 108/8)*, Vyšehrad, has dormitory-style doubles and bigger rooms with shared facilities at 420 and 370 Kč per bed. Book it through Domov mládeže (see the later Vinohrady section).

A recommended upmarket hostel is the quiet *Hlávkova kolej (Map 9; ☎ 29 00 98, Jenštejnská 1)*, two blocks west of Karlovo náměstí. Mini-suites are 900/1600 Kč, including breakfast.

Hotels – Budget Just south of the IP Pavlova metro station is *Pension Březina (Mini) (Map 9; ☎ 96 18 88 88, fax 24 26 67 77, email brezina@netforce.cz, Legerova 41)*, where basic rooms are 900/1100 Kč without shower and start at 1100/1300 Kč with. Legerova is pretty noisy.

Hotels – Mid-Range The overrated Art Nouveau *Grand Hotel Evropa (Map 6; ☎ 24 22 81 17, fax 24 22 45 44, Wenceslas Square 25)*, has some dreary mid-range rooms for 1280/2160/2790/3640 Kč without bath and 2450/3400/4350/5200 Kč with. This is good value for the location and the architectural charm, though some travellers have found the atmosphere creepy, such as for solo women.

The *Hotel Andante (Map 6; ☎/fax 22 21 16 16, email andante@netforce.cz, Ve Smečkách 4)* has modern-style rooms for 3080/3750/4830 Kč, with breakfast, TV and a choice of shower or bath. In a run-down lane south of Národní (Národní třída) is the *Hotel Koruna (Map 6; ☎ 24 91 51 74, fax 29 24 92, Opatovická 16)*, with rooms for 1650/2850/3600 Kč, including breakfast.

The *Novoměstský Hotel (Map 6; ☎ 24 91 16 74, fax 24 91 19 66, Řeznická 4)* near Karlovo náměstí has clean rooms with shower and TV for 2300/3000/4000 Kč, and the inexpensive Restaurace U Braunů downstairs. *Hotel 16 U sv Kateřiny (Map 9; ☎ 29 53 29, fax 29 39 56, Kateřinská 16)* has smallish, modern rooms with TV and shower for 2100/2800 Kč. It's a 10 minute walk from Karlovo náměstí.

Sandwiched between the raging traffic of Legerova and Sokolská is *Hotel Patty* *(Map 9; ☎ 24 26 11 81, fax 26 24 21 82, Fügnerovo náměstí 4)*, with rooms for 2890/3290 Kč.

Just below Vyšehrad is the *Hotel Union* *(Map 9; ☎ 61 21 48 12, fax 61 21 48 20, Ostrčilovo náměstí 4)*, where plain, clean rooms with shower and TV are 2800/3350 Kč, including breakfast. It's on the No 24 tram line to Wenceslas Square.

Hotels – Top End A block off Wenceslas Square is the executive-friendly, Art Nouveau *Hotel Palace (Map 6; ☎ 24 09 31 11, fax 24 22 12 40, email palhoprg@mbox .vol.cz, Panská 12)*, where rooms (including two barrier-free doubles) start at 7560/9000 Kč with breakfast (or how about the Presidential Apartment for 28,260 Kč?).

More top-end hotels are on Wenceslas Square (Map 6). At No 5-7, the *Ambassador* and *Zlatá Husa (☎ 24 19 31 11, fax 24 23 06 20, email ambassad@mbox.vol.cz)* form a single four star establishment with lots of restaurants, and 5120/6145 Kč rooms, mainly for groups. Rooms at the snooty, five star *Hotel Jalta (☎ 24 22 91 33, fax 24 21 38 66, email jalta@jalta.cz)* at No 45 are 7200/8400 Kč, with breakfast. Across the square at No 26 is the smallish, modern and pleasant *Adria (Map 6; ☎ 21 08 11 11, fax 21 08 13 00, email adria@ login.cz)* where singles/doubles (including two barrier-free doubles) with bath and satellite TV cost 4680/5580 Kč, including breakfast.

Opposite the Opera House, the five star *Hotel Esplanade (Map 6; ☎ 24 21 17 15, fax 24 22 93 06, Washingtonova 19)* looks like an embassy. Rooms start at 6600/8400 Kč.

The smart Best Western *City Hotel Moráň (Map 9; ☎ 24 91 52 08, fax 29 75 33, Na Moráni 15)*, right by the river, trams and the metro, has rooms with minibar and satellite TV for 5120/6110 Kč, including breakfast.

The high-rise *Hotel Forum (Map 10; ☎ 61 19 12 38/9, fax 61 19 16 73, email forum-reservations@ts-hotels.cz)*, beside Vyšehrad metro station and the Congress Centre (and not much else), has European-class service and 7470/8460 Kč rooms (including five barrier-free doubles), with breakfast. Curiously, American citizens who stay here could face criminal charges at home for doing business with a terrorist state, as the hotel is partly Libyan-owned.

Dejvice
All places in this section are on Map 3, unless otherwise noted.

Hostels A three minute walk from Dejvická metro station is *Hostel Orlík (☎ 23 31 12 40, Terronská 6)*, where a bed in a single/double/triple is 390/350/330 Kč.

Further up the road is the spartan but good-value *Berhanu Hostel (☎ 24 31 12 58, fax 24 31 11 07, Terronská 28)*, where beds are 250 Kč in small rooms with shared facilities, or 500/300 Kč per bed in single/double rooms in seven-room clusters, each room with its own key (400/200 Kč from July to March). Berhanu is also the BITA agency (see the Accommodation Agencies section earlier). In summer there are 400 beds – so walk-in odds are good – and a bar and breakfast room (breakfast costs 50 Kč).

Hotels – Top End The Soviet-style International Hotel, whose tower in Dejvice is visible from afar, was completed for the army in 1957. It has now been refurbished as a *Holiday Inn (☎ 24 39 31 11, fax 24 31 06 16, Koulova 15)*, with rooms from 5600/5900 Kč, including breakfast.

Dejvice's other deluxe hotels are the *Diplomat (☎ 24 39 41 11, fax 24 39 42 15, Evropská 15)*, with rooms (including five barrier-free) from 4800/5800 Kč; and the *Praha (Map 1; ☎ 24 34 11 11, fax 24 31 12 18, Sušická 20)*, starting at 5800/6800 Kč.

Bubeneč & Holešovice
Hostels The year-round, very basic *Hostel Spoas (Map 4; ☎ 80 48 91, Jankovcova*

63a) is only for those arriving on a late bus at Nádraží Holešovice metro station. Head away from the station and cross the bridge over busy Argentinská. A bed is 240 to 300 Kč, in two to six-bed rooms.

Hotels – Budget A 10 minute walk from Nádraží Holešovice metro station is *Hotel Standart (Map 4; ☎ 87 52 58, fax 80 67 52, Přístavní 2)*. It has plain rooms with shared bath for 620/800 Kč, or 350 Kč per bed dorm-style if you have an HI card – good value. If this is full, check out the friendly *Pension Vltava (☎ 80 97 95, Dělnická 35)*, where very quiet rooms are 500/800 Kč; the interior is a bit better than the grim way in.

Hotels – Mid-Range Rooms at the quiet *Hotel Splendid (Map 3; ☎ 37 33 51, fax 38 23 12, Ovenecká 33)* are 2170/3020 Kč with buffet breakfast. From Vltavská metro station, take tram No 1 or 25 two stops to Letenské náměstí.

The pleasant *Hotel Belvedere (Map 3; ☎ 20 10 61 11, fax 33 37 23 68, Milady Horákové 19)* has posh rooms for 2335/3120 Kč with breakfast. Take westbound tram No 1 or 25 two stops from Vltavská metro station.

Hotels – Top End Prices – 3740/4510 Kč with breakfast – at the stodgy *Parkhotel (Map 4; ☎ 20 13 11 11, fax 24 31 61 80, Veletržní 20)* reflect its proximity to the Fairgrounds. Take tram No 12 west from Nádraží Holešovice metro station, two stops to Veletržní.

Smíchov
Camping Grounds The *Yacht Club Karavan Park (Map 9; ☎ 54 09 25, fax 54 33 05)*, at the tip of Císařská louka, has fine views across to Vyšehrad. From Anděl metro station, take tram No 12 four stops to Lihovar, from where it's a 20 minute walk.

Hostels The small *Pension FD Tour* (see the following section) has a few dorm-style beds at 500 Kč in rooms with shared facilities.

Hotels – Budget Two blocks from Anděl metro station is the *Hotel Balkán (Map 9; ☎/fax 54 07 77, Svornosti 28)*, where basic rooms with bath or shower are good value at 1100/1400 Kč. The hotel also has a good restaurant. Across the road, the modest, helpful *Pension FD Tour (☎ 54 62 29, fax 54 86 88, Svornosti 33)* offers plain doubles from 1500 Kč (breakfast included), and you can arrange meals, excursions and other services here.

Hotels – Mid-Range The modern *Hotel Kavalír (Map 1; ☎/fax 52 44 23, Plzeňská 177)* has clean rooms, including five barrier-free doubles, for 2300/2650 Kč (100 Kč more on weekends), with breakfast. From metro station Anděl, take tram No 4, 7, 9 or 34, west to the fourth stop, Kavalírka.

Smíchov has two floating hotels (both Map 9): *Botel Admirál (☎ 57 32 13 02, fax 54 96 16, Hořejší nábřeží)* near Palackého bridge, with rooms for 2440/2560 Kč; and *Transbotel Vodník (☎ 57 31 56 67, fax 24 81 04 32, Strakonická)*, a five minute walk from Smíchovské Nádraží metro station, and better value at 1400/2200 Kč. Prices at both include breakfast.

At the northern end of Smíchov is the modern *Hotel Mepro (Map 9; ☎ 57 31 30 67, fax 57 21 52 63, Viktora Huga 3)*, with rooms from 1800/2500/3000 Kč, including breakfast.

In the quiet streets above Bertramka, *Hotel U Blaženky (Map 9; ☎ 57 32 08 63, fax 57 32 09 24, U Blaženky 1)* has comfortable, good-value rooms from 2400/2990 Kč, and a good restaurant. From Anděl metro station it's a 15 minute climb through woods on a footpath from the top of Ostrovského; or take bus No 137 three stops to the Malvazinky stop, then walk five minutes down U Mrázovky.

Hotels – Top End Isolated on the hill beside Kinského gardens is the *Hotel Vaníček (Map 5; ☎ 35 07 14, fax 35 06 19, Na Hřebenkách 60)*, with rooms from 4200/4400/4600 Kč, with breakfast. Take bus No 176 from Karlovo náměstí or náměstí Kinských.

Troja & Kobylisy

All places in this section are on Map 1.

Camping Grounds Along Trojská in Troja (Prague 7) are at least five grassy, quiet camping grounds, less than 10 minutes from Nádraží Holešovice metro station on bus No 112 (also nearby is the tram from náměstí Republiky, which runs all night).

Autocamp Trojská (☎ 83 85 04 87, fax 854 29 45), No 157 (Kazanka stop)
Camp Dana Troja (☎/fax 83 85 04 82), No 129 (Trojská stop), year-round
Camp Fremunt (☎ 83 85 04 76), No 159 (Kazanka stop), April to October
Camp-Pension Herzog (☎ 689 06 82), No 161 (Čechova škola stop), April to October
Camp Sokol Troja (☎/fax 854 29 08), No 171a (Čechova škola stop), June to August

Trojská is generally the most expensive but best-equipped; Fremunt is a bit cheaper than the others. All offer discounts for long stays, and for youth/student card-holders. There are pricey apartments at Dana Troja, and modest rooms and/or bungalows at the others; Sokol Troja also has dorm beds costing 200 to 220 Kč. All have hot showers, and all but Fremunt and Herzog have cookers for self-caterers. The closest restaurants are two or three stops north on the tram.

Hotels A recommended mid-range place is the quiet *Hotel Stírka* pension *(☎ 688 18 27, fax 688 67 36, Ke Stírce 11, Kobylisy).* Rooms with toilet, shower and TV are 1560/1940 Kč (breakfast included), and substantially less in the low season; credit cards are accepted. Book directly or through the AVE agency (see the Accommodation Agencies section earlier in this chapter). Take tram No 24 from Palmovka metro station or Wenceslas Square, or tram No 5 from náměstí Republiky, to the Ke Stírce stop.

Karlín & Libeň

A few places in Karlín, near Florenc and most easily reached from northern Nové Město, are listed in the Northern Nové Město section.

Hotels – Budget *Botel Neptun (Map 1; ☎ 66 02 93 04, fax 66 02 93 49, U Českých loděnic)* is a floating hotel in Libeň (Prague 8). Little cabins with toilet, shower and fridge are 700/900 Kč (including breakfast) in the high season and about 25% cheaper at other times. There are modest restaurants in the neighbourhood. From Palmovka metro station, walk five minutes north on Zenklova, turn left at Elznicovo náměstí and follow the channel.

Hotels – Mid-Range *Hotel Brno (Map 8; ☎ 24 81 18 88, Thámova 26),* by Křižíkova metro station, is a good deal at 1780/2700/3250 Kč, including breakfast. Pairs of rooms sharing a bath are a bit cheaper yet. There's a small restaurant.

Around the block is the well run *Hotel Ibis (Map 8; ☎ 24 81 17 18, fax 24 81 26 81, Šaldova 9/54),* where very comfortable rooms are 1990/2690 Kč from mid-March to early November, and about 40% cheaper the rest of the year.

A five minute walk from Invalidovna metro station is the sports-club-owned *Hotel Čechie (Map 1; ☎ 66 19 41 11, fax 683 01 37, U Sluncové 618).* Rooms in the new wing (including at least one barrier-free double) are 2400/3400 Kč, and those in the old wing 1600/2000 Kč; all have TV, shower and toilet. Guests may use the swimming pool, though all other facilities (tennis and squash courts, bowling alleys and fitness centre) are extra.

Beside Invalidovna metro station (Map 1) are the *Interhotel Olympik Praha (☎ 66 18 11 11, fax 66 31 05 59, Sokolovská 138),* with high-season rooms at 2462/3621 Kč; and beside it the *Interhotel Olympik II (or Olympik-Garni, ☎ 66 18 11 11, fax 66 31 01 06, U Sluncové 14),* which costs about 20% less and includes breakfast. Both mainly cater for groups. Neither is very friendly.

Žižkov

Camping Grounds Though just 3km from the centre, *Autokemp Žižkov (or Pražačka Camping; Map 1; ☎/fax 644 20 61, Koněvova 141a)* is only open in July and August, as it's in a school sports ground.

Hostels The *Clown & Bard Hostel (Map 6; ☎ 27 24 36, Bořivojova 102)*, with a café-bar, and beds for 200 to 250 Kč in dorms and 350 Kč in doubles with a shared kitchen, looks like one of Prague's most congenial hostels. It's in a quiet neighbourhood close to the Palác Akropolis (see under Alternative Venues in the Entertainment chapter). If it's booked out, go around the corner to the *Purple House (Map 6; ☎ 27 14 90, Krásova 25)*, where four-bed dorms are 330 Kč per bed. Get here from Seifertova (Husinecká stop on tram No 9 from Wenceslas Square or No 5 or 26 from náměstí Republiky).

Flats The Prague B&B Association has a block of comfortable *flats (Map 8; Seifertova 91)* by the tram lines on Seifertova. All have fridge, hotplate and utensils, and are about 800/1000/1400/1600 Kč per night for one/two/three/four people. They must be booked ahead with the Prague B&B Association (Map 5; ☎ 57 32 68 97, fax 57 32 68 99, email prague.b.and.b.ass@pha.pvtnet .cz), Kroftova 3, Smíchov, Prague 5.

Hotels – Budget The *Hotel Kafka (Map 8; ☎/fax 27 31 01, Cimburkova 24)* has scrupulously clean rooms for 1250/1700/ 2000 Kč, some with kitchens for an extra charge; this hotel can only be booked through its owner, the Vesta agency (see Accommodation Agencies in this chapter).

Hotels – Mid-Range Inner Žižkov has several good-value hotels, aimed at groups but with fair walk-in odds. All are near trams (No 9 from Wenceslas Square, Nos 5

and 26 from náměstí Republiký) or buses (No 133 or 207 from Florenc).

The *Bílý Lev (Map 8; ☎ 57 31 51 91, fax 57 31 29 83, Cimburkova 20)* offers renovated rooms for 1450/2700/3850 Kč with breakfast. Rooms (including four barrier-free) at the *U tří korunek (Map 8; ☎ 697 62 94, fax 22 78 01 89, Cimburkova 28)* are 1990/2690/3390 Kč, with satellite TV, buffet breakfast and an agreeable restaurant, and prices that drop by about *half* in the low season. A few blocks west is the small *Ostaš (Map 6; ☎/fax 627 93 86, Orebitská 8)*, with pleasant rooms for 1680/2480/2910 Kč with breakfast.

The *Olšanka Hotel (Map 8; ☎ 67 09 22 02, fax 27 33 86, Táboritská 23)* has overpriced singles/doubles with shower, toilet and TV from 2300/3000 Kč, with breakfast.

Vinohrady

Hostels A budget-end bargain, highly recommended, is *Domov mládeže*, also called *Penzion Jana (Map 1; ☎/fax 25 06 88, fax 25 14 29, Dykova 20)*, with bright singles/ doubles/bigger rooms with shared facilities for 500/400/350 Kč per bed, with breakfast. It's a block south of the Perunova stop on tram No 16 from náměstí Míru or Národní, or seven minutes walk from Jiřího z Poděbrad metro station.

Domov mládeže also has three other properties, which can be booked here; Penzion Máchova and Penzion Košická (see the following paragraphs) and Penzion Amadeus (see Southern Nové Město & Vyšehrad). *Penzion Máchova (Map 10; ☎ 25 41 89, Máchova 11)* has dorm beds in doubles/bigger rooms with shower and toilet for 520/470 Kč. *Penzion Košická (Map 10; ☎ 71 74 24 83, Košická 12)* has beds in big dorms for 350 Kč, and in dorm-style doubles with bath for 400 Kč. All prices include breakfast. Take tram No 22 from náměstí Míru or Národní, to the Jana Masaryka or Ruská stop, respectively.

The *Bulharský Klub (Map 10; ☎ 24 25 57 11, fax 24 25 67 19, Americká 28)* is an ageing but cheerful hostel for Bulgarians and other visitors. Doubles and triples with shower and toilet are 650 Kč per bed; bigger rooms with shared facilities are 400 Kč per bed.

The staid *Švehlova kolej hostel (Map 6; ☎ 57 09 31 11 ext 145, Slavíkova 22)* is a summer fall-back, at about 200 Kč per person. Walk here from Jiřího z Poděbrad metro station.

Hotels – Budget Recommended is *Hotel (or Pension) City (Map 10; ☎ 691 13 34, fax 691 09 77, Belgická 10)*, in a quiet neighbourhood two blocks from Náměstí Míru metro station. Plain rooms with bathtub, satellite TV and telephone are good value at 1110/1485 Kč (two rooms sharing bath) or 1590/2220 Kč (own bath), including breakfast. Bookings can be made directly or through Top Tour (see the Accommodation Agencies section earlier in this chapter).

South of Havlíčkovy park is *Hotel Hasa (Map 10; ☎ 71 74 71 28, fax 71 74 71 31, Sámova 1)*, with comfortable rooms for 800/1400 Kč, including breakfast.

Hotels – Mid-Range The Stop City accommodation agency (Map 6; ☎ 24 22 24 97, fax 24 23 12 33, Vinohradská 24) near náměstí Míru manages a big *boarding house* nearby, with doubles/triples/quads for about 1750/2300/2700 Kč in July and August (less at other times), and some two-room flats for 3000 to 4000 Kč, depending on occupancy.

Hotels – Top End The giant, four star, Austrian-built *Hotel Don Giovanni (Map 1; ☎ 67 03 16 03, fax 67 03 67 04, Vinohradská 157a)*, beside the Želivského metro and bus station, has rooms (four of them barrier-free) from 5700/6800 Kč, including a slap-up buffet breakfast.

North-West Outskirts (Prague 6)

All places in this section are on Map 1, unless otherwise noted.

Camping Grounds The year-round *Autokemp Džbán (☎ 36 85 51, fax 36 90 06, Nad lávkou 3, Vokovice)* is part of the Aritma sports complex (some 200m on from the sports ground). Facilities include huts and bungalows. From Dejvická metro station, take tram No 20 or 26, seven stops to the Nádraží Veleslavín stop.

Hostels *Kolej Kajetánka (☎ 20 51 31 18, Radimova 12, Střešovice)* has 150 single/double rooms at 395/345 Kč per bed. Take bus No 108 or 174 west from Hradčanská metro station to the Kajetánka stop; the hostel is in building No 1 of two tall, white towers. If the porter doesn't speak your language, go to the 'Ubytovací kancelář' office inside.

The BITA agency (see the Accommodation Agencies section earlier in this chapter) manages the huge *Hostel Suchdol*, with a year-round guesthouse at 300 Kč per bed (every two doubles share a shower, toilet and fridge), and dorm beds for 250 Kč from early July to mid-September. It's off Map 1, about 25 minutes from the centre by bus No 107 or 147 (night bus No 502) from Dejvická metro station.

The year-round *TJ Aritma Hostel (☎/fax 36 13 65)*, at the same address as Autokemp Džbán (see Camping Grounds), has beds in doubles and five-bed rooms for 280 Kč, and a restaurant.

The small *TJ Hvězda Praha Hostel (☎ 316 51 04, Za lány, Střešovice)* has beds for 300 Kč, though it's often full. From Dejvická metro station, take tram No 2, 20 or 26 west four stops to the Horoměřická stop.

In Dejvice's Šárka valley, the very basic *Tour Hotel (☎ 312 10 88, V Šáreckém údolí 84)* has beds in clean rooms for 250 Kč, with common shower and toilet, a lounge, and a public swimming pool. Take bus No 116 eight stops from Dejvická metro station to the Šatovka stop.

Hotels Doubles with bath at the *Hotel Markéta (☎/fax 20 51 32 83, Na Petynce 45, Střešovice)* are 1850 Kč, with breakfast. Take bus No 108 or 174 three stops to the Kajetánka stop from Hradčanská metro station.

The helpful, family-run *Pension BoB* (☎ *311 44 92, fax 311 78 35, Kovárenská 2, Lysolaje*) has rooms with shower and toilet for 965/1530 Kč, including breakfast. There's secure parking and a bar with TV. Take bus No 160 or 355 from Dejvická metro station to the Žákovská stop.

Hotel Pyramida (☎ *33 35 51 09, fax 33 35 81 62, Bělohorská 24*) has comfortable rooms for 2250/3300 Kč, with breakfast. Take tram No 8 from Hradčanská metro station or tram No 22 from Národní or Malostranská metro station, to the Vypich stop.

Hotels near Ruzyně airport, in the suburb of Veleslavín (beyond Map 1), include the *Krystal* (☎ *316 27 61, fax 316 42 15, José Martiho*), at 1500/2100 Kč (bus No 119 from Dejvická metro station), and the *Obora* (☎ *36 77 79, fax 316 71 25, Libocká 271/1*), at 1900/2600 Kč. The family-run *Ekipa Family Hotel* (☎ *20 61 00 86, fax 316 62 61, Na rovni 34*) has rooms from 2180/3020 Kč. All these prices include breakfast.

South-West Outskirts (Prague 5)
All places in this section are on Map 1, except as noted.

Camping Grounds *Caravancamp Motol* (☎ *57 21 50 84*, ☎ *52 47 14, Plzeňská 215a, Motol*) is seven stops from Anděl metro station on tram No 4, 7 or 9. To get to *Kemp Eva* (☎ *61 22 32 23, Strojírenská 78, Zličín*), off Map 1, take tram No 9 west from Wenceslas Square to the end of the line, then bus No 164 to the third stop.

Hostels At the year-round *Motorlet Císařka* (☎ *52 61 42, Podbělohorská 97, Císařka*), doubles and quads with shared facilities are 280 Kč per bed. From Anděl metro station, take bus No 191 to the fourth stop.

Hotels The big *Hotel Tourist* (☎ *52 46 45*, ☎ *52 44 07, Peroutkova 531/81, Košíře*) has rooms for 850/1300 Kč. From Anděl metro station, take bus No 137 to the end of the line and walk back several hundred metres.

The drab but clean and friendly *Hotel Golf* (*Map 1*; ☎ *52 32 51/9, fax 57 21 52 13, Plzeňská 215a, Motol*) has rooms with shower, toilet and TV for 2000/2500/3000 Kč, with breakfast.

South-East Outskirts (Prague 4 & 10)
All places in this section are on Map 1, except as noted.

Camping Grounds A peaceful site with a view across the Vltava is *Intercamp Kotva Braník* (☎ *44 46 13 97, fax 44 46 61 10, Braník, Prague 4*), which also has four-bed bungalows at 570 Kč per bed. It's a 25 minute trip south on tram No 3 from Wenceslas Square or eastbound on tram No 21 from Národní, to the Nádraží Braník stop, and a five minute walk west from there. It's open from April to October.

Sky Club Brumlovka (☎/*fax 42 35 19, Vyskočilova 2, Michle*) is right off 5.května (Highway E50/65), and half a kilometre east of Budějovická metro station (take bus No 118 or 178 one stop). Telephone bookings are accepted and youth/student discounts are available.

Hostels Behind Intercamp Kotva Braník (see Camping Grounds) is *Ubytovna Kotva Braník* (☎ *44 46 17 12*), where a bed is 125 to 225 Kč depending on the size of the room (two to six beds).

A popular place is *Hostel Boathaus* (Slavoj-Wesico; ☎ *402 10 76, V náklích 1A*), where dorm beds are 250 Kč. The peaceful riverbank setting makes you feel like you're in the country. It's just off the edge of Map 1; take southbound tram No 3 from Wenceslas Square or eastbound tram No 21 on Národní, to the Černý kůň stop, and walk five minutes west to the river, following the hostel signs.

At Hostel SPUS-managed *Hostel Podolí* (☎ *61 21 17 76 ext 128, Na Lysině 12*), in block B of a student dormitory complex, beds in doubles or triples start at 220 Kč. From Pražského Povstání metro station, take bus No 148 to the Děkanka stop.

PLACES TO STAY

At *Hotel Beta* (☎ *61 26 21 58, fax 61 26 12 02, Roškotova 1225/1, Krč, Prague 4*), a bed in a double or triple is 510 Kč. Take bus No 118 west for three stops from Budějovická metro station.

Hotels – Budget A recommended place along the river is *Pension Bohemians* (☎ *44 46 65 68, fax 44 46 37 76, Modřanská 51, Podolí*), where a room is 990/1290 Kč, with a hot breakfast. There are a few mediocre restaurants nearby. Take southbound tram No 3 from Wenceslas Square or eastbound tram No 21 on Národní to the Modřanská stop, walk around the back and go to the top floor.

The high-quality, five room *AV Pension Praha* (☎ *795 17 26, Malebná 1172*) is a four minute walk north from Chodov metro station. Bed and breakfast is 890/1280 Kč.

The small, well kept *Hotel Kačerov* (☎ *61 21 08 92, fax 42 76 43, Na úlehli 1200, Kačerov*) has basic rooms for 880/1320 Kč with breakfast, a fairly good restaurant and an overpriced bar. It's a 10 minute walk (or take bus No 106, 139 or 170) under the highway from Kačerov metro station.

The *Slavia Hotel* (☎ *67 31 24 71, fax 74 49 50, Vladivostocká 10, Vršovice, Prague 10*) has smart rooms with shower for 1500/1990 Kč including breakfast, and a restaurant. From Strašnická metro station, take westbound tram No 7 two stops, or No 19 to the terminus; the hotel is to the right of the sports complex at the No 19 terminus.

Hotels – Mid-Range *Botel Racek* (☎ *61 21 42 42, fax 61 21 43 90, Na Dvorecké louce, Podolí*) is a quiet, floating hotel with restaurant, café, and spartan cabins with shower and toilet for 2000/2520 Kč, including breakfast (cheaper during the low season). Walk-in prospects are good on weekdays. It's a five minute walk from the Dvorce stop on the No 3 or 17 tram line.

The business-oriented *Hotel ILF* (☎ *61 09 23 33, fax 42 25 55, Budějovická 15, Michle*) has plain, carpeted rooms (including seven barrier-free doubles) from 2000/2800 Kč with breakfast, and a dining room. It's a block from Budějovická metro station. There are also some rooms and services available for wheelchair users. Down the road is a smoky pub.

The smartly run *Hotel Globus* (☎ *792 77 00, fax 792 00 95, Gregorova 2115, Roztyly, Prague 4*), on the edge of the Michelský woodlands, has rooms (including eight barrier-free doubles) with bath and TV for 2200/2700 Kč, including breakfast – good value in this price range. The hotel has a restaurant, pub and nightclub. It's five minutes from Roztyly metro station; walk up left of the trees, then right on Gregorova, or take bus No 118 one stop.

Hotel Opatov (☎ *799 62 22, fax 791 48 48, U chodovského hřbitova 2141*) has one-plus-two mini-suites (ie a single and a double) from 1640/2250 Kč (with breakfast), a great bargain for three. It's the leftmost of two brown tower blocks on the edge of a housing estate east of Opatov metro station. Bookings can be made through Top Tour (see the Accommodation Agencies section earlier in this chapter).

Hotels – Top End At the high-rise *Hotel Panorama* (☎ *61 16 11 11, fax 61 16 63 61, Milevská 7, Pankrác*), rooms – including an impressive 24 barrier-free doubles and triples – are 5930/5660 Kč with breakfast. It's around the corner from Pankrác metro station. American citizens who stay here could face criminal charges at home for doing business with a terrorist state, as the hotel is partly Libyan-owned.

In a fine Art Nouveau house is the small, executive-friendly *Villa Voyta* (☎ *472 29 62, fax 472 29 18, K Novému dvoru 54/124, Lhotka*), with elegant rooms for 3870/4680 Kč with breakfast, and a very good restaurant. It's just off the southern edge of Map 1; take bus No 113, 171, 189 or 215 south from Kačerov metro station to the Sídliště Krk stop, and walk three blocks west on Na Větrově.

North-East Outskirts (Prague 8, 9 & 10)

Camping Grounds There are more camping grounds in this quadrant of the city than anywhere else. The following are out past the edge of Map 1:

Autocamp Sokol (☎ 81 93 11 12, *Nad Rybníkem, Dolní Počernice, Prague 9*) – 45 minutes out: from Palmovka metro station take bus No 250 or 261 to the Dolní Počernice stop, then a five to 10 minute walk

Bušek (☎ 859 18 52, *fax 22 36 17, U parku 6, Březiněves, Prague 8*) – take the No 12 tram from Palmovka metro station to the terminus and then bus No 258 to the end of the line

Triocamp (☎/*fax 688 11 80, Obslužná 43, Dolní Chabry, Prague 8*) – about 40 minutes from the centre: from Nádraží Holešovice metro station, take bus No 175 to Kobyliské náměstí, change to bus No 162 and go four stops

Hotels *Pension Praga* (☎ 66 31 07 32, *U lidového domu 11, Vysočany*) has renovated rooms with shower for 900/1320 Kč, including breakfast. From Českomoravská metro station, walk 700m east on Ocelářská and cross Freyova.

The renovated, high-rise *Hotel Rhea* (☎ 77 90 41/8, *fax 77 06 23, V úžlabině, Staré Strašnice, Prague 10*) has doubles in mini-suites for 2420 Kč, though there are few places to eat in the neighbourhood. It's popular with coach groups. From Želivského metro station, take tram No 11 to the Zborov stop.

PLACES TO STAY

Places to Eat

FOOD

Czech cuisine is typically central European, with German, Austrian, Polish and Hungarian influences. It's very filling, with meat, dumplings, potato or rice topped with a heavy sauce, and usually served with a vegetable or sauerkraut.

The standard meal, which is offered in just about every restaurant, is '*knedlo, zelo, vepřo*' (bread dumpling, sauerkraut and roast pork). Caraway seed, salt and bacon are the most common flavourings – most Czech chefs are rather generous with salt. Everything is washed down with alcohol, mainly beer. Diet food it isn't.

Prague's restaurant scene is changing fast, with new ethnic and international restaurants as well as western fast-food outlets. There seem to be Chinese restaurants around every corner (though some visitors report heavy use of monosodium glutamate).

For a full food glossary, see the Language chapter at the back of this book.

Breakfast

A typical Czech breakfast (*snídaně*) is *chléb* (bread) or *rohlík* (bread roll) with butter, cheese, eggs, ham or sausage, jam or yoghurt, and tea or coffee. Some Czechs eat at self-service *bufety* that open between 6 and 8 am – typically soup or hot dogs washed down with coffee or beer.

A hotel breakfast is typically a cold plate or buffet with cheese, sausage or meat, bread, butter, jam, yoghurt, and coffee or tea. Some also offer cereal and milk, pastries, fruit and cakes. Only at top-end hotels and a few restaurants can you get an American or English-style fried breakfast. Some eateries serving western-style breakfasts are noted in boxed text later in this chapter.

You can also go to a *pekárna* or *pekařství* (bakery), or to one of the French or Viennese bakeries, for *loupáčky*, like croissants but smaller and heavier. Czech bread, especially rye, is excellent and varied.

Lunch & Dinner

Lunch (*oběd*) is the main meal, but except on Sunday it's a hurried affair. Because Czechs are early risers, they may sit down to lunch as early as 11.30 am, though latecomers can still find leftovers in many restaurants at 3 pm. Even many of the grungiest spots are non-smoking until lunch

---

Spanish Birds & Moravian Sparrow

Many dishes bear names that don't offer a clue to what's in them, but certain words will give you hints: *šavle* (sabre), something on a skewer; *tajemství* (secret), cheese inside rolled meat or chicken; *překvapení* (surprise), meat, capsicum and tomato paste rolled into a potato pancake; *kapsa* (pocket), a filling inside rolled meat; and *bašta* (bastion), meat in spicy sauce with a potato pancake.

Two that all Czechs know are *Španělský ptáčky* (Spanish birds), veal rolled up with sausage and gherkin, served with rice and sauce; and *Moravský vrabec* (Moravian sparrow), a fist-sized piece of roast pork. But even Czechs may have to ask about *Meč krále Jiřího* (the sword of King George), beef and pork roasted on a skewer; *Tajemství Petra Voka* (Peter Voka's mystery), carp with sauce; *Šíp Malínských lovců* (the Malín hunter's arrow), beef, sausage, fish and vegetables on a skewer; and *Dech kopáče Ondřeje* (Digger Ondřej's breath), fillet of pork filled with an Olomouc cheese stick.

is over. Dinner (*večeře*) might only be a cold platter with bread.

Bufet, *jídelna* and/or *samoobsluha* are self-service buffets – sit-down or stand-up – for lunch on the run. Common items are *buřt* (mild pork sausages), *chlebíčky* (open sandwiches), *párky* (hot dogs), *klobásy* (spicy sausages), *guláš* (goulash) and good old *knedlo, zelo, vepřo*.

Most *hospoda* and *hostinec* (pubs), *vinárny* (wine bars) and *restaurace* (restaurants) serve sit-down meals with several courses until at least 8 or 9 pm. Some stay open until midnight.

Czechs start their meal with soup (*polévka*). Other common starters are sausage, the famous Prague ham and open sandwiches. Salads and condiments may cost extra. The most common main meal is dumplings (*knedlíky*), made from potato (*bramborové knedlíky*) or bread (*houskové knedlíky*), served with pork and sauerkraut. Beef may be served with dumplings and comes with a sauce – usually goulash, dill cream sauce (*koprová omáčka*) or mushroom sauce (*houbová omáčka*). A delicious Czech speciality is *svíčková na smetaně* – roast beef and bread dumplings covered in sour cream sauce, served with lemon and cranberries. Another Czech speciality is fruit dumplings (*ovocné knedlíky*).

Fish is common, and is usually carp (*kapr*) or trout (*pstruh*). Pike (*štika*) and eel (*úhoř*) are on more specialised menus. Seafood is found only in a handful of restaurants. Note that for a meal with a whole fish, the menu price is not for the whole fish but per 100 grams. Ask how much the trout weighs before you order it!

Poultry is common, either roasted or as *kuře na paprice*, chicken in spicy paprika cream sauce. Duck (*kachna*), goose (*husa*) and turkey (*krůta*) usually come roasted with dumplings and sauerkraut. Turkey is the traditional Christmas Day lunch.

A few restaurants specialise in game. Most common are venison (*jelení*), pheasant (*bažant*), hare (*zajíc*) and boar (*kanec*) – fried or roasted and served in a mushroom sauce or as goulash.

Vegetarian Meals 'Meatless' dishes (*bezmasá jídla*) are available on most menus, but some may be cooked in animal fat or even with pieces of ham or bacon! If you ask, most chefs can whip up something genuinely vegetarian. Useful phrases include:

I am a vegetarian.	*Jsem vegetarián/ vegetariánka* (m/f).
I don't eat meat.	*Nejím maso.*
I don't eat fish/ chicken/ham.	*Nejím rybu/kuře/ šunku.*

Some common meatless dishes are:

knedlíky s vejci
  fried dumplings with egg
omeleta se sýrem a bramborem
  cheese and potato omelette
smažené žampiony
  fried mushrooms
smažený květák
  fried cauliflower with egg and onion
smažený sýr
  fried cheese with potatoes and tartar sauce

Dessert

Most restaurants have little in the way of dessert (*moučník*). For cakes and pastries, it's better to go to a café (*kavárna*) or cake shop (*cukrárna*). Most desserts consist of canned/preserved fruit (*kompot*), either on its own or *pohár* – in a cup with ice cream (*zmrzlina*) and whipped cream. Pancakes (*palačinky* or *lívance*) are also very common. Other desserts you're likely to encounter are *jablkový závin* (apple strudel), *makový koláč* (poppy-seed cake) and *ovocné koláče* (fruit slices).

Snacks

The most popular Czech snacks are *buřt* or *vuřt* (thick sausages, usually pork) and *klobása* (spicy pork or beef sausages), fried or boiled, served with mustard on rye bread or a roll. Other snacks are *párky* (hot dogs), *bramborák* (a potato cake made from strips of potato and garlic) and *hranolky* (chips or French fries).

Locally produced *bílý jogurt* (natural white yoghurt) is a popular product that is much better than the imported versions. In autumn, street vendors offer roasted chestnuts (*kaštany*).

DRINKS
Coffee & Tea

Coffee (*káva* or *kafe*) and tea (*čaj*) are very popular. Basic coffee is the strong *turecká* (Turkish) – hot water poured over ground beans that end up as sludge at the bottom of your cup. *Espreso* is sometimes a fair equivalent of the Italian version. Viennese coffee (*Vídeňská káva*) comes closer to its Austrian counterpart.

Tea tends to be weak and is usually served with a slice of lemon; if you want it with milk, ask for *čaj s mlékem*.

Nonalcoholic Drinks

In Prague it's hard to find soft drinks (*limonády*) other than western imports. One Czech energy drink – clearly not being marketed just to track and field stars – is Erektus; another is Semtex, in honour of the infamous plastic explosive made in the former Czechoslovakia. Locally bottled mineral water is widely available, as many Czechs don't like the taste of their tap water. 'Juices' are widely available, but aren't always 100% juice.

Beer

Czech beer *(pivo)* is among the best in the world, with a pedigree that goes back to the 13th century. The world's first lager was brewed in Plzeň (Pilsen) in West Bohemia. The Czech Republic has for some years been the world's No 1 beer-drinking nation, with an annual per capita consumption of some 160L. Beer is served almost everywhere; even cafeterias and breakfast *bufety* have a tap. Most pubs close at 10 or 11 pm, but some bars and nightclubs are open until 6 am.

Most Czech beers are lagers, naturally brewed from hand-picked hops. Czechs like their beer at cellar temperature with a creamy, tall head. Americans and Aus-

tralians may find this a bit warm. When ordering draught beer, ask for a *malé pivo* (0.3L) or *pivo* (0.5L).

Most beer is either light or dark, and either *dvanáctka* (12°) or *desítka* (10°). This indicator of specific gravity depends on factors such as texture and malt content, and doesn't directly indicate alcohol content. Most beers are between 3% and 6% alcohol, regardless of their specific gravity.

The best-known Czech beer is Plzeň's Pilsner Urquell (Plzeňský Prazdroj in Czech), which is exported worldwide. Many Czechs also like another Plzeň brew, Gambrinus, but in 1997 Radegast, a North Moravian brew, was voted the best beer of the year. The most widely exported Czech beer is Budvar (Budweiser in German), the name of which was hijacked years ago for an unrelated American brew. The Czech Budvar's mild, slightly bitter taste is popular in Austria, Germany and Scandinavia. A new beer with a fine and very smooth taste is Velvet from North Moravia. Prague's home brand is Smíchovský Staropramen.

Some pubs brew their own beer; best known are the strong, dark beer served at U Fleků in Nové Město, and a light beer made by its neighbour, Novoměstský pivovar.

Most glass bottles can be returned to the point of purchase for a 3 to 10 Kč refund, a small boost for your beer budget.

Wine

Although not as popular as beer, wine (*víno*) is widely available in wine bars (*vinárny*), restaurants and pubs – but not in many beer halls. Dry wine is *suché víno* and sweet is *sladké*.

Reasonable local wines are available in Prague shops, but the best ones are bought straight from the vineyards. Bohemia's largest wine-producing area, around Mělník (see the Excursions chapter), produces good whites, though its reds don't measure up to Moravia's; most popular is the Burgundy-like Ludmila. The best Moravian label is Vavřinec, a red from the south-east; another good red is Frankovka. A good dry white is Tramín. Rulandské bílé is a semi-dry white, Rulandské červené a medium red.

Czechs seem to prefer sweeter whites. A popular summer drink is *vinný střik*, white wine and soda water with ice. In winter mulled wine is popular.

Spirits

Probably the most unique of Czech spirits (*lihoviny*) is Becherovka, from the spa town of Karlovy Vary, with its 'cough-medicine' taste. Another popular bitter spirit is Fernet. A good brandy-type spirit is Myslivecká.

Slivovice (plum brandy), fiery and potent, is said to have originated in Moravia, where the best brands still come from. The best commercially produced slivovice is R Jelínek from Vizovice. Other regional spirits include Meruňkovice apricot brandy and a juniper Borovička. If you have a sweet tooth, try Griotka cherry liqueur.

The deadliest spirit is locally produced Hills Liqueurs absinthe, made from worm-wood. While it's illegal in many countries, in part because of its high alcohol content, this green, slightly soapy tasting liqueur is legal in the Czech Republic. Arguments still rage about its safety.

Spirits are drunk neat, and usually cold (an exception is *grog*, a popular year-round hot drink: half rum, half hot water or tea, and lemon). Spirits, including western brands, are available in all restaurants and most pubs and wine bars.

WHERE TO EAT

There's no shortage of places to eat in Prague. If you like meat and dumplings you'll have no problems, though you may soon begin craving something else. The last few years have seen a boom in good restaurants serving more exotic cuisine, though the selection is constantly changing. Use this book as a guide, but have a look also at the *Prague Post* for current lists and reviews.

Opening hours are volatile, so don't be surprised if they're different from what we found. Most restaurants seem to stay open on national holidays, except Christmas Eve.

Funny, I Don't Remember Ordering That

Prague's restaurants are notorious for overcharging. In a 1996 survey by the Czech Commercial Inspectorate, over a third of inspectors' restaurant bills were inflated, so you can imagine what happens with foreigners. Some restaurants in tourist areas have two menus – one in Czech, and one in German, English or French with higher prices. You might be charged considerably more for Wiener schnitzel than for *telecí řízek*, which is the same thing.

If there's no menu, go elsewhere. If the menu has no prices, ask for them. Don't be intimidated by the language barrier; know exactly what you're ordering. When the waiter says 'rice or potatoes?', know how to ask, 'does it cost extra?' (*platí se zato zvlášt?*). If something's not available and the waiter suggests an alternative, ask for the price. Immediately return anything you didn't order and don't want, such as bread, butter or side dishes; don't just leave it to one side.

Many restaurants have a cover charge (*couvert*), typically 10 to 20 Kč, though some bury it so deep in the menu you'll never find it. In some places condiments like ketchup and mustard are not free, but if they charge you when you haven't used them, politely decline.

Finally, check your bill; better yet, estimate it before you let go of the menu. If you pay with a credit card, it's wise to keep track of it. See that the date and price are clear and correct on the sales slip, complete the 'total' box yourself, add a currency symbol before it with no space in between, and be sure only one sales slip is imprinted.

Main courses may stop being served well before the advertised closing time, with only snacks and drinks after that.

Prices soar as you approach Old Town Square and Malostranské náměstí, so if you're on a budget, eat outside the historical centre. We list price ranges for the main *hotová jídla* (ready-to-serve courses) and *jídla na objednávku* (courses to order), not totals for a full meal. Expect to pay half to two-thirds more than this if you order side dishes and drinks. A place calling itself a 'restaurace' will tend to be cheaper than a 'restaurant'.

Older Prague waiters still suffer from that affliction of the Communist-era service industry: surliness. It's nothing personal, and Czechs tend to ignore it. Many younger waiters are pleasant and professional.

Types of Eateries

Restaurace (restaurant) is a catch-all term. A *vinárna* (wine bar) may serve anything from small snacks to a full-blown menu. A *hospoda* or *hostinec* is a pub or beer hall serving basic meals; a *pivnice* is a beer hall serving no meals. A *bufet* is a cafeteria-style place with zero atmosphere but cheap soups and stodge. The occasional *kavárna* (café or coffee shop) has a full menu but most only serve snacks.

Reservations

In high season an advance booking is essential for dinner at most restaurants; for places near the city centre you may have to plan up to a week ahead. It's not unusual to find restaurants entirely 'reserved' – say, for coach parties – and at dinner time there are always a few anxious tourists marching up and down in search of a meal. That said, in months of Prague research, we mostly did just fine without making any reservations at all. The higher your standards and the larger your group, the more trouble you'll have.

Most places that see tourists have someone who can speak English, but if you'd rather dispense with bookings, try eating at odd hours, preferably early – start lunch by 11.30 am and dinner by 6 pm (many cheaper places run out of food after 3 pm and after 10 pm). Many pubs will serve you meat and dumplings at any time of the day. Don't forget the cheap stand-up *bufety* (buffets), some of which are tucked into the side of *potraviny* (food shops).

Tipping

See the Money section of the Facts for the Visitor chapter for some useful 'tip tips'.

Self-Catering

There are *potraviny* (food shops) and *samoobsluha* (supermarkets) everywhere, the best stocked and priciest being in flash department stores near the centre, such as those in the basement of Krone on Wenceslas Square (Map 6), and in Kotva on náměstí Republiky (Map 7). Cheaper are Bílá Labut on Na poříčí and Tesco on Národní (Národní třída; both Map 6). Other modest supermarkets are Julius Meinl, on

Eating Well & Where to Do It

To guide you to some of the best eating places that Prague has to offer, the authors' 10 personal favourites are listed below:

1. U Malého Glena, Malá Strana
2. FX Café, Vinohrady
3. Country Life, two branches in Staré Město
4. The Globe Café & Bookshop
5. U knihomola Café & Bookshop
   John King

1. U radnice, Žižkov
2. Vinárna v zátiší, Staré Město
3. Vinárna U Maltézských retířů, Malá Strana
4. Klub architektů, Staré Město
5. Le Saint-Jacques, Staré Město
   Richard Nebeský

Snap, Crackle & Pop

Plenty of *bufety* are open by 8 am, but you may not fancy soup and sausage at that time of day. Most restaurants that can cope with a western-style fry-up don't open until 10 or 11 am. But there's help for early risers.

Louvre/Gany's Café *(Map 6; upstairs at Národní 22)* opens at 8 am serving Czech, American and English breakfasts from 90 to 150 Kč (there's a Russian breakfast too, complete with a bottle of champagne and two shots of ice-cold vodka). Also in the neighbourhood is **Cornucopia** *(Map 6; Jungmannova 10)*, open weekdays from 7.30 am with a big, eggy menu (from 75 to 110 Kč) and hot muffins, and for brunch on weekends from 10 am to 4 pm.

Bar Rock *(Map 7; Pařížská 24, Josefov)* does eggs as you like, daily from 8.30 am for a not-so-cheap 165 Kč. **Red, Hot & Blues** *(Map 7; Jakubská 12)* does a western fry-up from 9 to 11.30 am daily and brunch (from 100 to 200 Kč) from 9 am to 4 pm on weekends. **Kavárna Obecní dům** *(Map 7; náměstí Republiky)* opens at 7.30 am, though it's pricey and service is not always cheerful.

Bohemia Bagel *(Map 5; Újezd 18, Malá Strana)* is open from 7 am with every kind of bagel and topping, all-day breakfast and a bottomless cup of coffee. **U Malého Glena** *(Map 5; Karmelitská 23, Malá Strana)* does brunch on weekends from 10.30 am to 4 pm; try their blueberry pancakes.

The 380 Kč price tag for buffet breakfast at the **Hotel Don Giovanni** *(Map 1; by Želivského metro station)* may take your breath away, but it's a breakfast like you've never seen.

28.října (Map 6), and Pronto Plus on náměstí 14.října in Smíchov (Map 9).

Note that some perishable supermarket food items bear a date of manufacture (*datum výroby*) plus a 'consume-within' (*spotřebujte do* ...) period, whereas others (such as long-life milk) have a stated minimum-shelf-life (*minimální trvanlivost*) date (after which freshness of the product is not guaranteed).

The city has quite a few open-air produce markets; see Open-Air Markets in the Shopping chapter for a list of some near the centre.

Prague Castle

Food prices here are as high as the castle itself. If you're on a budget, eat before you get here or bring a picnic! Refer to the Prague Castle map on page 82.

For cakes, good coffee, cold courses under 200 Kč or hot courses and grills from 240 Kč, try **Café Poet** (☎ 24 37 32 08, *Na baště*), to the left of the castle's main gate, open from 10 am to 8 pm. There might be

room among the tour groups at **Restaurace Vikárka** (☎ 53 51 59, *Vikářská 7*), open from 11 am to 11 pm with inventive Czech dishes, mostly 330 to 390 Kč. Alternatives are **Café Terasa** in Lobkowicz Palace, and a **bistro** in the courtyard of the Burgrave's Palace.

A 'cafeteria' called **U Kanovníků** serves overpriced sandwiches and apple pie to tourists at outdoor tables. Another entrance, on the left, leads upstairs to a simple canteen where castle staff fill up on Czech stodge for 50 to 70 Kč (clear your own tray), weekdays from 9 to 10 am and 11 am to 1.30 pm, and weekends from 11 am to 12.30 pm. It's not for the public but if you keep your mouth shut you might get away with it. On Sunday from 1 pm this is open to the public with a fixed meal costing about 150 Kč.

Near Golden Lane is **Bistro Zlatá ulička**, with overpriced drinks and Cellophane-wrapped sandwiches and pastries. Across the plaza, **Café Gallery** serves drinks from 9 am to 4 pm daily.

Hradčany

All places in this section are on Map 5.

West up the hill is an extraordinary tearoom called *Malý Buddha* (☎ *20 51 38 94, Úvoz 46)*, offering carefully prepared eastern dishes – vegetarian and otherwise – for just 50 to 100 Kč. It's open daily except Monday, from 1 to 10.30 pm. Nearby, *Restaurace Sate* (☎ *20 51 45 52, Pohořelec 3)* has good Indonesian dishes for around 100 Kč.

Moderately priced *U staré radnice* *(Loretánská 2)*, in the former Hradčany town hall, has a mock-medieval atmosphere but blasé service. Out of the mainstream is *U zlaté hrušky* (☎ *20 51 53 56, Nový svět 3)*, open daily from 11.30 am to 3 pm and 6.30 pm to midnight, with dishes from 400 to 550 Kč.

In the Strahov Monastery grounds is subterranean *Restaurant Peklo* (☎ *20 51 66 52, Strahovské nádvoří 1/132)*. The name means 'hell', referring to the fact that monks once did penance here, but it's anything but penitential now. The food is Italian and Czech, with dishes costing from 350 to 650 Kč. It's open daily from noon to midnight, except on Monday when it opens at 6 pm.

Malá Strana

All places in this section are on Map 5. Except as noted, typical opening hours are from 11 am to 11 pm daily.

Malostranské Náměstí & Around A

standout among Malostranské náměstí's touristy restaurants is *U tří zlatých hvězd* (☎ *53 96 60)* at No 8, with a good à-la-carte lunch menu including vegetarian dishes under 180 Kč. It closes at 4 pm. *Circle Line* (☎ *57 53 00 23)* at No 12 does inventive international dishes for 500 to 800 Kč. It's closed on Sunday.

At No 7 is cheerful *Jo's Bar & Garáž* (☎ *53 12 51)*, serving sandwiches and Mexican food to young expats from 11 am to 11 pm daily, and drinks till 5 am. Salad, soup and a sandwich is about 150 Kč, and they do a Sunday Mexican brunch.

A recommended place that cannot make up its mind to be a restaurant, bar or music club is laid-back *U Malého Glena* (☎ *535 81 15, Karmelitská 23)*. The ground-floor restaurant dishes up bagels, salads and grilled sandwiches for around 100 Kč. Later it morphs into a bar, with music in the basement, but the food rolls on until midnight (1 am on weekends).

The menu at *Waldštejnská hospoda* (☎ *53 61 95, Valdštejnské náměstí)* includes venison, rabbit and quail (260 to 380 Kč) and less exalted dishes from 175 Kč. On the 1st floor of the Pálffy Palace, the *Pálffy Palác Club Restaurace* (☎ *51 32 54 18, Valdštejnská 14)* serves fish and meat with mouthwatering sauces for 360 to 480 Kč – a fine place for a splurge.

If you like Greek food, try *Restaurant Faros* (☎ *57 31 69 45, Šporkova 2)*. Of course it has souvlaki and moussaka and more, with dishes from 150 to 300 Kč. *U sněděného krámu* (☎ *53 17 95, Lázeňská 19)* has a Czech and international menu with main courses from 125 to 170 Kč, and old-Prague décor.

Around Kampa Na Kampě square is lined with unexceptional restaurants and bistros, eg *U zlatých nůžek* (☎ *57 31 58 79)* at No 6, with salads and Czech dishes for 180 to 250 Kč. *Vinárna Čertovka* (☎ *53 88 53, Cihelná 24)* does small main courses for 150 to 350 Kč, but its main attraction is the view of Charles Bridge and Staré Město.

For better value, head for *Rybářský klub* (☎ *53 02 23, U sovových mlýnů 1)* at the south end of Kampa, with spicy Hungarian fish soup and lots of fish courses for 100 to 190 Kč. The riverside outdoor tables make a cool setting surprisingly hard to find in this riverside city. It's open daily from 11 am to midnight.

Southern Malá Strana Service at *Vinárna U Maltézských rytířů* (☎ *53 63 57, Prokopská 10)* is professional and the food top-notch, from a small menu of vegetarian and other dishes costing under 400 Kč. Book well ahead, and try for a downstairs table when Naďa Černíková gives her delightful spiel about the old building housing the restaurant.

Mazlova vinárna U malířů (☎ 57 32 03 17, *Maltézské náměstí 11)* is a French restaurant offering fish and shellfish from 420 Kč, pheasant and game from 550 Kč, and a blowout four course set dinner for 1290 Kč. It's open daily from 7 to 10 pm. Just off the square, *U modré kachničky* (☎ 57 32 03 08, *Nebovidská 6)* offers similar fare for much less, daily from noon to 4 pm and 6.30 to 11.30 pm.

Restaurant Canto (☎ 53 31 07, *Besední 3)* is a good choice for dinner before a concert – open from noon to 11 pm with seafood, fish and meat courses for 100 to 150 Kč, in a dignified, comfortable setting.

For relief from all this pricey food, try the sausages or goulash at *Snack U Kiliána* (☎ 561 81 40, *Všehrdova 13)*. Nearby is *Restaurace Bar Bar* (☎ 53 29 41, *Všehrdova 17)*, serving giant salads under 90 Kč and a zillion kinds of tasty crêpes, savoury or sweet, for 150 to 250 Kč, until midnight.

The self-service and *très américain Bohemia Bagel* (☎ 53 10 02, *Újezd 18)* is open from 7 am to 2 am daily with bagel sandwiches (100 to 125 Kč), quiches, soups, salads and all-you-can-drink soft drinks and coffee.

Across Újezd is the funicular railway up Petřín Hill. The halfway stop is at *Restaurant Nebozízek* (☎ 53 79 05, *Petřínské sady 411)*, with a varied menu of Czech standards and seafood dishes for 165 to 335 Kč. The salads are good, steaks and wines excellent (as are the views).

Josefov

All places in this section are on Map 7.

The *Košer jídelna* or Kosher Eatery in the Jewish Town Hall, on Maiselova, is open weekdays from 11.30 am to 2.30 pm with a daily four course menu for anywhere from 220 to 700 Kč. Book it at the Matana travel agency (☎ 232 19 54) at No 15.

Vinárna U Golema (☎ 232 81 65, *Maiselova 8)* is a quiet wine bar with not-too-overpriced fish, poultry and meat dishes

(120 to 200 Kč), open weekdays from 11 am to 10 pm and Saturday from 5 to 11 pm (closed Sunday). *Restaurace U městské knihovny (Valentinská 11)* has tasty Czech daily specials from 50 Kč and other dishes from 90 Kč.

The *Jewel of India* (☎ 24 81 10 10, *Pařížská 20)* has very good tandoori and north Indian specialities from 150 to 490 Kč. It's open daily from noon to 2.30 pm and 6 to 11 pm. *La colline oubliée* (☎ 232 95 22, *Elišky Krásnohorské 11)* offers a range of couscous specialities (from 150 to 450 Kč) and other north African fare from noon to 1 am (closed Sunday).

Staré Město

All places in this section are on Map 7, except where indicated.

Around Old Town Square Restaurants around Old Town Square tend to be predatory, but the food can be splendid. Worth a try is *Staroměstská restaurace* (☎ 24 21 30 15, *Staroměstské náměstí 19)*. The meaty Czech and international menu (from 40 to 240 Kč) is big, the food good and service pleasant. Try their fruit dumplings. Food and beer prices on the terrace outside are up to 50% higher than those charged inside.

In a pedestrian passage off the east corner of the square is the low-key *Restaurace Snack Bar U Černého slunce* (☎ 24 22 47 46, *Kamzíkova)*, good for a beer or a light meal from 10 am to 10 pm, with most dishes under 100 Kč – pretty good value for this area.

From behind Havelská market stalls, the stand-up *Safir Grill Bar (Havelská 12)* serves felafel, gyros (doner kebab) and other Middle Eastern goodies for 60 to 80 Kč a hit, plus good vegetable salads. It's open until 8 pm (closed Sunday).

An excellent French restaurant with pleasant service is *Le Saint-Jacques* (☎ 232 26 85, *Jakubská 4)*, with main courses from 170 to 490 Kč. It's open weekdays from 11 am to 3 pm and 6 pm to 1 am. Czechs trying to impress their friends take them to *La Provence* (☎ 90 05 45 10, *Štupartská 9)*,

PLACES TO EAT

with *Provençal* specialities from 200 to 600 Kč, daily from 8 to 1 am.

Around Dlouhá *Mikulka's Pizzeria* *(☎ 231 00 18, Dlouhá 8)* is open from 11 am to at least 11.30 pm, with pizzas for 70 to 123 Kč per person. If you're feeling wild and crazy, try a sweet pizza with chocolate. Another branch is called **Pizza-mania** *(☎ 231 57 27, Benediktská 16)*. Bookings are recommended for an evening meal at either.

U Benedikta *(☎ 231 15 27, Benediktská 11)* has salads, a few vegetable dishes and a menu of non-greasy poultry, fish, steak and game dishes for under 140 Kč. It's open until 11 pm (closed Sunday).

Around Náměstí Republiky *Red, Hot & Blues* *(☎ 231 46 39, Jakubská 12)* offers nachos, burgers and hot chilli for 130 to 160 Kč, New Orleans specials such as shrimp creole for up to 360 Kč, plus wicked desserts and a bottomless cup of coffee. It's open from 9 am to about midnight, with traditional jazz on the sound system and almost nightly jazz or blues live gigs.

Pivnice Radegast *(Templová 2, off Celetná)* has famously no-nonsense service but, for its location, cheap and very good traditional Czech food. The goulash with dumplings (54 Kč) is superior. Open daily from 11 am to midnight, it's popular with young Czechs.

The renovated Obecní dům has several places to eat well in Art Nouveau splendour, though not cheaply. In the basement the *Plzeňská restaurace* serves mainly Bohemian dishes for under 220 Kč, daily until 11 pm. At street level, prices at the excellent *Francouzská restaurace* or French Restaurant *(☎ 22 00 27 77)* run from 260 to about 600 Kč. It's open daily from noon to 3 pm and 6 to 11 pm. Light meals in the handsome *Kavárna Obecní dům* are 65 to 200 Kč per dish. It's open daily from 7.30 am to 11 pm.

Prague has come of age with its own *Planet Hollywood* *(☎ 24 21 27 50, Na příkopě 13 on Havířská)*, dispensing movie paraphernalia and big-screen film clips along with the hamburgers, pasta and big salads. Nothing costs over 400 Kč, and 0.5L of beer is 55 Kč.

Around Betlémské Náměstí Popular, subterranean *Klub architektů* *(Map 6; ☎ 61 50 17 60, Betlémské náměstí 5)* offers inventive Czech/international dishes, including vegetarian ones, for 90 to 130 Kč, from 11.30 am to midnight daily.

The top-notch *Vinárna v zátiší* *(☎ 24 22 89 77, Liliová 1)* also offers international and Czech dishes with a difference; try their duck with herb dumplings. Main courses cost from 300 to 600 Kč, with vegetarian dishes at the lower end. It's open daily from noon to 3 pm and 5.30 pm to 1 am. Opposite is *Restaurace U Betlémské kaple* *(☎ 24 21 18 79, Betlémské náměstí 2)*, offering a varied menu of tasty fish dishes (their carp is very good) for under 350 Kč, daily until 11 pm.

If you don't know what Icelandic food is, try the seafood at *Reykjavík* *(☎ 24 22 92 51, Karlova 20)* – such as the 'salmon plaice duette', with vegetables steamed to perfection. Per-dish prices are 300 to 450 Kč, and they're open daily until midnight.

Cheaper and a bit downmarket is *Restaurace U Ampezonů* *(Map 6; ☎ 24 21 13 99, Konviktská 11)*, whose solid Bohemian fare – such as roast chicken with potato dumplings – is better, and better value at 50 to 100 Kč per dish, than more expensive meaty items. It's open daily until 11 pm.

Bellevue *(Map 6; ☎ 24 22 13 87, Smetanovo nábřeží 18)* serves up pricey Italian cuisine (from 240 to 1200 Kč per course) with majestic views of the river, Charles Bridge and Hradčany (and traffic in the foreground if you dine on the balcony). Sunday features live jazz with Champagne Brunch from 11 am to 3.30 pm and with dinner from 7 to 11.30 pm.

Nové Město

Northern Nové Město The Hotel Palace's *Delicatesse Buffet* *(Map 6; Panská 12)* is good value, with a salad bar

A Table with a View, Please

Prague abounds in good viewpoints, and one way to enjoy them is over wine and a good meal. Many well placed restaurants have let the view go to their heads, and overpriced, mediocre food is the norm, but there are some exceptions:

Hanavský pavilón (Map 7; ☎ 32 57 92, Letenské sady, Letná) – main courses from 500 to 600 Kč, set seafood menu about 1800 Kč; in summer, dine on the terrace (daily until 10.30 pm) and enjoy a postcard-perfect view of the Vltava bridges; take tram No 18 from Malostranská metro station to Chotkovy sady

Restaurant Nebozízek (Map 5; ☎ 53 79 05, Petřínské sady 411, Malá Strana) – Czech standards and seafood for 165 to 335 Kč, good salads, and wide views across the Vltava to Staré Město; from Újezd, take the funicular railway to the midpoint

Restaurant La Perle de Prague (Map 6; ☎ 21 98 41 60, Dancing Building, Rašínovo nábřeží 80, Nové Město) – French specialities, main courses from 480 to 850 Kč or three course menu 900 Kč, with views of Malá Strana and Prague Castle; closed Sunday; four blocks west of Karlovo Náměstí metro station, or take tram No 3 from Wenceslas Square

Restaurace Televizní Věž (Map 8; ☎ 67 00 57 78, Mahlerovy sady 1, Žižkov) – in the TV Tower; so-so Czech dishes but modest prices (from 100 to 270 Kč per dish), renovations on the way; so high (63m) that you really can't see much; about four blocks north-east of Jiřího z Poděbrad metro station

(28 Kč per 100g) and a few meat dishes and sandwiches, served weekdays until 7 pm. Don't walk into the hotel's pricey restaurant instead!

The vaguely rustic, well regarded *Restaurace MD Rettigové* (Map 7; ☎ 231 44 83, Truhlářská 4) is named after Magdalena Dobromila Rettigová, a 19th century exponent of a culinary Czech National Revival. The menu is serious (poultry and meat under 260 Kč, including specials such as chicken breast with mushroom and liver) and the food is pretty good.

Pizzeria Mamma Mia (Map 7; ☎ 231 47 26, Na poříčí 13) rustles up very good pizzas (from 70 Kč) in a wood-fired oven, daily from 11 am to 11 pm (Sunday from 5 to 10 pm). Tucked away near the river is *Hacienda Mexicana restaurace* (Map 6; ☎ 21 85 10 95, Mlynářská), with tacky Mexican décor, a big Tex-mex menu and good strawberry margaritas.

Fakhreldine (Map 6; ☎ 232 79 70, Klimentská 48) has a big selection of excellent Lebanese dishes from 280 to 355 Kč, but desiccated baklava and slow service. It's open daily from noon to midnight.

Around Wenceslas Square The square is lined with atmospheric places where you generally pay over the odds, but there are some good exceptions.

In a courtyard at No 48, *Restaurace/hospůdka Václavka* (Map 6; ☎ 24 21 94 28) offers good Czech standards for 45 to 100 Kč, and fast service.

At the *Mayur Indický Snack Bar* (Map 6; ☎ 24 22 67 37, Štěpánská 61), deprived spice-heads will weep for joy over the curries and tandoori meats (about 120 Kč), soups, salads and fresh tandoori bread; there are also vegetarian dishes. It's open daily from noon to 11 pm. Next door is the *Mayur Indický Restaurant*, offering bigger main courses at bigger prices during the same hours.

In the Melantrich building at No 36 is the *Maso uzeniny* sausage shop, with a popular stand-up buffet at the rear serving soups, goulash, chicken and some of central

Prague's best bread dumplings, weekdays to 7 pm, Saturday to 6 pm and Sunday to 4.30 pm.

West of Wenceslas Square The self-service *Jarmark restaurace (Map 6; in a passage at Vodičkova 28)* has a big choice of good salads, chicken and meat dishes, and goulash for under 80 Kč. It's open daily to 10 pm.

The unpretentious restaurant and beer hall *Branický sklípek (U Purkmistra) (Map 6; ☎ 24 23 71 03, Vodičkova 26)* has a meaty but good-value Czech menu (main courses from 60 to 285 Kč), a few meatless items, and cheap beer. It's open from 9 am to 11 pm (weekends from 11 am). Try the unique, salsa-hot cuisine of the Texas-Mexico border at the mid-range *Buffalo Bill's Tex-Mex Bar & Grille (Map 6; ☎ 24 21 54 79, Vodičkova 9)*, from noon to midnight.

Smečky dietní restaurace (Map 6; Ve Smečkách 26) serves boring, low-calorie lunches in a manic atmosphere for under 70 Kč per dish, weekdays only from 10 am to 2.30 pm. It has some vegetarian dishes, and even a macrobiotic menu.

Around the block, *Česká hospoda V Krakovské (Map 6; ☎ 22 21 02 04, Krakovská 20)* serves Czech standards for under 110 Kč per dish, with light or dark Krušovice beer. Even better value is *Jihočeská restaurace u Šumavy (Map 9; Štěpánská 3)*, with tasty south Bohemian dishes for under 80 Kč. It's open daily except Saturday, from 11 am to 10 pm.

For a change, try Japanese favourites at *Miyabi (☎ 96 23 31 02, Navrátilova 10; Map 6)*, rather pricey at 125 to 620 Kč. It's open daily until 11 pm.

Around Národní The pseudo-Art Nouveau *Café-Bar Craull Evropa (Map 6; ☎ 26 20 80, Národní 23)* has snacks in the bar downstairs from 9 am, and a mid-range restaurant upstairs (from 120 to 610 Kč per course) with good Czech and international cuisine, open daily except Sunday, from noon to midnight.

Restaurace U medvídků (Map 6; ☎ 24 21 19 16, Na Perštýně 5-7) is a touristy beer hall plus wine bar plus non-smoking restaurant plus outdoor garden, all with the same meaty Bohemian menu (main courses from 75 to 220 Kč). It's open daily from 11.30 am to 11 pm. *Adonis bufet (Map 6; Vodičkova 30)* serves cheap kebabs, felafel and salads, to eat there or take away, weekdays from 11 am to 7 pm.

In the basement *Pizzeria Kmotra (Map 6; ☎ 24 91 58 09, V jirchářích 12)* you can wash down good, ungreasy pizzas (70 to 150 Kč) with cheap beer. Hours are 11 am to 1 am; by 8 pm crowd control is a problem, so go early. At No 2 is *Hospoda U Nováka (Map 6; ☎ 29 64 74)*, whose tasty Czech dishes (under 100 Kč) have already been discovered by tourists.

Around Karlovo Náměstí Czech specialities at *Vinárna U Čížků (Map 9; ☎ 29 88 91, Karlovo náměstí 34)* cost from 150 to 280 Kč per dish. It's open daily from noon to 3.30 pm and 5 to 10 pm.

The steaks are good at *Restaurant Buenos Aires (Map 6; ☎ 24 91 31 83, Křemencova 7)*, though the service doesn't measure up. Committed carnivores can order the 800g cut for 1200 Kč, while lesser mortals can make do with 150 to 320 Kč versions. It's open daily from 11 am to 11 pm.

Further south (and close to tram No 3 from Wenceslas Square) is *Diogenes Greek Restaurant (Map 9; ☎ 29 63 95, Gorazdova 22)*, with Greek standards from 95 to 275 Kč and pricier seafood. Down the road, the friendly *Šnek Bar* café *(Map 9; ☎ 29 73 21, Gorazdova 10)* offers 'Chinese' food and meaty variants on Czech dishes for a modest 70 to 80 Kč each, from 11 am to about 2 am (from 2 pm to midnight on Sunday).

At the central quay, *Restaurant Vltava (Map 9; ☎ 29 49 64)* serves cheap but unexceptional fish and meaty Czech dishes until 10 pm. The view is fine on a warm evening, but afternoon sunlight off the river turns it into a solar oven. Much better food

Click! One of the best views of the Vltava and its many bridges from Hanavský Pavilion in Letná.

JOHN KING

Taking in the pageant on Charles Bridge.

CHRIS MELLOR

Charles Bridge's Bruncvík and his golden sword.

RICHARD NEBESKÝ

The only place in the Old Town Square where you can sit down for free: around the Jan Hus statue.

Prague honours its history, both mythical and real: statue of Libuše and Přemysl (Vyšehrad), communism victims memorial (Wenceslas Square) and the Soviet liberation statue (near the train station).

(minus the view) is available above the quay at **Vinárna Nad přístavem** *(Map 9;* ☎ *29 86 36, Rašínovo nábřeží 64)*, daily until 11 pm. Dishes run from 90 to 230 Kč, and the carp is good.

A few blocks south of Karlovo náměstí, **U Čínského labužníka** *(Map 9;* ☎ *24 91 14 77, Vyšehradská 37-39)* offers authentic, good Chinese dishes from 90 to 380 Kč, including several vegetarian choices. It's open from 11 am to 3 pm and 5.30 to 11 pm daily. Take tram No 24 from Wenceslas Square.

Vyšehrad
Within the Vyšehrad walls (Map 9) are **Penguin's Café** between the Špička and Leopold gates, a *café* at Špička gate and a **snack bar** beside the remains of St Lawrence Basilica. The only restaurant is **Vinárna Na Vyšehradě** *(*☎ *24 23 92 97 or 0603 41 13 54)*, opposite the Church of SS Peter & Paul, with fish, meat and chicken dishes from 145 to 320 Kč.

Dejvice
All places in this section are on Map 3, except as noted.

Near Vítězné náměstí is a very good Lebanese restaurant, **U cedru** *(*☎ *312 29 74, Národní obrany 27)*, with chopped lamb, tabouli salad, stuffed vine leaves and more, mostly from 190 to 250 Kč per dish.

Popular with locals and foreigners, cheerful **Budvarka** *(*☎ *24 31 48 38)*, on the corner of Wuchterlova and Svatovítská, is good for a drink or something from the varied Italian, Chinese and Czech menu (mostly 40 to 60 Kč).

Restaurace Sokolovna *(*☎ *24 31 78 34, Dejvická 2)*, near Hradčanská metro station and Laundry Kings, serves cheap and cheerful pub lunches in the rear dining room, with ready-to-serve dishes under 50 Kč. This is a recommended stop while your laundry spins.

Restaurace U Adély *(*☎ *312 37 39, Jugoslávských partyzánů 5)* is a pivnice with a surprising menu of Chinese dishes (mostly around 100 Kč, with some vegetar-

ian options at 60 to 70 Kč), while Czech standards under 60 Kč are good value at lunchtime. **Pivnice U Švejka** *(Nikoly Tesly 1)*, at the corner with Jugoslávských partyzánů, is a popular pub with good grub for around 70 Kč. Unless you're staying round the block at Berhanu Hostel, walk (or take tram No 20 or 25 one stop) north from Dejvická metro station.

Bubeneč & Holešovice
Thang Long *(Map 4;* ☎ *80 65 41, Dukelských hrdinů 48)* has a Vietnamese name, but the food is Thai, Japanese and Czech; most courses are around 170 Kč. It's open from 11.30 am to 11 pm. The pleasant **Caffé Dante** *(Map 4;* ☎ *87 01 93, Dukelských hrdinů 16)* is open daily to 11 pm with tasty Italian food from 70 to 130 Kč, a salad bar and good coffee. Take tram No 12 west from Nádraží Holešovice metro station, two stops to Veletržní.

The **Hong Kong** Chinese restaurant *(Map 3;* ☎ *37 13 70, Letenské náměstí 5)* has an immense menu of dishes for 140 to 185 Kč; it's open from 11 am to 3 pm and 6 to 11 pm. Take tram No 25 or 26 from Vltavská metro station to the Letenské náměstí stop.

Hanavský pavilón *(Map 7;* ☎ *32 57 92, Letenské sady)*, built for the 1891 Prague Exposition, is now a pricey restaurant, with most main courses from 500 to 600 Kč. The attractions are the seafood (a set menu is about 1800 Kč) and the magnificent views of Prague and the Vltava. It's open daily from 11.30 am to 1 am, and in summer you can dine outside (the terrace is open from 11 am to 10.30 pm). Take tram No 18 from Malostranská metro station, one stop to Chotkovy sady.

Smíchov
Diana Snack Bar *(Map 5;* ☎ *53 17 35, Elišky Peškové 17)* has salads under 40 Kč, fish under 70 Kč and meaty dishes for under 100 Kč.

Vinárna U Mikuláše Dačického *(Map 9;* ☎ *54 93 12, Viktora Huga 2)* is open from 4 pm to 1 am (weekends from 6 pm) with fish and poultry dishes for under 100

Kč, and a variety of salads. **Snack Bar Angelika** *(Map 9; ☎ 54 09 03, Štefánikova 25)* is open daily with salads under 95 Kč, and Czech and Italian dishes for about 100 Kč.

Restaurant Penguin's *(Map 9; ☎ 57 31 66 55, Zborovská 5)* has unexceptional Czech and international dishes from 120 Kč, a big choice of pasta, and vegetarian items for under 90 Kč. If you're struggling to save pennies and fill your tummy, try noisy **Hospoda U Starého lva** *(Map 9; ☎ 54 73 07, Lidická 13)* – enter on Svornosti – dishing up fair helpings for under 50 Kč, daily until 10 pm (9 pm on Sunday).

Rising above it all near Bertramka is **Restaurant U Blaženky** *(Map 9; ☎ 57 32 08 63, U Blaženky 1)*, in the hotel of the same name. The food is good, and lunch-time specials are about 100 Kč, but an evening meal (book ahead and tidy up) will set you back a lot more. From Anděl metro station it's a 15 minute climb through woods on a footpath from the top of Ostrovského; or take bus No 137 three stops to the Malvazinky stop, then walk for five minutes down U Mrázovky.

Žižkov

A cheerful neighbourhood pivnice (with its own 10 person sauna, no less) is **U radnice** *(Map 8; ☎ 697 71 93, Havlíčkovo náměstí 7)*. Generous helpings of Czech standards are nearly all under 80 Kč; wash them down with Budvar. It's open weekdays from 10 am to 10 pm and Sunday from 3 pm (closed on Saturday). The sauna needs to be booked ahead.

Two other modest but popular, good-value places with Czech dishes for under 100 Kč, and attentive service, are **Restaurace U Ďasů** *(☎ 22 78 21 51, Miličova 25; Map 8)* and **Restaurace U Kroužků** *(Map 8; ☎ 27 01 25, Miličova 3)*, the latter open weekdays only.

Mailsi *(Map 8; ☎ 0603-46 66 26, Lipanská 1)* is Prague's first Pakistani restaurant. The decidedly downmarket décor could be anywhere except for the *qawwali* music. Service is courteous, the food good and prices modest (from 80 to 150 Kč per

course) for a speciality restaurant – though helpings are small. It's open daily from noon to 3 pm and 6 pm to 12.30 am.

Victoria Saloon *(Map 8; ☎ 27 05 81, Seifertova 44)* offers somewhat pricey but good European and American dishes, grill specialities from 150 to 300 Kč per dish, and some vegetarian offerings. The restaurant is downstairs from the bar.

The lively **Akropolis Café-Restaurant** *(Map 6; ☎ 27 21 84, Kubelíkova 27)*, beside the Palác Akropolis, does tasty meals, including lots of vegetarian options, nearly all under 80 Kč. The décor is charmingly oddball, though the air is very smoky. It's open from 4 pm to 2 am (to midnight on Sunday).

Restaurace Panda Palace *(Map 6; ☎ 697 66 10, Seifertova 18)*, at the corner with Přibyslavská, is a quiet place with attentive service and a vast menu of mainly northern Chinese food, including vegetarian items, from 100 to 120 Kč per course (except pricier duck and seafood). It's open daily (except Saturday morning) from 11 am to 3 pm and 5.30 to 11 pm.

For all the preceding places, take tram No 9 from Wenceslas Square or tram No 5 or 26 from náměstí Republiky to the Lipanská stop.

South of Olšany Cemetery is the popular **Crazy Daisy Restaurant** *(Map 8; ☎ 67 31 03 78, Vinohradská 142)*, opposite Flora metro station. International and seafood dishes are tasty and well priced at 100 to 150 Kč. Also on the menu are big salads and some good Czech meatless dishes. It's open daily from 11 am to 11.30 pm.

Vinohrady

The **FX Café** *(☎ 24 25 47 76, Bělehradská 120; Map 10)* has great salads, imaginative vegetarian dishes, pitta bread sandwiches and California-style soups and cakes, and stays open from 11.30 am to at least 2 am every day. Brunch is served until 3 pm on weekends, and Sunday night is Italian night. It's part of the Club Radost complex (see the Entertainment chapter), two blocks east of IP Pavlova metro station, or a 10 minute walk from the top of Wenceslas Square.

A Chinese restaurant in the same area is the small *Restaurace Zlatý Drak (Map 6; ☎ 24 23 76 57, Anglická 6)*, open daily from 11.30 am to 10.30 pm. Most main dishes are under 160 Kč.

South-east of náměstí Míru is the popular *Restaurace Pravěk (Map 10; ☎ 24 25 22 87, Budečská 6)*, with duck, venison and wild boar for 110 to 200 Kč per course, plus beer and wine. There are also some meatless dishes. Hours are 11 am to 11 pm daily.

In a quiet residential street where Vinohrady spills into the Nusle valley is *Restaurace Na Zvonařce (Map 10; ☎ 24 25 19 90, Šafaříkova 1)*. The patio commands a wide view across the valley, and the 'Plzeň-style' Czech dishes are good value at 70 to 150 Kč. It's open from 11 am to 11 pm daily. Get there by tram No 6 from IP Pavlova metro station, or on foot in 10 minutes from Náměstí Míru metro station.

South-East Outskirts

Restaurace Eureka (Map 1; ☎ 71 76 11 15, Roztylské náměstí 2, Prague 4) serves big portions of good Czech and international dishes at 60 to 150 Kč, plus a choice of salads. From Roztyly metro station, take bus No 118 seven stops to Roztylské náměstí, a few minutes walk from the restaurant.

Worth a splash-out is the elegant restaurant in the Art Nouveau *Villa Voyta (☎ 472 29 62, K Novému dvoru 54/124, Lhotka, Prague 4)*, with game and meaty international selections for around 450 Kč. It's past the southern border of Map 1; take bus No 113, 171, 189 or 215 south from Kačerov metro station to the Sídliště Krk stop, and walk three blocks west on Na Větrově.

VEGETARIAN

Indulge yourself with wholesome fresh food at *Country Life*, Prague's best health-food shop and vegetarian salad-and-sandwich bar (pizza and goulash too), and fill up for under 80 Kč. The original one

(Map 7; Melantrichova 15), with sit-down service at the back, is open from 11 am to 3 pm and 6 to 9.30 pm (Friday to 4 pm, closed Saturday). Another branch *(Map 6; Jungmannova 1 on the corner with Vodičkova)* is cafeteria-style, and open from 8.30 am to 6.30 pm (Friday to 6 pm, closed weekends). Both get densely crowded at lunchtime, so go early or get a takeaway.

Lotos (Map 7; ☎ 232 23 90, Platnéřská 13) has an all-vegetarian menu with many dishes modelled on Bohemian cuisine, for 50 to 130 Kč. It's open daily from 11 am to midnight.

Although *Bona Vita (Map 7; Dlouhá 2)* is not strictly vegetarian, vegetable and soya dishes (such as soya goulash) are plentiful, at 40 to 110 Kč. It's open daily from 10.30 am to 10 pm.

At *U Góvindy (Map 7; ☎ 24 81 60 16, Soukenická 27)*, a 'donation' of at least 60 Kč gets you a generous, imaginatively seasoned set meal of vegetable soup, salad, rice, cake and herbal tea. Hare Krishnas run it but nobody's preaching. It's open from 11 am to 5 pm (closed Sunday).

Splendid ice cream and fruit specialities can be found at the *Laguna Ice Cream & Fruit Parlour (Map 6; Štěpánská 6)*, open 10 am to 6 pm (weekends from 11 am).

CAFÉS
Hradčany & Malá Strana

All the cafés in this section are on Map 5.

Malý Buddha (☎ 20 51 38 94, Úvoz 46, Hradčany) has two dozen oriental teas and several varieties of 'healing wine' to go with, or instead of, its good vegetarian and other meals. It's open daily except Monday, from 1 to 10.30 pm.

Inexpensive coffee, beer and snacks are on offer at *U zavěšeného kafe* or The Hanging Coffee *(Radnické schody 7, Hradčany)*, along the steps to Ke Hradu and Prague Castle.

Slump into an armchair with your coffee at peaceful *St Nicholas Café (Tržiště 7, Malá Strana)*, in a quiet Gothic cellar at the heart of the tourist zone. This is our favourite midday refuge in Malá Strana.

Moravská vinárna (☎ 53 07 30, *Saská 1, Malá Strana*), under an arch of Charles Bridge, is about the coolest spot around on a summer day, though it's bang on the tourist track. To go with your coffee or wine are various gorgeous meat/cheese/salad plates from 45 to 75 Kč, as well as other light meals and desserts.

One of several suitable cake-and-a-drink stops in sunny Na Kampě square is *Kavárna Červená sedma* (*Na Kampě 5, Malá Strana*).

The cavernous but elegant *Café Savoy*, also known as the *Classique* (☎ 53 50 00, *Vítězná 5*), serves a range of coffees and sweets, plus meals, including salads under 55 Kč and grills at 100 to 180 Kč, daily from 9 am to 10 pm. While technically in Smíchov, it's more accessible from Malá Strana.

Staré Město

Kavárna Hogo Fogo (*Map 7;* ☎ 231 70 23, *Salvátorská 4*) is great for a hit of caffeine and pastry, or for lunch, and the music's good. A big list of vegetarian dishes has little that's more than 60 Kč. It's open from noon to midnight (Friday and Saturday to 2 am). Inside the Museum of Decorative Arts is a smoky *coffee house* (*Map 7; 17.listopadu 2*) with good coffee, good music and light meals. It's open daily from 10 am to 6 pm.

Upstairs at the divadlo v Celetné (enter through the courtyard) is *Café Gaspar Kaspar* (*Map 7; Celetná 17*) – pleasant, non-smoking and inexpensive, with a bar as well. Enjoy the relaxed atmosphere daily from 9 am to midnight.

Paris-Praha (*Map 6; Jindřišská 7*) is a prim food shop with a café at the back, offering cakes, coffee (French-style, with a mineral-water chaser) and light meals. Rather grander is the Art Nouveau kavárna at the *Hotel Paříž* (*Map 7; U Obecního domu 1*), worth the high price of a drink just to have a look around.

At *Galérie Jednorožec s Harfou* (*Map 6; Průchodní 4*), just off Betlémské náměstí, you can admire the work of young Czech

artists as you sip. It's open from 11 am to 11 pm (weekends from 1 to 10 pm). Around the corner is *Café Konvikt* (*Map 6; Konviktská 11*), popular with young Praguers and open from 9 to 1 am (from 1 pm at weekends).

Pay a bit more and enjoy top-notch Arabian coffee at *Káva.Káva.Káva* (*Map 6; Národní 37*), along with carrot cake and other American-style goodies.

The most famous of Prague's old café venues is the renovated, Art Deco *Kavárna Slavia* (*Map 6; Národní 1*), with tourist prices for coffee and snacks, but the same notoriously indifferent service.

Nové Město

As you steam in or out of Prague, pause at the *Fantova kavárna* (*Map 6*), at the main train station, for a drink and a gawp at the Art Nouveau grandeur of the station's old central hall. The café at the *Grand Hotel Evropa* (*Map 6; Wenceslas Square 25*) has some fine Art Nouveau décor, but second-rate cakes and coffee, and tourist prices (including a music cover charge after 3 pm).

Louvre/Gany's Café (*Map 6;* ☎ 29 76 65, *upstairs at Národní 22*) has 13 kinds of coffee, plus snacks and meals from 8 am to 11 pm, and a non-smoking room, though the pink walls don't agree with the high-ceilinged, Art-Nouveau ambience. Another place for a buzz is the nearby *Monica cukrárna* (*Map 6*), down an alley at Národní 32.

Kavárna Obecní dům (*Map 7; náměstí Republiky*) is an Art Nouveau masterpiece, complete with high ceilings, private booths and a grand piano. But staff have probably seen one too many tourists, and service tends to be curt. It's open daily from 7.30 am to 11 pm.

Scan the free English-language papers or gaze at one of Prague's prettiest and most historic squares from *Café Gulu Gulu* (*Map 6; Betlémské náměstí 8*), popular with foreigners and trendy Czechs. It's open daily from 10 am to midnight (weekends to 3 am).

For great ice cream with your coffee, try *Italská cukrárna (Map 6; Vodičkova 4)*. On the western side of Slovanský ostrov is *Posezení na řece (Map 6)*, an unexceptional café with exceptional views.

Tearooms A plus for Prague's café scene are the tearooms (*čajovny*) springing up around the city, with a peaceful atmosphere and brews from around the world. Unlike cafés, they tend to be non-smoking and booze-free.

Among those in Nové Město are the candle-lit *Dobrá čajovna (Map 6; Wenceslas Square 14)*, open from 11 am to 9 pm; and *Růžová čajovna (Map 6; Růžová 8)*, open from 10 am to 9 pm (Saturday 11 am to 10 pm, Sunday 11 am to 9 pm), with occasional live acoustic music or other entertainment in the basement.

Bubeneč & Holešovice

A relaxed and popular expat hang-out (sharing space with a first-rate English-language bookshop) is *The Globe (Map 4; ☎ 66 71 26 10, Jankovského 14)*, open daily from 10 am to midnight. The imaginative, healthy salads and sandwiches are pricey but good.

Vinohrady

The tiny but pleasant *Kaaba Café (Map 8; Lucemburská 15)* is already open at 6 am (7 am on Saturday, 10 am on Sunday) with coffee, cakes and local and foreign newspapers and magazines; it closes at 10 pm.

Medúza Kavárna (Map 10; ☎ 25 85 34, Belgická 17), a quiet spot in a quiet street off náměstí Míru, is open from 11 am to 1 am (weekends from noon) with snacks, juices and a long list of coffees. The front room is covered in old photos and the furniture is mix-and-match.

U knihomola (Map 6; ☎ 627 77 67, Mánesova 79) is an understated café in the basement of the bookshop of the same name. On offer is a different blend of good coffee every day, plus imaginative sweets,

salads and light meals (including vegetarian dishes). The café and bookshop are open from 10 am to 11 pm (except Friday and Saturday to midnight and Sunday from 11 am to 8 pm).

SELF-CATERING
Malá Strana

A fine food shop off Malostranské náměstí is *J+J Mašek & Zemanová (Map 5; Karmelitská 30)*. Nearby Nerudova has at least two mini-supermarkets.

Staré Město

All the following places are on Map 7, except where noted.

Fresh produce is sold at the daily *market* on Havelská, south of Old Town Square. *Michelské pekařství (Dlouhá 1)* is an excellent bakery, open from 6.30 am to 6 pm (Sunday from 11 am, closed Saturday). A smaller, pricier one is *Chléb pečivo (Kaprova 13)*.

Four floors of the renovated VJ Rott building now comprise an exclusive delicatessen, *Dům lahůdek (Malé náměstí 3)*, stocked with local and imported meat, cheese, wine and more. You can also sit down and nosh on the spot.

For supermarket supplies, try *Julius Meinl* (entrances at Rytířská 10 and 28.října 5; Map 6) or *Kotva (náměstí Republiky)*.

Nové Město

All the places noted here are on Map 6.

The concentration of department stores in Nové Město – *Krone*, *Tesco* and *Bílá Labuť* – should satisfy any shopping list. Krone's Julius Meinl supermarket tends to be the most expensive; and check use-by dates on goods bought here.

French wine, cheese, produce, sweets and more are on offer at *Fruits de France (Jindřišská 9)*, but not cheaply. Next door at No 7 is the similar *Paris-Praha*. For imported wines, try *Cellarius (Lucerna passage, from Wenceslas Square 36)*.

Entertainment

Across the spectrum from jazz to rock, ballet to bluegrass, theatre to tennis, there's a bewildering array of entertainment in this eclectic city. Prague is now as much a European centre for jazz, rock and post-rock as it is for classical music. Sports fans can catch a game of ice hockey in winter or the Czech Open tennis tournament in spring. And you can spend many a merry hour making Czech friends over wine or world-class beer.

For reviews, an up-to-the-minute directory of venues and day-by-day listings, consult the 'Night & Day' section of the *Prague Post*. Monthly listings magazines include *Culture in Prague* and PIS's *Prague Cultural Events* and Czech-language *Přehled*. The fortnightly pamphlet *Do města Downtown*, free at bars and restaurants, lists clubs, galleries, cinemas and theatre events. Even these publications don't cover everything, so keep an eye on the posters and bulletin boards.

Tickets

For classical music, opera, ballet, theatre and some rock concerts – even the most thoroughly 'sold-out' events – you can often find a ticket or two on sale at the box office a half-hour or so before concert time.

If you want to be sure of a seat, Prague is awash in ticket agencies. Their advantage is convenience: most are computerised and quick, and a few accept credit cards. Their drawback is a probable 10 to 15% mark-up. Touts will sell tickets at the door, but avoid them unless all other avenues have been exhausted.

At the box office, non-Czechs normally pay the same price as Czechs. Many venues have discounts for students, and sometimes for the disabled. Most performances have a certain number of tickets set aside for foreigners – for a premium price, of course.

'Wholesalers' with the largest agency networks are BTI (Bohemia Ticket International), FOK and Ticketpro (all Staré Město, Map 7); the others probably get their tickets from these.

BTI (☎ 24 22 78 32, fax 21 61 21 26, email btiinter@login.cz), Malé náměstí 13

FOK (☎ 22 00 23 36, fax 232 25 01), Obecní dům, U Obecního domu 1; mainly for the Prague Symphony

Ticketpro (☎ 24 81 40 20, fax 24 81 40 21, email orders@ticketpro.cz), Salvátorská 10, Josefov (this is the only Ticketpro branch accepting credit cards for payment)

For rock and jazz clubs you can front up at the door, but for big names advance bookings are recommended. A good Ticketpro agency for rock tickets is Melantrich (Map 6; ☎ 24 21 50 18, Rokoko passage, Wenceslas Square 36, Nové Město).

PUBS & BARS

Nothing to Do in Prague is a thorough, and thoroughly enjoyable, self-published guide to over 100 bars, clubs and cafés in Prague – locations, prices, clientele, deadpan reviews and shaggy-dog anecdotes – by two expats, Conor Crickmore and Nigel Robinson. It's sold, for about 150 to 200 Kč, at bigger hostels and most bookshops in the centre.

Pub Etiquette

Always ask if a chair is free before sitting down: *Je tu volno?* (Is it free?). Service is usually quick – in better places you may find a beer in front of you almost before your bum touches the seat – but if it's slow, chasing the waiter is a sure way to be ignored. Your bill is run up on a slip of paper left at your table, and at the end it's usually rounded up to the nearest koruna. Tipping is as in restaurants, that is 5 to 10% of the total.

Most pubs serve beer snacks, some of the most popular being *utopenci* (sliced sausage pickled in vinegar with onion); *topinky* (fried toast); and of course the famous Prague ham with gherkin. Many of the following places also serve inexpensive Czech food or pricier non-Czech food.

Hradčany & Malá Strana

All venues in this section are on Map 5.

A good pub serving hot snacks and cheap beer is *Pivnice U černého vola* (*Loretánské náměstí, Hradčany*). *Hostinec U kocoura* (☎ 53 89 62, *Neruda 2, Malá Strana*) enjoys its reputation as an old favourite of President Havel, and serves Czech pub grub for 40 to 70 Kč. Around the corner is *U krále Brabantského* (☎ 57 31 09 29, *Thunovská 15*), with cheaper beer and less atmosphere.

U Malého Glena (☎ 535 81 15, *Karmelitská 23, Malá Strana*) is a bar (with Guinness on tap), restaurant and jazz club (see also the Jazz section later in this chapter, and the Places to Eat chapter). You may catch a late-night live gig in the basement, and the kitchen stays open almost until the bar closes at 2 am (3 am at weekends).

Klub Újezd (☎ 53 83 62, *Újezd 18, Malá Strana*), a former live-rock venue tamed by noise complaints, remains an agreeable bar, with a wide range of music (harder sounds downstairs, mellower upstairs) and a slightly retro underground setting. No food is served. It's open daily from 6 pm to 6 am.

Ostroff (☎ 24 91 92 35, *Střelecký ostrov 336*) is a pricey club where professional bartenders serve a vast array of cocktails, wines and beers from behind an immense bar, while you look out at the river through floor-to-ceiling windows. It's open daily from 9.30 am to 2 am. Get there from the middle of most Legií (Legií Bridge). No shorts and flip-flops, puh-leez.

Off the south-eastern corner of Na Kampě is the snug *Hostinec U staleté báby* or Pub of the One-Hundred-Year-Old Granny, with fairly priced *guláš*, pizza and other grub.

Staré Město

All venues in this section are on Map 7.

Žíznivý pes, The Thirsty Dog (*Elišky Krasnohorské 5*), is a pleasant, uncongested spot for a drink or a meal, open daily from 5 pm to 1 am.

One old-town pub that has kept its prices down is writer Bohumil Hrabal's favourite hang-out, *U zlatého tygra*, The Golden Tiger (*Husova 17*). Two other pubs that have retained some old-town ambience, modest prices and loyal customers are *Pivnice U kata* (*U radnice 6*) and *Pivnice U milosrdných* (*Kozí 20*). *Kozička*, Little Goat (*Kozí 1*), a sedate basement bar with taped mainstream music and a young clientele, stays open until 4 am.

An expat bar that's very popular with tourists and Czechs alike, despite some bad-tempered staff, is *Chapeau Rouge,* on the corner of Malá Štupartská and Jakubská, open daily from 4 pm to 5 am (4 am in winter). Close by is *U Hynků* (*Štupartská 6*), with long tables and occasional live music.

Among several Irish-style pubs serving Guinness and Irish whiskies is candle-lit *Molly Malones* (*U obecního dvora 4*) in northern Staré Město, open daily from noon to 2 am. Another is the pricier *James Joyce* (*Liliová 10*), open daily from 10 am to 1 am. *O'Che's Cuban Bar* (*Liliová 14*) serves Guinness, Heineken and English beers during the same hours, and has sports-channel TV.

Nové Město

All the venues listed here are on Map 6, except where noted.

The jolly warren of drinking and eating rooms at *U Fleků* (☎ 24 91 51 18, *Křemencová 11*) is a Prague institution, increasingly clogged with tour groups high on oompah music and the tavern's own 13° black beer (49 Kč for 0.4L). Purists grumble but go anyway, because everybody has a good time, though tourist prices have nudged out many locals. You might still find an empty seat at 7 pm on a weekday. It's open daily from 10 am to 11.30 pm.

Novoměstský pivovar (☎ 24 23 35 33, Vodičkova 20) is another place that brews its beer on the premises, and suffers coach-party invasions. It's considerably cheaper (25 Kč for 0.5L) than U Fleků, and the food is very good, including a delicious *svíčková* (cream sauce with beef and dumplings).

For a pizza or an American-style cocktail in the middle of the night, try the **Zombie Bar** *(in a passage at Wenceslas Square 29)*, open daily from 3.30 pm to 3.30 am. Little **Cornucopia** *(☎ 24 22 09 50, Jungmannova 10)* is also a café, where you can watch sports TV between sips. *Jáma (V jámě 7)*, south off Vodičkova, is a well known rock bar with a tourist and young-Prague clientele, open daily from 11 to 1 am.

Pivnice U zpěváčků (corner of Vojtěšská and Pštrossova) is a cheap place to mix with Prague's young drop-outs, and gets very crowded. Bar/café/snack bar **Velryba** *(Opatovická 24)* is popular with young Czechs, and quiet enough to have a real conversation; don't overlook the back room and basement. It's open daily from 1 pm to 1 am (weekends from 5 pm).

The popular **Café Gulu Gulu** *(Betlémské náměstí 8)* livens up as the sun sets, and at weekends there may be live music in the basement.

While there are plenty of Irish pubs, Prague's only English-style pub is the **John Bull** *(Map 7; Senovážná 8)*, open weekdays from 8 to 2 am, Saturday from 10.30 am and Sunday to midnight.

Apart klub (Opletalova 38) is a student hang-out in the same building as the Kolej Jednota hostel, open from 6 pm to midnight.

Smíchov

For a taste of Ireland (including Guinness and Irish whiskies), try the **Irish Rover Pub** *(Map 1; ☎ 54 47 92, Holečkova 123)*, open daily from 6 pm to 3 am. From Anděl metro station, take tram No 4, 7, 9 or 34 west two stops to U Zvonu.

DISCOS & CLUBS

Club Radost *(Map 10; ☎ 24 25 47 76, Bělehradská 120, Vinohrady)* – DJ and occasional live music daily 10 pm to 5 am, early-evening fixtures 7 to 9 pm (poetry Sunday, films Monday, gay night Tuesday etc); **FX Café** is in the same location, open until 4 am

Disco Astra *(Map 6; Wenceslas Square 22, 1st floor, Nové Město)* – mainly techno, for a young tourist crowd, 9 pm to about 5 am

Klub Lávka *(Map 7; ☎ 24 21 47 97, Novotného lávka 1, Staré Město)* – disco with top-40 hits, nightly 9.30 pm to 5 am, 60 Kč

Klub Mánes *(Map 6; ☎ 29 94 38, Mánes Gallery building, Masarykovo nábřeží 250, Nové Město)* – bar from 11 am, Tropicana Latin American disco on weekends from 9 pm, live easy-listening or country music on weeknights

Student discos *(Map 5; Strahov, Malá Strana)* – dormitory blocks resound in summer to sounds from several discos, including **Club 001** (Block 10; also see the Rock & Post-Rock section on the next page about the Strahov 007 club here); bus No 143, 149 or 217 from Dejvická metro station

Variete Casino Admiral *(Map 6; ☎ 24 21 59 45, U Nováků building, Vodičkova 30, Nové Město)* – old-style dinner and floor show, popular with older tourists, daily except Monday, 7.30 am to 2 am (show runs from 9.30 to 11.30 pm)

GAY & LESBIAN VENUES

A-Club *(Map 8; ☎ 90 04 43 03, Miličova 25, Žižkov)* – 5 pm to 6 am (Sunday 3 pm to midnight), women-only on Friday, beer 20 Kč for 0.5L

Aqua Club 2000 *(Map 6; ☎ 627 89 71, Husitská 7, Žižkov)* – swimming pool and massage daily noon to 4 am, sauna Wednesday to Friday 3 to 8 pm, transvestite *(travestie)* show 9 pm on Wednesday, Friday and Saturday

Connection disco *(Map 6; ☎ 628 47 80, Husitská 7, Žižkov)* – entrance at No 7c, open daily from 9 pm

G&L Club *(Map 9; ☎ 29 62 87/32, Lublaňská 48, Nové Město)* – restaurant (meaty main courses 90 to 165 Kč) daily 8 to 10 pm, disco 8 pm to 4 am

Pivnice U dubu *(Map 10; Záhřebská 12, Vinohrady)* – open daily 6 pm to midnight

Podivnej bar *(Strange Bar; Map 6; Husitská 7, Žižkov)* – 8 pm until late

Sauna Babylonia *(Map 6; ☎ 24 23 23 04, Martinská 6, Staré Město)* – sauna, fitness room, jacuzzi, massage, daily noon to 3 am

Vinárna U starého songu *(Map 8; ☎ 22 78 20 47, Štítného 27, Žižkov)* – 6 pm to midnight, Friday and Saturday to 2 am

ROCK & POST-ROCK

Prague has a high-energy scene, with rock, metal, punk, rap and newer sounds at a score of legitimate DJ and live-music venues.

At the time of writing, noise had provided an excuse for the closure of several big venues, especially those, such as the venerable Bunkr, in city-owned properties. For current listings and reviews, see the entertainment periodicals noted at the start of this chapter – and watch the posters.

Except as noted, clubs have a bar, usually a dance floor, and cover charges of between 40 and 120 Kč.

Awika Klub (Map 7; ☎ 24 24 87 91, *Řetězová 10*) – New Age, relaxation or meditation music on most days from 10 am and 7 pm, but on Sunday from noon and 6 pm

Batalion (Map 6; ☎ 20 10 81 48, *28.října 3, Staré Město*) – anything from rock 'n' roll to punk from upcoming Czech bands (DJs on most Saturdays), for a young, mainly local crowd, bar open 24 hours, music from 9 pm

Klub Prosek (Map 1; ☎ 88 94 42, *Jablonecká 322, Prosek, Prague 9*) – rock bands on most nights from 7.30 pm; from Palmovka metro station take bus No 187, 258 or 279 to Sídliště Prosek stop

Kulturní dům Vltavská (*Bubenská 1; Map 4*) – dance club with local bands, in a big theatre hall with little atmosphere, 8 pm to 1 am

Lucerna Music Bar (Map 6; ☎ 24 21 71 08, *Vodičkova 36, Nové Město*) – quality venue now looking a little dog-eared, mainly Czech artists doing jazz, blues, pop, rock and more, increasingly touristy but still with a local feel, 8 pm to 3 am, inexpensive café 11 am to 5 pm, music from 9 pm, admission usually from 60 to 120 Kč

Malostranská beseda (Map 5; ☎ 53 90 24, *Malostranské náměstí 21, Malá Strana*) – anything from hard rock to bluegrass, for a young and mostly Czech crowd, daily 2 pm to 1 am (music from 8 pm)

Rock Café (Map 6; ☎ 24 91 44 16, *Národní 22, Nové Město*) – stripped-down venue for DJ and live rock, with a café downstairs, popular with locals but increasingly touristy, 10 am to 3 am (weekends from 8 pm), music from 9 pm and rock disco from 12.30 to 3 am

Strahov 007 (Map 5; ☎ 57 21 14 39, *Block 1, Strahov dormitory complex, Malá Strana*) – cheap beer and raw music from up-and-coming Bohemian bands, for a mainly student crowd, daily except Sunday, 7.30 pm to midnight (music from 8 pm); take bus No 143, 149 or 217 from Dejvická metro station

JAZZ

The following clubs have cover charges of between 50 and 100 Kč except as noted, and some double as restaurants:

Adria Jazz Club (Map 6; *Jungmannova 14, Nové Město*) – doubles as Adria Theatre café, live jazz Monday, Wednesday, Friday and Saturday from 9.30 to 11 pm

AghaRTA Jazz Centrum (Map 6; ☎ 22 21 12 75, *email artarec@vol.cz, Krakovská 5, Nové Město*) – venerable basement venue with 1970s décor, also a café and music shop, open from 5 pm, music from 9 pm to midnight (weekends from 7 pm)

Jazz'n Blues Café (Map 7; ☎ 24 22 87 88, *Rathova passage, Na příkopě 23, Staré Město*) – small venue, doors open 6 pm, live jazz or blues nightly from 9 pm to midnight, cover charge from 100 to 150 Kč

Malostranská beseda (Map 5; ☎ 53 90 24, *Malostranské náměstí 21, Malá Strana*) – jazz on some nights at 8.30 pm

Metropolitan Jazz Club (Map 6; ☎ 24 21 60 25, *email metropolitan@telecom.cz, Jungmannova 14, Nové Město*) – smallish basement venue, live jazz nightly 9 pm to 3 am; also a restaurant from 11 am (weekends from 7 pm)

Red, Hot & Blues (Map 7; ☎ 231 46 39, *Jakubská 12, Staré Město*) – restaurant with traditional American jazz on the sound system, and almost nightly live blues or jazz (check the board outside)

Reduta Jazz Club (Map 6; ☎ 24 91 22 46, *Národní 22, Nové Město*) – Prague's oldest jazz club, founded under communism, live jazz daily from 9 pm to whenever, 120 Kč cover charge; book a few hours ahead at the ticket office, weekdays from 3 pm, Saturday from 5 pm and Sunday from 7 pm

U Malého Glena (Map 5; ☎ 535 81 15, *Karmelitská 23, Malá Strana*) – restaurant/bar with great food, hard-swinging local jazz bands Friday, Saturday and Sunday from 9 pm to at least midnight, packed out for acid jazz Thursday, various types of live music on other nights

U Staré paní Jazz Club (Map 7; ☎ 26 49 20, *Michalská 9, Staré Město*) – jazz or blues nightly from 9 pm to midnight, bar 7 pm to 4 am, kitchen to 3 am, ISIC and Go25 card

ENTERTAINMENT

holders get 50% off the cover charge and some drinks

Železná Jazz Club (Map 7; ☎ 24 23 96 97, Železná 16, Staré Město) – renovated stone cellar with plenty of atmosphere, nightly live jazz from 9 pm to midnight, Sunday from 8 pm, bar from 3 pm

ALTERNATIVE VENUES

These are combined theatres and clubs with an underground look and feel. Mainly experimental venues, they feature bands, plays and films:

Palác Akropolis (Map 6; ☎ 697 64 11, email akropol@jk.anet.cz, Kubelíkova 27, Žižkov) – renovations were begun specifically with an alternative art venue in mind, but money ran low and compromises have been necessary; presently the *palác* features mostly modern musicals with some alternative bands, theatre and cultural shows; performances normally start at 8 pm

Roxy (Map 7; ☎ 24 81 09 51, Dlouhá 33, Staré Město) – a decrepit place with surprising longevity as an experimental venue; mostly avant-garde drama, dance and music; open nightly from 5 pm to 1 am

FOLK & TRADITIONAL MUSIC

Theatre na Klárově (Map 5; ☎ 53 98 37 or 53 98 45, nábřeží Edvarda Beneše 3, Malá Strana) is the venue for the Český Soubor Písní a Tanců (Czech Song & Dance Ensemble), the only professional troupe of its kind in the Czech Republic. Performances, a stylised amalgam of traditions from around Bohemia, are undeniable crowd-pleasers. You can see them at 8.30 pm on weekdays from May to September, and at least on Monday, Wednesday and Friday in April and October, for 340 Kč. The theatre is a block from Malostranská metro station.

An annual Folk Festival has been held in Prague since 1990, from July to September at the theatre in the City Library (☎ 688 54 16 or 684 01 02).

The Slovak dance ensemble Lúčnica has recently performed at the Křižík Fountain every year, in late August. Call ☎ 24 21 11 80 or 21 61 01 73 for information.

CLASSICAL MUSIC, OPERA & BALLET

Don't believe anyone who says it's impossible to get concert tickets. There are half a dozen concerts of one kind or another almost every day during the summer, making a fine soundtrack to the city's visual delights.

Many of these are chamber concerts by aspiring musicians in the city's churches – gorgeous but chilly (take an extra layer, even on a summer day) and not always with the finest of acoustics. An increasing number of church concerts have been second-rate, despite the premium prices foreigners pay.

For something a bit lighter, listen to recorded classical, rock or electronic music with visual accompaniment by the dancing Křižík Fountain (see Fairgrounds in the Things to See & Do chapter).

Hradčany

Prague Castle concert information: ☎ 24 37 23 64
Basilica of St George (Prague Castle)
Lobkowicz Palace (☎ 53 73 06, Jiřská 3, Prague Castle)
St Vitus Cathedral (Prague Castle)
Strahov Monastery (Map 5; ☎ 53 83 69, Strahovské nádvoří 1)
Wallenstein Palace (Map 5; Valdštejnské náměstí)

Malá Strana

The following venues are all on Map 5.

Liechtenstein Palace (☎ 53 09 43, Malostranské náměstí 13)
Nostitz Palace (☎ 57 31 15 90, Maltézské náměstí 1)
St Nicholas Church (☎ 53 69 83, Malostranské náměstí)

Staré Město & Josefov

The following venues are all on Map 7.

Chapel of Mirrors (☎ 24 22 95 00, Klementinum, Karlova)
Church of St Francis Seraphinus (Křižovnické náměstí)
Clam-Gallas Palace (Husova 20)
Convent of St Agnes (☎ 24 81 06 28, U milosrdných 17)

Estates Theatre *(Stavovské divadlo;* ☎ *24 21 50 01, Ovocný trh 1)* – opera and drama; equipped for the hearing-impaired and has wheelchair access (wheelchair bookings can be made up to five days in advance); for bookings, go round the corner to the Kolowrat Theatre, or to the National Theatre box office on Národní 4; stand-up tickets 10 Kč, sit-down tickets from 30 to 400 Kč

House at the Stone Bell *(*☎ *24 81 00 36, Old Town Square 13)*

Opera Mozart Theatre *(*☎ *21 08 22 88, Novotného lávka 1)* – chamber concerts, opera and some contemporary shows; the box office is open about half an hour before performances begin

Rudolfinum *(*☎ *24 89 31 11, Alšovo nábřeží 12)* – box office open from 10 am to 12.30 pm and 1.30 to 6 pm, and for one hour before performances; wheelchair access

Smetana Hall *(*☎ *22 00 21 21, Obecní dům, náměstí Republiky 5)*

St Nicholas Church *(Old Town Square)*

Unitaria Palace *(*☎ *24 22 95 92, Karlova 8)*

Nové Město

Bethlehem Chapel *(Map 6; Betlémské náměstí 1)*

Emmaus Monastery *(Map 9;* ☎ *24 91 53 71, Vyšehradská 49)*

National Theatre *(Map 6;* ☎ *24 91 34 37, Národní 2)* – mainly opera and ballet; box office at Nová Scéna, Národní 4, open weekdays 10 am to 6 pm, closed weekends from 12.30 to 3 pm; stand-up tickets 10 Kč, sit-down tickets 30 to 400 Kč; wheelchair access

State Opera House *(Map 6;* ☎ *26 53 53, Wilsonova 4)* – mainly opera and ballet; box office open daily 10 am to 5.30 pm (closed weekends from noon to 1 pm); admission 50 to 800 Kč

Vila Amerika *(Dvořák Museum; Map 9;* ☎ *29 82 14, Ke Karlovu 20)* – special Dvořák concerts

Vyšehrad

Congress Centre *(Map 9;* ☎ *61 17 27 11, 5.května 65)* – was known for musicals and chamber concerts, but the whole complex is to be reconstructed and its future as a music venue was uncertain at the time of writing

Bubeneč & Holešovice

Fairgrounds *(Výstaviště; Map 3)*

Smíchov

Bertramka *(Mozart Museum; Map 9;* ☎ *54 38 93, Mozartova 2/169)* – concerts of music by Mozart and other composers

Troja

Troja Castle *(Map 1;* ☎ *689 07 61)*

Prague Spring (Pražské Jaro)

This is the Czech Republic's best-known annual cultural event, and is now a major tourist event too. It begins on 12 May, the anniversary of Smetana's death, with a procession from his grave at Vyšehrad to the Obecní dům, and a performance there of his *Má vlast* song cycle. The festival runs until 2 June. The beautiful venues are as big a draw as the music.

If you want a guaranteed seat at a Prague Spring concert, book it by mid-March. Write to Prague Spring (MHF Pražské jaro; ☎ 53 02 93, fax 53 60 40, email festival @login.cz, Web site www.festival.cz), Hellichova 18, Malá Strana, 118 00 Prague 1. Bookings can also be made through Ticketpro (see the Tickets section at the start of this chapter).

A few seats may be available as late as the end of May: watch the papers. The cheapest tickets are at the official box office (Map 5) at Hellichova 18, off Karmelitská in Malá Strana, open weekdays from 10 am to 6 pm during the run-up to the festival, but only until 5 pm during the festival.

CINEMAS

Prague has about 30 movie theatres (*kino*), some showing first-run western films, some with Czech films. Admission costs from 80 to 110 Kč. The highest concentration is around Wenceslas Square (Map 6), where you'll find the **Lucerna** *(Vodičkova 36)*, **Hvězda** *(Wenceslas Square 38)* and **Jalta** *(Wenceslas Square 43)*. Prague's first multi-screen cinema, the **Galaxie multiplex** *(Map 1; Arkalycká 1/877, Jižní Město, Prague 4)*, is by the northern entrance to Háje metro station. Recent **summer cinemas** (*letní kino*) have been held at the Fairgrounds (Bubeneč) and on Střelecký ostrov.

THEATRE

Prague's most famous theatre feature is probably Laterna Magika (Magic Lantern), a multimedia show interweaving dance, opera, music and film, which caused a stir when it premiered in 1958 at the Brussels World Fair. Since moving from its birthplace (in the basement of the Adria Palace) to *Nová Scéna (Map 6; Národní 4)*, the New National Theatre building, it has become clever, expensive, mainstream entertainment, a set of rotating shows now enjoyed mainly by tourists.

Some agencies may tell you it's booked out, but you can often bag a leftover seat at the box office on the day before a performance, or a no-show half an hour beforehand. Tickets are about 500 Kč (650 Kč from Čedok or Ticketpro). The box office (☎ 24 91 41 29) is open from 10 am to 8 pm (weekends from 3 pm).

'Black-light theatre' is a hybrid of mime, drama and puppet theatre. Live or animated actors in phosphorescent costumes do their thing on a stage or in front of a black backdrop lit only by ultraviolet light, thus eliminating the usual distractions of stage management. It's a growth industry in Prague, with at least half a dozen venues.

In the past, mainstream western musicals were regularly presented at the *Congress Centre (Kongresové centrum; Map 9; ☎ 61 17 27 11, 5.května 65, Prague 4)*, formerly known as the Palace of Culture, but renovations are planned here. *Evita* had its Prague debut at the new *Spiral Theatre (divadlo Spirála; Map 3; ☎ 20 10 32 14, Fairgrounds, Bubeneč)*, a striking building that reminded one reader of the Thunderdome in *Mad Max III*.

Other venues for drama, experimental theatre, musicals and revues include:

Staré Město & Josefov

All the venues listed here are shown on Map 7 unless otherwise noted.

Estates Theatre (Stavovské divadlo; ☎ 24 91 34 37, Ovocný trh 1) – see the earlier Classical Music, Opera & Ballet section for details; some plays include simultaneous translation on headphones

Image Theatre (☎ 24 81 11 67, Classic Club, Pařížská 4) – mime and black-light theatre

Jiří Srnec Black Light Theatre (Map 6; ☎ 24 21 20 03, Lucerna Theatre), in the passage at Štěpánská 61 – Srnec was a founding member of the Black Light Theatre of Prague; performances most days from 8 pm, box office open from 3 pm weekdays and Saturday, 490 Kč

Kolowrat Theatre (☎ 24 21 50 01, Ovocný trh 6) – box office open weekdays 10 am to 6 pm, plus weekend performance days 10 am to 12.30 pm and 3 to 6 pm (or go to the National Theatre box office)

Puppet Kingdom (Říše loutek; ☎ 232 34 29, Žatecká 1), also called the National Marionette Theatre – performances by the Kladno puppet troupe of Mozart's *Don Giovanni*, 490 Kč

Theatre on the Balustrade (Divadlo Na Zábradlí) (☎ 24 22 19 33, Anenské náměstí 5) – Czech-language drama, including the occasional play by Václav Havel, box office open from 2 to 7.30 pm (two hours before showtime on weekends)

Southern Nové Město

Dramatic Club (Činoherní Klub) (Map 6; ☎ 96 22 21 23, Ve Smečkách 26) – Czech-language modern drama

Minor Theatre (Map 7; ☎ 24 22 96 75, Senovážné náměstí 28) – children's theatre on most weekdays at 3 and 7.30 pm; wheelchair-accessible

Reduta Theatre (Map 6; ☎ 24 91 22 46, Národní 20) – part of the jazz club of the same name, but with Czech-language drama at 7.30 pm on selected evenings, and occasional afternoon children's shows

Vinohrady

Vinohrady Theatre (Divadlo Na Vinohradech; Map 10; ☎ 24 25 76 01, náměstí Míru 7) – Czech-language drama, box office open daily except Sunday, 10 am to 7 pm

Karlín

Karlín Music Theatre (Hudební divadlo v Karlíně; Map 6; ☎ 21 86 81 49, Křížíkova 10) – Czech-language musicals and operettas

SPECTATOR SPORTS

Calcio Sport (Map 6; ☎ 24 91 73 47), Myslíkova 30, Nové Město, is a fan-shop for several of Prague's football and ice-hockey teams. Staff have details of upcoming matches and sell tickets. It's open on weekdays from 10 am to 6 pm, and on Saturday until noon. English is limited.

Prague International Marathon

The Prague International Marathon, started in 1989, is now an annual event (normally mid to late May), attracting more foreign runners than Czechs.

If you'd like to compete, contact Prague International Marathon (☎ 29 65 17 or 29 91 63), Záhořanského 3. The 1998 entry fee was US$15 for foreigners and 200 Kč for Czechs. Entries must be received 10 days before the race.

Ice Hockey

The Czech ice hockey (lední hokej) team has won the European championship 17 times, the world title seven times, and one Olympic gold medal. Sparta Praha and Slavia Praha are Prague's two big teams. The season runs from September to early April.

You can see Sparta play at the HC Sparta Sports Hall (Map 4; ☎ 66 71 25 47), by the Fairgrounds in Bubeneč (take tram 12 one stop west from Nádraží Holešovice metro station). Slavia plays at the winter stadium (zimní stadión) of the HC Slavia Praha complex (Map 1; ☎ 73 55 56), on Na hroudě in Vršovice. Cheap tickets are available at the ice rinks for Tuesday, Friday and Sunday games.

Tennis

Mention Czech sport stars and most westerners think of tennis (tenis). But you won't run into Ivan Lendl or Martina Navrátilová here: they've been US citizens for years. Tennis tournaments are held at the Štvanice club (TJ Slavoj Praha) on ostrov Štvanice (Map 4; tram No 3 from Wenceslas Square), and the Czech Open was played here in 1998.

Football

Slavia Praha and Sparta Praha are leading teams in the national football (fotbal)

league; two other Prague teams are Bohemians and Viktoria Žižkov. Each has its own stadium where you can see matches, mostly on Sunday afternoons. The season runs from August to December and February to June.

AC Sparta Praha stadium *(Map 3; ☎ 20 57 03 23, Milady Horákové 98, Bubeneč)* – tickets cost from 30 to 110 Kč; take tram No 1, 8, 25 or 26 east from Hradčanská metro station

FC Bohemians stadium *(Map 1; ☎ 71 72 26 20, Vršovická 31, Prague 10)* – take tram No 4 or 22 from Karlovo náměstí

FK Viktoria Žižkov stadium *(Map 6; ☎ 27 91 40, Seifertova, Žižkov)* – tickets cost from 30 to 50 Kč; take eastbound tram No 9 from Wenceslas Square or tram No 5 or 26 from náměstí Republiky

SK Slavia Praha stadium *(Map 1; ☎ 73 67 80, Vladivostocká 1460/2, Vršovice)* – tickets cost from 30 to 110 Kč; take tram No 4 or 22 from Karlovo náměstí

Horse Racing

Check out the racing (dostihy) scene at Chuchle závodiště (racecourse), Radotínská 69, Velká Chuchle, Prague 5 (off the edge of Map 1); take bus No 453 or 172 from Smíchovské Nádraží metro station. Races usually start after 2 pm on Tuesday and Sunday, between May and October. Contact PIS about other venues and events, as these constantly change. Tickets are cheap and usually available at the grounds.

There are four annual horse races at TJ Žižka Praha racecourse (jezdecké závodiště; ☎ 87 84 76) on Císařský ostrov (Map 1). Transport is awkward: take bus No 112 from Holešovice metro station to the Kovárna stop and walk south on Pod Havránkou across the bridge to the racecourse; or get off the PPS ferry to Troja (see the Boat section in the Getting Around chapter).

Shopping

The privatisation of retailing since 1989 has radically changed Prague's shopping scene. Consumer goods are easily obtainable and mostly of good quality. Imports carry western European prices, but Czech products are affordable for Czechs and cheap for westerners. While tourist-zone gift shops outside Prague (such as in Karlštejn or Mělník, see the Excursions chapter), have smaller selections, prices are significantly lower.

Prague's main shopping streets are Wenceslas Square and three streets around the edge of Staré Město: Na příkopě, 28.října and Národní (Národní třída). Here you should be able to find almost anything you need. For special needs, try the *Zlaté stránky* (Gold Pages) of the telephone book (which includes an English index), or ask your hotel receptionist or the people at PIS.

If you have bought what you think is a genuine antique or a piece of museum-quality art that may cause trouble at customs on the way out, you'd be wise to follow official procedures – see the Customs section in the Facts for the Visitor chapter (also for information on which goods are dutiable). In general, anything made before 1920 (among other criteria) is deemed nonexportable.

WHAT TO BUY
Ceramics

Well priced traditional-style ceramics are on offer at *Keramika (Map 6; ☎ 87 81 27)*, in a passage at Wenceslas Square 41, Nové Město. A good selection of work from the Slovácko region of Moravia and the Chodsko region of Bohemia is at *Tupesy lidová keramika (Map 7; ☎ 24 23 43 72, Havelská 21)*. *Obchod U Sv Jiljí (Map 7; Jilská, Staré Město)* offers offbeat ceramics along with toys and marionettes. For Slovak folk handicrafts, go to *Dům Slovenské kultury (House of Slovak Culture) (Map 6; Purkyňova 4, Nové Město)*; a smaller selec-

tion is at *Lidová jizba*, in a courtyard at Wenceslas Square 15.

Gemstones & Jewellery

Amber and gemstones (such as rubies and garnets) mined in the Czech Republic are good value, and popular as souvenirs or gifts. Amber (*jantar*) is better value here than over the border in Germany. This fossilised tree resin is usually honey yellow in colour, although it can be white, orange, red or brown. Ruby (*rubín*) is dark red, and the Czech garnet (*český granát*) is usually red but can be many other colours, or colourless.

Wenceslas Square, Na příkopě, Národní and Karlova abound in jewellers. A reliable shop for quality gems set in gold and silver is *Granát Turnof (Map 7; Dlouhá 28-30, Staré Město)*.

Gifts & Souvenirs

Czech Traditional Handicrafts (Česká lidová řemesla) (Map 7; Melantrichova 17, Staré Město) is the biggest of at least nine shops with the name between Prague Castle and Old Town Square, all with quality items of wood, ceramic, straw, textiles and other materials, handmade in traditional styles and/or with traditional materials. Things to look for include painted Easter eggs, wooden utensils, ceramic ware with traditional designs, linen with traditional stitching, and Bohemian lacework.

Stalls are everywhere in Wenceslas Square, Na můstku and Old Town Square, on Charles Bridge and along the steps to Prague Castle. Once a source of good drawings, paintings and photographs of the city, many of these stalls have now descended into kitsch.

Glass & Crystal

One of Prague's best buys is Bohemian crystal – anything from simple glassware to stupendous works of art, sold at some three dozen upmarket places in the shopping zone. Prices aren't radically different from shop to shop, though they are highest in the city centre. The most exclusive (and expensive) crystal shop is *Moser (Map 7; ☎ 24 21 12 93, Na příkopě 12)*, worth a browse as much for the décor as the goods: it's in an originally Gothic building called the House at the Black Rose (Dům U černé růže).

Other worthy shops include *Výtvarná Řemesla (Map 7; Karlova 23)* and *Sklo Bohemia (Map 7; Na příkopě 17)*. If all you want are a few souvenir tumblers, there are others to choose from as well.

Many accept credit cards, and most will ship goods abroad. If you want to ship them out yourself you must take your parcel, unsealed, to the customs post office (see Customs in the Facts for the Visitor chapter). Note that parcels containing glass and crystal are not accepted by the US, Australian and New Zealand postal systems.

Junk

You may not need a door knob, rusty bed springs or a cracked teapot, but drop in anyway at the old hardware/houseware shop of *Eduard Čapek (Map 7; Dlouhá 32, Staré Město)*, founded before WWI and doing a roaring trade ever since.

Music

Good buys are classical CDs of the works of the famous Czech composers (such as Smetana, Dvořák, Janáček and Martinů) as well as folk music – even *dechovka* (brassband 'polka' music) if you like it. There are almost as many music shops in Prague as bookshops.

A good option for classical music buffs is *Supraphon (Map 6; Jungmannova 20, Nové Město)*. Prague's music megastores are *Popron (Map 6; Jungmannova 30, Nové Město)* and *Bontonland (Map 7; Wenceslas Square 1-3, Nové Město)* in the basement of the Koruna building. *Chapeau Rouge (Map 7)* is a small, good classical-CD shop. It's on the corner of Jakubská and Malá Štupartská.

AghaRTA Jazz Centrum (Map 6;

Don't Forget Your Basket

Many supermarkets, grocery stores and even some shoe shops require customers to pick up a shopping basket or trolley when they enter, or to wait for one if there are none available. Those who enter without one may be set upon by angry staff. The intention is to keep a lid on the number of customers, making it easier for staff to spot shoplifters.

Krakovská 5, Nové Město) has its own jazz music shop, open from 3 pm to midnight (weekends from 7 pm).

Sporting Goods

A good sports shop with modest prices (and a range of serious backpacks) is at *YMCA Sport Centrum (Map 7; Na poříčí 12, Nové Město)*, open weekdays from 9.30 am to 6.30 pm and Saturday from 9 am to 1 pm. It's the separate entrance to the left.

Dům Sportu (Map 6; Jungmannova 28, Nové Město) is a collection of shops which sells a wide range of sporting goods and outdoor gear. Other good shops include Hudy Sport (Map 6; Slezská 10, Vinohrady) and Sport Slivka (Újezd 42, Malá Strana; Map 5); the latter also sells sleeping bags.

The big department stores also have sizeable sports departments. Locally manufactured equipment is moderately priced.

Toys

Czech Traditional Handicrafts (see the earlier section on Gifts & Souvenirs) sells wooden folk items and toys, and several of its branches specialise in toys. Another shop, which also has animated toys, is Beruška (Map 6). It's in a passage at Wenceslas Square 15.

Marionettes of wood (and more lifelike, delicate and expensive plaster ones) are available in many Staré Město shops (Map 7); worth a look are *Bonum (Husova 8)* and *Obchod U Sv Jiljí (Jilská)*.

WHERE TO SHOP
Bookshops

Prague is full of interesting bookshops (*knihupectví*), and those that stock English-language titles tend also to have books on Czech history and culture, and translations of well known Czech writers. Paperback English classics abound. Following are the best options for English-speaking book junkies:

Albatros *(Map 7; ☎ 24 22 93 22, Havelská 20)* – includes children's books and classical CDs

Big Ben *(Map 7; ☎ 231 80 21, Malá Štupartská 5)* – small but well stocked, English-language only, including Czech history, essays, fiction; bulletin board; weekdays to 7 pm, weekends to 6 pm

Cizojazyčná literatura *(Map 7; Na příkopě 27)* – maps, old prints, Czech literature in English and French; weekdays to 7 pm, Saturday to 6 pm, Sunday to 5 pm

Kanzelsberger *(Map 6; ☎ 24 21 73 35, Wenceslas Square 42)* – guides, Czech topics in English; daily to 7 pm

Nadatur *(Map 7; ☎ 24 61 75 39, Hybernská 5)* – heavy on civilian and military transport, publishes countrywide bus and train timetables; weekdays to 5.30 pm, Saturday to noon

Na můstku *(Map 7; ☎ 24 21 63 83, Na příkopě 3)* – maps, guides, souvenir books; weekdays to 7 pm, weekends to 6 pm

The Globe *(Map 4; ☎ 66 71 26 10, Jankovského 14)* – wide English-language selection, easy chairs; notice board; first-rate café; daily to midnight

U knihomola *(Map 6; ☎ 627 77 67, Mánesova 79, Vinohrady)* – very broad selection, including business, children's, and second-hand books, some foreign-language newspapers; excellent café; to 11 pm (Friday and Saturday to midnight, Sunday to 8 pm)

The second-hand bookshops (*antikvariát*) dotted around the Old Town and Malá Strana have few English titles but make great browsing. **Mapis** *(Map 5; ☎ 57 31 54 59, Štefánikova 63, Smíchov)* is a map specialist shop, open weekdays only, from 9.30 am to 6 pm.

Department Stores

The major department stores in the centre are:

Bílá Labuť *(Map 6; Na poříčí 23, Nové Město)*, and a smaller store at the corner of Wenceslas Square and Wilsonova

Kotva *(Map 7; náměstí Republiky 8, Staré Město)*

Krone *(Map 6)*, on the corner of Wenceslas Square and Jindřišská, Nové Město

Tesco *(Map 6; Národní 26, Nové Město)*

Open-Air Markets

The city has a number of open-air markets, where you can buy not only produce but souvenirs, clothing and the odd antique. The biggest one near the centre is the rather pricey daily produce and souvenir market on Havelská (Map 7), south of Old Town Square. Less expensive ones – mainly open in the morning, and closed Sunday – include:

Behind Tesco (Map 6); produce only

Dejvice (Map 3); take the Praha Dejvice exit from metro station Hradcanská and turn left into Dejvická

Dejvice (Map 3); just off Vítězné náměstí

Bubenské nábřeží, Holešovice (Map 4)

Arbesovo náměstí (Map 5) and nearby náměstí 14.října (Map 9), Smíchov

Traditional marionettes for sale, Hradčany.

Chill out in the shade at one of Prague's cafés.

Grab your armour ...

... and let the medieval games begin (Old Town Square).

The formidable stronghold of Český Šternberk looms over the Sázava River.

Welcoming statue in Konopiště's castle grounds.

Stunning Karlštejn castle on the Berounka River.

Excursions

The Central Bohemian countryside, within an hour's train or bus ride from Prague, is rich in landscapes, good walks, interesting architecture and historical sights. Following are a few day or overnight trips you can do on your own.

Top of the line, for our money, are photogenic Karlštejn Castle, harrowing Terezín, the silver-mining town of Kutná Hora and – barely outside the city limits – the park at Průhonice. Be ready for summer crowds at Karlštejn and Konopiště castles; staying the night, after the tour buses return to Prague, lets you see a place in a kinder light.

Of the castles and chateaux described here, Křivoklát and Karlštejn are open year-round, Mělník chateau from March to December, and the others from April to October. All the sights in this chapter are closed on Monday except the Terezín museum, the Lidice memorial, Mělník chateau and – in July and August – Křivoklát.

Tours

The risk of theft has prompted castles and chateaux to admit visitors only in guided groups, though most will let you pay the Czech price (from 30 to 60 Kč) and lend you a written English narrative. If you want to catch every detail, be prepared to fork out 60 to 110 Kč for an English-language tour (up to 240 Kč at Konopiště).

If you don't want to arrange a trip on your own, Čedok and other operators have a range of all-day excursions in the high season, with lunch included. See Organised Tours in the Getting Around chapter for more information.

Walks

Only a few walks are noted in this chapter, but many itineraries are described (in Czech) in the excellent series of 1:50,000 hiking maps produced by Klub českých turistů/VKÚ. Trails are well marked, with the same colours as shown on the maps.

MĚLNÍK
☎ 0206

On a prominent hill above the confluence of the Vltava and Labe, Mělník began as a 9th century Slavonic settlement. Mělník castle was the second home of Bohemia's queens from the 13th century until the time of George of Poděbrady. A solidly Hussite town, that was demolished by Swedish troops in the Thirty Years' War, and the original castle gave way to the present chateau.

The town, about 30km from Prague, is the centre of Bohemia's small wine-growing region. The best vineyards are descended from Burgundy vines imported by Charles IV.

This is an easy day trip, good for lazy strolling and wine tasting. On Monday some sights are closed, though the chateau remains open.

Orientation & Information

Across the road from the bus station, take any street that angles about 45° to the right (west). It's a 10 to 15 minute uphill slog to the town's old gate tower, Pražská brana (Prague Gate). Inside, bear right into náměstí Míru, an arcaded square lined with pastel-tinted Renaissance and baroque façades. Take the first left along Svatováclavská to the chateau and church.

The municipal Tourist Information Centre (☎/fax 62 75 03), náměstí Míru 30/16, offers town maps and accommodation help. It's open from 9 am to 5 pm daily from May to September and on weekdays only the rest of the year. Česká spořitelna banka on náměstí Míru and Komerční banka on Svatováclavská have currency exchanges and ATMs.

The Chateau

Marriage brought the Renaissance chateau

into the Lobkowicz family in 1753. Since getting it back from the state in 1990, they've opened it to the public.

A 60 Kč, 40 minute tour looks at the **former living quarters** on the top floor, crowded with the family's rich collection of baroque furniture and 17th and 18th century paintings. Additional rooms are given over to changing exhibits of modern works.

Another tour descends to 14th century **wine cellars** where you may taste the chateau's wines, for 80 Kč or 120 Kč depending on how many you want to try. Both tours go every half-hour. A shop in the courtyard sells the chateau's own label.

The chateau (☎ 62 21 21) is open daily from 10 am to 6 pm (but closed in January and February).

On the 1st floor, but independent of the family's operation, is a **district museum** (☎ 62 21 58) with a dreary exhibit on wine-making and a room full of baby carriages. It's open from April to October, from 9 am to 5 pm, daily except Monday.

Church of SS Peter & Paul

This 15th century Gothic church (kostel Sv Petra a Pavla), with baroque furnishings and tower, is worth a look. Remnants of its Romanesque predecessor have been incorporated into the rear of the building, south of the bell tower.

The old **crypt** is now an ossuary, packed with the bones of some 15,000 people dug up to make room for 16th century plague victims, and arranged in macabre patterns. It's open to the public from 9.30 am to 5 pm, daily except Monday, with an unintentionally hilarious show every half-hour. A single 30 Kč ticket also lets you have a look inside the church; children under five years get in free.

Lookout & Walks

The view from behind the chateau takes in the confluence of the Vltava and Labe, and a once-busy 10km canal from upstream on the Vltava. The big bump on the horizon to the north-west is a hill called Říp where, legend says, the brothers Čech and Lech

stopped on a journey from the east; the former stayed and founded the Czech nation, the latter went on to sire the Poles.

Lobkowicz vineyards carpet the wedge of land between the Vltava and the canal. To the right of the canal is thickly wooded Hořínský Park, to which you could descend for some pleasant walking. A 2km marked trail passes Hořín village, Hořín Chateau (the old Lobkowicz family home) and the canal lock, which is still in use.

Places to Stay

Autocamp Mělník (☎ 62 38 56, *Klášterní 717*) is north-east of the centre. Two modest and fairly central places have singles/doubles with shower and toilet: *Penzion V podzámčí* (☎ 62 28 89, *Seiferta 167*), at 400/800 Kč; and the *Hotel Jaro* (☎ 62 68 52, *17.listopadu 174*), at 940/1520 Kč. Both are two to three blocks from náměstí Míru, to the left as you face the chateau. The Tourist Information Centre can direct you to others. There are also *Zimmer frei* (rooms for rent) signs in the neighbourhood.

Places to Eat

The best local red and white wines are both called Ludmila, after the saint and grandmother of St Wenceslas. One of the best places to taste them is in the chateau. On the ground floor are the *Zámecká* restaurant, with a smashing view and good food (main dishes from 150 to 200 Kč, with cheaper vegetarian items), and a pricier *vinárna*, both open from 10 am to midnight. The *Stará škola* vinárna behind the church has similar views (and prices). For cheaper eats, try *U Tomáše* at Svatováclavská 3. Budget places are outside the tower gate.

Getting There & Away

On weekdays, buses run to Mělník every 30 to 60 minutes from Nádraží Holešovice metro station, and somewhat less often from Florenc bus station. On weekends you can only get there from Florenc, with departures every hour or so on Saturday and every hour or two on Sunday. The trip costs about 25 Kč and takes 45 minutes.

Returning from Mělník station requires some agility, as buses depart from several widely separated stands (at least stand Nos 7, 30 and 41). Note that most return only as far as Nádraží Holešovice.

TEREZÍN
☎ 0416

Even were it not for their savage use by the Nazis, the massive strongholds at Terezín (Theresienstadt in German) would be awesome. Though founded in 1780 by Emperor Joseph II as a state-of-the-art bulwark against the Prussians, they never saw action. In the 19th century the town within the Main Fortress was made a garrison, while the so-called Lesser Fortress served as a jail and a WWI prisoner-of-war camp.

In 1940 the Gestapo established a prison in the Lesser Fortress. At the end of 1941 they evicted the townspeople from the Main Fortress and turned it into a transit camp and ghetto, through which some 150,000 European Jews eventually passed en route to extermination camps.

Terezín became the centrepiece of an extraordinary public relations hoax. Official visitors to the fortress, which was billed as a kind of Jewish 'refuge', saw a clean town with a Jewish administration, banks, shops, cafés, schools and a thriving cultural life – a charade that twice completely fooled the International Red Cross, among others.

The reality was a relentlessly increasing concentration of prisoners (some 60,000 eventually, in a town built for a garrison of 5000), regular trains departing for Auschwitz, and the death by starvation, disease or suicide of some 35,000 Jews in the camp.

Though lacking the immediate horror of places like Auschwitz, Terezín has a potent impact. This is a highly recommended, and fairly straightforward, day trip from Prague.

Orientation

Public buses stop at náměstí Československé armády, the central square area of the town within the Main Fortress. The Lesser Fortress is a 10 minute walk east across the Ohře river, beside furious traffic on the Prague-Ústí nad Labem highway (which cuts through the middle of the village). In between is a huge tour-bus parking lot.

Information

A combined ticket for both branches of the Museum of the Ghetto and for the Lesser Fortress is 110 Kč (70 Kč for children). The museum has good multilingual self-guide pamphlets, a large selection of books for sale, and earnest guides for hire (a few of them ghetto survivors). For more information call ☎ 78 22 45.

Main Fortress

From the ground, the scale of the 4km of multiple walls and moats of the Main Fortress (*hlavní pevnost*) is impossible to grasp (but see the aerial photograph in the museum branch on Komenského).

Inside is the squared-off, colourless town of Terezín. There's little to look at except the chunky, 19th century Church of the Resurrection, the arcaded commandant's office, the neo-classical administrative buildings on the square – and the surrounding grid of houses with their awful secrets, where Jews were crammed increasingly tightly.

South of the square are the anonymous remains of a railway siding, built by prisoners, on which loads of further prisoners arrived. Two 'water gates' (for access to the river) remain.

The main attraction here is the absorbing **Museum of the Ghetto** (Muzeum ghetta), which has two branches. The main museum, on Komenského by the highway, explores the rise of Nazism and life in the Terezín ghetto, using artefacts, paintings, letters, photos and video documentaries.

A newer branch is in the former Magdeburg Barracks on Tyršova, which served as the seat of the Jewish 'government'. Here you can visit a reconstructed dormitory for prisoners, and look at exhibits on the extraordinarily rich cultural life – music, theatre,

EXCURSIONS

EXCURSIONS

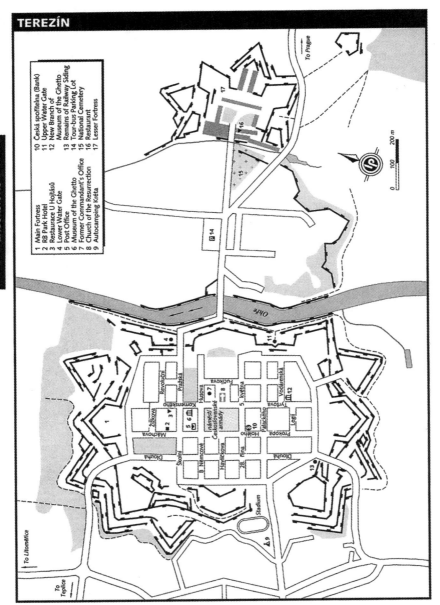

TEREZÍN

1 Main Fortress
2 RB Park Hotel
3 Restaurace U Hojtásů
4 Lower Water Gate
5 Post Office
6 Museum of the Ghetto
7 Former Commandant's Office
8 Church of the Resurrection
9 Autocamping Kréta
10 Česká spořitelna (Bank)
11 Upper Water Gate
12 New Branch of
   Museum of the Ghetto
13 Remains of Railway Siding
14 Tour-bus Parking Lot
15 National Cemetery
16 Restaurant
17 Lesser Fortress

To Prague

0   100   200 m

To Litoměřice

To Teplice

Ohře

Stadium

fine arts and literature – that somehow flourished among these condemned souls.

Both branches are open daily from 9 am to 6 pm (to 4.30 pm from October to April).

Lesser Fortress

You can take a self-guided tour of the Lesser Fortress (*malá pevnost*) through the prison barracks, isolation cells, workshops and morgues, past execution grounds and former mass graves. It would be hard to invent a more menacing, deathly place than these rooms, courtyards, and what seems an eternity of tunnels beneath the walls. The Nazis' mocking concentration-camp slogan, *Arbeit Macht Frei* (work makes you free) hangs above a gate. In front of the fortress is a **National Cemetery**, founded in 1945 for those exhumed from mass graves here.

The Lesser Fortress is open daily from 9 am to 6 pm (to 5.30 pm in winter).

Places to Stay

The thought of staying the night at a former concentration camp may make your skin crawl, but a camping ground, *Autocamping Kréta* (☎ 78 24 73), is open from April to mid-September by the stadium west of the Main Fortress; bungalows are 140 Kč per bed. The *RB Park Hotel* (☎ 78 22 60, Máchova 162) has basic rooms at 260 Kč per bed.

Places to Eat

In addition to bistros at the tour-bus parking lot, there's a restaurant in the former German officers' mess in the Lesser Fortress. There are also restaurants at *Autocamping Kréta* and the *RB Park Hotel*. Near the main branch of the museum, *Restaurace U Hojtášů* (☎ 78 22 03, Komenského 152) is open from 10 am to 11 pm – should you have any appetite after your tour.

Getting There & Away

Terezín is about one hour from Prague by bus. Useful direct buses from Florenc depart at about 7.50 and 10 am, and noon (Saturday 9 and 11 am, Sunday 10 am). Useful returning buses depart from Terezín at about 12.55, 2.25, 3.55, 5.10 and 5.40 pm (weekends 12.55, 2.25 and 4.20 pm; Sunday also 3.55 pm) – but all except the 5.10 (4.20) pm bus terminate at Vltavská metro station.

ČSAD buses between Prague and Ústí nad Labem also stop here, about hourly. Check at the PIS offices for the most current schedules.

LIDICE
☎ 0312

When Czechoslovak paratroopers assassinated Reichsprotektor Reinhard Heydrich in June 1942 (see the boxed text under History in the Facts about Prague chapter), the Nazis took savage revenge. Picking – apparently at random – the mining and foundry village of Lidice, north-west of Prague, they proceeded on 10 June to obliterate it from the face of the earth. All its men were shot, all the women and most children shipped to the Ravensbrück concentration camp, and the remaining children farmed out to German foster homes. The village was systematically burned and bulldozed so that no trace remained. Of its 500 inhabitants, 192 men, 60 women and 88 children died.

The atrocity electrified the world and triggered a campaign to preserve the village's memory and create a kind of symbolic Lidice. The site is now a green field, eloquent in its silence, dotted with a few memorials and the reconstructed foundations of the farm where most of the men were shot and buried.

This is a straightforward half-day trip from Prague.

Orientation & Information

The site is opposite the bus stop on the Prague-Kladno highway, on the far side of a never-completed, Communist-era monument. A small museum (☎ 92 34 42) recreates the village in photographs and multi-lingual text, along with chilling SS film footage of its destruction. It's open daily from 8 am to 5 pm, for 60 Kč (half-price for children and students).

Places to Eat

The only food as far as the eye can see is a snack bar across the road from the bus stop.

Getting There & Away

Lidice is on the bus line to Kladno, half an hour from Prague. Buses go from opposite the Hotel Diplomat, by Dejvická metro station. Direct (*přímý spoj*) routes to Kladno don't stop at Lidice, but anything serving Buštěhrad does: about every half-hour on weekdays, every hour on Saturday and every hour or two on Sunday.

BEROUN
☎ 0311

Though of little interest itself, Beroun acts as a jumping-off point for Křivoklát and Karlštejn castles, the Koněprusy Caves and hikes in the beautiful Berounka River basin.

The main square, Husovo náměstí, is a 10 minute walk straight out (north) from the train station. A not-very-useful municipal tourist office (☎ 65 43 21) is at the south-east corner of the square; it's open weekdays from 8 am to 12.30 pm and 1 to 6 pm, and Saturday to noon. Also on the square is a bank with a currency exchange. The bus station is east of the square, past the tourist office and across the river.

Places to Stay & Eat

Hotel U Blažků (*☎/fax 62 13 76, Česká 176*), off the square to the north-east, has good-value singles/doubles for 800/1150 Kč (with breakfast). Its restaurant also serves up big helpings of Czech standards for 40 to 80 Kč, until 9 pm.

Cheaper options include basic rooms with toilet and shower for 400 Kč a bed at *Hotel Český dvůr* (*☎ 214 11, Husovo náměstí 86*); and spic-and-span doubles with shower but shared toilet for 700 Kč (breakfast included) at the *Hotel Barbora* (*☎ 254 42*); from the train station, turn right beyond the highway. The big place with the illuminated 'Hotel' sign is *Hotel Litava* (*☎ 62 52 56, Havlíčkova*), where rooms cost 1020/1360 Kč.

Getting There & Away

From Prague to Beroun it's a beautiful train ride along the Berounka River – by itself, reason enough to go. Express trains leave about every three hours from Prague's main station, while local trains leave more frequently from the Smíchov station. An unreserved seat from the main station is 28 Kč. See the section on Křivoklát for more on timing.

KONĚPRUSY CAVES
☎ 0311

The tour through these impressive limestone caves (Koněpruské jeskyně in Czech), 6km south of Beroun and 600m deep, reveals colourful formations, the bones of humans and a woolly rhinoceros, and a 15th century underground forge used to make counterfeit coins.

The caves are open daily from April to October. In June, July and August the hours are 8 am to 5 pm; in May, weekdays 8 am to 4 pm and weekends 8 am to 5 pm; in April and September, 8 am to 4 pm; and in October, weekdays 8 am to 4 pm and weekends 8.30 am to 3.30 pm. Admission is 40 Kč. Take a pullover: it's a constant, chilly 10°C, and you'll be down there for 45 to 60 minutes.

There's no food to speak of except a snack bar at the caves.

Getting There & Away

Buses call at Koněprusy village below the caves on a motley timetable. On working days, useful departures from Beroun bus station include 9.25 am and 2.20** pm (for Zadní Třebáň) and 12.20 pm (for Příbram); and from Beroun train station, 11.30* am and 2.43** pm (for Liteň) and 2.35 pm (for Řevnice). They call at Koněprusy on the way back to Beroun at 12.57*, 1.04**, 3.30, 3.32**, 3.59 and 4.57 pm. Services that also run on Saturday are starred; those going every day have two stars.

It's obviously worth checking with the Beroun tourist office before you go (and the caves office when you arrive) about changes to this schedule!

KŘIVOKLÁT

☎ 0313

Křivoklát Castle was built in the late 13th century as a royal hunting lodge. In the 15th century Vladislav II gave it its present Gothic face. There's no hunting anymore: much of the upper Berounka basin, one of Bohemia's most pristine forests, is now the Křivoklát Protected Landscape Region and a UNESCO 'biosphere preservation' area.

Half the pleasure of going is getting there, by train up the wooded valley hemmed in by limestone bluffs. On weekdays you'll find none of the crowds associated with Karlštejn Castle (see the following section).

Orientation & Information

Křivoklát is a drowsy village, across the Rakovnický creek (a tributary of the Berounka River) from the train station. From the Hotel Sýkora, climb up the road for about 10 minutes to the castle turning. If you're driving, there's a petrol station further up the hill.

The Castle

Scarred on the outside by clumsy renovations, the castle's best features are inside. Its **chapel** is one of the Czech Republic's finest unaltered late-Gothic interiors, full of intricate polychrome carvings. The altar is decorated with angels carrying instruments of torture – not entirely surprising in view of the castle's 16th century use as a political prison.

Right under the chapel are the **prison** and the torture chambers. The **Knights' Hall** features a permanent collection of late-Gothic religious sculpture and painted panels. On the 1st floor is the 25m-long **King's Hall**, the second-biggest non-church Gothic hall in the republic, after Vladislav Hall in Prague Castle.

The castle is open from June to August from 9 am to noon and 1 to 5 pm; May and September to 4 pm; and the rest of the year to 3 pm. In July and August it's open daily; the rest of the year it's closed Monday. The only way to see it is to join separate tours to

the castle and to the main tower; foreign-language tours are 110 and 60 Kč, respectively (55 and 30 Kč for kids from six to 16 and students). If you're content to join a Czech-language tour you'll pay about half this.

Walking from Křivoklát to Skryje

If you've got the gear and an extra day or two, consider walking the fine 18km trail (marked red; if the markings disappear, follow the river) south-west up the Berounka valley to Skryje. It starts on the western side of Rakovnický creek near the train station. Beyond the bridge to Roztoky are the **Nezabudice cliffs** (Nezabudické skály), part of a state nature reserve, and the village of Nezabudice. Across the river from Týřovice village is **Týřov**, a 13th century French-style castle used for a time as a prison and abandoned in the 16th century. Surrounding this is another nature reserve.

The summer resort of **Skryje** has some old thatched houses. You can also walk back down the other side of the river for a closer look at Týřov. From Skryje, local buses travel down the valley to the train at Roztoky, or on to Beroun.

Placards around Křivoklát village (labelled *Okolí Křivoklát*) show you some shorter strolls through the woods.

Places to Stay & Eat

There are *camping grounds* about 3km up the Berounka River from Křivoklát at Višňová, across the river at Branov (cross at Roztoky), and at Skryje.

The courteous, family-run *Hotel Sýkora* (☎ 55 81 14) in Křivoklát village has basic doubles with shared toilet and shower for 1000 Kč (breakfast included), and a restaurant and beer hall with modest prices, open to 10 pm (to 9 pm Sunday). Both the restaurant and the hotel are closed on Monday.

At the top of the hill, a steep 15 minute climb from Křivoklát village past the castle, we found a small building being renovated as the *Hotel Montana*. Left and up from

EXCURSIONS

this is at least one house offering private rooms.

Getting There & Away

You can get from Prague to Křivoklát and back on a long day trip. There is just one departure from Prague's main station (about 8.10 am at the time of research) with a reasonable connection at Beroun, and just one similarly convenient return departure from Křivoklát (about 2.25 pm). Smíchov station gives you this train plus two or three other good connections, though these tend to be slower local trains. The journey takes 1¾ hours, a bit less coming back.

Staying the night at Beroun allows you to do more than just visit the castle. Rakovník-bound trains leave Beroun every two hours or so; Křivoklát is 50 minutes up the line.

KARLŠTEJN
☎ 0311

Karlštejn Castle was founded by Charles IV in 1348, as a royal hideaway and as a treasury for the crown jewels and his holy relics. Perched on a crag above the Berounka River, looking taller than it is wide, it's unquestionably the most photogenic castle in the Prague region – and the most popular, with coachloads of tourists trooping through all day. Get there early to beat the crowds.

Heavily remodelled in the 19th century, it's now in amazingly good shape. The best views are from the outside, so if the tours are sold out, relax and enjoy a good tramp in the woods (see the Walks section).

Orientation

It's a 10 minute walk from the train station to the village, and another 10 minutes up to the castle past a strip of overpriced restaurants and souvenir shops.

The Castle

The south-facing palace is where most of the open rooms are, including a handsome **audience hall** and the **imperial bedroom**. You must use your imagination since they have been largely stripped of their furnishings. Several scale models indicate just how drastic the 19th century renovation was.

North of the palace is the **Marian Tower** (Marianská věž), with Charles' private quarters and the Church of Our Lady (kostel Panny Marie), with fragments of its beautiful original frescoes. Charles' private St Catherine Chapel (kaple sv Kateřiny) is in a corner of the church.

The centre of the complex is the **Great Tower** (Velká věž), where the royal regalia, jewels and relics were kept. At its heart is the lavish Chapel of the Holy Cross (kaple sv Kříže), furnished in gilt, with thousands of semiprecious stones and scores of panels by Master Theodoric, Bohemia's best-known painter of the time. It's closed to the public for security reasons, so you must settle for photographs and a scale model in the sacristy behind the Church of Our Lady.

The castle is open year-round (except from noon to 1 pm, and Monday, the day after any public holiday, and Christmas Eve and New Year's Day) – during July and August from 9 am to 7 pm; May, June and September to 6 pm; April and October to 5 pm; and the rest of the year to 4 pm.

Foreigners are expected to pay 150 Kč for a 45 minute guided tour (plus 50 Kč to take photos or 150 Kč for video photography), commencing when there are enough people who speak your language. Or you can try in your best Czech for a 50 Kč ticket, and tag along with a Czech group.

Museum of Nativity Scenes

Below the castle on the road to the car park, in the 14th century parsonage, is this curious museum (Muzeum betlémů) with over two dozen nativity scenes, from a few centimetres across to several metres, made of everything from sugar to sheet metal. Some are even animated. It's open daily except Monday, from 9 am to 6 pm, for 30 Kč.

Walks

On a red-marked path east from Karlštejn village, it's 7km via Mořinka (not Mořina) village into the **Karlík valley** (Karlické údolí), a nature reserve where you can find the remains of Charles IV's Karlík Castle, abandoned in the 15th century. Karlík village, 1km down the valley, has a 12th century rotunda. From Karlík, a road and a green-marked trail run 1.5km south-east to Dobřichovice, on the Prague-Beroun railway line.

From Srbsko, one train stop west of Karlštejn, another red trail climbs 8km up the wooded valley of Bubovický creek to the ridge-top **Monastery of St John under the Rock** (klášter sv Jan pod Skálou), allegedly once an StB (secret police) training camp. About 1.5km further, on a blue-marked trail and just beyond the highway, is Vráž, with buses back to Beroun or to Prague.

Either walk takes less than three hours.

Places to Stay

A *camping ground* is on the northern side of the river, half a kilometre west of the bridge.

Avoid Karlštejn village's pricey pensions. The best deal is just north of the village at *Pension & restaurace Pod Dračí skalou* (☎ 68 41 77), where a double is 800 Kč (book ahead). At the tranquil, family-run *Pension Slon* (☎ 68 45 50), rooms with shared facilities are 600/1000 Kč; from the train station, turn right and right again over the tracks, then follow the elephant-shaped signs for 300m. *Hotel Mlýn* (☎ 68 42 08) – cross to the south side of the river and take the first left – has doubles with breakfast for 1150 Kč.

There are other riverside pensions on the road to Prague.

Places to Eat

An alternative to the overpriced restaurants on the path to the castle is a simple Czech *hospoda* about halfway up on the left, marked by a Krušovice beer sign. Here Czech standards will cost you from 50 to 180 Kč per dish.

Getting There & Away

Local trains depart at least hourly from Prague's Smíchov station for the 35 minute trip (20 Kč); note that express trains (which includes all departures from Prague's main station) don't stop at Karlštejn. There are return departures from Karlštejn until at least 10.30 pm.

Drivers must pay 80 Kč to use the village parking lot.

PRŮHONICE

In this village, just south of Prague, is a photogenic 13th century chateau, restored at the end of the 19th century in a mix of neo-Gothic and neo-Renaissance styles, fronting onto a 250-hectare landscaped park, one of the finest of its kind in Europe.

The **chateau** is now occupied by the Botanical Institute of the Czech Academy of Sciences and is closed to the public. The little **Church of the Birth of Our Lady** (kostel narození Panny Marie) beside the chateau, consecrated in 1187, still has some 14th century frescoes visible. It too is closed, unless you attend Sunday Mass at 5 pm.

But the **park**, now a state botanical park, is the main attraction. On weekends it's packed with Czech families, but on a drizzly weekday morning you could have the exotic gardens, sweet-smelling woods and three artificial lakes literally to yourself. In May, rhododendrons come out in rainbows.

The park is open daily, from 7 am to 7 pm from April to October and from 8 am to 5 pm the rest of the year. Admission is 10 Kč (5 Kč for children aged six to 15 and students). A map of the park, with some English text, is available at the entrance.

Getting There & Away

Buses to Průhonice leave from the ČSAD (not city bus) stand at Opatov metro station – but not many. On weekdays, several leave at commuter times (from about 5.30 to 7 am), one around 10 am and a couple at midday. Late buses back include departures around 4.45, 6.45 and 8 pm. Update these with PIS or ČSAD before you go. On weekends there are fewer buses. The 15 minute trip costs about 15 Kč.

EXCURSIONS

KONOPIŠTĚ
☎ 0301

The French-style castle at Konopiště dates from 1300. It had a neo-Gothic face-lift in the 1890s from its best-known owner, Archduke Franz Ferdinand, heir to the Austro-Hungarian throne, whose 1914 assassination set off WWI.

The archduke was an obsessive hunter, as you will see from a tour through the wood-panelled castle, packed with a grossly over-the-top collection of dead animals and an armoury of hunting weapons. In 25 years, he dispatched several hundred thousand creatures on the 225 hectare estate (and kept a tally of them all).

Nowadays the animals are back, and the English-style wooded grounds, dotted with lakes, gardens and statuary, are really the best reason to visit – and a relaxing antidote to the heavy tourist scene around the castle.

Orientation & Information

The nearest town is Benešov. Its train and bus stations are opposite one another and less than five minutes on foot from the town square, Masarykovo náměstí (turn left out of the train station, then right at Tyršova). The IPB bank on the square has a currency exchange and a Visa/MasterCard ATM.

The castle is 2km from town, a fine half-hour walk through the estate. Cross the bridge over the railway, take the first left into Ke stadiónu and the third right down Spartakládní. Drivers can go straight down Konopištská from the bridge.

The Castle

You have a choice of three tours, which tend to become little more than tedious inventories. For tours I and II (45 minutes each) you can join a Czech group for under 60 Kč, or take a 110 Kč English tour. The 60 minute tour III is 120 Kč in Czech or 240 Kč in English, making it the most expensive attraction in the Prague region.

All three take in the archduke's trophies, a forest of mounted heads, antlers, claws and teeth. **Tour I** also looks at the stately rooms with their Italian cabinets, Dürer graphics and Meissen porcelain. **Tour II** takes in hunting weapons, the chapel and a plush men's party room. **Tour III**, limited to groups of eight, is the most interesting and intimate, taking in the archduke's living quarters and the music salon of Princess Sophie.

If that's not enough, go round the back of the chateau to see the archduke's St George fetish: scores of paintings, statues and other renderings of the mythical dragon-slayer (and what you see here is only some 10% of the hoard).

The castle is open May to August from 9 am to noon and 1 to 5 pm; September to 4 pm; and April and October to 3 pm (weekends to 4 pm). The last tour starts one hour before closing time. The St George collection is open from May to August from 9 am to 1 pm and 2 to 5 pm; and during April, September and October on weekends only to 4 pm. Everything is closed on Monday, and the St George collection also on 14 April and 17 June.

Places to Stay & Eat

At the castle's car park is *Hotel Nová Myslivna* (☎ 224 96), with a touristy restaurant and plain doubles for 500 Kč with breakfast.

Benešov Cheapest is a 200 Kč hostel bed at the *Sport Hotel* (☎ 229 03), in the winter stadium (*zimní stadión*), off Hrázského in the eastern part of town.

The *Hotel Pošta* (☎ 210 71, Tyršova 162), off Masarykovo náměstí, has plain rooms with toilet and shower for 380/760 Kč (the price can more than double during busy times), and a breakfast restaurant.

Two monster motels sit south-west of town at the edge of the Konopiště estate. *Motel Švarc* (☎ 256 11, Ke stadiónu) has adequate doubles with toilet and shower for 820 Kč, plus a restaurant and 24 hour snack bar. *Motel Konopiště* (☎ 227 32), with modern rooms for 1450/1776 Kč, also has a *camping ground*, open from May to September.

Adequate cheap eats (main dishes 70 to 180 Kč) are available at the ***Hostinec U zlaté hvězdy*** pub in a corner of Masarykovo náměstí.

Getting There & Away

From Prague's main station, Benešov is a pleasant train ride through broadly rolling farmland and forests. There are 10 fast trains a day, taking just over one hour. Alternatively, coaches depart from Florenc and from Roztyly metro station about every two or three hours, taking 1½ hours. On weekdays there are at least four buses a day between Benešov and Konopiště castle.

ČESKÝ ŠTERNBERK
☎ 0303

This hulking castle, on a sheer ridge above the Sázava River, dates from the 13th century. It probably owes its survival not only to its impregnable position, but to being owned by the same family, the Sternbergs (Šternberk to the Czechs), for almost its entire life.

It succumbed to heavy baroque remodelling in the 17th and 18th centuries, and the only remaining traces of its Gothic personality are in the fortifications. Nowadays its most impressive features are the views – up from the river, and out from the castle windows. The scenery on the train journey up the Sázava River valley is itself worth the ride.

Don't get off at Český Šternberk station, but one stop on at Český Šternberk zastávka, across the river from the castle. A road and a shorter footpath climb around behind the castle.

The Castle

The tedious 45 minute tour reveals an Italian baroque renovation, very heavy on stucco ornamentation. Highlights include the rococo **St Sebastian Chapel** (kaple sv Šebestiána) and the **'Yellow Room'**, with fine views over the countryside. From here you can see trees marking out a 17th century French-style park across the river, the only part of a planned Sternberg chateau

that was completed before the money ran out.

The castle is open from June to August from 9 am to 6 pm, May and September to 5 pm. In April and October it opens only on weekends and holidays, to 4 pm. It's closed Monday. Tours in Czech cost 35 Kč (in other languages they're 95 Kč) and the last one commences an hour before closing time.

Places to Stay & Eat

Just above the rail stop (zastávka) is the ***Parkhotel Český Šternberk*** (☎ 551 68, fax 551 08), with smallish, clean rooms with shower for 540 Kč per person (with breakfast), and a restaurant. About 1km upstream from the castle is the small ***Pension Frigera***. The ***Hotel Vesna*** (☎/fax 551 02) is at a quiet spot on the river, a 25 minute trek downstream on the castle side, but it was closed when we were there.

The castle has a pricey ***vinárna***, and the ***Restaurace pod hradem*** in the hamlet below has cheap eats.

Getting There & Away

Change at Čerčany on the railway line to Benešov (see the earlier Konopiště section). From there, trains lumber up the Sázava valley about every two hours, taking about one hour to reach Český Šternberk.

KUTNÁ HORA
☎ 0327

It's hard to imagine today, but in its time this was Bohemia's most important town after Prague. In 1996 it was added to UNESCO's World Heritage List.

In the late 13th century, silver ore was found in these hills, and a town sprouted. In 1308, Wenceslas II imported a team of Italian minters and established his central Royal Mint here. The town's power grew, splendid churches and palaces rose, and in 1400 Wenceslas IV moved the royal residence here. In less than 150 years Kutná Hora had become one of Europe's biggest, richest towns, and Bohemia's economic mainstay.

EXCURSIONS

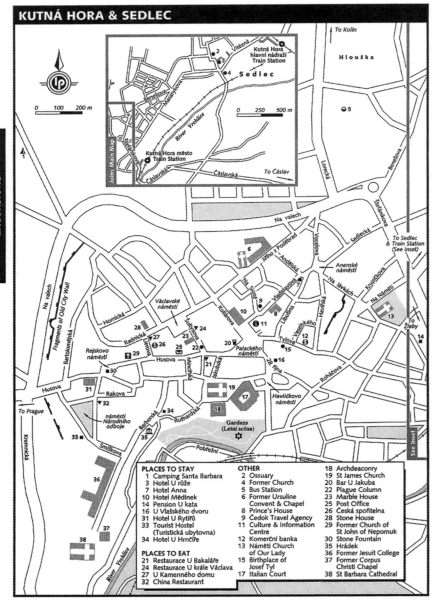

KUTNÁ HORA & SEDLEC

PLACES TO STAY
1 Camping Santa Barbara
3 Hotel U růže
7 Hotel Anna
10 Hotel Medínek
14 Pension U kata
16 U Vlašského dvoru
31 Hotel U Rytířů
33 Tourist Hostel
    (Turistická ubytovna)
34 Hotel U Hrnčíře

PLACES TO EAT
21 Restaurace U Bakaláře
24 Restaurace U krále Václava
27 U Kamenného domu
32 China Restaurant

OTHER
2 Ossuary
4 Former Church
5 Bus Station
6 Former Ursuline
  Convent & Chapel
8 Prince's House
9 Čedok Travel Agency
11 Culture & Information
   Centre
12 Komerční banka
13 Náměti Church
   of Our Lady
15 Birthplace of
   Josef Tyl
17 Italian Court

18 Archdeaconry
19 St James Church
20 Bar U Jakuba
22 Plague Column
23 Marble House
25 Post Office
26 Česká spořitelna
28 Stone House
29 Former Church of
   St John of Nepomuk
30 Stone Fountain
35 Hrádek
36 Former Jesuit College
37 Former Corpus
   Christi Chapel
38 St Barbara Cathedral

But in the 16th century the silver began to run out and decline set in, hastened by the Thirty Years' War. A baroque building boom came to an end with a devastating fire in 1770.

Today Kutná Hora is a fraction of its old self, but still dressed up in a collection of fine architectural monuments. With a pastel-hued square dotted with cafés, medieval alleys with façades ranging from Gothic to Cubist, and a cathedral to rival St Vitus, comparisons with Prague are hard to resist. Kutná Hora is certainly as densely picturesque as Prague, and blessed with warmer people and lower prices.

Orientation

The historical centre is compact enough to see on foot. Most attractions lie between the central square, Palackého náměstí, and the Cathedral of St Barbara in the south-western corner of town.

The bus station is a five minute walk north of the town centre. Although there's a train station near Kutná Hora's old town, trains from Prague stop only at Sedlec, 3km to the north-east.

The user-friendly town centre has almost too many signs. Quite a few places accommodate disabled visitors. Chronological (red) house numbers are in more common use than sequential (blue) ones.

Information

The helpful Culture & Information Centre (Kulturní a informační centrum; ☎ 51 23 78, fax 51 55 56, email kv.info.kh@ pha.pvtnet.cz, Web site webhouse.cz /kutna_hora), Palackého náměstí 377, can arrange accommodation, tours and guides. In summer the centre is open daily from 9 am to 7 pm (to 6 pm at weekends), and in winter it's open from 9 am to 5 pm on weekdays only.

The centre also has a terminal for Internet access, at 50 Kč per half-hour. A good 30 page booklet about the town is available from the centre, from Čedok (on the corner of Vladislavova and Na Sioně) and from newsagents.

Komerční banka is at Tylova 9/390, and Česká spořitelna has a Visa/Plus ATM at Lierova 148/2.

Italian Court (Vlašský Dvůr)

The Vlašský dvůr, on Havlíčkovo náměstí, was built by Wenceslas II as a royal seat and later became the Royal Mint. The old Czech name refers to its original Italian architects. A palace, chapel and tower were added a century later by Wenceslas IV, who made it his home.

When the mint closed in the early 18th century it became the town hall. The 20 Kč guided tour with translated text (or 50 Kč for a foreign-language tour) is worth it for a look at the few historical rooms open to the public. Tours are offered daily from 9 am – to 6 pm from April to October, to 4 pm in November and December, and to 5 pm the rest of the year.

The oldest remaining part, the (now bricked-up) niches in the courtyard, were **minters' workshops**. The original **treasury rooms** now hold an exhibit on coins and minting.

In Wenceslas IV's **Audience Hall** are 19th century murals of two important events that took place here: the 1471 election of Vladislav II Jagiello as king (the angry man in white is Matthias Corvinus, the loser), and an agreement between Wenceslas IV and Jan Hus (then rector of Charles University) to alter the university's German/Czech ratio.

About all that remains of Wenceslas IV's **Chapel of SS Wenceslas & Vladislav** (kaple sv Václava a Vladislava) is the oriel, which is best seen from the courtyard – although the 1904 Art Nouveau interior renovation is very striking.

The **Galérie Félixe Jeneweina**, just inside the courtyard, has changing art exhibits with the same opening hours as the mint.

From Vlašský Dvůr to St Barbara

Around the corner from Vlašský dvůr is the huge **St James Church** (kostel sv Jakuba), begun in 1330 but only completed a century later. Passing south of the church, you come to Ruthardská, a very old and photogenic lane running up beside the old town walls. It's named after Rozina Ruthard who, according to local legend, was sealed alive in a closet by her father, a medieval burgher.

At the top of the lane is the **Hrádek** (Little Castle), originally part of the town's fortifications. It was rebuilt in the 15th century as the residence of Jan Smíšek, administrator of the royal mines, who grew rich from silver he illegally mined right under the building. It's now the Museum of Silver and Medieval Mining, open daily except Monday, from 9 am to 6 pm (to 5 pm from October to April); admission costs 35 Kč. Non-claustrophobes can go down into Smíšek's tunnel for an extra 55 Kč.

The approach to the cathedral up Barborská ulice is between 13 crumbling **Gothic statues** and the former **Jesuit College** (1700), the biggest in the Czech Republic after Prague's Klementinum.

Cathedral of St Barbara (Kostel Sv Barbora)

The miners' guilds of Kutná Hora pipped Prague in the cathedral department: their Gothic masterpiece dedicated to the patron saint of miners is one of the finest Gothic churches in Europe.

Work was started in 1380, interrupted during the Hussite Wars and abandoned in 1558 when the silver began to run out. The rear (western) end was completed in neo-Gothic style only at the end of the 19th century.

Inside, eight **ambulatory chapels** surround the main altar, some with vivid frescoes – including mining scenes – dating from the 15th century. The lofty, bright **ceiling vault** is covered in a tangle of ribs, stars and floral patterns, and the coats of arms of the miners' guilds and local nobility. In the south-west chapel are **murals** of 15th century minters at work. The northwest chapel has an eye-popping mural of the *Vision of St Ignatius*.

The cathedral is open daily from 8 am to 5 pm in summer, and daily except Monday from 9 to 11.30 am and 2 to 3.30 pm in winter (entry is 20 Kč, including English text). On the hillside below the cathedral is the former **Corpus Christi Chapel** (kaple Božího těla), built in the 14th century.

Other Attractions

From the Jesuit College, walk through náměstí Národního odboje and turn left on Husova to see bits of the **old city walls**. Return along Husova to Rejskovo náměstí, with its 1495 Gothic Stone Fountain (Kamenná kašna).

Cross via Lierova to Radnická. The Gothic confection at No 183 is the **Stone House** (Kamenný dům), a burgher's house dating from 1490, now used for summer art exhibitions (open daily except Monday, from 9 am to 11.30 am and noon to 5 pm). Pop in just to see the inside of the house.

East and then south is Šultysova, once part of the town's medieval marketplace, and lined with handsome town-houses, in particular the **Marble House** (dům U Mramorů) at No 173. At the bottom of the street is a 1715 **plague column**.

Across Palackého náměstí, walk down Tylova to No 507, the **birthplace of Josef Tyl**, the 19th century playwright who wrote *Kde domov můj?* (Where Is My Home?) This later became part of the Czech national anthem. On the baroque façade is a statue of three miners.

Cross the square again to Kollárova and turn right on Jiřího z Poděbrad. Two blocks down is the former **Ursuline Convent** (klášter Voršilek), with a 1743 chapel by Kilian Dientzenhofer. In the convent there's an exhibit of furnishings from various chateaux in central Bohemia, open daily from 9 am to 5 pm from May to September, and to 4 pm on weekends only in April and October.

Places to Stay

Camping Santa Barbara (☎ 51 20 51 or 51 29 51) is north-west of town off Česká, near the cemetery.

At the budget end, the best place to stay is the year-round tourist hostel *Turistická ubytovna* (☎ 51 34 63, 51 49 61 or 0603 71 16 35, *náměstí Národního odboje 56*), with 160 Kč beds in rooms of six, communal shower and toilet, and a little kitchen (140 Kč with a youth or student card). Reception is open only from 4.30 to 5.30 pm. Rooms with shower and toilet at *Pension U kata* (☎ 51 50 96, *Uhelná 569*) are good value at 200 Kč per person. Many private homes have *Zimmer frei* (rooms for rent) signs, or you can book their rooms at the Culture & Information Centre for around 300 to 450 Kč per person.

Two good pensions are in listed 14th century buildings. Quiet *U Rytířů* (☎ 51 22 56, *Rejskovo náměstí 123*) has rooms of all kinds from 320 Kč per double. Romantic *Hotel U Hrnčíře* (☎ 51 21 13, *Barborská 24*) has plain doubles with shower and toilet for 500 to 1000 Kč per person, including breakfast.

Hotel Anna (☎/fax 51 63 15, *Vladislavova 372*) offers comfortable, modern rooms with shower, TV and breakfast, starting at 665/930 Kč. At the modern *Hotel U Vlašského dvoru* (☎ 51 46 18, fax 51 46 27, *28.října 511*), bright doubles with shower cost upwards of 1290 Kč, including breakfast. The run-down *Hotel Mědínek* (☎ 51 27 41, *Palackého náměstí*) offers overpriced singles/doubles with TV, toilet and bath for 740/1140 Kč, including breakfast.

Places to Eat

A few restaurants stay open until 11 pm. The *China Restaurant* (☎ 51 41 51, *náměstí Národního odboje 48*) serves respectable Chinese dishes costing from around 65 to 270 Kč, and helpings are generous; it's closed from 2 to 5 pm and on Monday.

Romantic, candle-lit *Restaurace U krále Václava* (*Šultysova 164*) offers inventive Bohemian dishes from 70 to 165 Kč; try *Šíp Mlýnských lovců* (The Arrow of the Hunters of Mlýn): beef and sausage with vegetable rice.

Restaurace U Bakaláře (☎ 51 25 47, *Husova 103*) has distracted service but

delicious chicken dishes (from 35 to 95 Kč), meatless main courses and pricier venison specials.

U Kamenného domu (*Lierova 4/147*) is a cheerful pub with cheap grub, and *Bar U Jakuba* (*Palackého náměstí*) has Guinness on tap.

Getting There & Away

Kutná Hora is about 70km south-east of Prague. By car, the fastest route is Highway 12 via Kolín and Sedlec; the prettiest is road 333 via Kostelec.

Several daily fast trains, taking about one hour, go to Kutná Hora hlavní nádraží (main station) in Sedlec, including four from Prague's main station and one from Masarykovo; and at least eight local trains, taking up to 1½ hours, go from Masarykovo. Each has a good connection by local train (taking eight minutes) to Kutná Hora město station, adjacent to the old town. There are also local buses (see Getting Around).

Long-distance buses take about 1¼ hours from Prague's Florenc station, departing about six times per weekday. There are also some local buses from Želivského metro station; however, there are few services on Sunday and almost none on Saturday.

Getting Around

Local (*městská doprava*) buses on Masarykova ulice go to/from Sedlec and the train station about hourly on weekdays, less often on weekends. Buy a ticket from the driver (4 Kč).

AROUND KUTNÁ HORA
Sedlec & the Ossuary Chapel of All Saints

Today Sedlec is a suburb of Kutná Hora, but it's been around longer, since the founding of Bohemia's first Cistercian monastery here in 1142.

After a 13th century abbot brought back some earth from Jerusalem and sprinkled it on the monastery's graveyard, its popularity mushroomed. Demand for grave plots was augmented by plague epidemics;

EXCURSIONS

within a century there were tens of thousands of graves, and bones began to pile up. The small 14th century All Saints' Chapel (kaple Všech svatých) was pressed into service as an ossuary.

When Joseph II abolished the monasteries, the Schwarzenberg family bought this one, and in 1870 a Czech woodcarver named František Rint turned the bones into the ghoulish artistic attraction you can see in the chapel cellar today. There are bone chalices and bone crosses; the Schwarzenberg coat of arms in bones; and an extraordinary chandelier made from at least one of every bone in the human body. Rint even signed his name in bones, at the foot of the stairs.

The ossuary is open in summer from 8 am to noon and 1 to 6 pm; in October to 5 pm; and in winter from 9 am to noon and 1 to 4 pm. It's open daily in July and August, and daily except Monday during the rest of the year. Admission costs 30 Kč, plus 30 Kč if you want to take photos or 50 Kč to video.

Down on the main road is the monastery's **Church of the Ascension of the Virgin** (kostel Nanebevzetí Panny Marie), renovated at the beginning of the 18th century by Giovanni Santini in his 'baroque-Gothic' style, unique to Bohemia. Nearby, the old monastery is now part of a tobacco factory and is closed to the public.

Places to Stay The *Hotel U růže (☎/fax 52 41 15, Zámecká 52)*, next to the ossuary, has clean, modern doubles with bath and TV for 1300 Kč.

Getting There & Away The ossuary is 2km from Kutná Hora by local bus. Some buses stop by the church, and some opposite the ossuary, two blocks up Zámecká from the church.

Žleby Chateau

This beautiful chateau, 18km south-east of Kutná Hora, dates from at least the 13th century. Its fairy-tale appearance – a sugary Gothic-Renaissance style meant to conjure up romantic visions of medieval castles – is the result of renovation by Duke Vincent Karl Auersperg in the late 19th century.

The Auerspergs lived here until 1945, when they fled to Austria, leaving everything behind. The chateau is therefore in immaculate – and authentic – shape, offering a glimpse of how the other half lived in Czechoslovakia earlier this century.

Inside it's all armour and mounted firearms, wood panelling and leather wallpaper, rococo flourishes and a treasure trove of old furniture. Highlights include the **Knights' Hall**, with a huge baroque cupboard and rows of Czech and German glass; the **Duchess Study**, with a replica Rubens on the ceiling and a fantastic door of inlaid wood; and the **kitchen**, fitted out with the 19th century's most up-to-date equipment.

From May to September the chateau is open daily except Monday, from 8 am to 4 pm (September from 9 am); in April and October it's open only on weekends from 9 am to 4 pm. It's also closed the day after each national holiday. Admission is 60 Kč. There are no crowds here, save for the occasional tour bus.

Getting There & Away The chateau is 55 minutes from Kutná Hora by bus. There are at least a dozen morning connections, but you must change at Čáslav. The whole trip takes about one hour. Get off at Žleby náměstí, the square at the foot of the chateau. Check return times, as buses peter out soon after 5 pm.

PŘEROV NAD LABEM

In this village east of Prague is the **Labe River Region Ethnographic Museum** (Polabské národopisné muzeum; ☎ 0325-978 72), the Czech Republic's oldest open-air museum of traditional architecture. It was begun in 1895, soon after the first such museum opened in Stockholm (the Swedish word for these museums, *skansen*, has stuck). Contrived as skansens are, they are a unique help in visualising life in an earlier time.

This one was started around an existing Přerov house: the 'Old Bohemian Cottage', dressed in herringbone clapboard and carved ornaments. Other exhibits have been brought in piecemeal from around the region: over a dozen houses have been reconstructed here, as well as bell towers, pigsties, decorated beehives and a pigeon house. Staff tend gardens and raise bees using traditional methods.

The museum is open from April to October, daily except Monday, from 9 am to 4 pm. It opens again in December (except the 24th and 31st) from 10 am to 4 pm, with a Christmas exhibition; admission costs 20 Kč. A detailed brochure is available, containing relevant information in English, at a cost of 10 Kč.

Getting There & Away

Trains from Prague's main station depart around 9.45 and 11.45 am (weekends about 1.15 pm plus Sunday about 9.45 am) for Čelákovice, where buses for Přerov meet the train; the whole trip takes about one hour. On Saturday only, there's also a direct bus to Přerov from Prague's Palmovka metro station, at about 11 am.

To get back on weekdays, a bus departs from Přerov at about 2 pm and reverses the route via Čelakovice, and a direct bus to Palmovka metro station leaves Přerov at about 4.15 pm. On Sunday there are direct buses at about 4.45 and 6 pm. The only way back on Saturday is on a bus at about 5 pm to Lysá nad Labem and then on a train from there. Check with PIS for information on current times.

Language

Czech (čeština) is the Czech Republic's main language. It belongs to the West Slavonic group of Indo-European languages, along with Slovak, Polish and Lusatian.

Lonely Planet's *Central Europe* and *Eastern Europe* phrasebooks have comprehensive Czech sections.

Pronunciation

It's not easy to learn Czech pronunciation, and you may have to abandon a few linguistic habits to do so (see the boxed text below). It is, however, spelt as it's spoken, and once you become familiar with the sounds, it's easy to read. Stress is usually on the first syllable.

Vowels

There are short and long vowels; the only difference is that long vowels take longer to say. Long vowels are indicated by an acute accent. The following approximations follow British pronunciation:

Bg Prdn?

The frustrating thing about Czech is its aversion to vowels. Many words contain nothing identifiable as a vowel. A famous tongue twister goes, *strč prst skrz krk*, which means 'stick your finger through your neck'. It's pronounced just as it's spelt!

---

a	as the 'ah' sound in 'cut'
á	as the 'a' in 'father'
e	as in 'bet'
é	as the word 'air'
i or **y**	as the 'u' in 'busy'
í or **ý**	as the 'ee' in 'see'
o	as in 'pot'
ó	as the 'aw' in 'saw'
u	as in 'pull'
ú or **ů**	as the 'oo' in 'zoo'

Diphthongs (Vowel Combinations)

aj	as the 'i' in 'ice'
áj	as the word 'eye'
au	an 'ow' sound as in 'out'
ej	as the 'ay' in 'day'
ij/yj	a short/long 'eey' sound
oj	as the 'oi' in 'void'
ou	as the 'o' in 'note', but both the 'o' and 'u' are more strongly pronounced than in English
uj/ůj	a short/long 'u' sound as in 'pull', followed by 'y'

Consonants

c	as the 'ts' in 'lets'
č	as the 'ch' in 'chew'
ch	a 'kh' sound, as in Scottish *loch*, or German *ich*
f	as the 'f' in 'fever', not as in 'of'
g	a hard sound like the 'g' in 'get'
h	as in 'he'
j	as the 'y' in 'year'
r	a rolled 'r', made by the tip of the tongue
ř	a rolled sound, 'rzh'; no English equivalent
s	as in 'sit', not as in 'rose'
š	as the 'sh' in 'ship'
ž	a 'zh' sound, as the 's' in 'treasure'
ď, ň, ť	very soft palatal sounds, ie consonants followed by a momentary contact between the tongue and the hard palate, as if a 'y' sound is added, as in the 'ny' in canyon. The same sound occurs with **d**, **n** and **t** followed by **i**, **í** or **ě**.

Greetings & Civilities

Hello/Good day.	*Dobrý den.*
	Ahoj. (ahoy) (informal)
Goodbye.	*Na shledano.* (NA-skhleh-dah-noh)
	Ahoj/čau. (informal)
Yes.	*Ano/*
	Jo. (informal)
No.	*Ne.*

Excuse me/Pardon.	*S dovolením.* (ZDO-vo-leh-nyeem)
May I? (Do you mind?)	*Dovolte mi?*
Sorry. (Excuse me/ Forgive me.)	*Promiňte.*
Please.	*Prosím.*
Thank you.	*Děkuji.* (DYEH-ku-yi)
You're welcome.	*Není zač.* (NYEH-ni-zahch)
Good morning.	*Dobré jitro/ Dobre ráno.*
Good afternoon.	*Dobré odpoledne.*
Good evening.	*Dobrý večer.*
Good night.	*Dobrou noc.*
How are you?	*Jak se máte?* (YAHK-seh MAA-teh)
Well, thanks.	*Děkuji, dobře.* (DYEH-ku-yi DOB-rzheh)

Language Difficulties

Do you speak English?	*Mluvíte anglicky?* (MLU-vee-teh AHN-glits-ki)
Does anyone speak English?	*Mluví někdo anglicky?* (MLU-vee NYEH-gdo AHN-glits-ki)
I speak a little ...	*Mluvím trochu ...*
I don't speak ...	*Nemluvím ...*
I understand.	*Rozumím.*
I don't understand.	*Nerozumím.*
Could you write that down?	*Napište mi to, prosím?*

Getting Around

What time does the train/bus leave?
Kdy odjíždí vlak/autobus?
What time does the train/bus arrive?
Kdy přijíždí vlak/autobus?
Excuse me, where is the ticket office?
Prosím, kde je pokladna?
I want to go to ...
Chci jít ... (khtsi yeet ...)

I'd like ...	*Rád bych ...*
a one-way ticket	*jednosměrnou jízdenku*
a return ticket	*zpáteční jízdenku*
two tickets	*dvě jízdenky*
a student's fare	*studentskou jízdenku*

Map Jargon

Terms you'll encounter on maps and throughout this book include the following:

dům	house
galérie	gallery, arcade
hora	mountain
hrad	castle
hřbitov	cemetery
kaple	chapel
kopec	hill
kostel	church
most	bridge
nábřeží	embankment (abbreviated *nábř*)
náměstí	square (abbreviated *nám*)
ostrov	island
palác	palace
potok	stream
řeka	river
sad(y)	garden(s), park(s), orchard(s)
silnice	road
třída	avenue
ulice	street (abbreviated *ul*)
ulička	lane
zahrada	gardens, park
zámek	chateau (live-in castle, manor)

1st class	*první třídu*
2nd class	*druhou třídu*
dining car	*jídelní vůz*
express	*rychlík*
local	*místní*
sleeping car	*spací vůz*

Directions

Where is ...?	*Kde je ...?* (GDEH yeh ...?)
Go straight ahead.	*Jděte přímo.*
Turn left ...	*Zatočte vlevo ...*
Turn right ...	*Zatočte vpravo ...*

behind	*za*
in front of	*před*
far	*daleko*
near	*blízko*
opposite	*naproti*

Accommodation

Do you have any rooms available?
Máte volné pokoje?
(MAA-teh VOL-neh PO-ko-yeh)
How much is it per night?
Kolik stojí jedna noc?
(KO-lik STO-yee YED-nah NOTS)

I'd like ...	*Přál bych si ...*
a single room	*jednolůžkový pokoj*
a double room	*dvoulůžkový pokoj*
a room with a	*pokoj s koupelnou*
bathroom	

cheap hotel	*levný hotel*
good hotel	*dobrý hotel*
nearby hotel	*blízký hotel*
bathroom	*koupelna*
room number	*číslo pokoje*
key	*klíč* (kleech)
toilet	*záchod* (ZAH-khot)/
	WC (veh-tseh)
men	*muži*
women	*ženy*
toilet paper	*toaletní papír*
cold/hot water	*studená/horká voda*
clean/dirty	*čistý/špinavý*

Signs

OTEVŘENO	Open
ZAVŘENO	Closed
VCHOD	Entrance
VÝCHOD	Exit
NOUZOVÝ	Emergency Exit
VÝCHOD	
INFORMACE	Information
VSTUP ZAKÁZÁN	No Entry
ZÁKAZ PARKOVÁNÍ	No Parking
ZÁKAZ KOUŘENÍ	No Smoking
PĚŠÍ ZÓNA	Pedestrian Zone
POLICIE	Police
TAM	Push
SEM	Pull
ZADÁNO	Reserved
WC/ZÁCHODY/	Toilets
TOALETY	
PÁNI or *MUŽI*	Men
DÁMY or *ŽENY*	Women

dark/light	*tmavý/světlý*
quiet/noisy	*tichý/hlučný*
cheap/expensive	*levný/drahý*

Around Town

I'm looking for	*Hledám ...*
(a/the) ...	
art gallery	*uměleckou galérii*
bank	*banku*
city centre	*centrum*
embassy	*velvyslanectví*
my hotel	*muj hotel*
main square	*hlavní náměstí*
market	*tržiště*
museum	*muzeum*
police	*policii*
post office	*poštu*
public toilet	*veřejné záchody*
telephone centre	*telefonní ústřednu*
tourist office	*turistické informační*
	středisko

What's the	*Jaký je kurs?*
exchange rate?	
What's the	*Jaký je poplatek?*
commission?	
Can I have my	*Můžete mě vrátit*
change?	*drobné?*

Time & Dates

What time is it?	*Kolik je hodin?*
When?	*Kdy?* (gdee)

in the morning	*ráno*
in the afternoon	*odpoledne*
in the evening	*večer*
today	*dnes*
now	*teď*
yesterday	*včera*
tomorrow	*zítra*
next week	*příští týden*

Days of the Week

Monday	*pondělí*
	(PON-dyeh-lee)
Tuesday	*úterý* (OO-teh-ree)
Wednesday	*středa* (STRZHEH-da)
Thursday	*čtvrtek* (CHTVR-tek)
Friday	*pátek* (PAA-tek)
Saturday	*sobota* (SO-bo-tah)
Sunday	*neděle* (NEH-dyeh-leh)

Dates in Museums

year	*rok*
century	*století*
millennia	*milénium* or *tisíciletí*
beginning of ...	*začátek ...*
first half of ...	*první polovina ...*
middle of ...	*polovina ...*
second half of ...	*druhá polovina ...*
end of ...	*konec ...*
around ...	*kolem ...*

Numbers

It's quite common for Czechs to say the numbers 21 to 99 in reverse; for example, *dvacet jedna* (21) becomes *jedna dvacet*.

0	*nula* (NU-la)
1	*jedna* (YED-na)
2	*dva* (dva)
3	*tři* (trzhi)
4	*čtyři* (CHTI-rzhi)
5	*pět* (pyet)
6	*šest* (shest)
7	*sedm* (SEH-dm)
8	*osm* (OH-sm)
9	*devět* (DEH-vyet)
10	*deset* (DEH-set)
11	*jedenáct* (YEH-deh-naatst)
12	*dvanáct* (DVAH-naatst)
13	*třináct* (TRZHI-naatst)
14	*čtrnáct* (CHTR-naatst)
15	*patnáct* (PAHT-naatst)
16	*šestnáct* (SHEST-naatst)
17	*sedmnáct* (SEH-dm-naatst)
18	*osmnáct* (OH-sm-naatst)
19	*devatenáct* (DEH-vah-teh-naatst)
20	*dvacet* (DVAH-tset)
21	*dvacet jedna*
22	*dvacet dva*
23	*dvacet tři*
30	*třicet* (TRZHI-tset)
40	*čtyřicet* (CHTI-rzhi-tset)
50	*padesát* (PAH-deh-saat)
60	*šedesát* (SHEH-deh-saat)
70	*sedmdesát* (SEH-dm-deh-saat)
80	*osmdesát* (OH-sm-deh-saat)
90	*devadesát* (DEH-vah-deh-saat)
100	*sto*
1000	*tisíc* (TYI-seets)
one million	*milión*

Emergencies

Help!	*Pomoc!* (PO-mots)
Please, call ...	*Prosím, zavolejte ...!*
a doctor	*doktora*
an ambulance	*sanitku*
the police	*policii*
dentist	*zubní lékař/zubař*
doctor	*doktor*
hospital	*nemocnice* (NEH-mots-nyi-tseh)
I'm ill.	*Jsem nemocný.* (m)
	Jsem nemocná. (f)
I'm lost.	*Zabloudil jsem.* (m)
	Zabloudila jsem. (f)
Where is the police station?	*Kde je policejní stanice?*
Where are the toilets?	*Kde jsou záchody?*
Could you help me please?	*Prosím, můžete mi pomoci?*
I wish to contact my embassy/consulate.	*Přeju si mluvit s mým velvyslanectvím/konzulátem.*

FOOD GLOSSARY
At the Restaurant

Bon appétit!	*Dobrou chuť!*
Cheers!	*Nazdraví!*
Table for ..., please.	*Stůl pro ... osob, prosím.*
The menu, please.	*Jídelní lístek, prosím.*
What is today's special?	*Jaká je specialita dne?*
I am a vegetarian.	*Jsem vegetarián.* (m)
	Jsem vegetariánka. (f)
The bill, please.	*Účet, prosím.*

Utensils

ashtray	*popelník*
drink	*pití*
fork	*vidlička*
glass	*sklenice*
knife	*nůž*
plate	*talíř*
spoon	*lžíce*
toothpick	*párátko*

LANGUAGE

Food & Condiments

biftek	beefsteak
brambory	potato
česnek	garlic
chléb	bread
cibule	onion
citrón	lemon
cukr	sugar
džem	jam
fazole	beans
houby	mushrooms
hovězí (maso)	beef
hranolky	chips/French fries
hrášek	peas
játra	liver
karbanátek	hamburger
kmín	caraway
knedlíky	dumplings
kotleta	cutlet/chop
křen	horseradish
kuře	chicken
květák	cauliflower
máslo	butter
maso	meat
med	honey
mrkev	carrot
okurka	cucumber/pickle
ovoce	fruit
paprika	capsicum
pepř	pepper
rajče	tomato
řízek	cutlet
ryba	fish
rýže	rice
smetana	cream

špenát	spinach
sterelizované zelí/	pickled cabbage
sterelizovaná	
kapusta	
sůl	salt
šunka	ham
sýr	cheese
telecí (maso)	veal
těstoviny	pasta
tvaroh	cottage cheese
vejce	egg
míchaná vejce	scrambled egg
omeleta	omelette
smažená vejce	fried egg
vejce na měkko	soft-boiled egg
vejce na tvrdo	hard-boiled egg
vejce se slaninou	egg with bacon
vepřové (maso)	pork
žampiony	mushrooms
zelenina	vegetables
zelí	sauerkraut

Cooking Terms

čerstvý	fresh
domácí	home-made
dušený	steamed
grilovaný	grilled/on the spit
pečený	roasted/baked
roštěná or	broiled
na roštu	
sladký	sweet
smažený	fried
uzený	smoked
vařený	boiled

Glossary

You may encounter the following terms and abbreviations while in Prague. For other terms, see the Language chapter.

autobus – bus

benzín – petrol/gasoline
bez poplatku – free of charge

čajovna – tearoom
ČD – Czech Railways, the state railway company
Čedok – the former state tour operator and travel agency, now privatised
celnice – customs
čeština – the Czech language
chrám – cathedral
cizinec, cizinci (pl) – foreigner
ČSA – Czech Airlines, the national carrier
ČSAD – Czech Automobile Transport, the state bus company
ČSSD – Social Democratic Party
cukrárna – cake shop

dámy – sign on women's toilet
divadlo – theatre
dům – house or building

fin-de-siècle – relating to the end of the 19th century, as in *fin-de-siècle* architecture

galérie – gallery

h. (hod) – hour; designates the hour in a time
hlavní nádraží – main train station
hora – mountain
hospoda – pub
hostinec – pub
hrad – castle
hřbitov – cemetery

impuls, impulsů (pl) – 'beep' or time interval used for determining telephone charges

jídelní lístek – menu

jízdenka – ticket

kaple – chapel
kavárna – café or coffee shop
Kč (Koruna česká) – Czech crown
kino – cinema
knihkupectví – bookshop
kolky – duty stamps, for payment at certain government offices, such as for a visa extension; sold at post offices and elsewhere
kostel – church

lekárna – pharmacy
lístek – ticket

maso uzeniny – meat, smoked meat and sausages
město – town
místenka – reservation (such as on a train)
most – bridge
muži – sign on men's toilet

nafta – diesel fuel
natural – unleaded petrol/gasoline
nábřezí – embankment
nádraží – station
náměstí – square
nemocnice – hospital

ODS – Civic Democratic Party
ostrov – island
otevřeno – open (such as a shop)
ovoce – fruit

palác – palace
paragon – receipt or docket
páni – sign on men's toilet
pekárna – bakery
pěší zóna – pedestrian zone
pivnice – small beer hall
pivovar – brewery
pivo – beer
platební karta – credit card
potok – creek
potraviny – grocery or food shop
Praha – Prague's Czech name

prádelna – laundry
přestup – transfer or connection

sad(y) – garden(s), park(s), orchard(s)
samizdat – underground press during communist years
samoobsluha – supermarket
samoobslužná prádelna – self-service laundry
sem – pull (sign on door)
sgraffito – mural technique in which the top layer of plaster is scraped away or incised to reveal the layer underneath
skansen – open-air museum of traditional architecture
sv (svatý) – Saint

tam – push (sign on door)
taximetr – taxi meter
tel. č – telephone number
toaletní papír – toilet paper
toalet – toilet
tramvaj – tram
třída – avenue

ubytovna – accommodation, usually of the dormitory-style
účet volaného – a collect or reverse-charges call

ulice – street
uložené zásilky – poste restante
úschovna – left-luggage office

vé cé (WC) – toilet
'Velvet Divorce' – separation of Czechoslovakia into fully independent Czech and Slovak republics in 1993
'Velvet Revolution' – bloodless overthrow of Czechoslovakia's communist regime in 1989
věž – tower
vinárna – wine bar
vlak – train
vstup – entrance
vstup zakázán – no entry
výstup – exit

zadáno – reserved
zahrada – gardens, park
zakázán – prohibited
zastávka – bus, tram or train stop
zavřeno – closed (such as a shop)
záchod – toilet
zámek – chateau
zelenina – vegetables
ženy – sign on women's toilet
Zimmer frei – German for 'rooms free', that is rooms for rent

LONELY PLANET

Phrasebooks

Lonely Planet phrasebooks are packed with essential words and phrases to help travellers communicate with the locals. With colour tabs for quick reference, an extensive vocabulary and use of script, these handy pocket-sized language guides cover day-to-day travel situations.

- handy pocket-sized books
- easy to understand Pronunciation chapter
- clear & comprehensive Grammar chapter
- romanisation alongside script to allow ease of pronunciation
- script throughout so users can point to phrases for every situation
- full of cultural information and tips for the traveller

'...vital for a real DIY spirit and attitude in language learning'
– *Backpacker*

'the phrasebooks have good cultural backgrounders and offer solid advice for challenging situations in remote locations'
– *San Francisco Examiner*

Arabic (Egyptian) • Arabic (Moroccan) • Australian *(Australian English, Aboriginal and Torres Strait languages)* • Baltic States *(Estonian, Latvian, Lithuanian)* • Bengali • Brazilian • Burmese • Cantonese • Central Asia • Central Europe *(Czech, French, German, Hungarian, Italian, Slovak)* • Eastern Europe *(Bulgarian, Czech, Hungarian, Polish, Romanian, Slovak)* • Ethiopian (Amharic) • Fijian • French • German • Greek • Hill Tribes • Hindi/Urdu • Indonesian • Italian • Japanese • Korean • Lao • Latin American Spanish • Malay • Mandarin • Mediterranean Europe *(Albanian, Croatian, Greek, Italian, Macedonian, Maltese, Serbian, Slovene)* • Mongolian • Nepali • Papua New Guinea • Pilipino (Tagalog) • Quechua • Russian • Scandinavian Europe *(Danish, Finnish, Icelandic, Norwegian, Swedish)* • South-East Asia *(Burmese, Indonesian, Khmer, Lao, Malay, Tagalog Pilipino, Thai, Vietnamese)* • Spanish (Castilian) *(also includes Catalan, Galician and Basque)* • Sri Lanka • Swahili • Thai • Tibetan • Turkish • Ukrainian • USA *(US English, Vernacular Talk, Native American languages, Hawaiian)* • Vietnamese • Western Europe *(Basque, Catalan, Dutch, French, German, Greek, Irish)*

Lonely Planet Journeys

JOURNEYS is a unique collection of travel writing – published by the company that understands travel better than anyone else. It is a series for anyone who has ever experienced – or dreamed of – the magical moment when they encountered a strange culture or saw a place for the first time. They are tales to read while you're planning a trip, while you're on the road or while you're in an armchair, in front of a fire.

These outstanding titles explore our planet through the eyes of a diverse group of international writers. JOURNEYS books catch the spirit of a place, illuminate a culture, recount a crazy adventure, or introduce a fascinating way of life. They always entertain, and always enrich the experience of travel.

MALI BLUES
Traveling to an African Beat
Lieve Joris (translated by Sam Garrett)
Drought, rebel uprisings, ethnic conflict: these are the predominant images of West Africa. But as Lieve Joris travels in Senegal, Mauritania and Mali, she meets survivors, fascinating individuals charting new ways of living between tradition and modernity. With her remarkable gift for drawing out people's stories, Joris brilliantly captures the rhythms of a world that refuses to give in.

THE GATES OF DAMASCUS
Lieve Joris (translated by Sam Garrett)
This best-selling book is a beautifully drawn portrait of day-to-day life in modern Syria. Through her intimate contact with local people, Lieve Joris draws us into the fascinating world that lies behind the gates of Damascus. Hala's husband is a political prisoner, jailed for his opposition to the Assad regime; through the author's friendship with Hala we see how Syrian politics impacts on the lives of ordinary people.

THE OLIVE GROVE
Travels in Greece
Katherine Kizilos
Katherine Kizilos travels to fabled islands, troubled border zones and her family's village deep in the mountains. She vividly evokes breathtaking landscapes, generous people and passionate politics, capturing the complexities of a country she loves.

'beautifully captures the real tensions of Greece' – *Sunday Times*

KINGDOM OF THE FILM STARS
Journey into Jordan
Annie Caulfield
Kingdom of the Film Stars is a travel book and a love story. With honesty and humour, Annie Caulfield writes of travelling in Jordan and falling in love with a Bedouin with film-star looks.

She offers fascinating insights into the country – from the tent life of traditional women to the hustle of downtown Amman – and unpicks tight-woven Western myths about the Arab world.

LONELY PLANET

Lonely Planet Travel Atlases

L onely Planet has long been famous for the number and quality of its guidebook maps. Now we've gone one step further and produced a handy companion series: Lonely Planet travel atlases – maps of a country produced in book form.

Unlike other maps, which look good but lead travellers astray, our travel atlases have been researched on the road by Lonely Planet's experienced team of writers. All details are carefully checked to ensure the atlas corresponds with the equivalent Lonely Planet guidebook.

- full-colour throughout
- maps researched and checked by Lonely Planet authors
- place names correspond with Lonely Planet guidebooks
- no confusing spelling differences
- legend and travelling information in English, French, German, Japanese and Spanish
- size: 230 x 160 mm

Available now: Chile & Easter Island ● Egypt ● India & Bangladesh ● Israel & the Palestinian Territories ● Jordan, Syria & Lebanon ● Kenya ● Laos ● Portugal ● South Africa, Lesotho & Swaziland ● Thailand ● Turkey ● Vietnam ● Zimbabwe, Botswana & Namibia

---

Lonely Planet TV Series & Videos

L onely Planet travel guides have been brought to life on television screens around the world. Like our guides, the programs are based on the joy of independent travel, and look honestly at some of the most exciting, picturesque and frustrating places in the world. Each show is presented by one of three travellers from Australia, England or the USA and combines an innovative mixture of video, Super-8 film, atmospheric soundscapes and original music.

Videos of each episode – containing additional footage not shown on television – are available from good book and video shops, but the availability of individual videos varies with regional screening schedules.

Video destinations include: Alaska ● American Rockies ● Australia – The South-East ● Baja California & the Copper Canyon ● Brazil ● Central Asia ● Chile & Easter Island ● Corsica, Sicily & Sardinia – The Mediterranean Islands ● East Africa (Tanzania & Zanzibar) ● Ecuador & the Galapagos Islands ● Greenland & Iceland ● Indonesia ● Israel & the Sinai Desert ● Jamaica ● Japan ● La Ruta Maya ● Morocco ● New York ● North India ● Pacific Islands (Fiji, Solomon Islands & Vanuatu) ● South India ● South West China ● Turkey ● Vietnam ● West Africa ● Zimbabwe, Botswana & Namibia

The Lonely Planet TV series is produced by: Pilot Productions
The Old Studio
18 Middle Row
London W10 5AT, UK

LONELY PLANET

Guides by Region

L onely Planet is known worldwide for publishing practical, reliable and no-nonsense travel information in our guides and on our Web site. The Lonely Planet list covers just about every accessible part of the world. Currently there are nine series: travel guides, shoestring guides, walking guides, city guides, phrasebooks, audio packs, travel atlases, diving and snorkeling guides and travel literature.

AFRICA Africa – the South • Africa on a shoestring • Arabic (Egyptian) phrasebook • Arabic (Moroccan) phrasebook • Cairo • Cape Town • Central Africa • East Africa • Egypt • Egypt travel atlas • Ethiopian (Amharic) phrasebook • The Gambia & Senegal • Kenya • Kenya travel atlas • Malawi, Mozambique & Zambia • Morocco • North Africa • South Africa, Lesotho & Swaziland • South Africa, Lesotho & Swaziland travel atlas • Swahili phrasebook • Trekking in East Africa • Tunisia • West Africa • Zimbabwe, Botswana & Namibia • Zimbabwe, Botswana & Namibia travel atlas
Travel Literature: The Rainbird: A Central African Journey • Songs to an African Sunset: A Zimbabwean Story • Mali Blues: Traveling to an African Beat

AUSTRALIA & THE PACIFIC Australia • Australian phrasebook • Bushwalking in Australia • Bushwalking in Papua New Guinea • Fiji • Fijian phrasebook • Islands of Australia's Great Barrier Reef • Melbourne • Micronesia • New Caledonia • New South Wales & the ACT • New Zealand • Northern Territory • Outback Australia • Papua New Guinea • Papua New Guinea (Pidgin) phrasebook • Queensland • Rarotonga & the Cook Islands • Samoa • Solomon Islands • South Australia • Sydney • Tahiti & French Polynesia • Tasmania • Tonga • Tramping in New Zealand • Vanuatu • Victoria • Western Australia
Travel Literature: Islands in the Clouds • Sean & David's Long Drive

CENTRAL AMERICA & THE CARIBBEAN Bahamas and Turks & Caicos • Bermuda • Central America on a shoestring • Costa Rica • Cuba • Eastern Caribbean • Guatemala, Belize & Yucatán: La Ruta Maya • Jamaica • Mexico • Mexico City • Panama
Travel Literature: Green Dreams: Travels in Central America

EUROPE Amsterdam • Andalucia • Austria • Baltic States phrasebook • Berlin • Britain • Central Europe • Central Europe phrasebook • Czech & Slovak Republics • Denmark • Dublin • Eastern Europe • Eastern Europe phrasebook • Estonia, Latvia & Lithuania • Finland • France • French phrasebook • Germany • German phrasebook • Greece • Greek phrasebook • Hungary • Iceland, Greenland & the Faroe Islands • Ireland • Italian phrasebook • Italy • Lisbon • London • Mediterranean Europe • Mediterranean Europe phrasebook • Paris • Poland • Portugal • Portugal travel atlas • Prague • Romania & Moldova • Russia, Ukraine & Belarus • Russian phrasebook • Scandinavian & Baltic Europe • Scandinavian Europe phrasebook • Slovenia • Spain • Spanish phrasebook • St Petersburg • Switzerland • Trekking in Spain • Ukrainian phrasebook • Vienna • Walking in Britain • Walking in Italy • Walking in Switzerland • Western Europe • Western Europe phrasebook
Travel Literature: The Olive Grove: Travels in Greece

INDIAN SUBCONTINENT Bangladesh • Bengali phrasebook • Bhutan • Delhi • Goa • Hindi/Urdu phrasebook • India • India & Bangladesh travel atlas • Indian Himalaya • Karakoram Highway • Nepal • Nepali phrasebook • Pakistan • Rajasthan • South India • Sri Lanka • Sri Lanka phrasebook • Trekking in the Indian Himalaya • Trekking in the Karakoram & Hindukush • Trekking in the Nepal Himalaya
Travel Literature: In Rajasthan • Shopping for Buddhas

LONELY PLANET

Mail Order

Lonely Planet products are distributed worldwide. They are also available by mail order from Lonely Planet, so if you have difficulty finding a title please write to us. North and South American residents should write to 150 Linden St, Oakland, CA 94607, USA; European and African residents should write to 10a Spring Place, London NW5 3BH, UK; and residents of other countries to PO Box 617, Hawthorn, Victoria 3122, Australia.

ISLANDS OF THE INDIAN OCEAN Madagascar & Comoros • Maldives • Mauritius, Réunion & Seychelles

MIDDLE EAST & CENTRAL ASIA Arab Gulf States • Central Asia • Central Asia phrasebook • Iran • Israel & the Palestinian Territories • Israel & the Palestinian Territories travel atlas • Istanbul • Jerusalem • Jordan & Syria • Jordan, Syria & Lebanon travel atlas • Lebanon • Middle East on a shoestring • Turkey • Turkish phrasebook • Turkey travel atlas • Yemen
Travel Literature: The Gates of Damascus • Kingdom of the Film Stars: Journey into Jordan

NORTH AMERICA Alaska • Backpacking in Alaska • Baja California • California & Nevada • Canada • Florida • Hawaii • Honolulu • Los Angeles • Miami • New England USA • New Orleans • New York City • New York, New Jersey & Pennsylvania • Pacific Northwest USA • Rocky Mountain States • San Francisco • Seattle • Southwest USA • USA phrasebook • Washington, DC & the Capital Region
Travel Literature: Drive Thru America

NORTH-EAST ASIA Beijing • Cantonese phrasebook • China • Hong Kong • Hong Kong, Macau & Guangzhou • Japan • Japanese phrasebook • Japanese audio pack • Korea • Korean phrasebook • Kyoto • Mandarin phrasebook • Mongolia • Mongolian phrasebook • North-East Asia on a shoestring • Seoul • South-West China • Taiwan • Tibet • Tibetan phrasebook • Tokyo
Travel Literature: Lost Japan

SOUTH AMERICA Argentina, Uruguay & Paraguay • Bolivia • Brazil • Brazilian phrasebook • Buenos Aires • Chile & Easter Island • Chile & Easter Island travel atlas • Colombia • Ecuador & the Galapagos Islands • Latin American Spanish phrasebook • Peru • Quechua phrasebook • Rio de Janeiro • South America on a shoestring • Trekking in the Patagonian Andes • Venezuela
Travel Literature: Full Circle: A South American Journey

SOUTH-EAST ASIA Bali & Lombok • Bangkok • Burmese phrasebook • Cambodia • Hill Tribes phrasebook • Ho Chi Minh City • Indonesia • Indonesian phrasebook • Indonesian audio pack • Jakarta • Java • Laos • Lao phrasebook • Laos travel atlas • Malay phrasebook • Malaysia, Singapore & Brunei • Myanmar (Burma) • Philippines • Pilipino (Tagalog) phrasebook • Singapore • South-East Asia on a shoestring • South-East Asia phrasebook • Thailand • Thailand's Islands & Beaches • Thailand travel atlas • Thai phrasebook • Thai audio pack • Vietnam • Vietnamese phrasebook • Vietnam travel atlas

ALSO AVAILABLE: Antarctica • Brief Encounters: Stories of Love, Sex & Travel • Chasing Rickshaws • Not the Only Planet: Travel Stories from Science Fiction • Travel with Children • Traveller's Tales

Lonely Planet Online
www.lonelyplanet.com *or* AOL keyword: lp

Whether you've just begun planning your next trip, or you're chasing down specific info on currency regulations or visa requirements, check out Lonely Planet Online for up-to-the minute travel information.

As well as mini guides to more than 250 destinations, you'll find maps, photos, travel news, health and visa updates, travel advisories, and discussion of the ecological and political issues you need to be aware of as you travel. You'll also find timely upgrades to popular guidebooks which you can print out and stick in the back of your book.

There's also an online travellers' forum where you can share your experience of life on the road, meet travel companions and ask other travellers for their recommendations and advice.

And of course we have a complete and up-to-date list of all Lonely Planet travel products including travel guides, diving and snorkelling guides, phrasebooks, atlases, travel literature and videos, and a simple online ordering facility if you can't find the book you want elsewhere.

Lonely Planet Diving & Snorkelling Guides

Known for indispensible guidebooks to destinations all over the world, Lonely Planet's Pisces Books are the most popular series of diving and snorkelling titles available.

There are three series: **Diving & Snorkelling Guides**, **Shipwreck Diving** series, and **Dive Into History**. Full colour throughout, the **Diving & Snorkelling Guides** combine quality photographs with detailed descriptions of the best dive sites for each location, giving divers a glimpse of what they can expect both on land and in water. The **Dive Into History** series is perfect for the adventure diver or armchair traveller. The **Shipwreck Diving** series provides all the details for exploring the most interesting wrecks in the Atlantic and Pacific oceans. The list also includes underwater nature and technical guides.

FREE Lonely Planet Newsletters

We love hearing from you and think you'd like to hear from us.

Planet Talk

Our FREE quarterly printed newsletter is full of tips from travellers and anecdotes from Lonely Planet guidebook authors. Every issue is packed with up-to-date travel news and advice, and includes:

- a postcard from Lonely Planet co-founder Tony Wheeler
- a swag of mail from travellers
- a look at life on the road through the eyes of a Lonely Planet author
- topical health advice
- prizes for the best travel yarn
- news about forthcoming Lonely Planet events
- a complete list of Lonely Planet books and other titles

To join our mailing list, residents of the UK, Europe and Africa can email us at go@lonelyplanet.co.uk; residents of North and South America can email us at info@lonelyplanet.com; the rest of the world can email us at talk2us@lonelyplanet.com.au, or contact any Lonely Planet office.

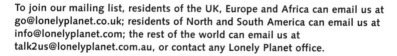

Comet

Our FREE monthly email newsletter brings you all the latest travel news, features, interviews, competitions, destination ideas, travellers' tips & tales, Q&As, raging debates and related links. Find out what's new on the Lonely Planet Web site and which books are about to hit the shelves.

Subscribe from your desktop: www.lonelyplanet.com/comet

Index

Text

Bold indicates maps.
Italics indicates boxed text.

Bold indicates maps.
Italics indicates boxed text.

Boxed Text

MAP 2 PRAGUE METRO

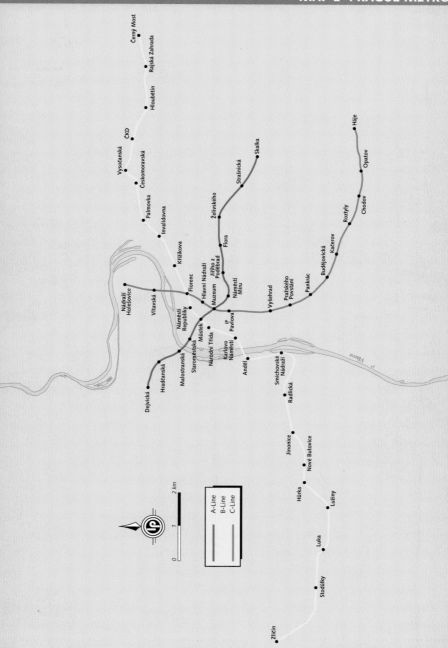

MAP 3

plavební kanál

0   200   400 m

Ve struhách

1 ■
Čínská

Koulova

Tram 20, 25

Zelená   Zelená
Ant. Čermáka

Nikoly
Tesly
2 ▼

3 ▼
Velflíkova

Maďarská

Terronská

4 ■

Lotyšská

Roosseveltova

Jugoslávských partyzánů

PRAHA 6

Stromovka

5 ●
Gotthardská

V. sadech

Wolkerova

K Starému

Verdunská

Českomalínska

Puškinovo
náměstí

Bubenečská

Pelléova

Sološnova

Národní obrany

6 ■

7 ●

Dejvická Ⓜ
evropská Tram 2, 20, 26, 57
Bubenečská

Vítězné
náměstí

Tram 2, 25, 26, 57

Na hutích

11 ▼

Národní obrany

Československé armády

Eliškova

Na Zátorce

Jaselská

Pod kaštany

Na Zátorce

Banskobystrická

Buzulucká

Kafkova

Generála Píky

9 ▼

Wuchterlova

Kafkova

Dejvická

12 ●

10 ✉

Václavková

Pod kaštany

15 ▼

14 ●
Dejvická

13

Hradčanská Ⓜ

Praha-
Dejvice

Tram 1, 8, 25, 26, 51, 56, 57

Pod hradbami

8 ⌀

Na valech

Na baště sv. Jiří

Tyršova

16

17 ●
Mickiewiczova

Tram 1, 8, 57
Badeniho

PRAHA 7

18 🏛

Kotkova

MAP 5

MAP 3

PLACES TO STAY
1 Holiday Inn
4 Berhanu Hostel & BITA
6 Hostel Orlík
20 Hotel Splendid
24 Hotel Belvedere

PLACES TO EAT
2 Pivnice U Švejka
3 Restaurace U Adély
9 Budvarka
11 Restaurant U cedru

15 Restaurace Sokolovna
21 Hong Kong Restaurant

OTHER
5 Dutch Embassy
7 Open-Air Market
8 Slovak Embassy
10 Post Office
12 Divadlo Spejbla a Hurvínka
13 Open-Air Market
14 Laundry Kings
16 Písek Gate

17 Canadian Embassy
18 Bílkova Vila
19 AC Sparta Praha Stadium
22 Post Office
23 National Technology Museum
25 Planetárium
26 Maroldovo Panorama
27 Křížík Fountain
28 Dětský svět
29 Spiral Theatre

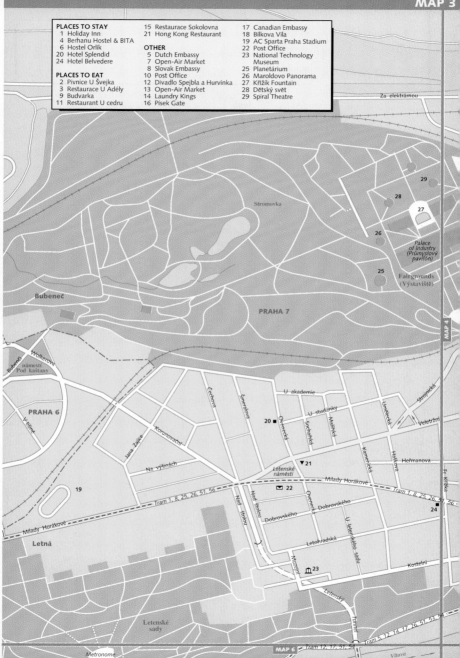

Za elektrárnou

MAP 4

29

28

27

Stromovka

26

25

Palace of Industry (Průmyslový pavilón)

Fairgrounds (Výstaviště)

Bubeneč

PRAHA 7

Wolkerova

Bubeneč náměstí Pod kaštany

PRAHA 6

V háji

Jana Zajíce

Korunovační

Čechova

Šimáčkova

Na výšinách

U akademie

U studánky

Ovenecká

Sochařská

Malířská

Umělecká

Veletržní

Strojnická

Heřmanova

Kamenická

Haškova

20

Letenské náměstí

▼ 21

19

Tram 1, 8, 25, 26, 51, 56

Milady Horákové

Tram 1, 8, 25, 26, 51, 56

Fr. Křížka

24

Milady Horákové

✉ 22

Nad Štolou

Dobrovského

Dobrovského

Ovenecká

U letenského sadu

Letohradská

Letná

Muzejní

Letohradská

Kostelní

🏛 23

Letenský

Letenské sady

Metronome

MAP 6

Tram 12, 17, 51, 54

Tram 5, 12, 14, 17, 26, 51, 53, 54

Vltava

MAP 4

PLACES TO STAY
1 Hostel Spoas
8 Parkhotel
16 Pension Vltava
17 Hotel Standart

PLACES TO EAT
7 Thang Long

10 The Globe Café & Bookshop
11 Caffé Dante

OTHER
2 Economic Chamber of
the Czech Republic
3 Capital Express
4 Ice Rink & HC Sparta Sports Hall

5 Lapidárium
6 American Medical Center
9 Trade Fair Palace & Centre
for Modern & Contemporary Art
12 Kulturní dům Vltavská
13 Štvanice Ice Skating Rink
14 Tennis Courts
15 Open-Air Market

0   200   400 m

Vltava

Tram 5, 17, 25, 53

Za elektrárnou

Praha-
Holešovice
Nádraží Holešovice
Vrbenského

Bondyho
Jankovcova
U Pergamenky
Vrbenského

Partyzánská

Plynární
Tram 12, 25, 54
Plynární

Poupětova

Železničářů

U měšť. pivovaru

Bubenská

MAP 3

U Výstaviště — Tram 5, 12, 17, 53, 54

U průhonu

Osadní

Holešovice

Přístavní
17

Strojnická

16

Dělnická

Schnirchova
Dukelských hrdinů
Jankovcého

Šimáčkova

6

7

Tovární

Argentinská

8
Veletržní
Tram 5, 12, 17, 53, 54

Tusarová

9

Jateční

Heřmanova

ppřk
Sochora
Veverkova

10

Jankovckého

Tram 1, 8, 25, 26, 51, 56

11
Bubenká

Vltavská
Tram 1, 8, 14, 25, 56

Za viaduktem

15

12

Dukel. hrdinů

Kulturní
dům Vltavská

Bubenské nábřeží — Tram 1, 3, 14, 25

Kostelní

nábřeží kpt. Jaroše

Tram 5, 12, 14, 17, 26, 51, 56
Hlávkův most

Ostrov
Štvanice
(Chase Island)

13
Tram 3, 8, 56

14

Vltava

MAP 6

A bird's-eye view of the Church of St Francis Seraphinus dome and the towers of the Old Town.

RICHARD NEBESKÝ

Loreta's baroque bell tower, Hradčany.

RICHARD NEBESKÝ

Waiting for business on the Old Town Square.

RICHARD NEBESKÝ

MAP 5

PLACES TO STAY
1 Kolej JA Komenského Hostel
2 Pension U raka
22 Hotel U krále Karla
37 Hotel Hoffmeister
60 Hotel U tří pštrosů
61 Hotel U Páva
80 Hostel Sokol
82 Kampa Hotel
102 Müller Hostel & Strahov 007 Club
103 Hostel SPUS & Travel Agency
104 Hotel Vaníček
105 Hostel ESTEC & Travel Agency
108 Hotel Coubertin

PLACES TO EAT
5 U zlaté hrušky
9 Malý Buddha
10 Restaurace Sate
13 Restaurant Peklo
16 Literární Kavárna U zavěšeného kafe
17 U staré radnice
25 Restaurant Faros
35 Pálffy Palác club restaurace
41 Waldštejnská hospoda
47 Circle Line
52 U Malého Glena
53 St Nicholas Café
54 U tří zlatých hvězd
55 Jo's Bar & Garáž
56 J+J Mašek & Zemanová Food Shop
62 Vinárna Čertovka
65 Kavárna Červená sedma
66 U zlatých nůžek
67 Moravská vinárna
71 U sněděného krámu
72 Mazlova vinárna U malířů
73 Vinárna U Maltézských rytířů
78 U modré kachničky
81 Rybářský klub
83 Restaurace Bar Bar
84 Snack U Kiliána
85 Restaurant Canto
88 Bohemia Bagel
89 Café Savoy
91 Diana Snack Bar
97 Restaurant Nebozízek

OTHER
3 Gambra Surrealist Gallery
4 Capuchin Monastery
6 Loreta
7 Černín Palace
8 Pivnice U černého vola
11 Strahov Picture Gallery
12 Strahov Library & Museum of
    Czech Literature
14 Strahov Monastery, Strahov Picture Gallery,
    Library & Museum of Czech Literature
15 Church of the Assumption
    of Our Lady
18 Sternberg Palace
19 Riding School
20 Archbishop's Palace
21 Schwarzenberg Palace & Museum
    of Military History
23 House of Two Suns
24 Lobkowicz Palace & German Embassy
26 Bretfeld Palace
27 House at the Golden Horseshoe
28 Church of Our Lady of Unceasing Succour
29 House of St John of Nepomuk
30 House of the Three Fiddles
31 Hostinec U kocoura
32 U krále Brabantského
33 British Embassy
34 Parliament House (Sněmovna)
36 Gočár's Cubist Houses
38 Theatre na Klárově
39 Wallenstein Riding School
40 Wallenstein Palace
42 House of the Golden Stag
43 Čedok
44 Smiřický Palace
45 St Nicholas Church
46 Liechtenstein Palace
48 Schönborn Palace & US Embassy
49 Irish Embassy
50 Exkod
51 Intercontact Agency
57 Malostranská beseda

58 Post Office
59 Malá Strana Bridge Tower & PIS
63 PPS Boat Landing
64 Hostinec U stalété báby
68 John Lennon Wall
69 French Embassy
70 Church of Our Lady below the Chain
74 Church of Our Lady Victorious
    & Infant of Prague
75 Prague Spring Box Office
76 Nostitz Palace
77 MXM Gallery
79 Sport Slivka
86 Church of St John at the Laundry
87 Klub Újezd
90 Ostroff
92 Open-Air Market
93 Prague B&B Association
94 Mapis (Map Shop)
95 Church of St Michael
96 Statue of Karel Hynek Mácha
98 The Maze
99 Petřín Tower
100 Church of St Lawrence
101 Štefánik Observatory
106 Esquo Relax Club (Squash Courts)
107 Strahov Stadium
109 Tennis Hall
110 Esquo Squashcentrum

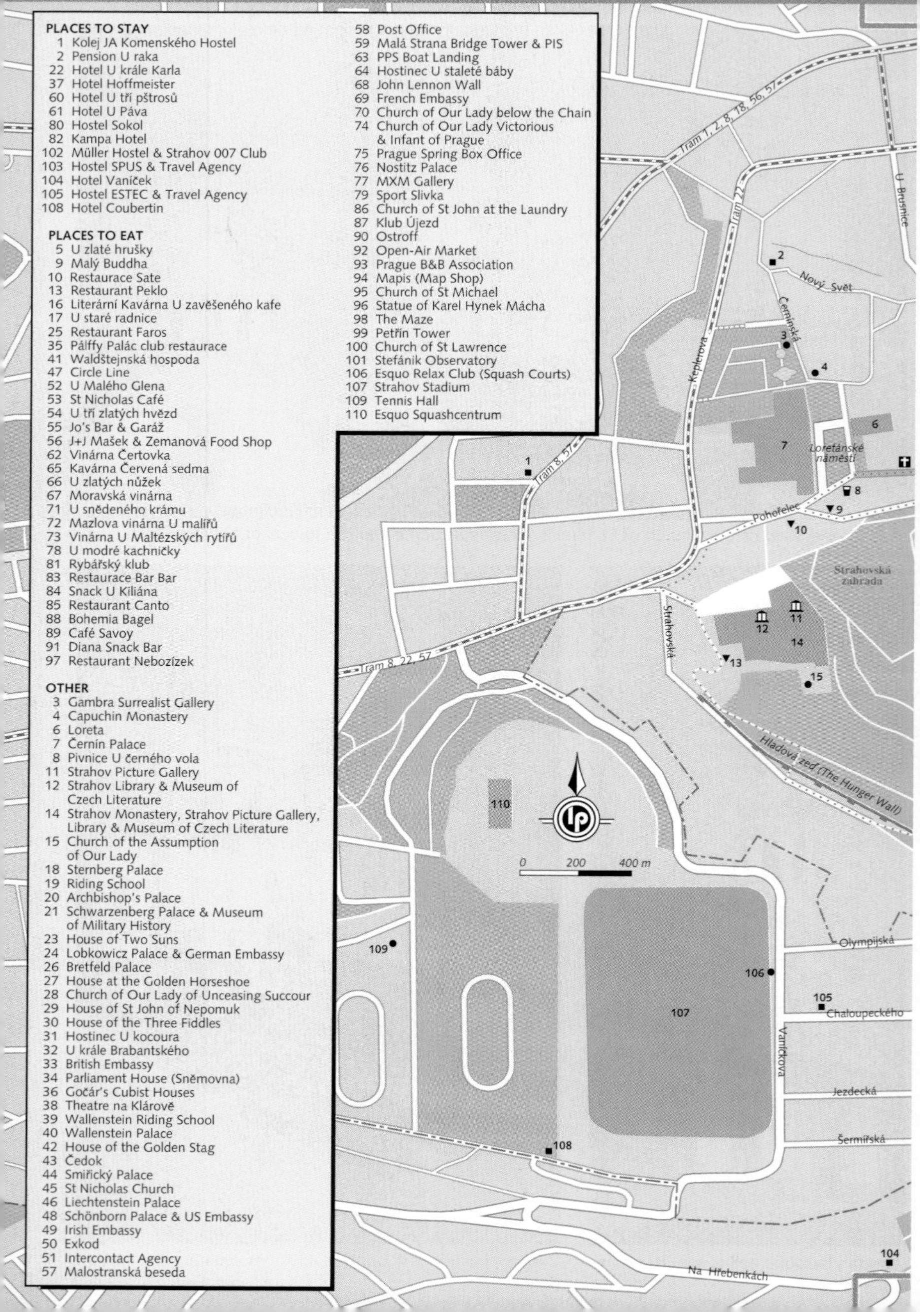

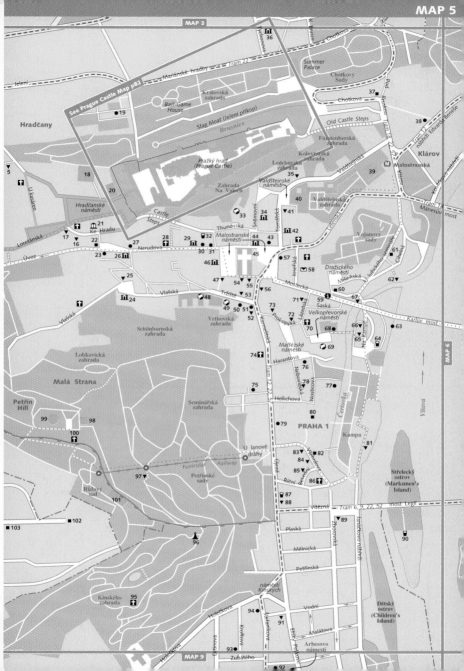

MAP 5

MAP 3

See Prague Castle Map p82

Hradčany

Summer Palace

Chotkovy Sady

Marianské hradby — Tram 22

Ball Game House

Královská zahrada

Chotkova

Jelení

Stag Moat (Jelení příkop)

Brusnice

Old Castle Steps

Klárov

Malostranská

Pražký hrad (Prague Castle)

Fürstenberská zahrada

Kolovratská zahrada

Ledeburská zahrada

Valdštejnské náměstí

Valdštejnská zahrada

Zahrada Na Valech

Hradčanské náměstí

Castle Steps

Snémovní

Thunovská

Tomášská

Vojanovy sady

U kasáren

Ke Hradu

Loretánská

Nerudova

Malostranské náměstí

Drážického náměstí

Míšenská

Úvoz

Vlašská

Tržiště

Mostecká

Karlův most

Vltava

Schönbornská zahrada

Vrtbovská zahrada

Saská

Velkopřevorské náměstí

Na Kampě

Lobkovická zahrada

Maltézské náměstí

Malá Strana

Harantova

Petřín Hill

Seminářská zahrada

Hellichova

Nebovidská

Nosticova

Čertovka

Kampa

PRAHA 1

U lanové dráhy

Funicular Railway

Petřínské sady

Střelecký ostrov (Marksmen's Island)

Růžový sad

Újezd

Vítězná — Tram 6, 9, 22, 52 — most Legii

Plaská

Mělnická

Petřínská

náměstí Kinských

Vodní

Kínského zahrada

Holečkova

Malátova

Eliščy Peškové

Dětský ostrov (Children's Island)

Arbesovo náměstí

Holečkova

Kroftova

Zborovská

Bítrnova

Matoušova

MAP 9

Zubatého

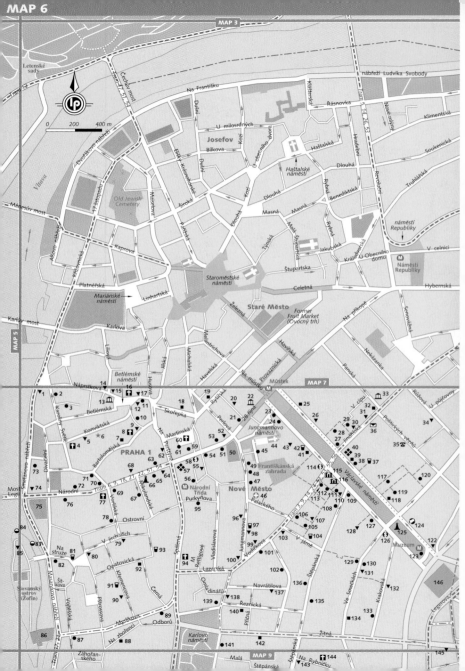

MAP 6

MAP 3

Letenské sady

náměstí Ludvíka Svobody

Na Františku

Josefov

Haštalské náměstí

U milosrdných

Bílkova

MAP 5

Old Jewish Cemetery

Kaprova

Vltava

Platnéřská

Mariánské náměstí

Linhartská

Karlov most

Karlova

Staroměstské náměstí

Staré Město

Former Fruit Market (Ovocný trh)

Celetná

Betlémské náměstí

Mariánské náměstí

Karlova

MAP 7

PRAHA 1

Nové Město

Slovanský ostrov (Žofín)

Karlovo náměstí

MAP 9

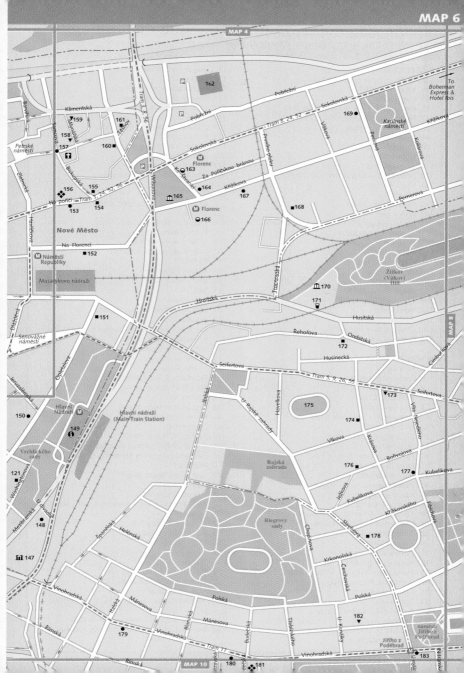

MAP 6

MAP 4

To
Bohemian
Express &
Hotel Ibis

162

Klimentská

159

161

158

157

160

Petrské
náměstí

Sokolovská

169

Karlínské
náměstí

Pobřežní

156

155

153 154

Na poříčí — Tram 3, 24, 52, 56

Nové Město

152

Na Florenci

Náměstí
Republiky

Masarykovo nádraží

Florenc

163

Za Poříčskou bránou

164

165

167

168

Florenc

166

151

Husitská

170

171

Žižkov
(Vítkov)
Hill

Senovážné
náměstí

Husitská

Řehořova

Orebitská

172

Husinecká

Seifertova

Tram 5, 9, 26, 55

Seifertova

173

175

174

Hlavní
Nádraží

Hlavní nádraží
(Main Train Station)

150

149

Vlkova

Vrchlického
sady

Rajská
zahrada

176

177

Kubelíkova

121

148

Kubelíkova

147

Riegrovy
sady

178

Vinohradská

179

Polská

Polská

Krkonošská

Mánesova

Mánesova

182

Vinohradská

náměstí
Jiřího z
Poděbrad

Jiřího z
Poděbrad

Římská

MAP 10

180

181

Vinohradská

183

MAP 8

MAP 6

PLACES TO STAY

- 7 Unitas Penzion & Cloister Inn
- 18 Express Hostel
- 19 Hotel U klenotníka
- 25 Ambassador Hotel & Hotel Zlatá Husa
- 32 Hotel Palace & Delicatesse Buffet
- 39 Grand Hotel Evropa
- 41 Hotel Adria
- 88 Hostel at Club Habitat
- 92 Hotel Koruna
- 118 Hotel Jalta
- 121 Hotel Esplanade & A-Rent Car/Thrifty
- 134 Hotel Andante
- 137 Miyabi
- 140 Novoměstský Hotel
- 142 Juniorhotel
- 151 Hostel Jednota & Pension, Universitas Tour Agency & Apart klub
- 152 Raketa Hostel
- 154 Hotel Axa
- 155 Hotel Harmony
- 160 Hotel Merkur
- 161 Hotel Opera
- 162 Hilton Atrium Hotel
- 168 TJ Sokol Karlín Hostel
- 172 Hotel Ostaš
- 174 Purple House
- 176 Clown & Bard Hostel
- 178 Švehlova kolej hostel

PLACES TO EAT

- 1 Bellevue
- 5 Restaurace U Ampezonů
- 9 Café Konvikt
- 12 Café Gulu Gulu
- 14 Vinárna v zátiší
- 15 Restaurace U Betlémské kaple
- 17 Klub architektů
- 20 Julius Meinl Supermarket
- 26 McDonald's
- 30 Paris-Praha Food Shop & Café
- 31 Fruits de France
- 34 Růžová čajovna
- 43 Dobrá čajovna
- 52 Káva.Káva.Káva
- 55 Monica cukrárna
- 62 Restaurace & Pension U Medvídků
- 64 Louvre/Gany's Café & Louvre Billiard Club
- 68 Café-Bar Craull Evropa
- 74 Kavárna Slavia
- 79 Pizzeria Kmotra
- 80 Hospoda U Nováka
- 85 Posezení na řece Café & Cruise Boat
- 90 Restaurant Buenos Aires
- 96 Adonis bufet
- 98 Cornucopia
- 99 Buffalo Bill's Tex-Mex Bar & Grille
- 100 Country Life Restaurant & Health-Food Shop
- 103 Branický sklípek (U Purkmistra)
- 107 Jarmark restaurace

- 110 Mayur Indický Snack Bar & Restaurant
- 122 McDonald's
- 128 Restaurace/hospůdka Václavka
- 131 Smečky dietní restaurace
- 132 Česká hospoda V Krakovské
- 138 Italská cukrárna (Ice Cream Shop)
- 143 Laguna Ice Cream & Fruit Parlour
- 145 Restaurace Zlatý Drak
- 158 Hacienda Mexicana restaurace
- 159 Fakhreldine Restaurant
- 173 Restaurace Panda Palace
- 182 U knihomola Café & Bookshop

OTHER

- 2 KMC (Klub mladých cestovatelů)
- 3 Drop In
- 4 Chapel of the Holy Cross
- 6 Police Station (Prague 1)
- 8 St Bartholomew Church
- 10 Galerie Jednorožec s Harfou
- 11 BS Foto
- 13 Náprstek Museum
- 16 Bethlehem Chapel
- 21 Batalion
- 22 Wax Museum
- 23 Baťa Shoe Store & Lindt Building
- 24 Peterkův dům
- 27 Former Office of Assicurazioni Generali (Kafka's Workplace 1907-08)
- 28 Beruška Toy Shop
- 29 Astera Laundrette
- 33 Mucha Museum
- 35 Telephone Bureau (Temporary Location)
- 36 Main Post Office
- 37 Zombie Bar
- 38 Best Tour, at Hotel Meran
- 40 Krone Department Store
- 42 Disco Astra
- 44 Church of Our Lady of the Snows
- 45 Austrian Cultural Institute
- 46 All-Night Emergency Medical & Dental Clinic & Pharmacy
- 47 Supraphon (Music Shop)
- 48 Dům Sportu
- 49 Popron (Music Shop)
- 50 Adria Palace, Theatre Animato & Adria Jazz Club
- 51 Balnea
- 53 Kodak Processing Lab
- 54 Václav Špála Gallery
- 56 Open-Air Market
- 57 Tesco
- 58 Thomas Cook
- 59 Western Union (at Sport Turist)
- 60 Church of St Martin in the Wall
- 61 Sauna Babylonia
- 63 Internet Café & Pražské Panoptikum (in Palác Metro Passage)
- 65 Reduta Jazz Club, Theatre & Rock Café
- 66 Memorial to Students Clubbed by Police on 17 November, 1989

MAP 6

Jazz music is popular on the streets of Prague.

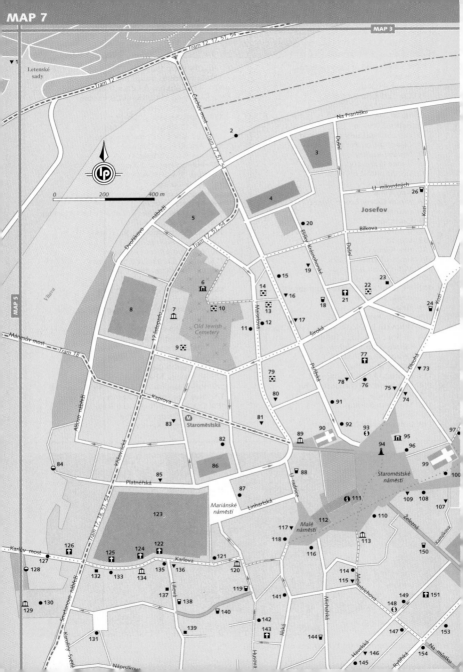

MAP 7

nábřeží Ludvíka Svobody

41

Tram 5, 14, 26, 53

Klášterská

Řásnovka

27

28

40
Novomlýnská
39
38 Nové mlýny

42
Soukenická

Klimentská

Petrské náměstí

44

43

45

Šaancova

U obecního dvora

25

29
Haštalská

Haštalské náměstí

Hradební

Revoluční

46

Zlatnická

MAP 6

33 34
Dlouhá

35 ▼ 36

Rybná

32
31
30
Dlouhá

Benediktská

54

53

Truhlářská

Havlíčkova

Na poříčí
Tram 3, 24, 52, 56

47

52

51

50

Masná
Masná

Malá
Rybná

55

63

64

Jakubská

Tram 3, 9, 14, 24, 52, 53, 56

Na Florenci

48

49
V celnici

Náměstí Republiky

72
71
70

Týnská
Štupartská

62

57
Králodvorská
U Obecního domu

56
náměstí Republiky

181

182

180

Masarykovo nádraží

66
67
68

61

65

58
59

Náměstí Republiky

60

98

69

Štupartská

101

102
Celetná

103

106
Staré Město

Former Fruit Market
(Ovocný trh)

105
104

173

174
175

176

178

177

Hybernská

179

Na Florenci

183

Senovážné náměstí
Tram 5, 9, 26, 56

Nové Město

171

170
Na příkopě

172

169

165
164

168
167
166

162

163

160

161

152

158

Havlíčkova

Provaznická

157

156

159

Můstek

155

188

186

187

189

190

185

184

Jeruzalémská

Nekázanka

Panská

MAP 7

PLACES TO STAY

3 President Hotel
4 Hotel Inter-Continental & Budget Car Rental
23 Hostel U synagogy
28 Hotel Casa Marcello
29 Maxmilian Hotel
33 Pension Dlouhá (Travellers' Hostel)
41 Botel Albatros
45 Kolej Petrská Hostel
48 Renaissance Hotel
52 Atlantic Hotel
57 Hotel Paříž
59 Grand Hotel Bohemia
63 Hotel Central
69 Hotel Ungelt
72 Hostel Týn
132 Hotel U zlatého stromu
137 Pension U Lilie
139 Accommodation U krále Jiřího & James Joyce
178 Hotel Meteor Plaza
186 Libra Q Hotel

PLACES TO EAT

1 Hanavský pavilon
16 Bar Rock
17 Jewel of India
19 La colline oubliée
35 U Benedikta
36 Pizzamania
42 U Góvindy
47 Pizzeria Mamma Mia
53 Restaurace MD Rettigové
60 Pivnice Radegast
62 Red, Hot & Blues
65 Le Saint-Jacques
68 La Provence
73 Mikulka's Pizzeria
74 Bona Vita
75 Michelské pekařství (Bakery)
78 Kavárna Hogo Fogo
80 Vinárna U Golema
81 Chléb pečivo (Bakery)
83 Restaurace U městské knihovny
85 Lotos
102 Café Gaspar Kaspar
107 Restaurace Snack Bar U Černého slunce
109 Staroměstská restaurace
115 Country Life Restaurant & Health-Food Shop
117 Dům lahůdek, in VJ Rott Building
136 Reykjavík
146 Safir Grill Bar
158 Planet Hollywood

OTHER

2 Evropská vodní doprava (EVD) Pier
5 Charles University Law Faculty
6 Ceremonial Hall
7 Museum of Decorative Arts
8 Rudolfinum & Rudolfinum Gallery
9 Pinkas Synagogue
10 Klaus Synagogue & Main Ticket Office
11 Matana Travel Agency
12 Jewish Town Hall & Košer jídelna
13 High Synagogue
14 Old-New Synagogue
15 Europcar Car Rental
18 Žíznivý pes
20 Novotný's Cubist Building
21 Church of the Holy Spirit
22 Spanish Synagogue
24 Kozička
25 Molly Malones
26 Pivnice U milosrdných
27 Convent of St Agnes
30 5 à Sec Laundrette
31 Granát Turnof Jeweller
32 Eduard Čapek's Junk Shop
34 Roxy
37 Terminal Bar
38 St Peter Church
39 Petrská Waterworks Tower
40 Postage Stamp Museum
43 GTS International Travel Agency
44 Avis Car Rental
46 Bohemiatour
49 ČSA Service Centre
50 YMCA & Sport Centrum
51 Insurance Firm where Kafka worked 1908-22
54 Prague Wheelchair Users Organisation
55 Kotva Department Store
56 Autoturist Agency
58 FOK Prague Symphony Ticket Agency
61 Top Tour Agency
64 St James Church
66 Chapeau Rouge Music Shop
67 Chapeau Rouge
70 Big Ben (Bookshop)
71 American Chamber of Commerce
76 Ticketpro
77 Church of the Holy Saviour
79 Maisel Synagogue
82 Puppet Kingdom (National Marionette Theatre)
84 Boat Rental
86 City Library
87 City Hall
88 Pivnice U kata
89 Franz Kafka's Birthplace & Exhibition & Josef Sudek Gallery
90 St Nicholas Church
91 Čedok
92 Image Theatre (Classic Club)
93 Thomas Cook
94 Jan Hus Statue
95 Kinský Palace
96 House at the Stone Bell
97 House at the Golden Ring
98 Týn Court (Týnský dvůr)
99 Church of Our Lady Before Týn
100 The Three Kings, Kafka's Home 1896-1907
101 U Hynků

MAP 7

View of Prague Castle across the Vltava River

RICHARD NEBESKY

MAP 8

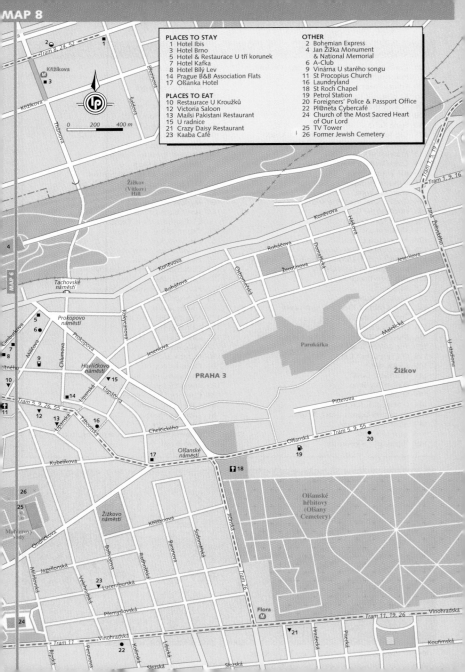

PLACES TO STAY
1 Hotel Ibis
3 Hotel Brno
5 Hotel & Restaurace U tří korunek
7 Hotel Kafka
8 Hotel Bílý Lev
14 Prague B&B Association Flats
17 Olšanka Hotel

PLACES TO EAT
10 Restaurace U Kroužků
12 Victoria Saloon
13 Mailsi Pakistani Restaurant
15 U radnice
21 Crazy Daisy Restaurant
23 Kaaba Café

OTHER
2 Bohemian Express
4 Jan Žižka Monument
   & National Memorial
6 A-Club
9 Vinárna U starého songu
11 St Procopius Church
16 Laundryland
18 St Roch Chapel
19 Petrol Station
20 Foreigners' Police & Passport Office
22 Pl@neta Cybercafé
24 Church of the Most Sacred Heart
   of Our Lord
25 TV Tower
26 Former Jewish Cemetery

A neoclassical frieze adorns the façade of the State Opera House, Nové Město.

Elaborate Art Nouveau portal.

Neo-Renaissance sgraffito, Staré Město.

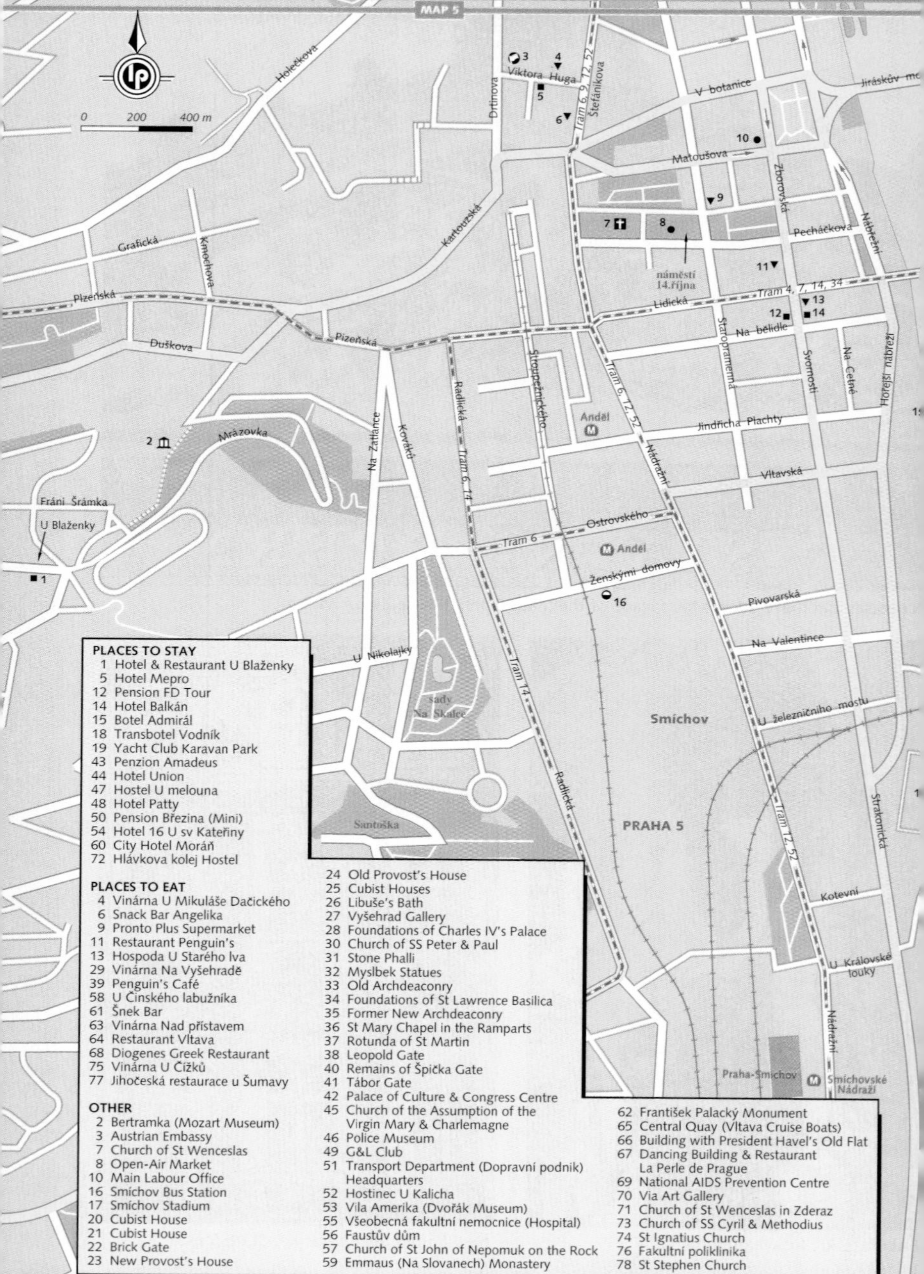

MAP 9

MAP 5

LP

0   200   400 m

Viktora Huga

V botanice

Jiráskův mc

Holečkova

Drtinova

Štefánikova

Matoušova

Zborovská

Nábřeží

Pecháčkova

Kmochova

Grafická

náměstí
14.října

11▼

Tram 4, 7, 14, 34

Lidická

Tram 6, 7, 12, 57

Plzeňská

Duškova

Plzeňská

Radlická

Na bělidle

Stroupežnického

Na bělidle

Štefánikova

Svornosti

Na Celné

Zborovská

Tram 6, 7, 12, 57

Mrázovka

Na zatlance

Kořenská

Tram 6, 7, 12, 57

Anděl
M

Jindřicha Plachty

Vltavská

Fráni Šrámka

U Blaženky

Ostrovského

Tram 6

Anděl
M

Ženskými domovy

16

Na Valentince

Pivovarská

U železničního mostu

U Nikolajky

Sady
Na Skalce

Smíchov

Radlická

Stroupežnického

Santoška

PRAHA 5

Kotevní

Tram 12, 57

Stroptnická

U Královské
louky

Nádraží

Praha-Smíchov

Smíchovské
Nádraží
M

František Palacký Monument

PLACES TO STAY
1 Hotel & Restaurant U Blaženky
5 Hotel Mepro
12 Pension FD Tour
14 Hotel Balkán
15 Botel Admirál
18 Transbotel Vodník
19 Yacht Club Karavan Park
43 Penzion Amadeus
44 Hotel Union
47 Hostel U melouna
48 Hotel Patty
50 Pension Březina (Mini)
54 Hotel 16 U sv Kateřiny
60 City Hotel Moráň
72 Hlávkova kolej Hostel

PLACES TO EAT
4 Vinárna U Mikuláše Dačického
6 Snack Bar Angelika
9 Pronto Plus Supermarket
11 Restaurant Penguin's
13 Hospoda U Starého lva
34 Vinárna Na Vyšehradě
39 Penguin's Café
58 U Čínského labužníka
61 Šnek Bar
63 Vinárna Nad přístavem
64 Restaurant Vltava
68 Diogenes Greek Restaurant
75 Vinárna U Čížků
77 Jihočeská restaurace u Šumavy

OTHER
2 Bertramka (Mozart Museum)
3 Austrian Embassy
7 Church of St Wenceslas
8 Open-Air Market
10 Main Labour Office
16 Smíchov Bus Station
17 Smíchov Stadium
20 Cubist House
21 Cubist House
22 Brick Gate
23 New Provost's House

24 Old Provost's House
25 Cubist Houses
26 Libuše's Bath
27 Vyšehrad Gallery
28 Foundations of Charles IV's Palace
30 Church of SS Peter & Paul
31 Stone Phalli
32 Myslbek Statues
33 Old Archdeaconry
34 Foundations of St Lawrence Basilica
35 Former New Archdeaconry
36 St Mary Chapel in the Ramparts
37 Rotunda of St Martin
38 Leopold Gate
40 Remains of Špička Gate
41 Tábor Gate
42 Palace of Culture & Congress Centre
45 Church of the Assumption of the
    Virgin Mary & Charlemagne
46 Police Museum
49 G&L Club
51 Transport Department (Dopravní podnik)
    Headquarters
52 Hostinec U Kalicha
53 Vila Amerika (Dvořák Museum)
55 Všeobecná fakultní nemocnice (Hospital)
56 Faustův dům
57 Church of St John of Nepomuk on the Rock
59 Emmaus (Na Slovanech) Monastery

62 František Palacký Monument
65 Central Quay (Vltava Cruise Boats)
66 Building with President Havel's Old Flat
67 Dancing Building & Restaurant
    La Perle de Prague
69 National AIDS Prevention Centre
70 Via Art Gallery
71 Church of St Wenceslas in Zderaz
73 Church of SS Cyril & Methodius
74 St Ignatius Church
76 Fakultní poliklinika
78 St Stephen Church

MAP 9

MAP 6

73
Resslova

76
75

77 78

Ječná   Tram 4, 6, 16, 22, 34, 51, 56

70
71
72
Nové
Město

67
66
68
69
Dittrichova

Václavská

Vyšehradská

Karlovo
náměstí

74

I P Pavlova

49

50

Trojanova

51

65

Na Moráni

60

Kateřinská

Na bojišti

53

52

64   63
61

Rašínovo nábřeží

Palackého most

62

Karlovo
náměstí

55
56

U nemocnice

Benátská

54

Viničná

Tyršova

Fügnerovo
náměstí

48

Pod Slovany
Slovanech

59

57

Botanická
zahrada

Apolinářská

Wenzigova

Trojická

Podskalská

58

Na slupi

Tram 18, 24

Albertov

Studničkova

46
45

47

MAP 10

Horská

Tram 7

Svobodova

Horská

Na slupi

20
Libušina

Vratislavova

21

Neklanova

Vnislavova

Na slupi

Sekaninova

Nuselský most

Štulcovy
sady

22

Oldřichova

Nezamyslova

Hořejší nábřeží

24
23

Vyšehradská

V Pevnosti

Ostrčilovo
náměstí

44

25

Slavín

Karlachovy
sady

Jaromírova

Tram 7, 18, 24

Čiklova

29

30

31

K. rotunda

36

Štulcova

35

37

43

Slavojova

18

19

28
27

32

Vyšehradské
sady

33

34

Lumírova

Krokova

Ciklova

Císařská
louka
(Imperial
Meadow)

26

Vyšehradská
skála
(Vyšehrad Rock)

38

39

40

42   Vyšehrad

41

Pankrácké
náměstí

Podolská

Na Pankráci

Sínkulova

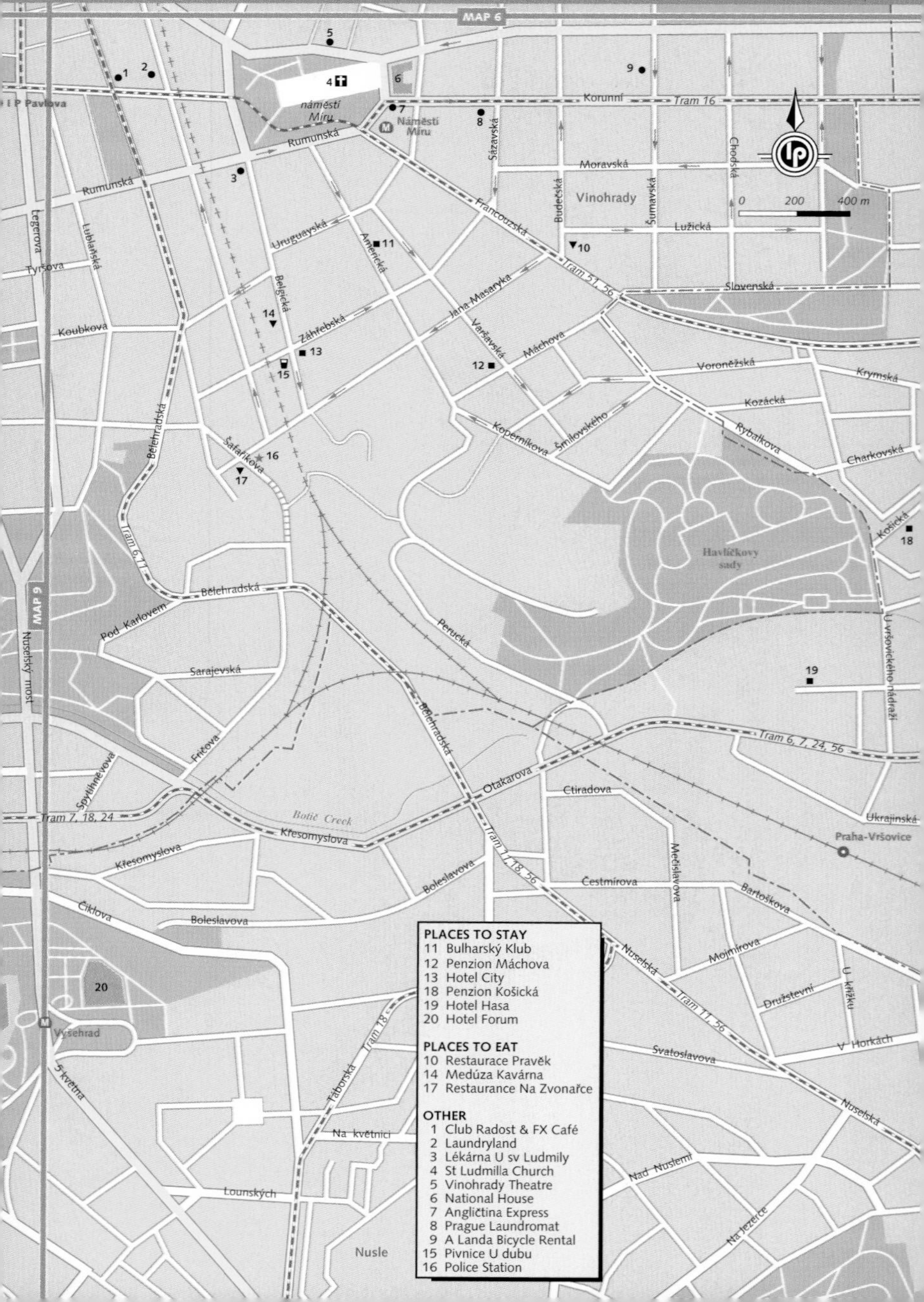

MAP 10

MAP 6

MAP 6

námeští
Míru

Náměstí
Míru

Rumunská

Korunní — Tram 16

Vinohrady

Moravská

Budečská

Šumavská

Lužická

Slovenská

Rumunská

Lublaňská

Koubkova

Tyrsova

Legerova

Uruguayská

Anglická

Šafaříkova

Bělehradská

Pod Karlovem

Sarajevská

Fričova

Spytihněvova

Tram 6, 11

Nuselský most

MAP 9

Tram 7, 18, 24

Čiklova

Boleslavova

Boleslavova

Vyšehrad

5. května

Lounských

Na květnici

Táborská

Nusle

Botič Creek

Křesomyslova

Křesomyslova

Otakarova

Ctiradova

Čestmírova

Nuselská

Petrská

Perucká

Francouzská

Tram 51, 56

Jana Masaryka

Varšavská

Máchova

Kopernikova

Smilovského

Voroněžská

Kozácká

Rybalkova

Charkovská

Krymská

Havlíčkovy
sady

U vršovického nádraží

Koperníkova

Tram 6, 7, 24, 56

Praha-Vršovice

Ukrajinská

Bartoškova

Moravská

U hřbitova

Mechlivská

Svatoslavova

V Horkách

Družstevní

Nuselská

Tram 11, 56

Nad Nuslemí

Na Petře?

Korunní

Chodská

Zahřebská

LP

0   200   400 m

Vinohrady

Vinohrady

PLACES TO STAY
11 Bulharský Klub
12 Penzion Máchova
13 Hotel City
18 Penzion Košická
19 Hotel Hasa
20 Hotel Forum

PLACES TO EAT
10 Restaurace Pravěk
14 Medúza Kavárna
17 Restaurance Na Zvonařce

OTHER
1 Club Radost & FX Café
2 Laundryland
3 Lékárna U sv Ludmily
4 St Ludmilla Church
5 Vinohrady Theatre
6 National House
7 Angličtina Express
8 Prague Laundromat
9 A Landa Bicycle Rental
15 Pivnice U dubu
16 Police Station

Vanity (holding a mirror) and Greed represent two of the four fears felt by 15th century Praguers.

The elaborate stucco on the Kinský Palace is one of Prague's finest examples of rococo decoration.

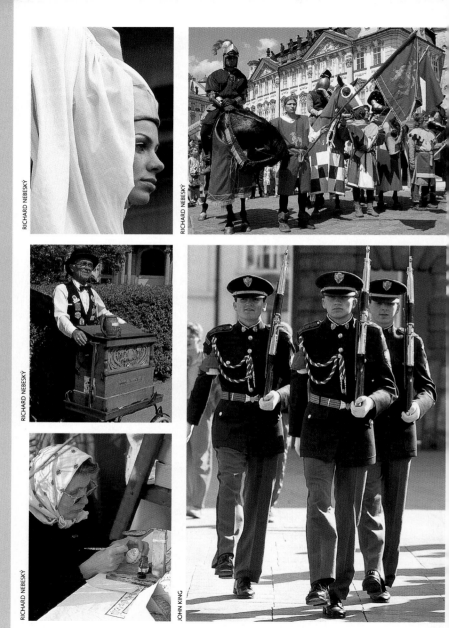

The many faces of Prague: the Charles IV celebrations and medieval games (top), busking in the sun (middle left), decorating Easter eggs (bottom left), changing guard at Prague Castle (bottom right).

MAP 11 AROUND PRAGUE

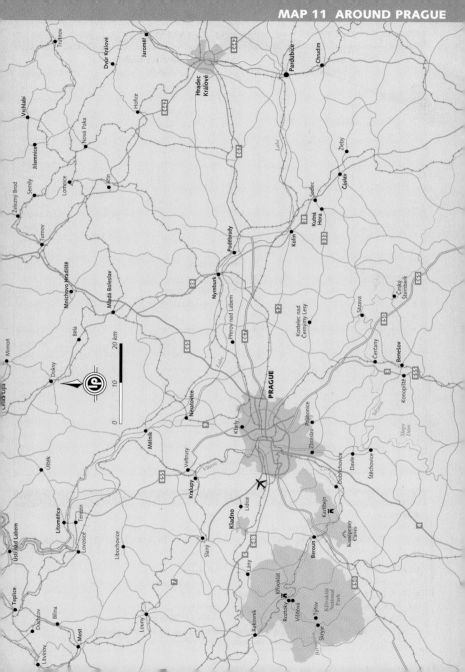

MAP LEGEND

BOUNDARIES

- International
- State
- Disputed

HYDROGRAPHY

- Coastline
- River, Creek
- Lake
- Intermittent Lake
- Salt Lake
- Canal
- Spring, Rapids
- Waterfalls
- Swamp

ROUTES & TRANSPORT

- Freeway
- Highway
- Major Road
- Minor Road
- Unsealed Road
- City Freeway
- City Highway
- City Road
- City Street, Lane

- Pedestrian Mall
- Tunnel
- Train Route & Station
- Metro & Station
- Tramway
- Cable Car or Chairlift
- Walking Track
- Walking Tour
- Ferry Route

AREA FEATURES

- Building
- Park, Gardens
- Cemetery

- Market
- Beach, Desert
- Urban Area

MAP SYMBOLS

✪	**CAPITAL** National Capital	✈	Airport	☂ National Park
◉	**CAPITAL** State Capital		Ancient or City Wall	One Way Street
●	**CITY** City	∴	Archaeological Site	Parking
●	**Town** Town	⌐	Beach	)(Pass
●	**Village** Village	☗	Castle or Fort	★ Police Station
○	Point of Interest		Cave	✉ Post Office
		ⓘ	Church	❖ Shopping Centre
■	Place to Stay		Cliff or Escarpment	Swimming Pool
⚠	Camping Ground	▭	Dive Site	Synagogue
⛺	Caravan Park	◉	Embassy	☎ Telephone
⌂	Hut or Chalet	○	Hospital	▮ Temple
		☪	Mosque	❶ Tourist Information
▼	Place to Eat	▲	Mountain or Hill	Transport
☕	Pub or Bar	⛫	Museum	Zoo

Note: not all symbols displayed above appear in this book

LONELY PLANET OFFICES

Australia
PO Box 617, Hawthorn, Victoria 3122
☎ (03) 9819 1877 fax (03) 9819 6459
email: talk2us@lonelyplanet.com.au

USA
150 Linden St, Oakland, CA 94607
☎ (510) 893 8555 TOLL FREE: 800 275 8555
fax (510) 893 8572
email: info@lonelyplanet.com

UK
10a Spring Place, London NW5 3BH
☎ (020) 7428 4800 fax (020) 7428 4828
email: go@lonelyplanet.co.uk

France
1 rue du Dahomey, 75011 Paris
☎ 01 55 25 33 00 fax 01 55 25 33 01
email: bip@lonelyplanet.fr
minitel: 3615 lonelyplanet *(1.29 F TTC/min)*

World Wide Web: www.lonelyplanet.com *or* AOL keyword: lp
Lonely Planet Images: lpi@lonelyplanet.com.au